# Privatization and State-Owned Enterprises

ROCHESTER STUDIES IN ECONOMICS AND POLICY ISSUES

Series Editor: Karl Brunner
University of Rochester, USA

Other titles in the series:

*Controlling the Growth of Monetary Aggregates,* by Robert H. Rasche and James M. Johannes

*Explaining Metals Prices,* by Paul W. MacAvoy

*Published in cooperation with*

The Bradley Policy Research Center
William E. Simon Graduate School
of Business Administration
University of Rochester
Rochester, New York

# Privatization and State-Owned Enterprises

## Lessons from the United States, Great Britain and Canada

**Paul W. MacAvoy**
University of Rochester

**W.T. Stanbury**
University of British Columbia

**George Yarrow**
Oxford University

**Richard J. Zeckhauser**
Harvard University

Kluwer Academic Publishers
Boston Dordrecht London

**Distributors**

*for the United States and Canada:* Kluwer Academic Publishers, 101 Philip Drive, Assinippi Park, Norwell, Massachusetts 02061 USA

*for the UK and Ireland:* Kluwer Academic Publishers, Falcon House, Queen Square, Lancaster LA1 1RN, UK

*for all other countries:* Kluwer Academic Publishers Group, Distribution Centre, Post Office Box 322, 3300 AH Dordrecht, The Netherlands

**Library of Congress Cataloging-in-Publication Data**

Privatization and state-owned enterprise.

(Rochester studies in economics and policy issues)
Includes index.
1. Privatization—United States. 2. Privatization—Great Britain. 3. Privatization—Canada. I. MacAvoy, Paul W.
HD3888.P77 1989 338.9 88-8425
ISBN 0-89838-297-1

Copyright © 1989 by Kluwer Academic Publishers

All rights reserved. No part of this publication may be reproduced, stored in a retrieval system or transmitted in any form or by any means, mechanical, photocopying, recording, or otherwise, without the prior written permission of the publisher, Kluwer Academic Publishers, 101 Philip Drive, Assinippi Park, Norwell, Massachusetts 02061.

Printed in the United States of America

## TABLE OF CONTENTS

## CHAPTER FOUR



## CHAPTER FIVE

# LIST OF TABLES

## LIST OF CONTRIBUTORS

**Walter Block** is Senior Economist at the Fraser Institute, Vancouver, British Columbia.

**Kenneth W. Clarkson** is Professor of Economics at the Law and Economics Center, University of Miami.

**Louis De Alessi** is Professor of Economics at the Law and Economics Center, University of Miami.

**Steve H. Hanke** is Professor of Applied Economics at the Johns Hopkins University, Baltimore, Maryland.

**Murray Horn** is Director, Economics Branch of the New Zealand Treasury.

**M. Bruce Johnson** is Professor of Economics at the University of California at Santa Barbara.

**Paul W. MacAvoy** is Dean and John M. Olin Professor of Public Policy and Business Administration at the William E. Simon Graduate School of Business Administration, University of Rochester, Rochester, New York.

**Sir Ian MacGregor** is a Director at Lazard Brothers and Company Ltd., London.

**George S. McIsaac** is AT&T Resident Management Fellow and adjunct Professor of Business and Public Administration at the William E. Simon Graduate School of Business Administration, University of Rochester, Rochester, New York.

**Kevin J. Murphy** is Marvin Bower Fellow at Harvard Business School and Assistant Professor of Business Administration at the William E. Simon Graduate School of Business Administration, University of Rochester, Rochester, New York.

**William Niskanen** is Chairman of the Cato Institute, Washington, D.C.

**Sam Peltzman** is Professor of Business Economics at the University of Chicago.

**Richard Schultz** is Director at the Centre for the Study of Regulated Industries and Professor of Political Science, McGill University, Montreal.

**W.T. Stanbury** is UPS Foundation Professor of Regulation and Competition Policy at the Faculty of Commerce and Business Administration, University of British Columbia, Vancouver.

**Fred Thompson** is Grace and Elmer Goudy Professor of Public Policy and Management at the Geo.H. Atkinson Graduate School of Management, Willamette University, Salem, Oregon.

**John Vickers** is Fellow in Economics at Nuffield College, Oxford University.

**Sir Alan Walters** is Senior Fellow at the American Enterprise Institute, Washington, D.C., and Economic Advisor at International Bank for Reconstruction and Development, Washington, D.C.

**George Yarrow** is Fellow in Economics at Hertford College, Oxford University.

**Richard J. Zeckhauser** is Frank P. Ramsey Professor of Political Economy at the John F. Kennedy School of Government, Harvard University.

# Privatization and State-Owned Enterprises

# Introduction*

In recent years privatization has been embraced by governments of all political stripes, at every level. Countries from Argentina to Zambia, with market-oriented and socialist governments alike, are exploring the implications of converting state enterprises to private ownership.

At a recent international gathering of senior government officials, the minister of finance of a socialist country was heard to say that the only way to ensure the future of socialism is to increase the rate of privatization. His belief underlying such surprising rhetoric was that privatization can serve a variety of purposes, from reducing budget deficits to restructuring industries to compete in the European Common Market. Despite a wide variance in political motivations, the results from privatizing tend to be similar across nations: higher productivity, a smaller public sector, and savings for the taxpayer.

To explore the growing trend toward privatization, the Bradley Policy Research Center of the University of Rochester hosted a conference on the subject of Privatization in November 1987. The aim was to bring together researchers in this area with those who had actually been involved with the process at a policy level. Participants included academics and government officials from Canada, Great Britain and the United States. This volume has been developed from the papers presented at the conference and the ensuing discussion.

---

* The authors acknowledge the substantial editorial assistance of Gordon A. Rogers, Research Associate, and Jeffery Ryan, Kalmbach Fellow, at the William E. Simon Graduate School of Business Administration, University of Rochester. Funding by the John M. Olin Institute as well as by the Bradley Policy Research Center at the University of Rochester for both the Conference in Washington, D.C., and the production of the book is gratefully acknowledged.

The book is divided into three major sections. The first presents a theoretical discussion that underlies the other essays. The second section deals with privatization issues from the perspective of the United States. The third describes research addressed to the U.K. and Canada.

In the first chapter, Richard Zeckhauser and Murray Horn develop a wide-ranging theoretical framework for assessing the capabilities and role of state-owned enterprises; it provides a foundation for the analyses that follow. In *The Control and Performance of State-Owned Enterprises*, they describe state-owned enterprises as an extreme case of the separation of ownership and control. The focus is on management -- the incentives it faces and the conflicts to which it is subjected. The distinguishing characteristics of public enterprise, the authors suggest, give it a *comparative advantage* over both public bureaucracy and private enterprise in certain situations. They argue that legislators are more likely to prefer SOEs over private enterprise when the efficiency of private enterprise is undermined by regulation or the threat of opportunistic state action, when the informational demands of subsidizing private production to meet distributional objectives are high, when it is difficult to assign property rights, or when state ownership is ideologically appealing. These considerations suggest why SOEs are usually assigned special rights and responsibilities, and they help explain observed regularities in the distribution of SOEs across countries and sectors.

Zeckhauser and Horn apply principal-agent theory to identify the key factors underlying the performance of state-owned enterprises. Ownership is diffuse and non-transferable in public enterprise, which impairs the mechanisms that help align the interests of management and those of the "shareholders". The position of the taxpayer-shareholder is weakened relative to others who can impose a claim on the operation of the enterprise -- such as consumers, suppliers, labor and management. The authors argue that the balance among these interests, and thus the performance of the organization, is determined by four main factors: the size of available surplus, the degree of competition the SOE faces (including the degree of "performance competition"), the extent of private shareholding in the enterprise, and the diversity of private interests affected by its operation. Zeckhauser and Horn summarize previous empirical findings on SOE performance to support their arguments. Their formulation also allows us to draw some conclusions about the impact of privatization. It is likely to yield the largest gains to taxpayers when the available pot is large and the interests of other claimants are concentrated. Efficiency gains are likely to be greater at the national rather than at the local level. Finally, even partial privatizations are likely to improve performance.

Paul MacAvoy and George McIsaac report on an investigation into the operation and structure of four major, federally sponsored enterprises: Conrail, Amtrak, the U.S. Postal Service and the Tennessee Valley Authority. Comparisons are drawn between those SOEs and the private-sector firms that operate in the same markets. *The Performance and Management of United States Federal Government Corporations* consists of two parts. First, after a review of the behavior of an index of all federal SOEs, the ten-year performance of the four SOEs is analyzed in terms of price and cost increases, capital formation and employment levels. MacAvoy and McIsaac find that these SOEs have done relatively poorly in terms of growth, price stability and cost containment. Then the authors examine the SOEs' peculiar organizational and management structures, from board composition to employment contracts, arguing that these factors explain why the market performance of the SOEs lagged behind that of the private-sector firms. Their implication is that only by restructuring their internal organizations in a way that makes the SOEs virtually identical to private-sector corporations will the performance of an SOE improve to achieve that are satisfactory and perhaps comparable levels to those of corporations elsewhere in the economy.

In *Privatization at the State and Local Level*, Kenneth Clarkson examines the various forms of privatization used to provide public services at the state and local level. The paper outlines recent experience and trends in privatization, focusing on the state of Florida, and examines the potential savings from privatization by service function. Before turning to the legal barriers to privatization, various elements impacting on the feasibility of privatization are discussed. Clarkson's review of the evidence on privatization reveals that there is no "hierarchy" of privatization candidates among regions; that governments tend to privatize those services that are "less public" (e.g. refuse collection as opposed to law enforcement); that higher levels of government expenditure increase the likelihood of privatization, while higher public employee compensation levels reduce it; and that the extent of privatization is determined in part by the institutions with which state and local officials are associated. The paper concludes with a review of the more commonly cited objections to privatization, which include difficulties with contract enforcement, excessive profit-taking, hidden costs, and the displacement of public employees.

The fourth chapter examines privatization in Great Britain and Canada. John Vickers and George Yarrow's *Privatization in Britain*, reviews the economic success of privatization under the Thatcher government. They discuss government policies concerning competition and regulation in the context of economic and political objectives, with particular emphasis on price regulation. Each of the newly privatized industries (British Telecom, British Gas, British Airports Authority, British Airways, and National Bus Company) is reviewed, and there is an in-depth discussion of the telecommunication industry.

Vickers and Yarrow conclude that incentive problems complicate the achievement of economic efficiency in the use of privatized resources. For example, Britain's method of price regulation encounters some of the same incentive problems that afflict rate-of return pricing used in the United States. Moreover, available evidence does not suggest that regulated private monopoly is more efficient than public monopoly. By and large, the Thatcher government has simply privatized public monopolies without increasing competition in the industry. But the privatization program has been successful politically because widening share ownership has created a constituency supportive of the program while reducing the public sector's need to borrow.

In responding to Vickers and Yarrow, Sir Ian MacGregor summarizes more than two decades of his career in public enterprise the Great Britain. A former chairman of several large state enterprises, including British Steel and the National Coal Board, Sir Ian outlines some of the dangers of state ownership. A major difference between management in state-owned enterprise and the private sector, he points out, is the amount of time devoted to labor matters: over seventy percent in the SOE.

Another personal perspective on the Thatcher government's privatization strategy is offered by Sir Alan Walters, a former economic advisor to the Prime Minister. He differs strongly with Vickers and Yarrow, particularly with respect to the importance of the "public sector borrowing requirement" in the success of privatization. He also offers some interesting comments on the mechanics of selling-off SOEs and the role of merchant banks in the transactions.

Finally, in *Privatization in Canada: Ideology, Symbolism or Substance*, W.T. Stanbury focuses on efforts by both the federal and provincial governments. In comparison to its southern neighbor, Canada has been generally perceived as a "public enterprise country", so that privatization is of particular significance there. Following a broad description of historical and current privatization activity at the federal and provincial levels, Stanbury examines several hypotheses to explain the nature and extent of privatization in Canada. The first is that privatization as an ideology has taken hold in governments across Canada. The second is that privatizing is a reaction to problems of management, financing, and control of "crown" corporations. The third hypothesis, for which Stanbury finds the most support, is that privatization in Canada between 1983 and 1988 was largely an exercise in symbolic politics designed to give the appearance of change while not really making much change at all. He also draws attention to several cases in which the sale of state enterprises resulted in highly complex transactions, which made it difficult to determine the actual proceeds the government received.

Stanbury notes, however, that the full extent of privatization in Canada is as yet undetermined because the process is still underway. With the announcement in 1987 that the extensive non-rail assets of Canadian National Railways would be sold, and the subsequent announcement that Air Canada would be privatized in stages, the federal government moved beyond a symbolic level of commitment to privatization. Moreover, the Province of British Columbia in early 1988 was undertaking the most innovative program of privatization in Canada. It was beginning to contract-out the services of line departments and had called for bids on the maintenance of all bridges and highways. Political and union opposition is intense, so the full program may not be implemented.

Each paper is accompanied by the comments of two readers who provide their own perspectives on the subject. The discussants draw on their experiences as policy advisors, academics and public enterprise managers.

In the promotion of competition, the generation of revenues from asset sales, or the improvement of the management of state enterprises, privatization has rejuvenated the economies of industrial and developing nations alike. The papers and comments contained in this volume all focus to some degree on the efficiency and management of government and private enterprises. The theme that emerges from this evidence is that as long as there is a discrepancy between the two, the trend toward privatization -- which began in earnest in the early 1980s -- should and will continue.

# CHAPTER ONE

# The Control and Performance of State-Owned Enterprises

Richard J. Zeckhauser and Murray Horn*

## INTRODUCTION

Society organizes economic activity in different forms chosen in response to varying transaction costs. If owners of enterprises could choose freely among organizational forms, we might expect that the forms observed in particular areas -- say between partnership and corporation or small business and monolithic enterprise -- were well chosen. Even if such choices were not made consciously, but any form could compete in any arena, forces of natural selection would push toward optimality.[1]

---

*Frank P. Ramsey Professor of Political Economy, Kennedy School, Harvard University, and Director, Economics Branch of the New Zealand Treasury, respectively. Darryll Hendricks and Scott Feira provided able research assistance. Nancy Jackson, Kevin J. Murphy, Sam Peltzman and participants in the Conference on Privatization in Britain and North America (Washington, D.C., November 1987) gave us helpful comments. We would also like to thank Preston Robert Tisch (Postmaster General, U.S. Postal Service) and W. Graham Claytor, Jr. (Chairman and President of Amtrak), both of whom we interviewed in November 1987 as part of this research. Zeckhauser's more general research on business-government relationships is sponsored by the Business and Government Center, Harvard University.

[1] It is usually assumed that organizational forms in the private sector survive because they represent the lowest-cost way to meet the market demands of consumers (Jensen 1983, p. 331). The implicit assumption is that the resulting competitive outcome is simply accepted: Affected groups do not turn to the political system, which has a monopoly on force, to favor one

The real world is not so simple, however, and we cannot be confident that state-owned enterprises (SOEs) spring up where they are most efficient.

State-owned enterprises represent a response to significant transaction costs, most notably contracting costs and insecure property rights. But political concerns also play an important part, loading onto these enterprises many additional responsibilities beyond the efficient production of goods. This makes their task more difficult to perform and their performance more difficult to judge. Enterprises burdened in this manner must be given real economic advantages if they are to survive. And so they are. State-owned enterprises are often protected from competition by edict, and/or they receive subsidies, either cash or a cheap or free resource.[2] And as government-owned entities, SOEs are relieved of many tax and regulatory obligations.[3]

The introduction of political or distributional criteria does not make efficiency irrelevant, however. We expect politicians to try to minimize the dead-weight loss associated with achieving any given income distribution. If redistribution were costless, more efficient organizational forms would be expected to dominate less efficient ones (Pareto superior arrangements would secure unanimous approval). Redistribution is generally assumed to be costly, however, and Pareto inferior organizational forms may survive if they benefit politically powerful groups. Public ownership can provide a vehicle for these groups to influence pricing, production, and investment decisions. But public ownership is just one of many devices that can be used to benefit private interests. The choice between forms of intervention, such as public ownership and regulation, will be influenced by the dead-weight costs of the alternatives.

The more an SOE is insulated from competitive pressures, and the less able citizens are to direct the manner in which it operates, the less confident we can be that it is an appropriate organizational form or that it is performing effectively. By contrast, where competitive pressures are significant, we would expect superior performance. Thus the University of California at Berkeley, which intends to remain a leading research university, must work hard to keep up with its private competitors. And within the

---

organizational form over another.

[2] For example, only the U.S. Postal Service is allowed to deliver the mails, Amtrak is subsidized directly and the Tennessee Valley Authority (TVA) borrows from the Federal Financing Bank at the cost of funds to the federal government.

[3] Utilities, for example, may set prices without impositions by regulatory authorities.

airline sector, we would expect a state-owned international carrier to be better operated than its domestic counterpart, assuming the latter is a monopoly.[4]

The question of state-owned enterprises is usually framed in terms of absolute advantage vis-a-vis one alternative: how do state-owned enterprises perform relative to their private counterparts?[5] Our analysis will focus primarily on comparative advantage and will look at two alternatives: In which areas will state-owned enterprises perform relatively the best and worst in comparison with (1) public bureaucracy and (2) their private counterparts? (To be realistic, we suspect many of our readers will try to distill absolute advantage conclusions.[6]) Our findings should be helpful even in a society where the overall level of government participation cannot be significantly altered, but areas of responsibility can be shifted between state firms and the private sector.

Private for-profit corporations are not the only alternative to state-owned enterprises. Nonprofit organizations, such as those that run most higher education institutions, hospitals, and museums in the United States, should be considered as well.[7] And moving in the opposite direction, toward greater centralization, it is important to consider direct bureaucratic production, such as we find in the patent office, or bureaucratic procurement, as when a city contracts with private garbage haulers. When making these comparisons, we are interested in how the distinctive characteristics of public enterprise affect its comparative performance. Will the emphasis on produc-

---

[4] Indian colleagues inform us that in their homeland the domestic state-owned Indian Airlines is generally perceived as significantly less efficient than Air India, the international state-owned carrier.

[5] There are many dangers in the absolute advantage approach. It brings to the fore ideology and preconceptions as the basis for judgement. Moreover, since each form has advantages and disadvantages, few conclusions can be reached predominantly on a conceptual basis.

[6] We believe that virtually no one is objective about this area. Test yourself. Look around the world and compare the performance of SOEs on average with that of a perfectly functioning private market. Now compare the performance on average of private firms and the perfect private market. If we now gathered these pairs of scores for a number of perfectly objective researchers, we should find no correlation in scores for the two sectors. If individuals were optimists or pessimists, or easy or hard graders, then we would get a positive correlation. If people differentially recognized the costs of information transfer and incentives that confront both sectors, then we should find a positive correlation as well. Our speculation, however, is that we would get a negative correlation due to non-objectivity: If you like SOEs, you dislike private firms, and vice versa.

[7] See Hansmann (1980) for a discussion of the behavior of nonprofit organizations, a subject beyond the scope of this analysis.

ing goods and services for sale lead public enterprises to be treated, and to behave, differently from the rest of the public sector? And what impact will government ownership have on the performance of a business enterprise?

Our plan of attack is as follows. First we define the distinguishing features of SOEs, describe the more prevalent types found in industrialized countries, and highlight their important shared features.[8] Subsequent analysis explores the consequences of these characteristics for SOE performance and, hence, for the roles they are asked to play. Second, we define some of the reasons why a society might choose to adopt state-owned enterprises. This section of the paper compares public enterprise first with bureaucracy and then with private enterprise. The third section of the paper examines the performance of SOEs on both a conceptual and empirical basis. Relative performance is related to the characteristics inherent in state ownership, such as diffuse and nontransferable ownership, the lack of a stock price to indicate performance, the organization's possible subjection to claims of the political process, and its insulation from the dissatisfaction of its residual claimants. We assume throughout that the political process is far more responsive to concentrated interests -- those with a large per-capita stake -- than to diffuse interests (Peltzman 1976).

Our focus is on management -- the incentives it faces and the conflicts to which it is subjected. The performance of labor has fewer distinctive characteristics. In terms of their freedom in dealing with labor, most SOEs end up somewhere between private firms and the bureaucracy with its rigid civil service rules and personnel procedures. Presumably then, SOEs suffer a greater agency loss in their labor dealings than do private firms.

## DEFINITION AND DESCRIPTION OF SOEs

State-owned enterprises are business enterprises owned by governments. Aharoni (1986, p. 6) argues that they have three distinguishing characteristics: "First ... they must be owned by the government. Second, ... [they] must be engaged in the production of goods and services for sale ... Third, sales revenues of SOEs should bear some relationship to cost."

---

[8] Our predominant interest is in the role of SOEs within a developed nation with a liberal democracy and a significant commitment to free enterprise. In practice, state-owned enterprises have been most prominent in socialist and communist nations, particularly in developing countries. But we believe it would be dangerous to draw too many lessons from the experiences which are so different from those of the developed liberal democracies.

In contrast to the for-profit corporation, the SOE is not a well-defined legal form. State-owned enterprises are often created to meet special circumstances, and they differ significantly among themselves in several dimensions, such as independence of boards, the role of private shareholders, levels of government subsidy, and the extent to which the government is a customer.

## Government Ownership

Government ownership of enterprise assets has far-reaching implications. Asset ownership is more diffuse than in the private sector, and so long as individuals remain taxpayers it is nontransferable and compulsory.[9] While SOEs can be sold, or privatized, by collective action, individual taxpayers can "sell their shares" in a public enterprise only by moving outside the political jurisdiction of the owning government. In the private sector, where shareholding is both transferable and voluntary, ownership can become concentrated in the hands of those who believe they know how to better manage the firm. This is virtually impossible in public enterprise. Furthermore, because the individual taxpayers' interests in an SOE are so diffuse, they have very little to gain from monitoring management.

Two aspects of government ownership are likely to be particularly important. First, the government need not own all of the SOE's shares. If the characteristics of government ownership are important, we would expect the performance of SOEs to vary in a systematic way with the degree of private participation. Second, we expect that the level of government -- national, state, or local -- may be important. Spann (1977) observes that voter mobility is likely to be a greater constraint on local than federal government. We believe other features of localized government are also likely to influence SOE performance and that these features make government ownership more attractive at the local level.

---

[9] If the public enterprise were fully responsive to the interests of the broad citizenry, the allocation of its benefits would still be a complex matter. Increased revenues from an enterprise would be divided between reducing taxes and increasing expenditures, say in the ratio T to 1-T. Citizen i gets it of any tax reduction and ie of any expenditure increase. His share of an increased dollar from an enterprise would be Tit+(1-T)ie. Prudent fiscal management of SOEs is often identified as principally a taxpayer concern. It is important to recognize that those who benefit from the expenditures of government are also stakeholders in an SOE's financial success.

## Business Character

SOEs are distinguished from other parts of the public sector by their business character. While bureaus rely primarily on periodic budgetary grants to finance their activities, SOEs typically depend on revenues from the sale of goods or services.[10] Thus they specialize in the production of goods and services that can be readily sold; that is, transactions costs are not inordinately high. By implication, the costs of defining the amount of a good or service consumed and of identifying consumers are low. Furthermore, it must be relatively easy to ensure payment -- to charge for service and to exclude those who do not pay. It would be hard to establish the State Department as an SOE because of the difficulty of defining its output and the tradeoffs between its various objectives; moreover, since foreign policy is a quintessential public good, exclusion is not possible. We argue that production of salable goods and services makes it easier for those both inside and outside the enterprise to monitor its management. There is, then, less need for bureaucratic procedural controls that limit management flexibility; moreover, the costs of imposing noncommercial objectives on the enterprise become more transparent.

## Diversity of SOEs

Even in the industrialized countries, SOEs are extremely diverse; they operate in a range of market environments, have markedly different histories, and are justified in many different ways. Some SOEs can be thought of as essentially resource preserving. In these cases the government assumes ownership to preserve private rents, to maintain a "vital" industry (which may produce a number of externalities), to avoid the costs associated with disruptive resource reallocation, or to operate a natural monopoly (which, perhaps because of declining costs, can only be operated most efficiently at a loss). These are often enterprises taken over by government because they could not continue operations profitably under private ownership; should they cease operation, there would be a loss of efficiency.

---

10 This distinction is weaker in some cases than others. We would classify Amtrak as an SOE even though its operating revenues covered only a little over half of its operating expenses in 1985 and 1986 (Amtrak 1986 Annual Report, p. 26). However, we do require a degree of independence from government bureaucracy, with some insulation from the annual budget cycle.

A second class of SOE might be thought of as essentially resource hoarding. In these cases, governments find it difficult to allocate the property rights to natural resources that are widely perceived as belonging to the community as a whole. The TVA might be an example.

When the government wishes to promote noncommercial values, it sometimes employs SOEs. In an extreme case, they may produce public goods. Government-owned laboratories, for example, might also take some commercial contracts or license patents. A number of governments are launching such efforts in leading-edge, high-technology fields such as microelectronics and biogenetics.[11] Other SOEs are kept within government ownership because it is believed to be a more secure way of promoting values. The state might own vital industry, for example, because of a concern about resource availability under conditions of war. A final group in this third class of values-promoting SOEs arises in situations where the government may not trust private producers. Though public schools and nursing homes are not strictly SOEs, since their revenues are not significant relative to their costs, society's general reluctance to privatize these institutions probably relates to the belief that for-profit firms will be less able to promote civic values in the first instance, or will take advantage of citizens in the second. Prisons, also not strictly SOEs, provide an interesting mixture of value protection and resource hoarding. A hesitancy in turning prisons over to private hands reflects both a desire to preserve the government's monopoly on the right to incarcerate and use force, and a concern that society's valuation of humane treatment would not be respected.

Our fourth class of SOEs falls in the category described by Gordon (1981) as rent collectors. She points out, for example, that Canadian governments became involved in some resource-based industries in order to share the rents created by the large increase in commodity prices during the early 1970s. Fiscal monopolies that are granted by the state to raise revenue -- as for tobacco and liquor -- are the more traditional sources of such rents.

This summary description of SOEs only hints at the diversity of their

---

[11] The human genome project, a monumental attempt to map the genetic structure of man, provides an intriguing example of various ways to produce information, which is often described as the quintessential public good. Some propose that the project be undertaken within the government, in a manner that parallels the Manhattan Project. Other proposals call for the government to contract out. Walter Gilbert, the Nobel Prize winner, has made the more startling proposal that a private firm undertake the effort, and then sell the information.

activities and the motives for their creation.[12] And it does not tell us much about why governments have turned to ownership rather than some other means such as regulating or subsidizing private production.

**Common Features**

Despite their diversity, many SOEs have important features in common. Their responsibilities and resources are often very different from those of private firms. State enterprises are frequently created to meet redistributive objectives -- for example, to favor certain consumers, regions, domestic suppliers or employees -- as well as commercial objectives. Moreover, various groups can pressure the enterprise to meet possibly conflicting objectives. Vernon (1981, p. 11) notes that "in the several nationalizations of British steel, for instance, numerous motivations were evident. Those in the Labor Party who were committed to a socialist ideology, for instance, saw it in part as a transfer of national power from the private to the public sector . . . Those tied more closely to the rank and file of Britain's labor movement, however, tended to see it as a way of improving labor's bargaining power . . . Those in the Board of Trade hoped that nationalization could be used to improve the productivity of the steel industry and improve its exports. And so on." This "confusion of goals" has an important impact on enterprise performance. SOEs are also typically given special privileges, including both rights and resources.[13] This creates an invisible surplus -- what we term the "available pot" -- that can be used for redistribution without the

12 Lewin (1982, pp. 57-8) suggests that "there is no clear pattern to explain why state-owned enterprises came about in mixed economies. Case studies of the origins of individual SOEs suggest many additional motives for their creation: Political retaliation (e.g. Renault and Berliet), historical accident (e.g. potash and ammonia production in France), promote political and ideological tenets (e.g. redistribution of wealth), balance social and commercial costs and benefits (e.g. railroads), exploit profits from scarce resources (oil, coal) or commodities made artificially scarce (fiscal monopolies), redistribute wealth and employment, provide a 'window in the industry', preserve declining industries, boost exports, curtail imports and improve the balance of payments, control strategic industries, provide investment in infant industries (aerospace), protect domestic industries, cross-subsidize downstream industries, encourage regional development, control inflation, promote national security and national prestige, reduce dependence on foreign technology and raw materials, improve productivity, provide leadership in mixed industries, and foster high risk and/or high technology industries."

13 Rights include legal monopoly, relief from regulation or implicit price guarantees. Resources include the use of rivers, land, or even inputs like capital and energy, at well below competitive market prices.

enterprise suffering visible losses.[14] As Aharoni argues, this can enable the government to achieve objectives that it does not necessarily want to make public, such as subsidizing certain sectors of the economy or benefiting certain groups or regions. Consequently, governments may be less likely to create SOEs when there is a difficulty in assuring the enterprise of this available pot.

A comparison of the SOE sector in various countries reveals two interesting regularities. First, the contribution of SOEs to GNP was about 10 percent on average for the industrialized countries in 1980, and most countries, including developing nations, are clustered in the 5 to 15 percent range (Table 1.1).[15] The outliers are the communist countries, where state enterprises are obviously much more important, and the United States, where their share is much smaller than average. Second, SOEs tend to be important in the same sectors everywhere. They are virtually never involved in agricultural production in Western nations. But SOEs are prevalent in postal service, which is a state-owned monopoly in all industrialized countries, and in utilities and infrastructure.[16] Production in many of those sectors is monopolistic, which may make it easier to generate an available pot for redistribution. Moreover, these sectors are widely regarded as strategically important. Both of these factors create pressure for government intervention, which usually takes the form of ownership or regulation. While these kinds of intervention are not perfect substitutes, the choice between them -- which often determines the importance of SOEs in these sectors -- will be influenced by their relative cost. Cost considerations are also likely to be important in determining the role of SOEs in other sectors of the economy. While

---

[14] The "available pot" is the surplus that could be generated from the resources given to the SOE if it were run as a private, for-profit firm. The pot can be increased by extending other privileges to SOEs. In some countries SOEs are exempt from laws - including tax laws - that govern private firms. Moreover, SOEs need not pay dividends; they enjoy lower financing costs (e.g. via access to the tax-exempt bond market), and they may receive purchasing and sales preferences from government.

[15] Table 1.1 reproduces some of the data collected by Short (1984, p. 115) comparing the quantitative importance of SOEs across countries. These data illustrate both the atypically low share of SOEs in the United States and the broad similarities among countries. Short notes that, while the investment share of developing countries was much higher than it was in industrial countries, "the majority of countries in both groups had investment shares of between 10 percent and 25 percent and output shares of between 5 percent and 15 percent." However, he also cautions that "these similarities probably result in part from differences in the coverage of public enterprise statistics."

[16] The "utilities and infrastructure" category includes transportation (rail and airways), energy (electric utilities and gas), and telecommunications. See Short (1984), Lewin (1982), and McCraw (1984).

Table 1.1 Output and Investment Shares of Public Enterprises

| | Years | % Share in GDP at Factor Cost[1] | % Share in Gross Fixed Capital Formation[2] |
|---|---|---|---|
| Australia | 78-79 | 9.4 | 19.2 |
| Austria[1] | 78-79 | 14.5 | 19.2 |
| Belgium | 78-79 | .. | 13.1 |
| Canada[2] | 78-81 | .. | 14.8 |
| Denmark | 1974 | 6.3 | 8.3 |
| Finland[2] | 74-75 | .. | 13.6 |
| France | 1974 | 11.9 | 14.0 |
| Germany(FRG) | 78-79 | 10.2 | 10.8 |
| Ireland | 1978 | .. | 11.8 |
| Italy[1] | 1978 | 7.5 | 16.4 |
| Japan[2] | 78-81 | .. | 11.2 |
| Luxemburg | 1974 | .. | 9.6 |
| Netherlands[2] | 1978 | .. | 12.6 |
| Norway | 78-81 | .. | 22.6 |
| Spain[1] | 1979 | 4.1 | 16.6 |
| Sweden[1] | 78-80 | .. | 15.3 |
| United Kingdom | 78-81 | 10.9 | 16.8 |
| United States | 1978 | .. | 4.4 |
| India | 1978 | 10.3 | 33.7 |
| Korea[2] | 74-77 | 6.4 | 25.1 |

SOURCE: Short(1984)

[1] Share in GDP at market prices where indicated.

[2] Share in gross domestic capital formation, including change in stocks, where indicated

agricultural production may be very important for some countries, public enterprise is likely to be comparatively inefficient in this sector, as a number of communist nations have learned to their dismay.

## WHAT ROLE FOR SOEs?

SOEs represent a compromise between production within a bureaucracy and a private corporation. They may appear to escape much of the political discipline imposed on the public sector and the market discipline imposed on the private sector. The fact that government production is considered at all indicates the presence of some market imperfections in the arena where the SOE operates. But does an SOE represent an effective compromise, or would either private or bureaucratic production be preferable in each case? We address this question by comparing SOEs first with bureaucracy and then with private firms.

### Public Bureaucracy versus Public Enterprise

Niskanen (1971, p. 15) defines bureaus as "nonprofit organizations which are financed, at least in part, by a periodic appropriation or grant". Nonprofit organizations are defined as those in which neither managers nor owners can appropriate the difference between costs and revenues as personal income. A public bureau is one that is owned by government and financed primarily by government grants. SOEs, in contrast, specialize in the production of output for sale and tend to rely on the revenue from these sales, rather than on grants, to finance their activities.

Government bureaucracy can be used to supply the goods and services that are often supplied by SOEs. Indeed, many SOEs -- like the Canadian National Railway and the U.S. Postal Service -- assumed roles previously carried out by bureaus. The two forms have some distinctive advantages and disadvantages.

**The Advantages of Public Enterprise.** SOEs have several advantages over bureaus when it comes to the public supply of goods and services. First, because the sale of output makes it easier for those inside and outside the firm to monitor the performance of managers, there is less need to rely on the very restrictive procedural constraints that are applied to the rest of the public sector. These constraints -- like civil service rules on hiring, firing, pay and promotion, budgetary controls and operating procedures -- severely limit managerial flexibility and the ability to delegate decision-making power to those best able to use it. These constraints also tend to distort resource allocation, as when a department head strives to spend the full amount allotted for each line item in the budget (Walsh 1978, p. 225). When the output of the organization is sold, financial performance can be used to monitor management; there is less need to rely on procedural constraints to limit the abuse of managerial discretion. Moreover, to the extent that managers look to the private sector for future job opportunities, they will have an incentive to signal their ability through measurable indicators like good financial performance.

These considerations suggest that SOE managers are likely to be less constrained than the rest of the public sector by either budgetary controls or civil service regulations. This is indeed the case. For example, Walsh (1978, p. 40) notes that public authorities are usually free "from the civil service systems and pay scales of parent governments; from central budget administration; from detailed pre-audits and post-audits by government auditing agencies; from government regulation on contracting, purchasing, and price setting". In fact, she observes, "Even public authorities whose employees are legally part of city, state or federal civil service have less rigid job classifications and procedural rules" (p. 239).

The ability to do without bureaucratic procedural controls will vary. Financial measures of performance are more meaningful when the special responsibilities and resources often accorded SOEs are less significant -- so that, for example, managers find it difficult to excuse a poor financial showing by citing demands placed on them to meet noncommercial criteria.[17] Management is also likely to worry more about financial performance when it is competing for customers (who can go elsewhere if the SOE's prices are too high), or when taxpayers or potential employers can compare the SOE's performance with that of similarly situated firms. Finally, managers are unlikely to be permitted substantial discretion when problems of moral hazard are particularly severe -- for example, in the determination of management compensation. Despite the greater flexibility noted by Walsh, senior

---

[17] Such excuses are more easily avoided if the government subsidizes the SOE directly for the cost incurred in meeting noncommercial criteria.

management compensation is often tied to civil service pay scales and may be substantially below private-sector levels.[18]

A second advantage of SOEs is that they allow politicians to distance themselves from public-sector activities that create popular discontent. This may be one reason why considerable emphasis is placed on the independence of these enterprises.[19] Tierney (1984) suggests that this was an important motive for Congress' willingness to give up direct responsibility for the operation of the postal office, which, as a focus of citizen complaint, provided few opportunities to win votes.

The desire to distance themselves from trouble does not explain either why politicians should favor public ownership over the regulation of private enterprise or why bureaus' commercial activities should be a focus of this desire. The first question is addressed in the next section of the paper. Two considerations are likely to be important in answering the second. First, it would be difficult for politicians to distance themselves if they retained control of an organization's financing. The ability to finance the organization from sales may be important to make this distancing credible. Second, the goods and services sold by SOEs tend to be ones whose quality, quantity, and cost are easily judged by consumers. Thus, services such as mail delivery, telephone communications, and passenger railroads are bound to attract criticism because their deficiencies are highly visible; delays, losses, breakages and service costs are easily monitored by consumers. The characteristics that make these goods and services easy to sell could also make them a continual source of political embarrassment if they remained part of the bureaucracy.

Reducing political interference is also widely perceived as improving efficiency. Thus Priest (1975, p. 68) notes that "Congress determined that among the principal causes of the [post] office's decline was the political influence to which the office had been subjected since 1792." To purge this political influence, the Postal Reorganization Act of 1970 established the Postal Service as an independent entity. Gordon (1981, p. 57) makes a similar point with respect to the Canadian National Railroad: "The Drayton-Acworth

---

[18] For example, the salary of the current head of Amtrak is linked to executive-level civil service pay rates and is considerably below that paid to executives with similar positions in the private sector. Unlike his private-sector counterparts, he receives no stock options.

[19] Tierney (1984, p. 78) makes this point: "It is no coincidence that the legislative records attached to laws creating these organizations are filled with pointed references to the independence these organizations are to be granted." The desire at least to give the appearance of independence may also help explain why members of SOE boards are often appointed for fixed and staggered terms (Walsh 1978, p. 172).

Commission rejected a departmental form of managing the railway. Partisanship and public scrutiny had made management of the Intercolonial Railway, which was run as a government department, difficult and inefficient. To put distance between the government and the state railway -- and thereby minimize political interference -- a crown corporation, Canadian National Railways, was established." Even if individual politicians or parties could gain from intervening in the commercial operation of bureaus, they may be better off by collectively denying themselves this opportunity. Moving an activity into an "independent" SOE may help achieve this objective because it raises the individual's cost of interference. In this case, commercial activities are vested in SOEs because either the individual's net political gains from interference are slight or the collective efficiency losses are large.

A third advantage is that SOEs allow politicians to meet voter demands with a minimum of budgetary expenditure. This consideration has been particularly important in the creation of SOEs at the state and local level in the United States, where politicians have been confronted by constitutional limits on public borrowing (Walsh 1978, pp. 23-24).[20] Even when limits are not made explicit, there are political constraints on the extent to which taxes can be used to meet demands for public spending. Taxpayers cannot establish contingent controls on spending; they can only restrain these demands through some sort of cap on subsidies. Given these gross restrictions, one way to meet voter demands is to "corporatize" those parts of the public sector that produce goods and services. The important characteristic of the SOE in this regard is its ability to finance its activities largely from sales revenues.[21]

Employees and managers may also favor the "corporatization" that comes through the creation of a public enterprise, since it makes possible higher salaries and greater financial independence (Aharoni 1986, p. 36). Demsetz (1983) argues that managers differ in their tastes for nonpecuniary consumption and that managers, and presumably other employees, who prefer

---

[20] The case of Pennsylvania is particularly dramatic. Nineteenth-century defaults resulted in constitutional revisions restricting municipal borrowing to 7 percent of assessed property valuation and putting a cap on state debt. These restrictions became particularly severe in the 1930s, when property prices were falling. Shortly after the passage of a 1935 act exempting government-owned corporations from municipal debt restrictions, over 50 local corporations were established. By 1973 Pennsylvania had 1,872 municipal authorities, most of which simply issue revenue bonds and invest the proceeds in construction of facilities that are then leased back to a government agency (Walsh 1978, pp. 119-22).

[21] SOEs may issue bonds to smooth out capital needs. However, the absence of risk capital might be a constraint: for example, in building a power plant that might not be licensed for operation.

more of this type of consumption will be attracted to enterprises where monitoring costs are high. As long as the relevant labor markets are reasonably competitive, these managers will receive lower pecuniary rewards.[22] If the population of managers is reasonably heterogeneous in this regard, there will be a demand for an array of institutional forms that offer different mixes of pecuniary and nonpecuniary benefits. Because the behavior of managers is easier to monitor when financial measures of performance are available, public-sector workers who favor a higher ratio of pecuniary to nonpecuniary rewards will favor corporatization of those public-sector activities that can provide useful financial monitoring data. Not surprisingly, pecuniary compensation in SOEs tends to be higher than in the rest of the public sector -- where monitoring is more difficult -- and lower than in the private sector -- where monitoring is easier (Walsh 1978, p. 247; Aharoni 1986, p. 68).

**The Limits of Public Enterprise.** Given the advantages of SOEs, why not abandon grants and sell all public services -- or, where they cannot be sold direct to consumers, fund them on the basis of per unit subsidies?

For one thing, significant costs are associated with attempting to strike, and enforce, separate contracts for each good or service produced by a bureau. Contracting for many services supplied by bureaus would be extremely difficult because of the difficulty of measuring outputs or of defining goals and the tradeoffs among goals (Zeckhauser 1986a).[23] The ability to measure an organization's output is an obvious precondition for the sale of that output at a per-unit rate. Moreover, compensating suppliers only on the basis of characteristics that are easy to define (like quantity) creates a financial incentive to ignore characteristics (like quality) that are harder to define.

Even if it were possible to define bureau output well enough to contract for its supply, it might be extremely expensive to compensate it on a per-unit basis because of transactions costs (Coase 1937; Cheung 1983). Many very detailed contracts might be needed if the activities performed by a bureau varied greatly or changed frequently, or if they -- or the tradeoffs among them -- were difficult to specify in advance. A bureau's annual appropriation

---

[22] For example, Paul Volcker accepted a much lower salary as Federal Reserve chairman than he could have expected in the private sector and derived satisfaction from "getting something done" (Wall StreetJournal, July 24, 1987).

[23] Niskanen (1971, p. 20) argues that "the primary functional reason for choosing bureaus to supply these services [rather than contracting with profit-seeking organizations], I suspect, is the difficulty of defining the characteristics of the services sufficiently to contract for their supply."

resembles Coase's employment contract: Rather than meet specific contractual obligations in return for specified unit payments, bureau heads agree, within certain limits, to obey the directions of government in exchange for a certain annual grant. There is then no need to draw up detailed contracts in advance because attention can be restricted to events as they unfold.

Finally, even if transactions costs did not prohibit "selling" output on a per-unit basis, politicians might continue to use bureaus as a way of disguising redistribution. The histories of the U.S. Post Office and Canada's Intercolonial Railway illustrate that politicians find it relatively easy to interfere in the commercial operations of departments. Given the relative independence of SOEs, the greater emphasis placed on financial performance, and the ease of measuring this performance, the cost of requiring these organizations to meet noncommercial criteria becomes more transparent; thus they are less desirable instruments for meeting legislators' distributional objectives.

## Public versus Private Enterprise

Aharoni (1986, p. 4) identifies a number of ideological, political, economic, social, and administrative reasons for state ownership. For example, he notes that "public enterprise may be a pragmatic response to economic problems, such as the need to eliminate, reduce or control a monopoly or to ensure an adequate supply of essential goods and services at reasonable prices when excessive financial and technical risks deter private-sector investment or in cases where the private sector is not able to deliver what the government feels is required in the public interest." Here we develop a framework for considering the political and economic factors that are likely to favor establishing a public enterprise. We do not wish to suggest, however, that the very existence of a state-owned enterprise implies the desirability of that organizational form, or vice versa. The performance of public enterprises is discussed in the next section of the paper.

Given that the ownership structure is the essential difference between public and private enterprise, we must look to differences in ownership to explain any preference for SOEs. Government ownership is extremely diffuse, and asset owners are in a much weaker position than their private-sector counterparts to resist the claims of more concentrated interests, like consumers and input suppliers, who have an interest in the operation of the enterprise. Moreover, conflicting claims are settled by political, as well as market, influences. Furthermore, government ownership also has ideological currency. Finally, nationalization, like privatization, signals a dramatic change in circumstances, and in some cases this may produce favorable effects.

In this section of the paper we will examine, in some detail, four classes of situations where the creation of SOEs may be desirable: to overcome problems caused by government opportunism; to meet distributional objectives; to overcome difficulties in assigning property rights; and to respond to ideological demands. What are the special characteristics of government that may favor public over private enterprise?

First, government can not credibly promise not to expropriate private profit once irreversible investments have been made (Rodrik and Zeckhauser 1987). This implicit threat may be particularly important if markets offer the potential for surpluses, as they may if they are not competitive or if they offer rents (such as the ownership of natural resources or fertile land).

Second, government is responsible for ensuring the supply of goods and services that are difficult to sell on markets, such as defense or flood control, and for redistributing income. It may be easier -- certainly politically -- to promote these objectives in conjunction with an operating entity. When many objectives are mixed in together in this way, it may be difficult to allocate production costs or to determine an appropriate level for a subsidy. This may lead government to favor public enterprise.[24]

Third, government is responsible for allocating property rights. When these rights are hard to define or value, government may want to hold on to the rights for resources controlled by public enterprises rather than allocate them to private owners. Major hydroelectric projects may fall into this category.

Fourth, the government is assigned responsibilities and has economic interests that stretch beyond those of any private-sector participants. For example, the price of keeping a troubled enterprise alive may be less than the cost of the social transfers that would be engendered by a failure. Government participation in an industry often yields externalities to parties who could not be charged, yet the government, following the cost-benefit tradition, may feel

---

[24] For example, the TVA and Bonneville Power Authority (BPA) dams were originally built for three purposes - navigation, flood control, and power; the government met the costs allocated to the first two, essentially public, goods and used the public authority to recover the cost of power generation via consumer charges. For example, only 32.5 percent of the cost of constructing the Bonneville dam was attributed to power generation and had to be recovered by the BPA in power charges. The histories of the TVA and BPA also illustrate the importance of redistribution. Part of the rationale for government involvement was that competition from public suppliers would encourage the private sector to develop low-rate, high-volume business that would extend electricity to all.

it appropriate to count those benefits.[25] Assuming rigidities in wages or prices, the government may also act to achieve economically efficient outcomes that can not be achieved through ordinary bargaining. Workers, for example, may be receiving rents from the continued operation of a firm; yet its representatives may be unwilling to cut wage demands even close to opportunity cost. Many bailouts of English firms have fallen (or have been thought to fall) into this category.

Fifth, an SOE presumably has an incentive, independent of its long-term reputation or profitability, to consider the welfare of its customers. Because SOE managers do not appropriate any of the difference between costs and revenues as personal income, they have much less of an incentive to "rip off" their customers by compromising on those aspects of output, like quality, that are hard to measure. (We leave aside the question of how effective private markets are in preventing such behavior.) By this reasoning, SOEs should be more effective than private firms in markets where information is difficult to transmit, customers are poorly informed, and quality is hard to measure. These considerations provide an argument for government-owned hospitals and nursing homes.

Sixth, nationalization may also form part of a "throw the rascals out" strategy, switching back and forth between public and private as one form or the other becomes ossified. For example, the creation of Amtrak allowed the major players in passenger rail service to break out of unproductive relationships that had become firmly entrenched.[26]

Seventh, nationalization, or continued state ownership, often has ideological appeal. It would be difficult to explain some of the cross-country variation in the importance of SOEs, or some of the patterns of nationalization and denationalization, without some reference to ideological factors. We now examine some of these situations in more detail.

---

[25] Presumably the rescue of the U.S. rail system fell into this category: Otherwise discomfited customers of the railroads gained more from the continuation of rail freight-hauling than it cost the government.

[26] The effect on work rules provides an important illustration. When Amtrak took on railroad employees, it was not obliged to hire them under their existing contract. The new contracts abolished old work rules that linked pay to miles traveled and engine weight. Paying on the basis of hours worked, rather than a day's pay per 100 miles, reduced the cost of running a train from Washington to Florida from 24 man-days to eight. The creation of Amtrak may have sent an important signal to employees of the plight of the railroads, convincing them to give ground when negotiating new contracts.

**Lack of Commitment: The Problem of Government Opportunism.** Government cannot commit itself not to increase its regulation or taxation of private firms opportunistically. Moreover, because governments change, they may have less incentive than long-lived private firms, whose share prices incorporate reputational capital, to build a reputation for consistency. The risk of adverse policy changes increases the cost of private production and may, in the extreme, discourage private investment altogether.[27] In cases where these costs are high, public production may be favored. Indeed, one of Aharoni's main economic arguments for public enterprise is that it can ensure essential supplies when excessive risk deters private investment.[28] He did not address the opportunism issue, but it certainly creates the type of risk that inhibits private actors. We explore this argument in more detail here, using the term "opportunism" to denote any pernicious intervention by government that it would not have undertaken had it been able to commit its actions in advance.

The threat of expropriation reduces the efficiency of private production; it creates uncertainty about future profitability, attenuates incentives for profit-seeking (especially if -- as seems usual -- higher profits increase the probability of exploitation),[29] creates incentives for rent-seeking, and distorts the implicit factor prices faced by firms. Several conditions tend to make the pernicious regulation style of expropriation more likely.[30] First, activities that involve substantial economic rents or quasi-rents create an opportunity for low-visibility redistribution. When a firm is a private monopoly, our society may seek to promote efficiency through rate regulation

---

[27] For example, Kydland and Prescott (1977, p. 486) suggested that "rational agents are not making investments in new sources of oil in the anticipation that price controls will be instituted in the future."

[28] Somewhat parallel arguments may explain why organized crime tends to run illegal activities.

[29] Yarrow and Vickers (this volume, p. 229) argue that even the British RPI-X system of rate regulation has this feature in practice. (The RPI-X system limits the annual increase in the average price charged to the rate of inflation of the retail price index (RPI) minus X percent). They argue that "[t]hus, RPI-X by itself does not avoid the incentive problems of rate-of-return regulation."

[30] Some regulation may improve the profitability of incumbent private firms by restraining competition. It therefore may be demanded by the owners of these firms. See Stigler (1971) and Peltzman (1976). We do not explore this case here since we are attempting to explain the demand for public enterprise rather than for regulation.

(to give "normal" profits).[31] However, regulation is not a simple task, and the power to regulate becomes the power to confiscate. For example, some utilities built nuclear power plants that are not now allowed to operate, yet their construction costs are excluded from the rate base. Second, a firm making large profits from firm-specific capital (e.g. because the original investment was very risky) may attract taxation. In this situation the temptation to tax may be particularly strong because the investments have already been made and are sunk costs to the company. Third, governments have less of an incentive to maintain a commitment when it is not possible to carry much of a reputation between elections (e.g. when the political scene is unstable and party discipline weak). Finally, government opportunism is more likely when the gains to the private firm of avoiding regulation are widely dispersed among shareholders. Demsetz and Lehn (1985, pp. 171-173) find that among electric utilities in the United States, less stringent regulation is associated with more concentrated ownership. Although they suggest that causation runs from regulation to ownership concentration, the evidence is also consistent with the opposite interpretation.[32]

Government opportunism is likely to be particularly expensive when production requires a great deal of firm-specific capital (making asset owners vulnerable to expropriation) and regulation is complex so that nonproductive effort is invested in evading regulation and monitoring the firm's compliance. Moreover, regulations may not be adequately adjusted when cost and demand conditions change. These losses are likely to be lower when simple, easily enforced rules can be used (e.g. when demand and cost conditions are reasonably predictable, administrative price maladjustment poses less threat to regulated profit). This may be why regulation is concentrated on homogeneous goods in monopolistic industries like electricity, water, gas, and

---

[31] That regulated private enterprise is often the alternative to public enterprise is illustrated by recent experience with privatization in Canada and Britain. See Stanbury's discussion of Teleglobe Canada (this volume, pp. 284-291) and Vickers and Yarrow (this volume, Chapter Four).

[32] They suggest that when the regulatory climate is less stringent (i.e. considered by Salmon to be more favorable for investment purposes), owners have greater potential for wealth gain by effective monitoring of management performance because there are fewer restrictions and less commission monitoring of management. However, it is also possible that the more concentrated the ownership, the more powerful will be the ownership interests, and the less likely that regulators will be stringent.

telephone service.[33] (Presumably these factors are nearly in balance in arenas where regulated private and public enterprise coexist in the same industry.)

Expropriation is not merely a transfer because it distorts resource decisions along the way.[34] When the dead-weight losses associated with opportunism are large, there is a tradeoff between evils. Consumers may prefer public enterprise despite the additional agency costs it introduces. It is helpful to think of three cases. First, when the expropriation potential is so potentially expensive as to discourage all private production, public enterprise is a potential Pareto improvement if it is efficient enough to generate any cost/benefit surplus, and an actual Pareto improvement if it runs at a profit. Moreover, because there is no private supplier, there will be little political resistance to the demands of potential consumers (and public producers). Without subsidy, which we discuss in the next section of the paper, private ownership cannot substitute for public ownership.

However, the expropriation threat may not be prohibitively expensive. In this second case -- which we might imagine as a comparison of the cost of using an SOE or a regulated private monopoly to meet the demands of a powerful consumer group -- public ownership may have an advantage, often ascribed to nonprofit enterprises, because there is less need to expend resources in monitoring or restricting management actions. Since the owners (citizens) cannot liquidate their residual claims, and since managers as such have no ownership stake in the enterprise, the producer has less incentive to raise prices or cut corners to increase profits.[35] Moreover, because the pecuniary rewards of SOE management are relatively low, these jobs are more likely to be filled by people who derive some satisfaction from providing more,

---

33 Hansmann (1980, p. 886) makes the point that "the simplicity and homogeneity of the services provided by utilities make it relatively easy to determine when a utility has engaged in excessive cost-cutting by reducing the quality of service...[and] also make it relatively easy to establish a price schedule." He also argues that the fact that utilities are monopolies reduces uncertainty about demand and makes it easier to ensure that in setting a price ceiling "the firm receives neither too much nor too little income to cover its costs" (p. 887).

34 Even the threat of regulation or taxation is likely to cause distortions that will increase costs and reduce the efficiency of private production. For example, firms are less likely to engage in high risk/return projects because if they work, the resulting surplus may be taken as a signal that the firm is exploiting its position, and that increases the risk of opportunism. However, these distortions are unlikely to be as serious because suppliers can pick the least-cost way of meeting consumer demands (i.e. of holding off opportunistic government action).

35 A surplus offers some benefits to the management; it is likely to provide resources for future expansion.

and higher-quality, service.[36] A second advantage is that monitoring public enterprise may be easier, since information should be more readily accessible and the burden of proof can be shifted to management. Regulators have to identify a standard and prove that the private firm is not in compliance. Public-sector corporations can be structured so that management has to prove that it is fulfilling its charter. Third, consumers have less need to rely on restrictive ex ante regulation in the case of public enterprises because more flexible ex post disciplining devices are available. While it may be impossible to turn to an alternative supplier, management can be replaced if it is "not responsive". Perhaps more significant, consumers can use the courts. For example, many public-sector utilities are not subject to the normal controls of public utilities commissions; instead the public can ask the courts to judge the "reasonableness and uniformity" of prices and service.

Finally, public enterprise can reduce the distributional conflict that prompts exploitation (by producers acting via the market, or by consumers acting via regulation). At the extreme, when consumers and taxpayer-owners are the same, consumers have no incentive to try to use the firm as a distributive device.[37] Moreover, these owners/consumers, like those of the private corporation, will be able to concentrate their attention on minimizing the agency loss generated by the separation of ownership and control.

These arguments suggest that government ownership may make more sense at the local than the national level. At the local level there is less distributional conflict (since there is greater identity between taxpayers and consumers); moreover, local oversight makes it easier to reduce agency loss to management.[38] Other features of local ownership tend to reinforce this conclusion. Taxpayers have a larger per-capita stake and are therefore more

---

36 Hansmann (1980) makes similar arguments with respect to the management of private nonprofits. Selective factors are also likely to give an important advantage to volunteer organizations, which are used extensively in the provision of various public safety services. The importance of these incentive and selective factors is suggested by the extent to which volunteer and nonprofit organizations are used when governments turn to the private sector. Data in Table 3.1 of Clarkson (this volume) indicate that these forms are more common than private for-profit firms in supplying health and human services, parks and recreation services, and some public safety services. For-profit firms dominate when governments use the private sector to supply transportation services and physical environment/public works (e.g. solid waste collection).

37 As we argue at length, however, if consumers are but a small set of taxpayers, the problem arises in a different form with SOEs.

38 And among SOEs at the federal level, there will be less inefficiency when customers are widely spread, as they are with the U.S. Postal Service, than when they are concentrated, as with the TVA.

likely to invest effort in monitoring. At the same time, the potential for comparison with similar enterprises in other districts facilitates the task of monitoring. Our general argument presents a disturbing conundrum. SOEs will be most vigorously sought where the distributional gains to concentrated parties are greatest, namely when there is little overlap between a small clientele of the SOE and the taxpayers at large. Unfortunately, this is the time when the efficiency costs of SOEs are likely to be greatest.

The third case to consider is one in which public enterprise increases the costs of production. When consumers and taxpayers are sufficiently dissimilar, consumers may still attempt to shift production from private to public enterprise because the resulting diffusion of producer interest strengthens their position (e.g. regulation would be a counterproductive strategy for consumers if producer interests were sufficiently concentrated to be able to "capture" the regulatory process). However, in many cases established private producer interests will be more concentrated than those of consumers, and it will be difficult to establish SOEs, as private owners will resist the introduction of privileged competitors. The major exception will be when private producers are in trouble and seek a government buy-out as a means of "socializing" their losses.[39] Taxpayers will have difficulty resisting the coincidence of producer and consumer interests (witness the number of public enterprises formed from failed, and/or heavily regulated, privately owned firms).[40]

This discussion suggests the following two propositions:

First, public enterprises are more likely to be established when the risk of costly government interventions is high. Factors that increase this risk include capital intensity and asset specificity, high risk (especially firm-specific risk), lack of competition, difficulty in defining outputs or allocating costs, and frequent turnovers in political parties that reduce the political cost of

---

[39] See our discussion of Pashigian's analysis of the causes of public ownership of urban transport in the final section of the paper.

[40] Taxpayers will be better able to constrain the discretion of public enterprises when these enterprises run deficits and must therefore take their place in the normal budgetary process (Aharoni 1986, p. 297). The consumer's subsidy (and the subsidy to labor) will then be subject to ongoing scrutiny; taxpayers may be able to limit this burden or escape it altogether by privatization.

opportunism. Other forms of private production, such as nonprofits, may overcome some of these difficulties but invariably run afoul of others.[41]

A disproportionate number of the relatively most efficient public enterprises are likely to be organized by local governments and owned by local taxpayers (especially those enterprises that have most of their impact on local consumers). This pattern may be more prevalent in the United States (because of debt constraints on local government), but it should also occur in other countries.

**Distributional Objectives.** Public enterprises are often assigned a set of responsibilities and resources quite different from those of the private sector. SOEs may be asked to meet various noncommercial objectives, such as maintaining employment, restraining price increases, maintaining activity in or service to particular regions, purchasing inputs from domestic suppliers, and favoring certain classes of consumers. There are at least two reasons for using public, rather than subsidized private, enterprise to carry out this redistribution. First, even if subsidizing private production is more efficient, it may generate political problems for recipients and donors. Explicit subsidies make the choice between competing budget claims a matter for legislative deliberation, rather than leaving it to a public-sector enterprise's management. Moreover, they place such expenditures on the same budgetary basis as other social spending, thus inviting a less biased comparison between them. And when subsidies are explicit, it is easier to distinguish them from the effects of management inefficiency. These effects may not be welcomed by recipients -- who may prefer a less obvious, and presumably more secure, form of redistribution -- or by managers, who may want their management performance veiled. Note how infrequently the United States government employs straight cash transfers, whether to support farmers or assist import-affected industries.

Second, even if subsidized private firms would be more efficient, they may not be the best instrument available to meet the distributional demands placed on politicians -- because it is often difficult to determine the minimum sufficient subsidy and to ensure that it is optimally distributed to meet these demands. Two problems make it difficult to determine the extent of subsidy required when the subsidized "good" must be jointly produced with a private

---

41 For example, nonprofits either will find it difficult to raise high-risk capital (because of the difficulty of assuring a return to risk or the damage to a creditor's public relations in the case of foreclosure (see Hansmann 1980, p. 877)), or, if they rely on government sponsorship, they will be more sensitive to political instability.

firm's main activity. First, it may be difficult to determine the degree of cross-subsidization that would occur without government intervention. For example, Aharoni (1986, p. 146) suggests that "an airline may decide it is worthwhile to lose on certain short-haul lines because they serve as feeders of passengers for long flights. If a subsidy is offered, an airline may always claim that the short lines are losing in the national interest of serving one community or another. The distinction in this and many other cases is not easy to make." Second, because the subsidized activity is only a part of the firm's total activity, it is often extremely difficult to allocate costs to the performance of this activity.[42]

Managers of profit-seeking private firms have an incentive to exaggerate the size of the subsidy required and to provide consumers with as little of the subsidized redistribution as they can get away with. Public enterprise managers also have an incentive to exaggerate the size of the subsidy required (although they may not want to risk privatization or incur large deficits that would reflect on their reputation as managers or attract procedural interference from budgetary authorities). However, with government ownership the resulting surplus will be differently distributed. Parties with a concentrated interest in the operation of an SOE can use various mechanisms to influence its management. They can have direct representation on supervisory boards.[43] They also influence SOE managers directly by threatening to take up time in hearings, initiating legal claims, exerting community pressure (if management resides in the community that benefits from the operation, as do the managers of the TVA), and holding out the prospect of lucrative opportunities for future employment outside the enterprise. They can also influence SOE management indirectly through the political system and the Congressional oversight process. Moreover, SOE management has less incentive to use its discretion to favor shareholders over these other groups because the link between shareholders' interests and those of management is much weaker (as discussed in more detail in the next section of the paper). While private firms are likely to distribute surpluses to

---

[42] Many nations have operated their airlines through SOEs. The argument was that they aided prestige and helped bring externalities to the nation through tourism and business access. In its early days Pan American functioned virtually as an arm of government. It was heavily subsidized for carrying mail, whereas its primary purpose may have been to show the flag.

[43] MacAvoy and McIsaac (this volume, pp. 109-110) point out that the "Boards of Amtrak, Conrail, TVA, and the Postal Service have ... represented the interests of important constituencies such as the employees, the business community of that region, or specific consumer groups." They also note that there is often a strong relationship between lower levels of management and constituent groups (p. 116).

shareholders, SOEs are structured so that any subsidies they receive are more likely to be distributed among groups that have a concentrated interest in their operation.[44] Politicians may choose SOEs to meet the demands of these groups, rather than subsidize private firms, because they realize that managers of publicly owned firms are likely to be much more responsive to these demands.

Some observers have suggested that SOE managers are more noble or socially committed than their private-sector counterparts -- that they can be better trusted to promote overall welfare. The experience of SOEs whose endeavors provide widely dispersed benefits suggests otherwise. For example, many government-owned firms have an undistinguished record with environmental protection. Military installations have been laggards in complying with CERCLA, the legislation governing the cleanup of hazardous waste sites. The TVA, though now behaving responsibly, long resisted undertaking appropriate air pollution control measures. The Eastern Bloc countries of Europe, with their heavily socialist production, are now facing a pollution crisis (*New York Times*, October 25, 1987, p. 18). We believe that SOEs respond to concentrated interests, and are likely to be as responsive or unresponsive as private firms to environmental concerns which provide diffuse benefits.

**The Problem of Allocating Property Rights.** Many SOEs are awarded special property rights. These rights frequently derive from the government's unique position as owner of newly created or identified property rights (such as the radio spectrum), its monopoly on the legitimate use of force, and its ability to exert its ownership or control over activities, such as delivering the mails, when it deems that such control will be in the national interest.

Why might the government wish to maintain ownership of a bridge or throughway, the shoreline, or the post office? The answer sometimes rests with symbolism. Most citizens think it appropriate for the government to own the Grand Canyon, and more efficient utilization of the resource is not a significant concern. Sometimes an SOE, by invoking the other powers of government, will have an advantage in operation. (Laval Wilson, Boston's superintendent of schools, recently declared striking school bus drivers to be

---

[44] To illustrate the principle more generally, consider other organizations afflicted with the same pressures. Note, for example, the difficulty that private universities, with their unclear ownerships, have in resisting pleas to provide services to surrounding communities, to pay heed to social issues with their portfolios, and in general to promote the goals of particular interest groups that may compete with supposed goals of education and research.

city employees; such employees are forbidden to strike.)

Some government rights are difficult to alienate, such as the use of force. That may help explain why the United States did not privatize the Panama Canal long before it was returned to Panama, and why many citizens are queasy about privatizing prisons. Sometimes the property right is difficult to define. What right would a private dam owner have to a river? Could he raise its temperature, add to its pollution, slow its rate of flow, or siphon off some water for irrigation? Given such questions, it may be simpler and more legitimate to keep the river as property of the government. Obviously private polluters get some implicit entitlements to dump, but they can be limited.

Even if property rights can be defined, legislators may be hesitant to auction them. There is a certain tawdriness associated with selling the national heritage. More pragmatic considerations also come into play. A sale is a one-shot operation; the taxpayer beneficiaries are hardly likely to notice the difference.[45] The SOE, by contrast, can be a source of political support for generations. Rent-seeking, it is true, may be a wasteful activity on net, but it may benefit the solicited legislators and bureaucrats.

Finally, if the government has a continuing interest in a resource, the transactions costs associated with its sale may be excessive. Maintaining ownership of forests may make it easier to produce public goods such as the control of erosion and fires. Britain maintained its BBC monopoly for years, in part on the theory that it made it easier to produce the public good of educating the citizenry. Often it proves desirable to franchise, which is the United States approach to grazing and timber rights. This maintains the symbolism and flexibility that come with owning the resource, but allows for private-sector production. When it would be difficult to define appropriate restrictions if an asset were sold, but relatively easy to determine whether a specific use has remained within bounds, then the government may retain ownership while licensing a use. If the use is hard to monitor, the government may maintain control of the commercial activity.

**The Impact of Ideology.** Various special circumstances surrounding the creation of some SOEs are difficult to account for in terms of the preceding discussion. Consider, for example, government confiscation of the property of an enemy during wartime or of native collaborators, which was the case with Renault in France and with much of Austria's industrial establishment (Vernon 1981, p. 8). While these actions may be examples of "oppor-

---

[45] The claimants on the available surplus will notice, however. Customers of the Bonneville Power Authority have fiercely opposed any plan to privatize it.

tunism", they are founded on unique historical circumstances. Moreover, it is difficult to explain some of the cross-country variation in the relative size of the SOE sector, or the variation in the importance of SOEs over time, without some reference to ideology. The difference between communist countries and the United States in the importance of public enterprise is probably due in large part to differences in ideology. Similarly, ideology is likely to play an important role in explaining why the same industries in the same country are nationalized by one regime and denationalized by others (Aharoni 1986, p. 317). Ideology may also help explain some of the cross-country variations in the types of activity conducted by SOEs. For example, in countries where private ownership is the accepted norm, such as in the United States, SOEs will be established primarily where private enterprise is failing (as in the case of Conrail) or where private enterprise is a direct beneficiary (e.g. Export-Import Bank, Small Business Administration). Some commentators have also argued that an important "reason for growth [in size of SOE sectors in the market economies since World War II] has been a shift in public opinion regarding the appropriate role of the state in economic affairs" (Vernon 1981, p. 8). Presumably, they would argue that the current, and very widespread, interest in privatization has been influenced by growing skepticism about the ability of governments to manage these affairs. While public opinion has no doubt been influenced by reports of poor SOE performance, it is also likely to have been affected by the experience of government management in other areas of the economy. The point is that these changes in opinion cannot be satisfactorily explained by reference to SOEs alone.

The arguments advanced earlier are consistent with a role for these "ideological" factors. In particular, the political balance is more likely to tilt in favor of the sort of opportunism discussed above in countries, or during periods, where extensive government intervention in economic management receives strong popular support. Indeed, that discussion may help us to identify those aspects of ideology that are likely to be particularly important in explaining the development of the SOE sector.

While ideology may help explain some outcomes, its importance has been moderated by more pragmatic considerations in a great many situations.[46] Aharoni (1986, p. 51) makes the point that "outside these [communist] countries, however, both the share of the SOEs out of GNP and their distribution by industries is very similar in countries with totally different ideological beliefs, such as South Korea and India. Moreover, Sweden

---

46 Stanbury (this volume) makes a similar argument with respect to the pattern of recent privatizations in Canada.

nationalized more firms in the short period in which it was governed by a conservative Fladen government than it did in the previous 30 years in which it was dominated by a Socialist government, and right-of-center parties in Canada have created more Provincial Crown Corporations than the socialist party ... The Conservative British government in the 1970s was responsible for the nationalization of firms such as Rolls Royce and British Leyland, and the socialist-dominated coalition in Israel sold more SOEs to the private sector than the liberal government that followed it."

## HOW DO SOEs PERFORM?

We shall advance three major arguments in this section. First, the diffuseness and nontransferability of ownership, the absence of a share price, and indeed the generic difficulty residual claimants would have in expressing "voice" (much less choosing "exit"),[47] all tend to magnify the agency losses associated with SOEs. Second, SOEs in different statuses are likely to encounter different problems. SOEs with large available pots (i.e. the ones that are potentially profitable if run like private-sector firms) will experience the greatest pressures to dissipate profits through transfers to concentrated constituencies, predominantly employees and customers. SOEs that are created to preserve an unprofitable industry will be less generous and, since they spill red ink, more closely monitored. Third, many SOEs have protected markets. Even if they do, it will be beneficial to judge their performance relative to comparable organizations.

The separation of ownership and control in any enterprise creates an agency problem. In private corporations, the shareholders' ability to sell their stock or to vote out management creates incentives for those who control the enterprise to serve the interests of owners. The very diffuse, nontransferable shareholding that characterizes government ownership, by contrast, reduces these incentives. Consequently, those who control the public enterprise pay less attention to the interests of their taxpayer shareholders, and groups with

[47] Beyond mere loyalty, Hirschman (1970, p. 4) identifies two strategies that the members of an organization have to influence the behavior of its leaders. Management is stimulated to reduce dissatisfaction amongst consumers and/or members of the organization in response to either "exit" (i.e. members of these groups abandon their relationship with the organization) or "voice" (i.e. the dissatisfaction is expressed "directly to management or to some other authority to which management is subordinate"). The taxpayer shareholders of SOEs have difficulty using either of these mechanisms.

more concentrated interests, such as suppliers, consumers and employees, can influence management to favor them over the taxpayers.

The critical question we address here is whether -- if we imitate the corporate form, only substituting public for private ownership -- we can replicate the benefits of private ownership. Our answer is no, on two scores. First, some features of private ownership are not replicable with public ownership. There is no share price, no ability to increase or decrease one's holdings, no large shareholders, and no stock options. Second, public ownership brings with it attention to certain classes of government goals and practices. For example, salaries for top executives will be very low by industry standards. Politics will inevitably play some role in the operation of the enterprise.

## Separation of Ownership and Control: Differences Between SOEs and Private Firms

Diffuse ownership reduces the incentive for shareholders to monitor management. An individual shareholder reaps all the benefits from "shirking" a monitoring role while the costs of that dereliction are spread thinly over all shareholders. The more concentrated the ownership, the more likely that the benefits and costs of monitoring are shared by the same owner (in the extreme case of a single owner, there are none of these "externalities"). Shareholding in the SOE is so diverse that we expect individual shareholders to have very little incentive to monitor the ongoing management of the enterprise.

**Private Firms**. Diffuse shareholding offers many advantages, notably the relative ease of raising large amounts of capital and spreading shareholder risk. In private firms, presumably, the level of diffusion is set roughly so that advantages offset the costs of weakened monitoring incentives.[48] Monitoring is undertaken for at least two purposes: to oversee management and encourage improved performance, and to determine whether to purchase or sell holdings. The latter kind of monitoring can be undertaken by stock-

---

[48] Demsetz and Lehn (1985, p. 1176) examine the relationship between ownership concentration and accounting profit rate in over 500 U.S. firms and find no significant relationship between these variables, "and especially no significant positive relationship". We expect firms with concentrated shareholding to earn higher profits so as to compensate large shareholders for the larger risk they face. In a subsequent article, Demsetz (1986) argues that insider trading offers a secondary source of compensation to controlling shareholders.

brokers or, as cocktail party conversation suggests, by relatively small investors who might wish to increase their holdings.[49] This suggests that even if ownership is highly diffuse, so long as it is transferable there will be monitoring to ensure that share price reflects informed current opinion about value.

Private corporations have features that help to ensure that the organization is run by managers who can earn the most from the firm's assets and who are sensitive to shareholders' interests even when ownership is diffuse. Even managers with shareholders' interests at heart will vary in their ability to earn a return on the firm's assets. The board of directors oversees management and can fire poor performers. In theory, outside members of the board typically earn only a small proportion of their income from a single firm and cannot afford to tarnish their reputations by colluding with management and neglecting their fiduciary duty to shareholders.[50] A takeover provides another mechanism for replacing incumbent managers (in this case by those who think that they can do a better job and are prepared to invest in that judgment).

The threat of a takeover may also provide some incentive for incumbent management to behave in shareholders' interests.[51] However, a number of other mechanisms are likely to be more important in this regard.[52] First is the market for managers inside and outside the firm (Fama 1980).

---

49 Elsewhere, Zeckhauser (1986b) has labeled this behavior poaching. He suggests that the potential for poaching makes any arena more efficient. Monitoring for purposes of poaching need have no efficiency objectives, but only a desire to find share prices that are out of line. In contrast to monitoring for efficiency, where the social gains exceed the private gains, the private gains of monitoring for poaching exceed the social gains.

50 Weisbach (1987), for example, finds that firms with more outside directors are more likely to replace management when it is performing poorly.

51 Shareholders may also be able to discipline management with a proxy contest or a derivative suit. Clark (1986, p. 396) argues that "the shareholder-sponsored proxy contest is not an adequate solution to the rational apathy problem or the free rider problem. Partly, this results from the practical difficulties that would arise from trying to identify deserving insurgent shareholders and compensate them for their costs and risks they incur. Even more important, the proxy contest is limited because current law doesn't even try to provide for such compensation as a matter of right." The derivative suit is an action brought on behalf of the corporation by a shareholder's attorney who is compensated, in a risk-adjusted way, if successful. However, Clark suggests that the derivative suit is "well designed only for remedying violations of legal norms, not for policing under-performance, slack or incompetence"(p. 397).

52 Hostile takeovers can require large sums of capital and incur substantial transactions costs. Such takeovers were rare in the United States until the 1960s, although before that there were often bitter proxy contests seeking to wrest control of corporations.

The value of a manager's human capital is likely to depend on the value of the firm as revealed in its share price. Managers have an incentive to seek a high return for shareholders because their association with a successful firm increases their own value in the market for managers.[53] Second, management will try to maintain the value of the firm's shares, and its reputation in the bond market, in order to minimize the cost of capital to the firm.[54] A concern for share price also creates some incentive for managers to inform investors of the firm's prospects. Third, privately owned firms can tie management compensation to corporate performance through bonuses and stock options. This link is very important in practice. On the basis of evidence on the compensation of about 500 executives in 73 of the largest U.S. manufacturing firms from 1964 to 1981, Murphy (1985, p. 13) concludes that "corporate performance, as measured by the rate of return realized by shareholders, is strongly and positively related to managerial remuneration." Fourth, for reasons of pride and self-esteem, no one wants to head an organization that is clearly signaling its lack of success. Managers will be worried about their share price even if they have no intention of going to the bond or equity market and have little concern about losing their jobs.

**SOEs.** All of these mechanisms are less effective or nonexistent in the SOE. Because SOE shares are nontransferable, takeovers are impossible. Politicians, who have the power to dismiss managers, are subject to pressure from more concentrated interests such as customers and employees, who do not want to see profits achieved at the expense, say, of low prices or high wages. While taxpayers have the power to vote in a new set of political leaders, they are unlikely to do so purely on the basis of how SOEs are handled. (One does not sell a mutual fund to discipline the managers of one firm of the fund or attempt a hostile takeover of a department store because its accessories department is poorly managed.) Hence, in comparison with private owners, politicians have relatively little incentive to replace management for poor financial performance. Seeking involvement in a public firm that is performing poorly is not good strategy for the politician. It is likely to continue to perform unacceptably, tarnishing those associated with it.

---

53 As Fama (1980, p. 292) phrases it, "the signals provided by an efficient capital market about the value of a firm's securities are likely to be important for the managerial labor market's evaluation of the firm's management."

54 Demsetz (1983, p. 387) notes that "even shirking managers desire cheaper financing of amenities."

Moreover, many SOE board members are appointed, as in the TVA, for fixed terms: "Authority directors are usually appointed for fixed and staggered terms ... [and frequently] ... stay in office for longer periods of time than the mayor or governor or local councilmen who selected them" (Walsh 1978, p. 172).

Unsatisfactory performance by SOEs may well go undetected. The lack of a share price exacerbates the monitoring problem and limits performance competition (see below). Management knows that it can avoid the sanctions, such as cuts in salaries and perquisites and public censure, that come from poor performance. As a result, poor management performance will not be automatically reflected in a higher cost of capital.[55] Lack of a share price also makes it overwhelmingly less likely that poor management performance will be perceived in the outside market for management.

Finally, SOEs are severely restricted in their ability to link management compensation to financial performance. Where government owns all the shares, managers cannot be given stock options. In the absence of a share price, it is difficult to find a measure of financial performance that is beyond manipulation and thus provides a valid basis for bonus payments. Moreover, the link between good managerial decisions and financial performance is seriously weakened by the noncommercial demands of those who are politically responsible for the enterprise. Finally, compensation of SOE managers may be subject to a politically acceptable upper limit.[56] This limit restricts the extent to which pecuniary compensation can be increased as the enterprise's financial performance improves.[57] Whatever the reason, heads of the federal SOEs in the United States tend to have their salaries linked to

---

[55] Walsh (1978) suggests that public enterprise managers try to maintain a good reputation in the municipal bond market, to be able to raise capital on the best terms and with a minimum of restrictions written into their indenture agreements. She suggests that this motivation encourages managers, who are more reliant on bonds than are private firms, to be more commercially oriented. However, the interests of bondholders and taxpayers do not coincide.

[56] This may result from the difficulty of making tacit contingent agreements between taxpayers and their political representatives (i.e. a tacit version of the debt limitations discussed above). Taxpayers find it hard to know which jobs are important or which candidates are especially deserving. Moreover, moral hazard is particularly strong here; high-paying SOE jobs would be a valuable source of patronage. So taxpayers are more likely to eschew contingent payments and look to some restrictive wage norm, which may not attract good applicants for management positions.

[57] Limits on executive compensation in SOEs will have strong selection effects. Those who differentially gain nonpecuniary rewards from providing the service, or those who need not be worried about money, are attracted; these may be people who are committed to public service or have already achieved great financial success elsewhere.

executive-level salaries paid in the civil service. For these managers, we have to rely on nonpecuniary benefits that vary with enterprise performance to create performance incentives. To the extent that these benefits are much more significant for the CEO than other senior managers, performance incentives for the latter may be particularly weak.

## Factors Underlying SOE Performance

While government ownership weakens the influence of shareholders and the link between their interests and those of management, it also provides a channel through which other interests can influence the performance of the enterprise. Various features of the environment will determine the relative influence of taxpayers, managers, and other groups on the SOE. SOEs that meet different purposes, or which are structured in different manners, will perform dramatically differently.

**The Size of the Available Pot.** Enterprises that would have the potential to generate large surpluses if run like private firms will find it harder to resist pressures to distribute benefits to groups like powerful consumers and employees at the expense of efficiency and shareholder welfare.[58] It is not obvious that their managers wish to resist such pressures.[59] Moreover, because SOEs lack strong measures of financial success, the pressure for profits is attenuated; it is difficult to judge the salience of any change in the cash surplus generated by the enterprise (especially in the absence of an opportunity value of the enterprise's resource endowment).

---

[58] The tendency for redistributive pressure to increase with the profitability of the enterprise when the asset owners are weak has more general applicability. For example, socialist states use subsidies and taxes to redistribute profits between firms, which has the effect of improving the position of underperformers and equalizing performance overall (Kornai 1986; Kornai and Matits 1984). Robert Eccles (1985) has argued that transfer pricing within firms is frequently used for equivalent purposes, which is quite contrary to what economists prescribe. By contrast Harvard University sets "each tub on its own bottom", holding each of its ten schools responsible for its own fiscal well-being. Redistribution among schools is limited; incentives are maintained. This system is frequently cited in explaining the success of Harvard.

[59] For example, port authorities, receiving extraordinary valuable resources for free, are frequently highly profitable. Some of them have gone into ancillary businesses, real estate development, manpower training programs, and so on. Such programs may be advantageous for the manager's image as a forward-looking, responsible civic figure. The same sort of agency loss is incurred when corporate executives are celebrated for their "generous" corporate donations.

If there is deficit financing, by contrast, its extent is easily monitored. (The size of the subsidy to the U.S. Postal Service has long been a subject for lively political discussion.) Taxpayers are more likely to notice an enterprise that is continually dipping into the public purse than one that is probably yielding a poor return on assets. Enterprises that make losses automatically attract the attention of politicians and become subject to budgetary scrutiny. There is considerable evidence that management puts more emphasis on increasing efficiency at the expense of favoring groups with a concentrated interest, when the enterprise is suffering sizable losses. Conrail is a good case. Since its inception it has abandoned over 20 percent of its lines,[60] cut employment dramatically and shed responsibility (to "other agencies") for loss-making commuter operations.

The attitude of Amtrak's current management illustrates how the importance of financial performance changes as the enterprise moves into the black. While Amtrak continues to register an operating loss, management intends gradually to increase the proportion of operating costs covered by revenues. However, once operating expenses are covered, this emphasis on financial performance is likely to give way to demands for improved service.[61] There seems to be little perceived benefit in returning operating "profits" to the Treasury. If there are private shareholders, however, their concentrated interest in financial performance will lead them to look for profits -- not just break even.

**Competition and Comparability.** It is useful to distinguish between two elements of competition that are not usually treated separately: competition for market share and what we have called "performance competition". We usually think of competition in the former sense: consumers abandon firms that fail to provide an attractive price-quality package. Performance competition arises when incentives for management can be

---

60 Between 1981 and 1986, Conrail abandoned about 23 percent of its total route mileage (from 17,700 to 13,700 route miles). Moreover, when Conrail was formed, about 6,000 route miles of track owned by its bankrupt predecessors was abandoned (Conrail Annual Reports).

61 W. Graham Claytor (Amtrak) told us that rail rates are currently set to maximize revenues. Robert Tisch (U.S. Postal Service), by contrast, told us that the Postal Service tries to break even and would think it inappropriate to raise postal rates even if that would increase net revenues. The "return on assets" figures presented by MacAvoy and McIsaac (see their Table 2.11) indicates that the Postal Service has tended to run only very small surpluses or deficits since 1977, while private mail services have earned a consistently high return. (They find that all four of the federal SOEs they examine earn a lower return on assets than private firms in broadly comparable businesses. See p. 98, this volume).

created on the basis of the enterprise's performance relative to its peers. Thus, a municipal waste company may not lose customers if it charges more than neighboring companies, but it may still come under substantial pressure to reduce its prices. Failing that, its management may be replaced.

When an SOE is competing with private firms in a single market, it is likely to act more like its private-sector counterparts. Thus, Berkeley is not unlike Yale in salaries or management styles, and Express Mail bears many similarities to Federal Express. If an SOE is competing for market share, the enterprise must meet the demands of consumers to survive (if only performance competition is involved, responsiveness to consumers will depend on how concentrated their interest is). If the enterprise is also competing in the same factor markets, its financial performance can be directly compared with that of its private-sector counterparts. This comparison highlights the cost of meeting noncommercial objectives and should lead managers to emphasize measurable financial success in order to maintain a reputation for good management. However, if firms operate across markets or if factor markets are different, it may be difficult to compare costs (e.g. Air New Zealand competes with American airlines but also services domestic routes and faces different factor prices; electric utilities in the United States face performance competition, but costs depend on the mode of generation). When special circumstances provide a more convincing excuse for poor performance, taxpayers are in a relatively poor position to hold off demands from other concentrated interests.

If the public comes in close contact with SOEs, they may be subject to some absolute evaluation as a form of monitoring. Citizens, for example, have frequently complained of the poor performance of the post office, something that might be determined merely by observing disorganization or laziness. British Telecom is currently having great difficulty with its customers on quality issues.

Comparability can also make it easier for the enterprise to reduce the benefits captured by concentrated interests when it is under pressure to improve its performance. In 1981, for example, Congress was informed that "Conrail cannot be made self-sufficient unless the proportion of its revenues paid out in labor costs is ultimately reduced to a level typical of other railroads" (Conrail 1981).

**Diversity of Private Interests.** Efficiency of performance is likely to be strongly affected by the extent to which the benefits of enterprise operations can be concentrated on some group (so that their members have a large per-capita stake). This does not mean that any single interest "captures" the enterprise; it merely means that those with more at stake will invest more in increasing their share of the available pot.

Street cleaning is not subject to a great deal of political influence because the benefits are widely spread and the per-capita benefit is low. In this situation the claims of both consumers and taxpayer shareholders are likely to be relatively weak; management will have considerable discretion. Urban renewal, on the other hand, creates big winners and is highly subject to political influence. We expect these political demands to be reflected in inefficient pricing by the enterprise, and in costs above the minimum level. It will be in the interest of the closely involved parties to disguise these costs and prices. An urban renewal effort might offer cheap land and subsidized loans, but impose costs for hiring local construction workers, building facilities for the community, limiting some rents, and so on.

The performance of SOEs is also likely to be influenced by the extent to which concentrated private interests conflict over its operation. Disadvantaged groups are likely to try to restrict the extent to which SOEs can benefit competitors. During the early years of the Bonneville Power Authority's operation, its low rates for electric power gave it -- and its public utility clients -- a competitive advantage over private utilities which did not have equal access to the Authority's wholesale resources. As long as equal access was denied, private utilities had an incentive to monitor the size of any subsidy received by the BPA and work to reduce it.

**Private Shareholding in SOEs.** In an enterprise wholly owned by the state, asset ownership is extremely diffuse and shareholders are likely to exhibit rational apathy. However, in SOEs with some private shareholding, large private shareholders may be represented on the board, and they may counteract the demands of other groups. The interests of these private shareholders and the taxpayers are not necessarily identical, because dividend payments may be financed by injections of public funds. When private shareholding is transferable, however, there is likely to be a greater emphasis on profits, strengthening the position of taxpayer shareholders. While government ownership a precludes takeover, some other benefits of transferable shares are retained. Moreover, the existence of a share price draws attention to the cost of meeting the interests of other groups.[62]

**Summary.** Managers of state-owned enterprises may perform poorly on two dimensions. First, they may be getting less out of their resources than they should; that is, they may suffer from what Leibenstein has labeled X-inefficiency. If so, it is probably because of government-related strictures on the way they can operate. Second, even if they do not suffer production inefficiencies, they may slight the interests of their taxpayer shareholders by subsidizing customers, suppliers and other concentrated interests. If so, it is primarily because the disciplinary mechanisms that operate on private firms are absent.

Numerous interests pressure SOEs. Management is most likely to be concerned about the profitability of the enterprise when it is in the red, when there is private participation in shareholding (especially if that shareholding is transferable), when benefits are widespread, and when comparability with other organizations makes it easier to judge profitability. On the other hand, a "behavioral" model of SOE performance is likely to be more appropriate when these conditions are reversed. When the available pot is large, and when the incentive to stress profitability is weak, the dispersion of benefits will depend on the pressures that can be brought by particular groups.

## The Empirical Evidence

A large number of studies suggest that managers of SOEs do tend to make decisions with respect to prices, risk, and input mixes that differ from those of comparable private firms. Moreover, these differences are in the direction suggested by the arguments presented above: SOEs tend to favor groups that have a larger stake in the operation of the enterprise, and there is greater agency loss to managers of SOEs. The importance of these factors is also likely to depend on the degree of competition and regulation in the

---

62 Eckel and Vining (1982, p. 218) note two instances where the prospect of greater government interference in the affairs of jointly held companies caused stock prices to fall. After the Canadian Development Corporation directors refused to bail out the ailing Massey-Ferguson Ltd. in 1980, newspapers reported that the government wanted greater influence on the company, which was 49 percent government-owned. "All this publicity was not lost on stockholders. Stock prices fell 8 percent during this period ..." Similarly, they report the stock prices of Domtar Ltd. fell on the news that two provincial crown corporations had secretly increased the government's interest from 23 percent to 42 percent in 1980.

market. However, these studies do not provide evidence on all the dimensions that seem likely to be important. In particular, there are very few studies comparing the performance of SOEs that differ along the four dimensions discussed above: the size of available pot, the degree of competition, the diversity of private interests, and the extent of private shareholding. We can draw some inferences on the basis of the work already completed, but these are more indicative than conclusive.

**Public Bureaucracy versus Public Enterprise.** We have found no studies that compare the performance of government enterprise and bureaucracy. However, the recent experience of New Zealand is suggestive. Early in 1987 the government created nine new SOEs to take over trading activities that had been previously run by government departments. While it is too early to complete a systematic study of the effect of this transition, recent statements from the government illustrate both the poor performance of the bureaucracy and some dramatic improvements spurred by corporatization.

Bureaucratic operation resulted in large operating losses and benefits for some consumers, employees and regional interests over the taxpayer. Before corporatization, the Forest Service sold logs "at a price which barely recovered the cost of cutting the trees down", and the State Coal Mines maintained employment at a cost that should have been prohibitive (New Zealand Minister of Finance 1987b, p. 26). The government summarized its experience with these bureaucratic operations in its Economic Statement on Expenditure Reform (19 May 1986, p. 11): "Over the last 20 years successive governments have ploughed $5 billion (1986 dollars) of taxpayers' money into departmental trading activities of the airways system, the Lands and Survey department and Forest Service, the Post Office, the State Coal Mines and the Electricity Division of the Ministry of Energy. Together these organizations have assets valued at over $20 billion and employ around 60,000 staff. This year, the net-after-tax cash return to the taxpayer from these organizations will be zero."

Some dramatic improvements have already been made since corporatization. The government's 1987 Budget noted that "The Government Property Services Corporation has already effected reductions of $1.3 million in overheads alone. They have also, for example, identified in prime central city locations four Crown-owned sites with a market value of around $50 million which are providing no return at all. The Forestry Corporation, which inherited a system running an annual deficit of about $70 million, expects this year to run a surplus of $30 million. . . There are many more such examples

... With only a third of the original workforce, [workers at the Strongman coal mine] have achieved a 20-percent increase in production" (New Zealand Minister of Finance 1987a, p. 21).

The New Zealand experience supports our argument that bureaucratic operation of trading activities is likely to be relatively inefficient, because of the increased difficulty of monitoring, the greater likelihood of political interference, and the need to rely on procedural forms of control. The change to an enterprise form has been accompanied by changes in managers' employment conditions and a substantial increase in managerial flexibility.

**Public versus Private Enterprise.** Our discussion suggests two types of differences in the performance of public and private enterprise. First, because the claims of stakeholders are weaker in the public sector, we expect public enterprise to make pricing and other decisions that are more sensitive to other interests (including those of management). There is considerable evidence to support this conclusion. Second, we expect the relative performance of public enterprise to vary along the four dimensions discussed above. While empirical studies are not available on all of these dimensions, the information that is available is supportive of our hypotheses.

**Distributional Issues.** Who benefits from public ownership? To answer this question, one can compare the pricing, output, and input mix decisions of public and private managers in the same sector. Another approach is to identify the groups that support, or oppose, continued public ownership and/or the decisions of SOE managers.

Much of the evidence on the distributional impact of SOE pricing decisions comes from studies of how ownership affects the pricing decisions of U.S. electric utilities. Given the relatively weak position of their shareholders, we would expect publicly owned utilities to charge lower prices and favor large users. Moore (1970) estimated the profit-maximizing price and compared it with the prices charged by 62 regulated private and seven municipal U.S. power companies. He concluded that regulation had a slightly negative effect on the prices charged by private utilities but that "the municipal owned companies are charging between 10 percent and 22 percent less than monopoly price" (p. 372). Peltzman (1971) found that prices charged by public utilities were lower for all customer groups, and he indicated that virtually all of this difference could be accounted for by lower operating costs that result from their tax-exempt status. He also found that "government relative prices tend to be lower for the small non-residential group than for the large residential group. This pattern may occur because a small group, like the non-residential customers, has lower internal costs of organizing political pressure (and, because of its high consumption rate, each member of the group can expect a substantial payoff to political pressure) than large groups" (p. 127). MacAvoy and McIsaac (this volume) also find that the price of TVA power was lower than that of private utilities and that ... "if TVA had the same cost of debt and were obligated to pay taxes at the same rate as private utilities, their rates would not have differed significantly from those charged by private utilities" (footnote 32, p. 107; see also their Appendix One: TVA's Relative Price Performance).

Mann and Seifried (1972) attempted to explain the prices that publicly owned electric utilities charged residential, commercial and industrial consumers on the basis of scale, cost, property taxes and other variables. They found that cost factors were important in explaining only residential prices and that "utility scale is significant and negatively related only to the industrial price indicating that industrial consumers may be the primary beneficiary of any economies of size attained by publicly owned electric utilities" (p. 87). In a similar study of privately owned electric utilities, Mann and Mikesell (1971) found that the prices charged all categories of customers were sensitive to costs. The evidence suggests that the publicly owned utilities are used to favor consumers over taxpayers, and large industrial users over residential groups whose interests are more diffuse.[63]

Pashigian's (1976) study of the determinants of public ownership of urban transit facilities illustrates the power of consumers. He suggests that users demand public ownership because they can expropriate more from public owners than they can from regulating private owners. He presents evidence from 40 cities to show that "government ownership is associated with lower profit margins and lower revenue per vehicle-mile" (p. 1257). Both the severity of regulation and the probability of public ownership, he also suggests, can be explained by the political balance between users and nonusers. Pashigian demonstrates that private profits are higher, and the probability of public ownership is lower, when transit systems are regulated by state rather than local authorities. He argues that state commissions are less responsive to the demands of users because of opposition from voters in rural and smaller urban and suburban communities. He also demonstrates that "public

63 In another study that suggests the importance of the political influence of users in setting electricity prices, Mann (1974, p. 440) found that "there is evidence that those publicly owned electric utilities (POEUs) located in counties dominated by one political party have lower residential bills than POEUs located in counties having more political instability." He suggested that either the political dominance variable proxies other factors, or that dominant parties were better able to use utility prices as a means of perpetuating their position.

ownership of transit facilities did occur first in cities where users represented a larger share of all voters" (p. 1231). Finally, he shows that the change in the balance of users and nonusers affected the profit margin of transit firms between 1960 and 1970. He finds that "after controlling for changes in vehicle miles, smaller decreases in profit margin were experienced by transit systems located in urban areas with (a) larger increases in autos per household, (b) larger increases in the percent of upper income families, (c) smaller increases in workers per household, and (d) smaller household growth rates (p. 1256). . . While the decline in the profit margin of transit systems from 1960 to 1970 was pervasive, it was smaller or negligible in urban areas where the political strength of nonusers increased most" (p. 1258).

These results are hard to reconcile with the argument that private transit firms faced difficulties primarily because of declining demand. If this were the case, smaller decreases in profits should have been associated with smaller increases in autos and larger increases in workers rather than vice versa. Rather, it seems to be the balance between nonusers and users that is crucial in determining profitability and the probability of government ownership. This may help explain why government takes over "lame duck" industries in some situations and allows them to fold, or subsidizes them directly, in others.

**Management Monitoring.** Evidence from U.S. electric firms and Australian banks provides some support for the argument that weaker incentives to monitor management in government-owned firms allow management more room to act in its own interests and that this is likely to affect input mixes adopted by SOEs. De Alessi (1974, p. 28) interpreted a number of Moore's and Peltzman's results as indicating that SOE managers have little incentive to seek the profit-maximizing rate structure, and have greater freedom to adopt simpler, more convenient pricing rules. For example, Peltzman (1971, p. 146) found that "government firms will tend to classify customers into broader groups than private firms and will give up opportunities for profitable price discrimination." De Alessi (1977) also found that SOEs use less peak-load pricing and that their rate structure is less complex than that of private firms. Moore discovered that the ratio of peak demand to total capacity was lower for city- and county-owned electric power companies than for private establishments (although not significantly lower). This is more likely to reflect the risk preferences of management than of the taxpayer-owners, who are extremely diffuse and thus should be risk neutral (Arrow and Lind 1970). The expected value of lost income resulting from an inability to meet peak demand is likely to be very low. The risk to SOE managers may be very high, however, because failure is observable and because their human capital investment is concentrated in the enterprise. While both private and public firms face this problem, we would expect the reduced incentive to monitor managers' behavior in the state sector to be reflected in more risk-averse decisions.

Davies' (1981) study of the impact of ownership in the Australian banking system adds considerable weight to the view that public-sector managers have a greater opportunity to increase their well-being at the expense of shareholders. He suggests that SOE managers are likely to want to trade returns for lower risk; they cannot appropriate any of the payoff from successful high-risk investments, yet they suffer the risk of transfer, demotion, or dismissal as a result of a highly visible disaster. Davies compared the privately owned Bank of New South Wales (BNSW) with the government-owned Commonwealth Trading Bank (CTB), and privately owned savings banks with the government-owned Commonwealth Savings Bank (CSB). Most of this research rests on a comparison of the two trading banks, which were similar in size, as well as several other important characteristics, and operated under virtually identical legal and regulatory constraints (including liability for income tax). The government savings bank also operates under the same regulation as private savings banks. The government-owned banks have some advantages,[64] and there is no evidence that they fulfill any special extra social allocative or redistributive functions. In sum, "the few differences in the business environment we discovered appear to favor the competitive position of government banks" (p. 121).

Davies finds several indications that the agency loss is larger for the SOE. First, in the decade ending in 1972, the CTB had a lower ratio of loans to assets in every year but one. Loans yield a higher return but entail more risk than investments. Moreover, with respect to the composition of investments, "In all years the Wales bank . . . as well as the combined total for all private banks, holds a larger share of total investments in higher yielding but riskier non-government securities than the taxpayer-owned firm" (p. 122).

---

[64] The federal government and the four smaller states give all their banking business to the Reserve Bank of Australia and the CTB; the CTB and CSB have a privileged position with respect to school savings accounts, and they have no direct shareholders' funds (so they rely on capital injections from central bank operations rather than their profit performance to obtain funds and therefore have a much lower ratio of capital and reserves to total liabilities).

The evidence from savings banks is weaker.[65] Second, Davies points out that granting loans and advances is not only more risky but also much harder work than managing a portfolio of government securities. Furthermore, other evidence suggests that "the government bank has consistently held a significantly larger proportion of deposits on which it must pay interest. . . This strategy. . . is easy and conducive to the growth of deposits, but not necessarily profits. . . " (p. 129). He concludes that SOE managers "also arrange their banks' affairs so that they have easier, less arduous lives .. and that their firms grow more rapidly and have larger staffs ..." (p. 136). Finally, these differences, and the larger staffs employed by SOE managers, produce the "substantially lower profit rates manifested in the public sector" (p. 111). Government trading and savings banks consistently had higher expenses to net earnings, and lower profits to expenses, to deposits, and to capital, than did privately owned banks.

**Employee Claims.** The employees of the enterprise also have a concentrated interest in the way it is managed and thus should be able to capture some of the enterprise's incipient surplus. Funkhauser and MacAvoy (1979) compared private firms and SOEs in Indonesia and found that lower profit margins in SOEs were due to higher input costs rather than the use of different factor input ratios or the desire to provide more output. Because there was no strong central control, SOE managers came under pressure from local interests to maintain employment and to purchase material from certain suppliers at higher prices. The authors conclude that SOEs have been used to increase payments to factors rather than dividend payments.

In a review of recent evidence on local government provision of services in the United States, Donahue (1987) suggests that employees capture much of the surplus from public enterprise. In reviewing Stevens' (1984) study of the cost of municipal delivery of eight types of service, he argues that "Stevens' finding that contractors pay no less on average than municipal departments is an artifact of aggregating (without weighting) the wage data for all services. . . For most services, in fact, lower labor costs -- both wages and benefits -- are a major part of the contractor's cost edge" (Donahue 1987, p. 226). The other factors found to be important in giving private contractors a

---

[65] The private trading banks were not permitted to operate savings banks until 1956. Davies suggests that the early years of his sample period may be influenced by the behavior of private banks, which were only just entering the savings bank business. The one piece of evidence he cites that runs counter to his conclusions is that the major private savings banks generally had a larger ratio of government securities to assets.

cost edge are their more flexible use of labor, a richer array of incentives and penalties (e.g. greater wage dispersion), and often a more precise allocation of accountability (e.g. not using centralized motor pools to handle equipment maintenance).

**Who Supports Privatization?** The identity of the groups who support, or oppose, public ownership and the decisions of SOE managers provide another source of data on the distributional impact of SOEs. There are numerous instances of concentrated consumer and employee interests supporting public ownership or opposing privatization. For example, Aharoni (1986) notes that "labor unions have been the strongest opponents of privatization schemes."[66] Our arguments here imply that groups that lack a concentrated interest will not benefit from government ownership. After reviewing a number of studies, Aharoni (1986, p. 46) concludes that "SOEs also do not have a very good record as a tool for income redistribution [from rich to poor]" and that "there is ground to believe that SOEs are not more socially responsible than their private-sector counterparts." Among other observations, he points to SOEs' poor record in meeting the demands of diffuse constituencies, and complying with pollution regulations and government-imposed boycotts (such as British Petroleum and Rhodesia).

Finally, we would expect SOE managers to be much less consistent in their opposition to privatization than other groups with a concentrated stake. As long as the market for managers is reasonably competitive, the greater opportunities that public sector managers have to extract nonpecuniary rewards from their positions, the lower the pecuniary component of their job should be. While those who value the nonpecuniary aspects of the job are more likely to be attracted to SOE management, those who are forced to overconsume these nonpecuniary benefits will prefer the improved opportunities for monitoring manager behavior -- and hence improved pecuniary rewards -- that are likely to accompany privatization. These arguments receive some support from the evidence. Aharoni (1986, p. 327) notes that "managers, generally, did not oppose being part of the private sector; what they objected to was remaining as managers of SOEs while having to hive off to the private sector some of their more profitable subsidiaries."

**Regulation and Competition.** Comparisons of the efficiency of private and public enterprise are complicated by the effects of regulation and

---

[66] Clarkson (this volume, p. 177) cites evidence to show that union/employee resistance is a major obstacle to privatization at the local level in the U.S.

competition. We suggested above that pernicious regulation was likely to reduce the efficiency of private firms by distorting their implicit factor prices (the Averch-Johnson effect), and by creating uncertainty about future profitability due to possible administrative error or the threat of political pressure for expropriation.[67] Such regulation also restricts the residual available to owners and, therefore, reduces their incentive to monitor management.[68] Thus, while SOEs may charge different prices and face different input costs, regulated private monopolies may not be any more cost efficient than publicly owned monopolies. In their discussion of privatization in Britain, Vickers and Yarrow (this volume, p. 219) cite a number of studies that indicate that "with respect to the major utility industries, the available evidence does not suggest that regulated private monopoly . . . is decisively more efficient than public monopoly." Moreover, the empirical evidence from U.S. electric and water utilities tends to suggest no significant differences in overall cost efficiencies between public and private utilities. Atkinson and Halvorsen (1986) review six empirical studies of electric utilities and three of water utilities and conclude that, while some of the earlier studies indicated that one or the other sector was more cost efficient, the more recent, and better, studies showed no significant difference.[69] Their own study, of 123 privately owned and 30 publicly owned steam-electric generation utilities, reached a similar conclusion: "The results indicate that publicly-owned and privately-owned electric utilities in the United States are equally cost inefficient" (Atkinson and Halvorsen 1986, p. 293).

We have argued that competition should improve the efficiency of SOEs as well as private firms. Primeaux (1977) provides evidence that supports this argument. He found 49 cities in 1966 with populations of 2,500 or more where a municipally owned electricity firm competed directly (virtually always with a private firm) for customers. To assess the effect of

---

[67] Pashigian's study of urban transit showed that stringent local-authority regulation had a much more dramatic effect on the profitability of private firms than on publicly-owned firms.

[68] In a study of ownership concentration in 511 private firms, Demsetz and Lehn (1985) find evidence that supports this latter argument. They suggest that regulation reduces the potential wealth gain achievable by more effective monitoring of managers by owners and therefore should be associated with less concentrated ownership. They find that "average concentration of ownership for regulated firms is significantly less than for other firms" (p. 1167).

[69] In particular, they cite Fare, Grosskopf and Logan (1985) for electric utilities and Feigenbaum and Teeples (1983) for water utilities. The latter study is complemented by additional research in Teeples, Feigenbaum and Glyer (1986), which supports their earlier findings.

competition on the cost of public production, he compared "the costs of municipally-owned firms facing competition with cost levels of municipally-owned firms in selected monopoly cities" (p. 105). Primeaux regressed average costs for the firm against variables he considered important in explaining costs, such as sales, capacity, cost of power source, and market density, and included a dummy variable for the competitive cases. He found that competition caused the publicly owned firms to reduce their costs. "The dummy variable shows that average cost is reduced, at the mean, by 10.75 percent because of competition" (p. 107). This competitive effect was stronger for smaller firms.

While competition should improve the efficiency of SOEs, the inability to transfer shares should mean that publicly owned enterprises perform worse than private firms even if output markets are competitive. However, the evidence on comparable performance in a competitive environment is both mixed and relatively sparse. Caves and Christensen (1980) compared the total factor productivity of the wholly government-owned Canadian National Railways (CN) and its private competitor, Canadian Pacific (CP). The railroads are of roughly equal size and compete for traffic.[70] On the basis of the total factor productivity measure, Caves and Christensen found "no evidence of inferior efficiency performance by the government-owned railroad. We conclude that in the case of Canadian railroads the beneficial effects of competition have been sufficient to overcome any tendency toward inefficiency resulting from public ownership" (p. 961). However, these measures of productivity do not necessarily mean that CN is as economically efficient. It is possible, for example, to improve one's physical productivity at the expense of profitability by cutting prices and increasing output. In a study of financial data for these railroads during the period 1971-76, Gordon (1981) found that "for total CN and CP operations -- including non-rail activities -- CP clearly comes out ahead. In 1972-76 the average annual return on invested capital was 7.4 percent for CP, compared with only 1.6 percent for CN. . . For railway operations alone . . . operating profit margins also showed a great discrepancy -- an annual average of 11.7 percent for CP, compared to 0.6 percent for CN . . . In 1972 [CN's ratio of wages and salaries to revenues in railway operations] was 57 percent, but it had declined to 52 percent by 1976. Nevertheless, this was still worse than for CP, whose ratio was 47 percent in 1972 and 45 percent in 1976" (Gordon 1981, p. 64).

---

[70] CN may be at some disadvantage because it is affected more by government restrictions (e.g. on grain rates) than is CP (see Gordon 1981).

Davies' (1981) comparative study of Australian banks provides evidence that government-owned enterprises are likely to be less financially efficient even when they are competing with privately owned banks and have some competitive advantages. He concluded that the government-owned banks incurred higher costs to earn a dollar of income and had a lower ratio of profit to assets, to expenses, to employees, to deposits, and to capital.

In sum, the empirical evidence provides support for some of the main arguments advanced in this paper. First, SOEs tend to use their available pot in a way that favors concentrated private interests -- be they consumers, employees, or suppliers. The evidence from U.S. electric utilities indicates that consumers, especially small groups with a large electric demand, are direct beneficiaries of the privileges that are provided to publicly owned firms. On the other hand, public ownership does not tend to benefit diffuse interests. Second, there is evidence of a greater agency loss from shareholders to management when the enterprise is state-owned (Davies' study is particularly important in this regard). However, this difference appears to narrow when SOEs are compared with regulated private firms. While ownership form of U.S. electric utilities appears to matter for both costs and prices, Atkinson and Halvorsen find no significant effect on cost efficiency. Third, competition improves the cost efficiency of SOEs.

## CONCLUSION

State-owned enterprises represent an extreme case of the separation of ownership and control. Ownership interests are extremely diffuse and cannot be sold. Thus there is no share price, and no incentive to monitor the firm for investment purposes. All of the mechanisms that help align the interests of management with those of shareholders in the privately owned corporation are weaker or nonexistent in the SOE. Moreover, managers who have difficulty securing a return on assets are less likely to be replaced. Ownership participation is fixed, in effect, by the individual's debts and receipts from the government. Thus there are no large holders to threaten the removal of management, and no danger of takeover. The political process offers clumsy oversight. No single enterprise is a substantial portion of government, yet administrations are changed as a whole.

We have argued that the performance of a firm depends on who owns, or might own, it. With some concentration of ownership or potential ownership, management will find it desirable to push for profits and efficiency, rather than enjoy the smooth sailing and more comfortable existence that comes with "reasonable concessions" to concentrated interest groups. In stark contrast to owners, these groups -- such as customers, suppliers, and employees of the state-owned enterprise -- can exert significant pressure for favorable treatment. The empirical evidence suggests that they do so successfully at the expense of citizen shareholders. SOEs receive special privileges such as subsidized resources, legal protection from competition, and tax-exempt status. These privileges are extended in exchange for the SOE's acceptance of special responsibilities, such as preserving a valuable resource, maintaining an uneconomic production facility, or subsidizing certain classes of customer -- responsibilities that the political process has chosen not to entrust to private firms.

When is privatization likely to be most promising? First, transferring ownership is likely to have a greater impact on enterprise efficiency when the available pot is large and/or when the benefits of enterprise activity are concentrated on a relatively small group. Unfortunately, privatization is likely to be most fiercely resisted in these cases. One non-obvious conclusion from our analysis is that there is likely to be more to gain from privatizing enterprises owned at the national, rather than at the local, level. Second, if it is impossible to transfer an entire enterprise to the private sector, there are likely to be considerable efficiency gains from selling some proportion of the shareholding and allowing these shares to be traded. Third, privatization -- like nationalization -- may be particularly useful if current organizational relationships are entrenched in an especially unattractive way. Finally, the gains from privatization are likely to vary with the degree of regulation of the firm and competition in its markets. Privatization will offer the least gains, we suspect, at the two extremes. Many of the factors supporting creation of SOEs imply that a privatized firm will be heavily regulated; that is, it will be subject to many of the same efficiency-restraining forces that hinder SOE performance. A SOE in a competitive industry, admittedly not a common occurrence, is likely to mimic its private competitors in most important ways.[71] Privatization should perhaps be most seriously contemplated in areas where a privatized firm would operate relatively freely but enjoy some market power. When the drive for efficiency of competitive forces is weakened -- by market structure, rents, or other enterprise-specific claims on the "pot" -- monitoring

---

[71] Vickers and Yarrow (this volume, p. 217) draw a broadly similar conclusion from the British experience: "Thus, while privatization may have seemed most appropriate for enterprises operating in competitive product markets, these were precisely the enterprises whose internal efficiency performance was most readily improved by reforms to the public monitoring system."

by the firm's shareholders and the market for control of the enterprise achieve their greatest import. Privatization will offer its greatest advantages there.

When the potential for government opportunism is significant, by contrast, privatization is not likely to be very helpful. The risks will be excessive. Probably no private firm would open a steel plant in a militant socialist nation; the risk of expropriation at some future date would seem too large. Similarly, investments in resource industries are vulnerable to price controls or excess profit taxes, should there be a great increase in world price. Given that state utility commissioners have substantial latitude to set "unfair" rates, private utilities are likely to have their projects built on too small a scale, and to invest too little in total. When the risk of opportunism looms large, the arguments for limiting state ownership are weaker.

Symbolic concerns may weaken the potential for privatization. The value of a resource to society may be tied up in its ownership. It is not only the costs of contracting with private vendors, say to cap prices and maintain standards, that prevents the United States from selling the Grand Canyon for use in power generation. Hydroelectric dams, which use the "national resource" of a river, are disproportionately publicly owned around the world, in contrast to oil and gas plants.

SOEs are likely to be established when there is an argument for subsidy. Many of the arguments used for subsidies may be employed to justify state participation in production. Education is a prime example. The virtues of educating the citizens on their democratic rights and providing equal opportunity for all seem to warrant subsidy -- and may seem threatened when private institutions take on these tasks. Except when private firms' very survival is threatened, our society does not like direct subsidies for private firms. (The argument is not so much that their shareholders may be wealthy; rhetoric often fails to pierce the corporate veil. Rather, corporations themselves are not seen as worthy beneficiaries.)

Given a certain level of government responsibilities in society, it would be desirable to allocate particular activities between the public and private sectors according to principles of comparative advantage. Some powerful forces push in that direction. Compared with private firms, however, SOEs are likely to be much more subject to, and the subject of, the demands of the political process. The bias in that process toward concentrated interests influences the industries in which SOEs participate. This tension between concerns with efficiency and distribution -- as well as the influence of symbolism, history, and ideology -- leads to a haphazard division of responsibilities that to some extent reflects, but by no means reproduces, the pattern that comparative advantage dictates.

Our analysis identifies those factors that are likely to have the greatest influence on the performance of SOEs. In particular, we have emphasized the importance of market competition, the size of the "available pot," the diffuseness of private interests and the degree of private shareholding. We have also stressed the importance of "performance competition" when these enterprises are insulated from market pressures. The less opportunity there is for competitors to poach on the markets of a poorly performing firm, the clumsier the mechanism to change its management or ownership, the more desirable it is to be able to monitor its performance on a relative basis. Once the lessons about the operation of SOEs in different sectors are well understood, it may be possible not only to improve their performance, but to select superior organizational forms for undertaking a number of the central tasks of society.

# The Control and Performance of State-Owned Enterprises: Comment

Kevin J. Murphy*

Professors Zeckhauser and Horn have written a careful and thought-provoking analysis of an interesting organizational form, the State-Owned Enterprise (SOE). They pay particular attention to the economic efficiency of public and private firms, and the managerial incentives in these alternative organizational forms. They argue that there is an implicit trade-off between efficiency and other social objectives, and that SOEs survive in large part because of their ability to satisfy these other objectives. In this comment, I expand on Zeckhauser and Horn's analysis of managerial incentives in SOEs, and confirm their conclusion that managers in SOEs lack incentives to maximize the value of their enterprises. The absence of value-maximizing incentives does not, however, imply that SOE managers have incentives to maximize other social objectives such as providing higher quality products or redistributing income in a socially desirable way. Rather, the absence of both value and redistributive incentives suggests that managers in SOEs will pursue goals and set agendas that maximize their own well-being. The chance that the manager's own agenda replicates society's seems pretty remote.

---

* Marvin Bower Fellow, Harvard Business School, and Assistant Professor, William E. Simon Graduate School of Business Administration, University of Rochester.

## MANAGERIAL INCENTIVES IN STATE-OWNED ENTERPRISE

The owners of SOEs are the voting population, and Zeckhauser and Horn argue that these owners have two potential social objectives: maximizing the size of the overall pie and allocating slices of the pie in some socially desirable way. These two objectives cannot be simultaneously maximized, and presumably there is some trade-off at the margin between total wealth and redistribution that maximizes society's "utility function". The challenge to the owners of SOEs is to hire the right managers and to structure the right incentive contracts to balance complicated dual objectives and achieve the optimal combination.

Managers of SOEs, like all people, tend to take actions that increase their utility and avoid actions that cause their utility to decline. Managers will act in the interest of owners if they are made better off by doing so, and their behavior, therefore, depends in large part on the incentives they face. Incentive structures that reward value maximization motivate managers to increase the size of the overall pie, and incentive structures that reward optimal redistribution motivate managers to allocate slices in the socially appropriate manner. Incentive structures independent of pie size and slice allocation cause managers to maximize their own utility without regard to value or redistributive objectives.

The rewards for satisfying the owners' objectives can take many different forms, including praise from politicians and the media, implicit promises of future opportunities in the public and private sectors, feelings of self-esteem that come from superior achievement and recognition, and direct and indirect cash rewards for achieving results or taking particular actions. Monetary rewards are often especially important in determining behavior because money represents a generalized claim on resources and is therefore in general preferred over an equal dollar value payment in kind.

## DO MANAGERS IN SOEs HAVE INCENTIVES TO MAXIMIZE VALUE?

There are several forces which potentially induce value-maximizing managerial behavior. Some of these forces are internal to the organization, such as compensation and termination policy. There are also important external forces providing incentives, including nonmonetary external pressures as well as competition in the product, labor, and control markets. Many of these forces are present, to at least some extent, for managers in widely held open corporations. Most of these forces are absent, however, for managers in state-owned enterprises.

## INTERNAL FORCES PROVIDING VALUE-MAXIMIZING INCENTIVES

Compensation policies which provide cash rewards for increased firm value are virtually nonexistent in SOEs. With a few exceptions, managers in U.S. SOEs are paid according to civil service wage scales. Most Chief Administrators of independent agencies, including, for example, the Tennessee Valley Authority, FDIC, Export-Import Bank, and the Federal Home Loan Bank Board, fall into Level III of the Executive Schedule. Salaries under the Executive Schedule are set by Congress. Year-to-year variations chiefly reflect changes in the cost of living and do not reflect performance. There is, therefore, no pay-for-performance for top managers in these SOEs.

Zeckhauser and Horn argue that the absence of pay-for-performance policies in SOEs reflects the absence of market measures of performance such as stock prices. But share price is at best a performance measure for the highest level managers in publicly traded firms. Different measures of performance are routinely used for managers of divisions, heads of venture capital groups within larger firms, partners in partnerships, lower-level managers, and employees of sole proprietorships and closely held organizations. Performance measures used for salary and bonus decisions are often based on accounting numbers, and sometimes valuation consultants or investment bankers are brought in to estimate a true market value. These measures are presumably available for SOEs as well; the evidence suggests that they just aren't used. The absence of market prices can therefore not explain the lack of incentive compensation in SOEs.

In addition to compensation policy, termination policy can be used to discipline poorly performing managers. Zeckhauser and Horn suggest, however, that lousy managers are rarely ousted from SOEs. The turnover that does occur is usually politically motivated and I suspect largely independent of performance. The internal incentive structure of SOEs, therefore, does not provide managers with incentives to operate efficiently and maximize the value of their enterprises.

## EXTERNAL FORCES PROVIDING VALUE-MAXIMIZING INCENTIVES

Competition in the product market will drive managers toward efficiency, since competitive firms managed by CEOs pursuing non-profit objectives will earn negative profits and will be driven out of the market. In most cases, SOEs are explicitly and legally spared the indignities of competing in the product market; therefore SOE managers do not get any incentives in this dimension. In cases where SOEs do compete in the product market, they are invariably subsidized. SOE managers, therefore, are not driven toward efficiency and value maximization by product market competition.

Most SOEs in the U.S. are "natural monopolies" in the sense that they produce goods such as postal services and energy at declining average costs. An argument can be made that it is optimal to have only one firm in these industries, and that this one firm should not maximize profits (and value) but rather should set price at marginal cost even though this generates negative profits. It is worth noting, however, that if their monopoly power were so "natural", we wouldn't need legislative restrictions on competition.

Competition in the managerial labor market will also motivate managers to make value-maximizing decisions when reputational human capital depends on the manager's observed performance (Fama 1980). Zeckhauser and Horn argue that the managerial labor market is less efficient in public firms than in private firms since the lack of share-prices makes it more difficult to measure managerial performance. This conclusion seems unwarranted since, as argued above, other performance measures are available. Moreover, the managerial labor market in private firms is generally internal to the firm and not external; top managers in private firms usually leave only upon retirement. Therefore, what we think of as the managerial labor market is not very active for top management in the private sector. In contrast, it seems that managers of SOEs are more mobile, leaving their SOE posts for other jobs in the government or private industry where they can exploit their political connections. The managerial labor market will therefore be active for SOE executives, but this activity will not in general provide incentives to maximize value since the external opportunities are likely to be based on factors other than SOE performance.

Competition in the market for corporate control will not provide incentives for SOEs since the shares are not transferable other than by taxpayer mobility. As noted by Zeckhauser and Horn, SOE shareholders will have no incentive to monitor managers, since ownership is diffuse and is legally unconcentrated. Moreover, there is no threat of takeovers to discipline managers.

Nonmonetary rewards such as power, prestige, and honor definitely affect the level of monetary compensation necessary to attract properly qualified people to the SOE, and nonpecuniary aspects of compensation may explain why salaries in SOEs and government are low relative to private-sector salaries. But nonmonetary rewards provide value-maximizing incentives only if they vary positively with the value of the enterprise. Nonpecuniary rewards associated with success and accomplishment, and nonpecuniary punishments associated with failure, do provide incentives for SOE managers. But what kinds of incentives? Managerial conformance to pressures to maintain employment, peace with unions, or major contributions to communities by keeping unprofitable plants open can easily become synonymous with "success" and its nonpecuniary rewards at the expense of value and efficiency.

## VALUE-MAXIMIZING INCENTIVES IN WIDELY HELD FIRMS AND SOEs

Managers of SOEs do not have incentives to operate efficiently and maximize the value of their organization. Salaries depend only on rank and are independent of performance. Inefficient managers are retained, and competitive forces in the product, managerial labor, and control markets are generally absent. It is inappropriate, however, to condemn this particular organizational form without comparing the managerial incentives in SOEs to incentive structures in private organizations.

Jensen and Murphy (1988) argue that the internal incentive structures of private open corporations are grossly inadequate. Pay is positively related to performance, but the relation is far from that necessary to provide incentives for CEOs to maximize value. CEOs in poorly performing firms are more likely to be replaced, but the empirical relation between performance and termination is weak. Stock ownership can provide incentives, but CEO stock ownership is small in magnitude and has been systematically declining over the past several decades. And, while the takeover market can serve to discipline and replace bad managers, the evidence suggests that a manager can waste about 40 percent of the value of his firm before there is any serious risk of takeover. Moreover, the increased activity in mergers and acquisitions is not a natural outcome of a well functioning incentive system but is rather a symptom of there being major problems with the internally provided incentives. Thus, the private sector fails to provide value-maximizing incentives to managers. Nonetheless, the forces providing incentives in private firms are much stronger than the corresponding forces in SOEs.

## DO MANAGERS IN SOEs HAVE INCENTIVES TO REDISTRIBUTE INCOME?

Implicit in Zeckhauser and Horn's theory is that society's "utility function" depends on both the size of the available pie and the distribution of the slices. The absence of internal and external value-maximizing incentives implies that SOE managers do not have incentives to maximize the size of the pie. Managers will have distributional incentives if they are rewarded for distributing the slices of the pie in a socially desirable way. There is no evidence, however, that managers in SOEs have these incentives.

Zeckhauser and Horn argue that SOE managers have incentives, independent of their long-term reputation or profitability, to "consider the welfare of its customers. Because SOE managers do not appropriate any of the difference between costs and revenues as personal income, they will have much less of an incentive to rip off their customers by compromising on those aspects of output, like quality, that are hard to measure." There are two fundamental flaws in the analysis and conclusion. First, value-maximizing managers in a competitive market have incentives to make correct marginal trade-offs between quality and quantity; therefore, managers in competitive firms are more likely to make optimal quality decisions than their SOE counterparts.

Second, and more important, the fact that managers lack incentives to maximize value does not imply that they will instead behave in the interest of customers or suppliers, and that this behavior is optimal for society. We can fully expect that SOE managers will pursue goals and set agendas that maximize their own well-being. This agenda will probably include granting special favors to powerful customers and suppliers, and will also be reflected in a propensity to hire and a reluctance to fire one's friends in the organization. But the chance that the manager's own agenda replicates society's seems pretty remote.

There are no internal and few external incentives motivating SOE managers to redistribute income in a socially desirable way. The civil service wages of SOE managers, indicating the absence of value-maximizing compensation incentives, also imply that SOE managers do not receive bonuses for maximizing the social good. The low turnover of SOE managers, apart from turnover associated with changes in political administrations, implies that termination policy is not structured to penalize deviations from redistributive objectives. External political redistributive pressures can of course influence managerial behavior, but these pressures cannot be reflected through legal pecuniary rewards, and it is difficult to make the manager's nonpecuniary wealth vary with observed redistributional performance. Finally, the absence of competition in the product and control markets implies that SOE managers have more latitude in pursuing their own objectives. But these objectives will not in general be the same as society's.

## WHAT KIND OF MANAGERS CAN SOEs ATTRACT?

Individuals accept employment opportunities when the value of working for a particular organization in a particular capacity exceeds the value of the best alternative occupation. Many factors affect the value of a job, including current and future monetary compensation, working conditions, honor, prestige, power, and potential future opportunities. Few individuals accept job offers solely on the basis of money, and the importance of non-pecuniary rewards is particularly evident in the government sector where political influence effectively substitutes for cash compensation. There is no shortage of Presidential candidates, for example, even though the meager annual salary of $200,000 is (hopefully) trivial compared to their opportunity cost.

It is well known that managers in SOEs are paid less than managers in comparable private firms, but the salary differential is surprisingly large. For example, the Postmaster General of the U.S. Postal Service, one of the largest business organizations in the world, received a 1986 salary of $88,800. The Deputy Postmaster General made $87,500, followed by the Associate Postmaster General with $86,500 and the Senior Assistant Postmaster General with $80,500. In comparison, CEO Fred Smith of Federal Express made $493,000 in 1986, more than five times the salary of the Postmaster General. Of course, comparing the salary of the Postmaster General to that of Smith isn't quite fair since Smith is the founder of Federal Express. But, it should be noted that 1986 was a relatively paltry year for Smith, whose 1982 total compensation of $52 million still tops the all-time compensation list.

Conrail, even before it became privatized in March 1987, was an exception among SOEs in its effort to pay competitive wages to its top executives. In 1986, Conrail's CEO received salary and bonus of $348,760, and the Senior Vice President made $195,000. These salaries are high by government standards, but still pale in comparison with Conrail's competitors. The CEO of Norfolk Southern, for example, took home $1.7 million in 1986, followed by CSX, Union Pacific, Burlington Northern, and Santa Fe Southern Pacific which paid their CEOs $1.6 million, $1.3 million, $1.1 million, and $800,000, respectively.

The Tennessee Valley Authority (TVA) is one of the nation's largest electric utilities. In 1986, the chairman of TVA made $82,500. In comparison, the median 1986 pay for 73 publicly-traded electric and gas utilities was $361,000, and the best paid CEO received $1,600,000. Sixteen of the 73 CEOs made more than $500,000; only five made less than $200,000.

The salary differential between SOEs and private firms is often attributed to nonpecuniary aspects associated with SOE management. Nonpecuniary rewards in the government sector are important, and can undoubtedly explain why the President of the USA earns substantially less than the president of USX. It's more difficult, however, to argue that nonpecuniary benefits explain why the head of TVA received $500,000 less than the CEO of Public Service Company of New Mexico.

Given the absence of internal or external mechanisms motivating SOE managers to pursue value-maximizing or redistributive objectives, the government must rely on appointing especially talented managers with intrinsic agendas that closely parallel society's objectives. Zeckhauser and Horn argue that, given the low salaries and potential political clout, SOEs will attract managers with higher tastes for nonpecuniary consumption. It is a tremendous leap in logic, however, to argue that individuals with high tastes for nonpecuniary consumption will work for low salaries and will take socially desirable actions.

Intrinsic motivation is a desirable attribute, of course, but the government sector is not a monopsonist in the market for intrinsically motivated workers. Shareholders would love to hire individuals who receive high intrinsic rewards from being a good CEO, since these individuals would not need a high salary or artificial incentives such as bonuses and stock options in order to maximize firm value. Textile firms could eliminate piece rates for intrinsically motivated machine operators, and large hierarchical organizations could eliminate promotion opportunities for intrinsically motivated middle managers. The facts that these private-sector organizations cannot hire qualified workers without paying competitive salaries, and cannot motivate workers without providing incentives, are also applicable to the government sector.

Jensen and Murphy (1988) argue that risk-averse, low-skilled individuals will choose organizations where pay is independent of performance, while more talented and less risk-averse individuals join firms where the pay/performance relation is stronger. In other words, firms that pay people like entrepreneurs are likely to attract entrepreneurial talent, while firms that pay people like bureaucrats will attract bureaucrats. There's no disagreement about how people at SOEs are paid; it's only a matter of following the logic to predict what sort of managers SOEs will attract.

## WHAT IS THE SOCIAL GOOD?

Critical to the analysis is Zeckhauser and Horn's implicit assumption -- evident through phrases such as "the value of a resource to society" and "society does not like subsidies for private firms" -- that society is an entity with a well defined utility function. I'm uncomfortable with the very notion of society's "utility" and the Social Good, since "socially desirable redistribution" is ultimately subjective and depends on the nonuniform opinions of individuals. Society is comprised of millions of self-interested individuals, each with his or her own set of desires and objectives. Measuring the Social Good obviously entails somehow adding up the utilities of all these individuals, using some appropriate set of weights. The weights utilized depend on the identity of the counter, and therefore measuring the Social Good is always ambiguous if not impossible.

A major focus of the Zeckhauser and Horn paper is that private and public organizations are not "black boxes" but are rather comprised of self-interested individuals. Under this framework, the performance of the organization depends on internal and external incentive structures and also on the utility functions of managers and shareholders. Unfortunately, their desire to open up the firm's black box does not extend to society. Zeckhauser and Horn have opened up one important black box, but they have left an equally important one closed. And I find this asymmetry troubling and disappointing.

## IS PRIVATIZATION THE ANSWER?

Privatization encourages economically efficient behavior by creating alienable rights to the organization. Before concluding that privatization is appropriate, however, we need a positive theory of privatization. The same politicians who are currently engaged in political theft through opportunism and rent-collecting SOEs are unlikely to transfer the SOE to its highest valued user. Selling the SOE to the highest bidder would solve the problem, but this solution is unlikely because no single politician can realize the benefits of the exchange. More likely, the privatization transfer will be political, and many non-economic restrictions will be placed on the new entities -- such as limitations on transferability, compensation, and ownership concentration. The inefficiently managed corporations established by the Alaskan Native Claims Settlement Act are a disastrous example (Karpoff & Rice 1987).

# The Control and Performance of State-Owned Enterprises: Comment

Sam Peltzman*

Zeckhauser and Horn (ZH) offer a long menu of explanations for the emergence and survival of state-owned enterprises (SOEs). They are so successful that there is hardly an SOE anywhere, be it the TVA or the Grand Canyon Lodge, that cannot be recognized somewhere in this paper. But this taxonomic success comes at a price: Somehow it fails to distill the essence of the phenomenon. That the economist's passion for bringing order out of chaos is not requited by this paper is perhaps understandable. The economic theory of institutions, especially political institutions, is rudimentary at best, and some fishing around for possible elements of such a theory is probably inevitable. Nevertheless, I think it is possible to put SOEs into sharper focus than they appear in the ZH paper.

Given the theoretical vacuum, it may be useful to work backwards. Let's look at what SOEs do and try to figure out what seems general about these activities. ZH define a SOE as an entity legally owned by the state but deriving a substantial share of revenues from sales of output. On this definition, a very clear pattern emerges that ZH recognize early on in their paper, but do not make enough of subsequently. This is the very heavy concentration of SOEs in a handful of industries. These include transport (mainly air and rail), energy (mainly electric, water and gas utilities) and communications (mainly telephone and post). Most of these industries are

* Graduate School of Business, University of Chicago

SOEs in most developed countries. Collectively, the industries account for something between 5 and 15 percent of GDP in these countries. Since, ZH tell us, <u>total</u> SOE activity falls in this 5 to 15 percent range, it seems clear that these few industries dominate the SOE total. Once we get beyond this core group of industries, what remains is a scattered collection. SOEs operate steel mills, auto plants, banks, gas stations, etc., but, in each case, they do so only in a handful of countries. Any theory of SOEs must, I believe, come to grips with this heavy concentration in a few industries. It must also come to grips with a characteristic of these industries that is obvious to the most casual observer: Where they are not SOEs, these industries are or have been regulated -- and regulated in very much the same way. That is, a state agency restricts entry and sets minimum and/or maximum rates. Thus the SOE domain is mainly limited to a small group of industries which seems universally to attract a particular type of state intervention.

Once this is understood, we can, I believe, simplify ZH's discussion considerably. The reader can test any purported reason for the survival of SOEs against a simple standard. "Is this reason really much more important for utilities, communication and transportation than for virtually any other industry I can think of?" If the answer is "no", the reason is probably wrong -- or at least peripheral. For example, ZH argue that the SOE is a way of overcoming potential government opportunism. The fear of expropriation supposedly dries up private capital and requires the state to make up the shortfall. This argument implies that SOEs will tend to flourish where private capital is easily appropriated, e.g. industries where there is a lot of immobile capital. Now, to be sure, immobile capital is an important input in most of the core-SOE industries. But there are many more industries with a similar technology which are neither SOE-dominated nor pervasively regulated. Just as a start, consider agriculture, urban real estate and mineral extraction. In all of these site-specific rents could easily be expropriated, but each seems nevertheless able to attract enough private capital to avoid the need for SOEs. To anticipate a rejoinder, these particular industries are hardly exemplars of <u>laissez-faire</u>. They are all subject to unusual taxes or subsidies, price regulation, and, occasionally, nationalization. My point here is not to deny that immobile capital attracts state intervention, but rather that the state usually seems to have sufficient ammunition short of ownership (or even continuing, pervasive regulation) to accomplish its objectives in industries with much immobile capital. Accordingly, we can safely ignore fear of government opportunism as an <u>important</u> reason for the survival of SOEs.

It is unnecessary to continue this dialogue with ZH to make my general point clear: An understanding of why SOEs survive has to follow from an understanding of why the state intervenes in a particular way in a few industries. Here a few simple observations about the nature of the industries that seem to attract this intervention may be helpful. Most of them are or have been characterized by some combination of scale and density economies. This suggests that, absent state intervention, these industries would either be organized monopolistically or that resources would be wasted in rivalry. (On my short list of SOE-prone industries, this old story is least applicable to airlines.) Most important, I believe, is that however they're organized, these industries would sell, in the absence of state intervention, essentially similar services at vastly different prices to differently situated customers. For example, the small, isolated customer would pay substantially more for electricity, gas, and telephone service than the large buyer in a dense market. The pervasive tendency of state intervention has been to suppress these differences, usually by creating monopoly rents which are partially dissipated either in cross-subsidies or via explicit subsidies to the high-cost customers.

It would take us too far afield to push the inquiry a step back and ask why there is a political propensity for suppressing cost differences. If we take that propensity as a given, the next question -- the question facing this volume -- is how the burden of acting on this propensity is shared between SOEs and regulation of privately owned firms. Once it is understood that both the SOE and its privately owned counterpart are going to be constrained to do pretty much the same thing, the question is more about details than substance. (See the paper by Vickers and Yarrow in this volume for a particularly timely discussion of the similar constraints facing SOEs and their privately owned counterparts.) The conjecture I share with ZH is that the important detail lies in the tension between the political objective and the costs of achieving it. Consider the ultimate subsidy -- giving the output away. This attains the political objective of treating differently situated consumers similarly, but it wastes resources. The government must either supply enough to eliminate excess demand for the "free" good, or enforce a costly rationing scheme. For most markets served by SOEs, demand is sufficiently elastic and marginal cost sufficiently high to restrain the political impulse to give the output away: hence the self-financing constraint on SOEs or the tolerance for profit-seeking private ownership in these industries. But profit-seeking creates an "agency-problem". It strengthens the incentive to avoid or subvert the political objective of below-cost pricing for some customers. The SOE becomes the efficient form when the weight on the political objective becomes suitably large.

As just stated, this criterion for SOE efficiency is not very informative. To make it informative, one would have to specify the conditions under which the political objective gets a higher weight relative to cost minimization. However, by focusing on the tension between the two objectives, we can, I think, come closer to understanding where SOEs are likely to survive and where they are likely to fail.

If market forces reduce substantially the ability to attain the monopoly rents required for cross-subsidization, the SOE is unlikely to survive or flourish. On this argument, state-owned input suppliers (e.g. steel mills or coal mines) are living on borrowed time. The internationalization of markets has sharply reduced the opportunities for such SOEs to spread rents around. Today those rents would have to be generated by taxing imports, which renders the input-using industries uncompetitive, or via explicit subsidies, which doesn't require SOEs. Similarly, the demise of IATA and tight control of entry into international airline markets has, I believe, made the state-owned airline obsolete. If Air France, Air Canada or Alitalia remain SOEs, they will either lose market share or become operationally indistinct from private firms. The case of state-owned railways is a little more complicated, but their decline and ultimate substantive privatization can, I think, be predicted with some confidence. The reason is the same as that which led to the substantial reduction of railroad regulation in the U.S.: Inroads of competitive forms of transport ultimately doomed the ICC's rear-guard attempt to preserve cross-subsidies by eliminating the rents from which these subsidies were drawn. In Europe, these same competitive forces have necessitated enormous explicit subsidies (around 1 percent of GDP in France and Germany, and 3 percent in Italy in the early 1980s. On a U.S. scale, the Italian subsidy would be around $150 billion per year.) Given the growing availability of alternatives, it is hard to believe that tolerance for such subsidies will continue unabated. However, density economies are more important for the state railways than for the state airlines. This suggests that outright privatization is more likely for the airlines than for the railways. As long as the railways are constrained to provide some light density service to remote customers, the political incentive to cross-subsidize them will be more easily attained through an SOE than a privately owned rail system. No similar rationale for the SOE exists for the state airlines, at least on international routes. Accordingly, railway privatization may lag airline privatization. But the important point is that competition from alternative modes is shrinking the ability to cross-subsidize light density rail traffic, and this will create corresponding pressures to shrink the size of the state railway sector.

Where, then, are SOEs likely to flourish? If my analysis of the source of demand for SOEs is correct, the first answer is: in those industries where monopoly rents and cross-subsidies can be retained. The most obvious examples are the industries that continue to be price-regulated where they are privately owned, i.e. local telephone service, electricity, gas, etc. I recognize that, had I written this comment just a year or two ago, I would have failed to anticipate the privatization of British Gas and British Telecom. But I would not have failed to anticipate the continuing heavy role of regulation in the prices of these nominally private firms. (Again, see Vickers and Yarrow's article in this volume for elaboration of this point.)

There is also room for SOEs where the government's political objective of transforming monopoly rent into subsidies runs into severe agency problems. An emerging example of this may be banking, where SOEs have so far been only sporadically important. Here governments, more or less everywhere have guaranteed, *de facto* or *de jure*, the banks' liabilities, so that the banks' cost of acquiring them is essentially identical to the government's own cost of debt. The putative motive for this subsidy is to use the banks as the government's agents for providing a cheap, liquid substitute for government money. The quid for this quo is that banks should refrain from using their access to the government guarantee simply to maximize profits. In some cases, this has meant that banks (or similarly privileged institutions) were supposed to channel credit to socially "worthy" sectors, like housing. But, the inherent difficulty of regulating the flow of credit among sectors has always limited this form of cross-subsidy. The more relevant restraint on banks has been that they should not take the full degree of risk that their guaranteed depositors' lack of concern would permit and make attractive. However, banks in many countries have been demonstrably unable to be bound by that restraint. The recent sharp increase in loan losses and erosion of bank capital is the most obvious symptom of the breakdown of the restraint on using the government guarantee to acquire risky assets. In the U.S. this has already led to an increase in government intervention. One large bank has become a SOE and the guarantor agency has, willy nilly, gotten into the business of running a large portfolio of distressed loans. It is still unclear whether resolution of this agency problem will entail transfer of many more banks to state ownership. But, at the least, the problem is bound to attract increased regulation of bank portfolios. And the general rule that SOEs flourish in regulated markets should not be ignored.

In closing, I want to emphasize a point that informs both my remarks and the ZH paper. This is that overemphasis on form can obscure substance. There is no simple dichotomy between SOEs and privately owned firms with respect to the behavior we can expect from them. ZH emphasize the difference between bureaus and less constrained SOEs, while I emphasize the difference between regulated and unregulated markets. What is globally important about these distinctions is less a matter of who owns what than what the government is trying to accomplish and what constraints it faces in the process. This is why I have argued that the substantive differences between, say, British Air and Air France are likely to be less important than the differences between any international airline, whoever owns it, and either the "private" British Telecom or the state-owned PTT. ZH are, I think, correct in stating that similarly large differences in objectives and constraints can lead to similarly large differences in results within the state sector. They are also correct, I believe, in arguing that the interests of politically important groups (such as the high-cost customers I have been emphasizing) will shape the government's objective in an important way. A good illustration of what ZH are talking about, and of the need to look beyond form of ownership, is provided by the experience of the U.S. Postal Service. It is a SOE, and it was a SOE before the 1971 reorganization. However, the absence of ownership change did not preclude considerable substantive change.

The first column of Table 1.2 summarizes the pre-organization situation. Productivity was hardly growing, while wages of workers (the organized interest) were growing faster than in the rest of the economy. In a business where wages were and are around 80 percent of costs, the increases in wages thus translated directly into cost increases. Prices covered only part of the cost increase (compare lines 3 and 4), and the result was a substantially growing charge on the Treasury. The 1971 reorganization can be understood, in retrospect, as an attempt to preserve the E part of SOE -- i.e. to keep revenues covering a substantial part of costs, while also preserving the politically important organized interest of the workers. The only way this could be done was by a substantial reversal of the previous lag in productivity growth. That is precisely what the reorganization accomplished, as shown in the second column of Table 1.2. In an economy where productivity growth generally decelerated, Postal Service productivity accelerated by over 3 percent per year. Who benefitted from this dramatic productivity improvement? Not the unorganized patrons who continued to face rising real prices. The workers benefitted -- their wages relative to other workers' wages rose even faster than before -- and Congress benefitted from the declining unit costs which, together with the price increases, shrank the burden of the deficit.

The point of this brief history is not that the Postal Service is today a paragon of efficiency. It is not that reorganization has done everything that privatization might have done. It is that ownership is only part of the story. The rest, and probably the biggest part, lies in understanding the supply and demand forces in the political market which give rise to institutions like SOEs.

Table 1.2: U. S. Postal Service.
Pre and Post Reorganization Performance Data

| Item | | Average Annual Growth Rate | |
|---|---|---|---|
| | | 1960-1970 | 1970-1983 |
| 1. | Productivity (Pieces per employee) | 0.1% | 3.3% |
| 2. | Relative Wages (Postal Wage per employee) U.S. Mfg. Wage) | 1.1 | 2.0 |
| 3. | Unit Costs (Costs per piece/ GNP deflator) | 1.2 | -1.0 |
| 4. | Prices (Revenues per piece/ GNP deflator) | 0.7 | 1.1 |

SOURCE: Statistical Abstract of the U.S.

# CHAPTER TWO

# The Performance and Management of United States Federal Government Corporations

Paul W. MacAvoy and George S. McIsaac*

## INTRODUCTION

The Federal Government's production of goods and services has come under increased scrutiny in recent years, as regulatory reform and constraints on federal budget expenditures have begun to take hold in the far corners of government. Although there is less public enterprise in the United States than in the United Kingdom or Canada, the scale and scope of operations of the Federal companies are still considerable. Their size and strategic importance make the case for an evaluation of the public nature of their operations. Where poor results follow because the government is the producer, then reform policy should center on divestiture of these federal organizations.

There are at least fifty major federal enterprises. They employ over a million people, generate annual revenues of $22 billion, and in fiscal year 1983 received as subsidies federal outlays of at least $3.5 billion. Their production has until recently included more than 15 percent of the nation's electric power, most of the freight rail service in the northeast quadrant of the country, all intercity rail passenger service, and residential along with the

---

* W.E. Simon Graduate School of Business Administration, University of Rochester. With the material assistance of Taj Bindra, Patricia L. Gray, Eric Leavitt, Gordon A. Rogers, and Jeffrey Ryan, all Olin Fellows at the W.E. Simon Graduate School of Business Administration.

major part of commercial mail delivery. They have played a major role in the provision of credit and finance throughout the economy, with borrowing authority through the Treasury of nearly $47 billion and potential funding capacity of nearly $166 billion in federal loan guarantees.

The public rhetoric is that they developed to this extent because private markets had failed to meet the full measure of consumer demands. The government had to assume responsibility for providing supplies in markets where private companies had exited, or where they were in the bankruptcy process threatening to exit. A more comprehensive justification has not been articulated, but in each case specific goals have been put into the record -- including increasing the higher rates of regional development, enhancing standby services when abandoned by private companies, and extending services to rural or low-income consumers. In each case, the demands for more or higher quality service could be determined, but they were insufficiently remunerative for private corporations.[1]

Even given such public goals, these enterprises have operated like businesses, supplying their services at prices that in most cases have generated substantial cash-flow over operating costs. Their income statements do not differ in kind from those of private electric power companies or railroads. Indeed, the distinctive pattern in their market behavior has not resulted from the "public" nature of their goals. Rather, their prices in general have been increasing more -- not less -- rapidly than those of comparable private companies. And they have experienced less growth in service, but more growth in costs, than the private companies in similar markets.

Evaluating this behavior as particularly "public" requires both a general review and a more detailed analysis of a select few of the important federal public enterprises. Performance is assessed relative to the prices, costs, and productivity of less than perfectly efficient private companies in the same industry. The initial set of comparisons are between general indices of federal enterprise prices and costs, and those indices of the same prices and costs for companies in sectors of the economy which provide similar services. Subsequent comparisons are between price and cost patterns of four important public enterprises -- Conrail, Amtrak, the Tennessee Valley Authority, and the Postal Service -- and those of private companies in the same industries. Both sets of comparisons establish that the public companies have not done as well

---

[1] These arguments are described for the major public corporations on pages 107 to 128 of this chapter.

in meeting basic efficiency and sales-growth objectives inherent in the concept of public "service" as have private firms.

The "privatization" issue arises at this point in the findings. The four public enterprises are then subject to a detailed management analysis to determine whether there are structural elements and procedures that make price and cost control less likely. Five inherent obstructions are found to be common to the four select public companies. These characteristic deviations are explainable by the management approaches common to these companies only because they are public enterprises. This failure of the uniquely public-sector management scheme makes the case for selling-out to private investors.

## GENERAL INDICES OF PUBLIC AND PRIVATE CORPORATE PERFORMANCE

The assessment of performance of the public companies has to be based to some extent on the intentions of the Congress in setting out corporate charters for these organizations. These charters have stated in the most general way that the public-sector corporations are expected to provide more service than private-sector corporations carrying on in the same sector of the economy. But whether in providing insurance for bank deposits, or electricity in a rural community, these corporations have still been expected to generate revenues to cover operating and capital costs. The tradeoff toward "public service" has required lower rates of profit and higher sales. These characteristically "public" operations would be achieved by charging relatively low prices, thereby adding to demands for service, which would be met by larger capacity, employment and production.

Whether such "public" operations go far enough to achieve the aims of the charter cannot be determined. But they have to go farther than the private company. A straightforward appraisal of public-sector company performance is to compare that company's price and production growth with those of private companies in the same or similar markets (Funkhauser and MacAvoy 1979). There is no immediate reason that demands should differ between private and public companies for the same services, or that choices of technology should be more limited for one than the other -- given that demand is not predictable. In extending service in recent years the public corporations should have done better in holding down prices and increasing sales, if their productivity growth were to match that of comparable private corporations they were to extend or supplant.

In fact, they have not done as well. This conclusion follows from comparisons based on indices of "government enterprise" compiled from the income statements of eighteen federal government corporations by the Bureau of Economic Analysis of the Department of Commerce.[2] From 1975 to 1980, a period of economic expansion, the index for government-enterprise prices increased at half the rate of prices for private companies in the transportation, electric power, and finance industries, but at approximately the same rate as those in communications.[3] But since 1980, a period in which the economy was in recession for two out of five years, with a much lower inflation rate than in the 1970s, the prices for government enterprises increased on average by half again as much as prices for private companies in the same sectors of the economy. The relatively high rate of public-sector price increase potentially can be explained in a number of ways: Profit margins have increased, or costs have increased, with or without more rapid increases in demand. But production rates (in Table 2.2) rule out the possibility that they have followed from greater demand growth. The gross national product of the public enterprises in the index has not increased substantially since 1980, although the economy has undergone substantial expansion since then, while the private-sectors, except transportation, have experienced GNP increases in real terms of 20 percentage points (and the relative decline in transportation was accompanied by relatively less price increase).

The sharply rising prices and constant output of the public enterprises were most likely the result of relative cost increases. Their profit margins have declined, while their costs have increased in comparison with the four counterpart private industries. Profit margins on sales for the public companies in the index values were notably negative during 1975, a recession year, and even during the expansion of the late 1970s, as well as from 1980

---

[2] These eighteen corporations are as follows: The Alaska Railroad Company; The Bonneville Power Administration; The Canteen Service Revolving Fund of the Department of Energy; The Credit Share Insurance Fund; FDIC; The Federal Home Loan Banking Board Revolving Fund; The Federal Savings and Loan Insurance Corporation; The United States Government Printing Office; The National Capital Airports; The Department of Defense Nonappropriation Fund; The Overseas Private Investment Corporation; The Pension Benefit Guarantee Corporation; The United States Postal Service; The Southeast Power Administration; The Southwest Power Administration; The Tennessee Valley Authority; The Upper Colorado River Water Storage Corporation; The Lower Colorado River Water Storage Corporation.

[3] Changes in price levels in Table 2.1 are defined as changes in the implicit price deflator for that sector of the economy. This deflator is calculated by dividing the annual gross national product for the industry in current dollars by GNP in 1982 constant dollars (U.S. Department of Commerce 1983). The four industries selected are the same industries as for public corporations included in the public-enterprise indices.

Table 2.1: Price Indices

(1982 = 100)

| Year | Government Enterprises | Finance and Insurance | Transportation | Communication | Electric and Gas Utilities |
|---|---|---|---|---|---|
| 1975** | 63.22 | 55.60 | 53.56 | 72.46 | 52.73 |
| 1976* | 66.67 | 55.60 | 57.30 | 77.11 | 59.40 |
| 1977* | 66.05 | 63.14 | 61.01 | 78.84 | 66.04 |
| 1978* | 69.43 | 73.88 | 65.31 | 81.24 | 70.44 |
| 1979* | 76.86 | 84.50 | 71.31 | 82.07 | 70.11 |
| 1980* | 78.15 | 90.12 | 81.70 | 84.95 | 80.00 |
| 1981** | 92.41 | 92.36 | 92.68 | 92.27 | 87.69 |
| 1982** | 100.00 | 100.00 | 100.00 | 100.00 | 100.00 |
| 1983* | 103.06 | 112.56 | 105.98 | 104.23 | 108.95 |
| 1984* | 118.22 | 118.14 | 109.16 | 110.57 | 112.71 |
| 1985* | 123.08 | 115.12 | 115.69 | 116.42 | 115.29 |

SOURCE: Bureau of Economic Analysis: Department of Commerce and as described in the text.

* Period of economic expansion as defined by National Bureau of Economic Research, Inc.

** Period of economic recession as defined by NBER, Inc.

Table 2.2: Gross National Product By Industry

(1982 billion $)

| Year | Government Enterprises | Finance and Insurance | Transportation | Communication | Electric and Gas Utilities |
|---|---|---|---|---|---|
| 1975** | 20.6 | 104.2 | 110.5 | 55.2 | 80.6 |
| 1976* | 20.7 | 107.6 | 119.2 | 58.1 | 79.8 |
| 1977* | 21.5 | 112.4 | 126.2 | 61.9 | 80.4 |
| 1978* | 22.9 | 116.8 | 134.9 | 67.7 | 82.2 |
| 1979* | 22.9 | 121.4 | 137.7 | 72.5 | 83.3 |
| 1980* | 23.8 | 124.7 | 129.5 | 78.4 | 85.5 |
| 1981** | 23.7 | 128.9 | 121.6 | 82.8 | 91.8 |
| 1982** | 22.2 | 132.4 | 110.8 | 85.6 | 92.0 |
| 1983* | 22.9 | 136.3 | 113.7 | 92.1 | 95.0 |
| 1984* | 23.6 | 141.1 | 124.4 | 92.7 | 99.9 |
| 1985* | 24.7 | 144.8 | 124.9 | 93.2 | 105.3 |

SOURCE: Bureau of Economic Analysis: Department of Commerce.

NOTE: * is a period of expansion, and ** is a period of recession, as defined by the National Bureau of Economic Research, Inc.

through 1983, a period of economic stagnation. On the contrary, they were positive for private-sector industries during that time (see Table 2.3). Both declined over that period, but the public-enterprise index recovered in 1985 and 1986 by larger relative magnitudes.

Cost increases lie behind the squeeze in margins. Expenditures on wages and salaries per unit of production have been systematically higher and growing in the public companies relative to those of private firms in the service sectors (see Table 2.4). From 1975 to 1980, a period of economic growth, public enterprises saw their unit labor costs increase by 20 cents per dollar of real GNP, which is 50 percent more than the average of private-sector firms. Since 1980, the government companies on average have realized an increase in labor costs of 34 cents per dollar of real GNP -- more than twice the increases of private firms in all sectors (except the financial sector, where the difference was 15 percent greater than that sector's favor).

That the source of relative price increases in the public companies has been cost-based is further indicated by the limited growth in productivity relative to that in the private companies (see Table 2.5). The government enterprises have most recently experienced no increase in total factor productivity, while private firms in two of the private service sectors on average realized growth of productivity of approximately six to seven points (or 15 to 20 percent). Declining demand in transportation has kept that sector's factor productivity constant, while increased service quality has probably had the same effect in the finance and insurance sector. Thus the public companies did not exceed any of the four sectors in productivity growth, and they fell short in two sectors.

In the latter half of the 1970s, government-enterprise price increases were in line or below those of the private-sector. After the fact, in the 1980's the public-sector companies have increased their relative prices, and have probably thereby reduced relative demands for their services. The price increases have been in line with rising production costs relative to those of private companies in a low-inflation economy. Public-sector wage and salary rates have not increased out of line with those in the counterpart private industries (see Appendix Two), but public-company costs have increased more, per unit of output. Without productivity gains from technology or from increased scale, the public companies, by adding to employment, brought on these higher costs per unit of output.

Table 2.3: Profit as a Percent of Sales

(Shown in percent)

| Year | Government Enterprises | Finance and Insurance | Transportation | Communication | Electric and Gas Utilities |
|---|---|---|---|---|---|
| 1975** | -18.18% | 5.32% | 2.07% | 9.45% | 13.27% |
| 1976* | -1.45 | 7.24 | 4.74 | 12.39 | 15.66 |
| 1977* | -4.93 | 8.87 | 5.23 | 13.35 | 16.54 |
| 1978* | -1.26 | 10.19 | 5.00 | 15.32 | 15.68 |
| 1979* | 0.00 | 8.71 | 4.56 | 12.69 | 13.34 |
| 1980* | -6.45 | 5.73 | 3.53 | 11.31 | 14.20 |
| 1981** | -2.28 | 3.77 | 1.95 | 10.67 | 14.50 |
| 1982** | -4.05 | 1.93 | 0.13 | 9.18 | 14.01 |
| 1983* | -5.08 | 3.25 | 3.72 | 9.44 | 14.09 |
| 1984* | 3.58 | 1.97 | 4.96 | 11.45 | 17.87 |
| 1985* | 5.59 | 2.74 | 4.69 | 10.66 | 15.06 |

SOURCE: Bureau of Economic Analysis: Department of Commerce

NOTES: For all industries except Government Enterprises, the values calculated are Corporate Profits Before Tax as a percentage of GNP. For Government Enterprises, Current Surplus, defined as sales receipts and subsidies received from other levels of government less current expenses, is used as a proxy for corporate profits.

NOTE: * denotes a period of expansion, and **, a period of recession, defined by the National Bureau of Economic Research, Inc.

Table 2.4: Unit Labor Costs by Industry

(Labor costs per dollar of real GNP)

| Year | Government Enterprises | Finance and Insurance | Transportation | Communication | Electric and Gas Utilities |
|---|---|---|---|---|---|
| 1975** | 0.63 | 0.42 | 0.37 | 0.36 | 0.16 |
| 1976* | 0.68 | 0.38 | 0.39 | 0.37 | 0.18 |
| 1977* | 0.69 | 0.41 | 0.41 | 0.39 | 0.19 |
| 1978* | 0.70 | 0.46 | 0.43 | 0.40 | 0.21 |
| 1979* | 0.77 | 0.51 | 0.48 | 0.43 | 0.23 |
| 1980* | 0.83 | 0.57 | 0.55 | 0.45 | 0.26 |
| 1981** | 0.95 | 0.62 | 0.62 | 0.49 | 0.27 |
| 1982** | 1.04 | 0.68 | 0.69 | 0.53 | 0.31 |
| 1983* | 1.08 | 0.75 | 0.69 | 0.51 | 0.32 |
| 1984* | 1.14 | 0.80 | 0.69 | 0.51 | 0.33 |
| 1985* | 1.17 | 0.86 | 0.71 | 0.52 | 0.33 |

SOURCE: Bureau of Economic Analysis: Department of Commerce

NOTE: Unit Labor Costs are wages and salaries and supplements in current dollars divided by constant dollar Gross National Product.

NOTE: * is a period of expansion, and ** is a period of recession, as defined by the National Bureau of Economic Research, Inc.

Table 2.5: Total Factor Productivity

| Year | Government Enterprises | Finance and Insurance | Transportation | Communication | Electric and Gas Utilities |
|---|---|---|---|---|---|
| 1976* | 12.80 | 51.97 | 23.43 | 27.44 | 57.74 |
| 1977* | 13.27 | 51.43 | 24.04 | 28.29 | 56.98 |
| 1978* | 13.51 | 51.50 | 24.52 | 29.47 | 55.58 |
| 1979* | 13.50 | 50.89 | 24.19 | 29.95 | 54.52 |
| 1980* | 13.79 | 49.99 | 23.84 | 31.39 | 54.63 |
| 1981** | 13.76 | 50.01 | 23.07 | 32.39 | 57.05 |
| 1982** | 13.34 | 50.07 | 22.47 | 33.17 | 56.13 |
| 1983* | 13.60 | 50.51 | 23.16 | 39.12 | 56.99 |
| 1984* | 13.72 | 49.48 | 23.29 | 37.90 | 59.04 |
| 1985* | 13.75 | 49.38 | 22.76 | 38.40 | 60.97 |

SOURCE: Bureau of Economic Analysis: Department of Commerce

NOTES:

1. Productivity is a constant dollar product for the sector divided by total labor hours for that sector. While termed "total factor", this measure does not take explicit account of capital and materials inputs. This measure reflects the joint effect of changes in technology, capital investment, capacity utilization, organization of production, managerial skills, and the characteristic of the work force. However substitution of labor by capital is not accounted for.

* Period of economic expansion as defined by National Bureau of Economic Research, Inc.

** Period of economic recession as defined by NBER, Inc.

## THE RELATIVE PERFORMANCE OF FOUR PUBLIC CORPORATIONS

To begin to determine the sources of this anomalous public-sector behavior, we investigate in detail four public-sector corporations. Their rationales for operations are explored in more detail, along with the distinctive characteristics of their price and output behaviors. The same pattern of more rapidly rising prices, based on relative increases in costs, is observable for these companies in the 1980s -- as compared to their behavior in the 1970s.

The four companies were established to provide services for which there were already substantial revenue-generating demands. The Tennessee Valley Authority (TVA) was founded because of a perceived public argument for accelerating economic growth and environmental improvement along the Tennessee River in the early 1930s.[4] President Roosevelt called for a new government corporation to use resources made idle by the Depression of 1929-1933 for economic development and agricultural reform.[5] Region-wide coordinated projects undertaken by a government agency would accomplish what had not been forthcoming from the comparatively low levels of market-growth throughout the valley during the early 1920s. In the late '60s, the provision of "universal and equitable mail service" was seen to be possible only if there were an independent government corporation. Indeed, at the time of

---

4 Government expenditures toward economic and agricultural and environmental development in the Tennessee Valley were substantial in the early years. It can be said with a great deal of confidence that TVA preserved the objective originally set. A question remains, however: How much has TVA's commitment to its objective changed since 1933. The table below shows non-power versus power-related expenditures from 1938 to 1985.

| Year | % Power | % Non-Power |
|---|---|---|
| 1936 | 8.35 | 91.15 |
| 1939 | 39.13 | 60.87 |
| 1944 | 61.97 | 38.03 |
| 1949 | 56.55 | 43.42 |
| 1954 | 79.99 | 20.01 |
| 1959 | 86.67 | 13.33 |
| 1964 | 85.09 | 14.91 |
| 1969 | 83.79 | 16.21 |
| 1974 | 96.47 | 3.53 |
| 1979 | 96.37 | 3.63 |
| 1984 | 96.11 | 3.89 |

5 The Tennessee Valley Authority was formed to "improve navigability, provide for flood control, reforestation and the proper use of marginal lands in the Tennessee Valley" (Source: The Tennessee Valley Authority Act of 1933).

the inauguration of the United States Postal Service, there was substantial concern that service would be subverted by more efficient private-sector organizations. The removal of postal governance from the inhibitions of political dominance was seen as an essential step to counter these concerns. The roots of Conrail's existence can be traced to the bankruptcy of the seven northeastern railroads in the late 1960s. Their financial reorganization threatened to reduce rail service in any consolidated system owned by a private-sector corporation. Conrail was set up to respond to a condition which was perceived by politicians to be one of emergency -- the imminent cessation of a substantial amount of the rail service in the northeast quadrant of the country. The solution was to "provide assistance so that they could continue rail services that were in danger of being halted". Amtrak was created by the Rail Passenger Service Act of 1970 (Public Law 91-518) to salvage domestic rail passenger service, which had declined from 40 billion passenger-miles in 1947 to just over 6 billion in 1970 (U.S. House of Representatives 1976).

Each of these organizations has operated in a sector of the economy, and indeed sometimes in particular markets, served by private-sector corporations. The TVA is only one of many large electric utilities in the country.[6] TVA has a natural regional monopoly in the generation and distribution of hydropower electricity but not in the basic generation of energy. In fact this public company is part of a distribution network of hydrocarbon-fired and nuclear generating stations in the South, and within this network are alternative sources of energy which provide competition. Conrail operates in wholesale distribution markets served by two other major railroads and a multiplicity of trucking firms that alternatively can deliver rail freight.[7] While Amtrak is the country's sole provider of intercity rail passenger service, it competes with airline, bus and automobile transportation. The Postal Service operates under a statutory monopoly in first-class mail and carrier-delivered third-class mail, but it faces competition in the parcel post and express mail markets from a number of private corporations (among them are United

---

[6] But unlike most private utilities, only a small amount of TVA's generated electricity is sold directly to commercial and residential consumers. TVA sells most of its electricity to municipalities and cooperatives for resale to final consumers.

[7] Approximately 85 percent of Conrail's traffic can be handled by either competing railroads or trucking lines (Conrail Annual Report 1986).

Parcel Service and Federal Express).[8] None of these four enterprises has operated to any general extent as a monopoly. Only in certain well-defined markets for specific services have they done so under the terms of the original statutory mandates.

Their performance has differed substantially from that of counterpart companies in the private-sector. The evidence requires the separation of the four companies from other firms providing similar service, but not as might be expected from the statutory mandates on grounds of distinctiveness in their service offerings. Rather, these organizations have been given to producing a high-cost pattern of response to generic market conditions.

The pricing behavior of these four companies in the last decade departed from that of other companies in their respective industries. The prices charged by TVA for electricity increased more rapidly -- 50 percent -- as compared to 40 percent in the counterpart private company from 1980 through 1986.[9] Conrail rail-service charges increased to one-third more than those of the private-sector railroads. (See Table 2.6. The exception was that Conrail rail-rates were increasing substantially more than those of other railroads from 1978 to 1986, but not thereafter when this company was in the final stages of transition to becoming a private-sector railroad.) Postal Service charges increased slightly over the last ten years, in real terms, but those of other firms in the same industry declined by almost 20 percentage points in the same period.[10] While Amtrak fares increased, those for the private-sector airlines and bus companies in roughly the same short-distance intercity service markets were constant in 1982 dollars (See Table 2.6).

---

[8] In heavily populated areas, the Postal Service also faces competition in the delivery of second-, third- and fourth-class mail. Such competitors include: large magazine publishers, national newspapers, advertisers, book and record clubs, and tele-marketers. 1985 market shares for companies in the overnight courier service are: Federal Express - 46 percent, USPS - 19 percent, UPS - 16 percent, Airborne - 8 percent, Purolator - 6 percent, Emery - 5 percent (U.S. Postal Service 1984).

[9] The TVA's rates of investment grew relative to private industry utilities between 1977-1984, which forced a significant increase in prices due to increased costs of debt service. Prior to 1975, TVA's rates for electricity were 50 percent of the national average; in 1985, TVA rates were only 17 percent lower than the average for U.S. investor-owned utilities (U.S. Senate 1985a).

[10] Postal Service prices for "same day/next day" mail (and other classes) do not necessarily reflect the cost of provision. The Postal Service costing mechanism permits charging a disproportionately high share of institutional costs to first class mail. However, this anomaly should not affect the time-series behavior of prices of individual classes of USPS mail.

Table 2.6: Prices

(1982 = 100)

| Year | Electric Utilities | | Railroads | | Mail Services | | Passenger Services | |
|---|---|---|---|---|---|---|---|---|
| | Industry | TVA | Industry | Conrail | Industry | USPS | Industry | Amtrak |
| 1976 | 53.66 | 34.38 | 61.03 | 61.59 | n/a | n/a | 80.79 | 42.00 |
| 1977 | 56.10 | 46.88 | 66.54 | 64.04 | n/a | n/a | 81.66 | 48.00 |
| 1978 | 63.41 | 50.00 | 71.61 | 68.99 | 110.17 | 98.15 | 82.10 | n/a |
| 1979 | 70.73 | 62.50 | 77.41 | 75.53 | 114.35 | 96.21 | 81.22 | 50.00 |
| 1980 | 78.05 | 75.00 | 86.40 | 83.64 | 112.24 | 92.77 | 89.52 | 62.00 |
| 1981 | 87.80 | 84.38 | 97.46 | 95.96 | 150.77 | 99.65 | 101.75 | 69.00 |
| 1982 | 100.00 | 100.00 | 100.00 | 100.00 | 100.00 | 100.00 | 100.00 | 100.00 |
| 1983 | 117.07 | 128.13 | 98.90 | 100.31 | 98.68 | 96.74 | 75.11 | 104.00 |
| 1984 | 119.51 | 140.63 | 100.00 | 104.46 | 96.50 | 94.18 | 82.10 | 110.00 |
| 1985 | 124.39 | 131.25 | 102.39 | 104.62 | 92.74 | 100.79 | 81.66 | 113.00 |
| 1986 | 117.07 | 128.13 | 106.08 | 100.33 | 90.99 | 107.94 | n/a | n/a |

SOURCES: COMPUSTAT Annual Industrial and OTC file, Quarterly Utilities file and annual Research file for Industry data. Various Annual Reports are used for individual company reports; Edison Electric Institute Statistical Yearbook (1981-1985) and Association of American Railroads "Railroad Facts" (1986).

LEGEND: n/a - not available

The larger price increases of the public companies were not able to establish profit margins at levels comparable to the private sector companies. The margins for prices over direct costs were negative throughout the 1975-1980 period (as seen in Table 2.7; the exception was TVA, which was in the process of capital expansion while not charging depreciation). While these margins increased after 1980, only TVA and Conrail achieved levels close to those for comparable private sector companies (again see Table 2.7; Conrail's margins approached those of a comparable "privatized" company, which it was to become).

These more rapid rates of public-company price increase were reflected in adverse sales growth in the 1980s. The increases in total dollar sales in the four public enterprises were not as large as those of private-sector firms in the industries of which they were part (see Table 2.8). Taking account of larger price increases for TVA, USPS, and Amtrak as compared to their private-sector counterparts, their lower rates of growth of dollar sales indicate a much lower relative growth in physical units of sales. (In the extreme case, while there still was substantial sales growth in the southeastern private-sector railroads, Conrail's sales in dollars were declining.)[11] Production measures confirm that the four public-sector corporations were lagging behind (see Table 2.9, where TVA and not Conrail was the most seriously deficient in relative growth).[12]

As public enterprises, then, these four corporations have raised their prices more than have comparable private-sector enterprises.[13] They have not succeeded in raising profit margins above those of the private companies. There have to be other reasons for higher prices. Perhaps they are the result of extraordinary market forces, or particular types of regulation imposed on the operations of public-sector firms.

---

[11] This exception proves the rule. The mandate of Conrail for privatization was to stem the heavy losses that had been incurred by the bankrupt railroads; a strategy by which this was accomplished was a significant reduction in the scale of operations. Over 25 percent of the route structure was eventually abandoned by this railroad.

[12] Prior to the late 1970s, demand for electricity in the Tennessee Valley was extremely high due to the relatively low rates charged by TVA. When rates began to rise in the mid 1970s, demand-growth reduction (or "conservation") became a priority to valley residents. This resulted in sales-increase figures not commensurate with previous increases in investment in utility plant by the TVA.

[13] The major source of increased costs for TVA were interest costs resulting from their aggressive expansion program and nuclear fuel inventory costs which were nearly ten times those of the private utilities.

Table 2.7: Profit as a Percent of Sales

(Annual Percent)

| | Electric Utilities | | Railroads | | Mail Services | | Passenger Services | |
|---|---|---|---|---|---|---|---|---|
| Year | Industry | TVA | Industry | Conrail | Industry | USPS | Industry | Amtrak |
| 1975 | 25.8% | 3.93% | 9.4% | n/a | 8.1% | -8.9% | 4.1% | -124.4% |
| 1976 | 27.7 | 13.71 | 12.1 | -6.6 | 9.1 | -8.4 | 4.6 | -139.7 |
| 1977 | 25.1 | 14.14 | 11.5 | -11.0 | 11.4 | -4.1 | 4.9 | -151.9 |
| 1978 | 23.0 | 16.39 | 10.8 | -11.1 | 11.3 | -2.3 | 5.2 | -165.2 |
| 1979 | 21.9 | 21.24 | 12.6 | -4.5 | 10.5 | 1.7 | 5.7 | -154.0 |
| 1980 | 21.1 | 26.52 | 12.4 | -4.7 | 10.8 | -2.1 | 3.9 | -157.2 |
| 1981 | 23.1 | 29.05 | 12.1 | 1.6 | 9.1 | -2.1 | 4.6 | -152.3 |
| 1982 | 24.3 | 33.78 | 9.2 | 1.4 | 10.0 | 2.1 | 2.3 | -106.0 |
| 1983 | 26.8 | 34.65 | 12.3 | 9.4 | 9.6 | 1.2 | 0.9 | -103.1 |
| 1984 | 29.5 | 31.20 | 14.3 | 13.8 | 6.8 | -0.7 | 7.2 | -95.7 |
| 1985 | 30.9 | 31.30 | 13.8 | 12.4 | 6.9 | -1.8 | 7.4 | -89.7 |

SOURCES: COMPUSTAT Annual Industrial and OTC file, Quarterly Utilities file and annual Research file for Industrial data. Various "Annual Reports" for individual company reports.

NOTE: Profit margin as a percent of sales is equal to sales revenues minus operating expenses divided by sales revenues.

Table 2.8: Total Sales

(1982 = 100)

| Year | Electric Utilities | | Railroads | | Mail Services | | Passenger Services | |
|---|---|---|---|---|---|---|---|---|
| | Industry | TVA | Industry | Conrail | Industry | USPS | Industry | Amtrak |
| 1975 | 37.94 | 25.99 | 31.44 | n/a | 18.80 | 49.56 | 55.82 | 40.06 |
| 1976 | 44.34 | 41.72 | 36.58 | 67.58 | 23.00 | 55.10 | 58.14 | 44.04 |
| 1977 | 53.18 | 48.76 | 41.74 | 90.92 | 34.62 | 63.12 | 62.04 | 49.36 |
| 1978 | 58.98 | 61.06 | 46.48 | 96.54 | 45.24 | 68.02 | 71.40 | 49.62 |
| 1979 | 64.54 | 68.88 | 59.52 | 108.86 | 62.12 | 76.48 | 81.14 | 59.48 |
| 1980 | 76.18 | 83.82 | 83.16 | 110.10 | 75.12 | 80.46 | 90.62 | 67.96 |
| 1981 | 90.02 | 99.97 | 101.42 | 116.16 | 88.16 | 87.56 | 98.56 | 78.72 |
| 1982 | 100.00 | 100.00 | 100.00 | 100.00 | 100.00 | 100.00 | 100.00 | 100.00 |
| 1983 | 104.68 | 103.17 | 119.22 | 85.06 | 128.96 | 104.56 | 80.28 | 105.34 |
| 1984 | 115.22 | 114.30 | 155.36 | 93.44 | 171.98 | 108.62 | 92.68 | 120.30 |
| 1985 | 121.12 | 119.61 | 150.92 | 88.70 | 207.88 | 119.00 | 104.16 | 130.92 |

SOURCES: COMPUSTAT Annual Industrial and OTC file, Quarterly Utilities file and annual Research file.

Total sales for the industry are cumulative sales for the selected firms in that sample for that industry.

Sales for electric utilities are dollar expenditures on KwH generation, for railroads are revenue ton miles, for mail services are dollar expenditures for total pieces delivered, and for passenger services are traffic receipts. Thus for these industries the estimates are determined by both price and quantity changes.

Table 2.9: Total Production

(1982 = 100)

| Year | Electric Utilities | | Railroads | | Mail Services | | Passenger Services | |
|---|---|---|---|---|---|---|---|---|
| | Industry | TVA | Industry | Conrail | Industry | USPS | Industry | Amtrak |
| 1976 | 86.74 | 100.16 | 110.88 | 155.62 | n/a | 77.63 | 72.18 | 108.00 |
| 1977 | 87.39 | 112.38 | 109.94 | 150.00 | n/a | 80.86 | 76.45 | 115.00 |
| 1978 | 89.35 | 108.66 | 109.58 | 147.75 | 39.72 | 84.98 | 87.45 | 113.00 |
| 1979 | 90.54 | 105.66 | 118.41 | 151.69 | 55.43 | 87.53 | 100.55 | 113.00 |
| 1980 | 92.93 | 111.09 | 117.64 | 134.27 | 73.93 | 93.22 | 101.64 | 103.00 |
| 1981 | 99.78 | 105.81 | 114.53 | 123.60 | 89.14 | 96.56 | 97.36 | 108.00 |
| 1982 | 100.00 | 100.00 | 100.00 | 100.00 | 100.00 | 100.00 | 100.00 | 100.00 |
| 1983 | 103.26 | 97.87 | 101.89 | 102.25 | 136.18 | 104.68 | 107.18 | 102.00 |
| 1984 | 108.59 | 100.44 | 112.67 | 107.87 | 206.33 | 115.34 | 113.55 | 101.00 |
| 1985 | 114.46 | 95.39 | 104.03 | 102.25 | 302.22 | 122.84 | 128.36 | 105.00 |

SOURCES: "National Income and Product Accounts", Bureau of Economic analysis, Department of Commerce; Various "Annual Reports" for company data; "Energy Electricity Handbook", United States Department of Energy.

NOTE: Total production volume for railroads is revenue ton miles; for electric utilities it is kilowatt per hour; for mail services total number of pieces are used; and for passenger traffic, passenger miles are used.

Each of these four organizations has faced competition in the markets served. But this has not changed in ways that would affect relative prices. TVA and Conrail have faced the same extent of competition as have their private-sector counterparts.[14] Amtrak provides less than one half of one percent of the total intercity passenger miles, and even discounting automobile passenger supply as competitive this company has less price-setting power than at its inception (U.S. Congressional Budget Office 1982a). The Postal Service has been faced with more competition and the threat of entry of new competition in the provision of express service and bulk commercial mail in the past decade.[15]

There have been some disparities in the extent of regulation between private- and public-sector counterparts. TVA has been relatively unencumbered by the regulatory process since it does not seek approval for prices before state public utility commissions.[16] But this has been the mode of operation since inception; it cannot be the cause of large relative price increases in the 1980s.[17] In the first five years of its existence, Conrail was

---

[14] As is the case with other U.S. utilities, TVA faces limited direct competition in the generation of electricity in specified geographic regions. It does face a threat of new entry, however, with municipalities and cooperatives able to terminate their franchise relationship with the TVA to form their own electricity-generating utilities or to wheel power in from outside the region. This threat is nearly the same across all electric utilities.

[15] The growth of courier services over the last decade and the development of self provided delivery of bulk advertising at the local level has been spectacular.

[16] In the TVA enabling legislation, a three-person board of directors was given total autonomy over management and immunized from any regulatory body. President Roosevelt took the position that by putting the operation of TVA in the hands of a technocracy, management problems could be solved on ostensibly "non-political" grounds by using scientific, engineering and administrative expertise without the constraints of regulatory intervention. As Roosevelt desired, this management structure allowed TVA to "... be clothed with the power of government yet enjoy the flexibility and initiative of private enterprise" (Sources: The Tennessee Valley Act of 1933 and U.S. Senate 1985a).

[17] The rates of growth in electricity rates for TVA versus the U.S. average for electric utilities are as follows (U.S. Senate 1985a):

| Year | TVA | U.S.Average |
|---|---|---|
| 1977 | -3% | 4% |
| 1978 | 8% | -1% |
| 1979 | 2% | -1% |
| 1980 | 1% | 4% |
| 1981 | 15% | 4% |
| 1982 | 11% | 3% |
| 1983 | 22% | 4% |
| 1984 | 9% | 5% |

more heavily burdened by the regulatory process than its competitors. Protracted branch-line abandonment procedures and delays in regulatory agency evaluation of proposed increases in rates hampered this railroad's attempts to control costs. But general deregulation of railroad rates has largely lifted these burdens from Conrail as well as the rest of the railroad industry. In addition, the Northeast Rail Services Act of 1981 granted Conrail expedited track abandonment, route closings, and flexibility in using boxcar capacity. Thus Conrail moved along the continuum from being more regulated than the rest of the industry, to achieving measures of deregulation more quickly than the other major railroads. This may have allowed Conrail to increase rates relative to the rest of the railroads (although in the later 1980s, Conrail greatly moderated its rate increases as it became more free of controls).

To allow Amtrak maximum flexibility, the Rail Passenger Services Act exempted the corporation from ICC jurisdiction over its routes, fares, abandonments, and services. Amtrak was also granted exemption from tate laws applying to passenger rail operations, which provided the opportunity to test the market potential of rail passenger service. Similarly, although the Postal Service sets rates for its services (which are regulated by the Postal Rate Commission), any rate finding by the regulator can be rejected by the Postal Service's Board of Governors. Whether this constitutes more or less regulation than imposed on private service is doubtful. The opportunities to provide these new services have therefore been unencumbered by a policy process, whether done publicly or privately. Thus, there is no general pattern of reduced regulatory constraint that would explain relative price increases in public-sector companies.

It is necessary to look to the organization of the public-sector corporation itself for the sources of differences in performance. There are two potential sources. The first is that set of "factor market conditions" which provide the costs of capital, labor and raw materials. The second is the management structure and style of these organizations, given that they have public-statute foundations, public reporting processes, and lack private debt and stockholders.[18]

---

[18] Of Conrail's total 1982 capitalization of $5.5 billion, approximately $900 million was represented by long-term capital leases on equipment (rolling stock) with private financing. TVA's publicly traded bonds represent 10 percent of its total capitalization. The Postal Service's bonds sold on the market account for 8 percent of long term debt. (Source: Annual Reports of Conrail, TVA and USPS.)

## THE RELATIVE COSTS OF SERVICE FROM PUBLIC CORPORATIONS

The public enterprises have common conditions for access to capital that influence their pricing and operational behavior. Capital has been available from the Federal Financing Bank (FFB) for each of these enterprises at interest charges less than market rates. Both TVA and the Postal Service (USPS) financed their placements of debt with the FFB in the 1970s, and paid only a 12.5 basis-point premium above Treasury bond rates for interest on their issues. This rate of interest is lower than on bonds of companies with comparable financial performance, as the price spread between TVA and Treasury bonds exceeded that between comparable private utilities and Treasury bonds by more than 60 basis points.[19] Over the period 1971-1981, Amtrak has not only issued bonds for more than $900 million, but has received direct capital grants.[20] If these four organizations had not had access to FFB financing, the additional interest charges which they would have incurred probably would have exceeded $5 billion over the last decade.[21]

At the same time, labor costs have also been greater for the public than private enterprises. The public companies have experienced, over the

---

[19] Based on a time series (a sample of monthly data from 1/75 to 12/86) comparing the yields of publicly traded TVA bonds and comparable Treasury bonds, it was found that the yield on TVA bonds is on average 77.21 basis points higher than Treasury bond yields. This spread can be recognized as a market-assessed risk premium placed on TVA bonds.

[20] Federal assistance to Amtrak (in millions of dollars):

| Amtrak Operating Grants | Amtrak Capital Loans | Amtrak Capital Grants | Northeast Corridor Program | Total Federal Assistance |
|---|---|---|---|---|
| $4083 | $930 | $882 | $1957 | $7853 |

(Source: U.S. Congressional Budget Office 1982a)

[21] From *The Budget of the United States Government*, 1975-1985, and Standard and Poor's *Bond Guide*, 1975-1985.

Conrail had exhausted its initial appropriation of $2 billion within the first three years of its existence, and then requested and received another $1 billion. Capital budgeting decisions were not based on rate-of-return criteria, but on a measure called "funds required". Conrail received no further federal funds after 1981, but in that year announced that it would never be able to repay the debt it owed the federal government and that it should be forgiven in order to allow it "renewed access to private capital markets" (Conrail 1981).

decade, problems containing or controlling labor costs. In part this was due to the effectiveness of unions of public employees in achieving demands for job security. The unions have had substantial bargaining strength particularly in Postal Service and Conrail -- derived both from plausible threats of strikes to disrupt service and the lack of mechanisms within the public-sector firm to restrain excessive costs.[22]

Resistance in the firm to excessive capital and wage costs is reduced because TVA, Postal Service, and Conrail have a "margin" of slack that comes from not hiring in competitive markets and avoidance of state and local taxes. Even more basic, employment on principles analogous to those for civil service, with emphasis on independence and seniority, has reduced resistance to higher labor costs.[23]

The effects of these differences are apparent. The accumulation of assets by TVA and Postal Service has been relatively rapid, in comparison to private firms in industries in which they are part. (See Table 2.10. The four-fold growth of capital in TVA is more than twice the industry rate,[24] and the growth of Postal Service capital exceeds that of the mail services industry by 50 percent since 1980.)[25] While neither Conrail nor its industry in general has been growing, due to substantial declines in the demands for rail transport services Conrail has exceeded the industry average rate of capital growth once adjustments have been made for the relatively low regional demand in the

---

[22] It is a widely held belief that excessive labor costs were in part responsible for the collapse of the northeast rail system that led to Conrail's establishment. Nevertheless, the enabling legislation contained provisions that protected every employee on the payroll from being laid off when the properties were conveyed. This clause guaranteed each protected worker an inflation-indexed wage until normal retirement. Its inclusion in the 3R Act was necessary in order to get labor's support for the bill, which was in danger of being defeated. The clause was repealed in the Northeast Rail Services Act of 1981 (Public Law 97-35).

[23] One of the reasons for establishing Conrail was to remove its rail service from the rules and regulations of the bureaucracy. Conrail has been the most successful in reducing labor costs.

[24] In the middle to late 1970s, TVA's forecasted annual growth of electricity demand was approximately 7.5 percent as opposed to roughly 4 percent for private utilities. In order to accommodate this increase in demand, it was deemed necessary to extend capacity by as much as 40 percent. From 1977 to 1984 net utility plant investment increased by 47 percent. Because of TVA's favorable financing relationship with the Federal Financing Bank, they were able to accumulate this amount of debt.

[25] While the Postal Service's assets have grown by an average annual rate of 14 percent since 1976, the growth rate of sales per employee has been half that.

Table 2.10: Total Assets

(Million current $)

| Year | Electric Utilities | | Railroads | | Mail Services | | Passenger Services | |
|---|---|---|---|---|---|---|---|---|
| | Industry | TVA | Industry | Conrail | Industry | USPS | Industry | Amtrak |
| 1975 | 2956 | 4793 | 2983 | n/a | 35 | 7482 | 805 | 538 |
| 1976 | 3271 | 5096 | 3141 | 3761 | 43 | 10685 | 844 | 826 |
| 1977 | 3707 | 6442 | 3358 | 4406 | 81 | 12292 | 891 | 1024 |
| 1978 | 4158 | 8028 | 3523 | 4823 | 115 | 13379 | 994 | 1300 |
| 1979 | 4806 | 9628 | 3884 | 5426 | 195 | 16392 | 1108 | 1705 |
| 1980 | 5471 | 11285 | 5477 | 5628 | 263 | 17205 | 1261 | 2036 |
| 1981 | 6005 | 12875 | 6007 | 5705 | 368 | 17487 | 1410 | 2591 |
| 1982 | 6905 | 13914 | 7677 | 5505 | 462 | 19807 | 1633 | 3074 |
| 1983 | 7420 | 14875 | 10031 | 5703 | 659 | 20864 | 1891 | 3376 |
| 1984 | 8307 | 17345 | 10530 | 6236 | 815 | 21560 | 2106 | 3623 |
| 1985 | 8907 | 19477 | 11121 | 6568 | 982 | 27060 | 2499 | 3807 |

SOURCES: COMPUSTAT Annual Industrial and OTC file, Quarterly Utilities file and annual Research file for Industrial data. Various "Annual Reports" for individual company reports. The "industry" estimates are the average levels of assets per company for the counterpart private sector firms.

LEGEND: n/a - not a meaningful number

Northeast.[26] Amtrak, while approximately the same size as the counterpart private companies in 1976, had assets 52 percent larger by 1985 (see Table 2.10).

This high-level growth of the public companies took place despite low levels of returns on assets. Although public corporations are not expected by Congress to generate profits, they should generate returns on invested capital which are comparable to those which alternative uses of government funds would generate. TVA had rates of return on assets one third less than those of companies elsewhere in its industry, and Conrail had rates of return one half the returns of other railroads. The Postal Service realized negative returns -- as did Amtrak, which had negative returns at about 20 percent or more per annum (see Table 2.11). These returns do not attain levels of private-sector returns or of the bond interest on FFB issues, so that they have not been comparable to those on alternative public investments.

Various measures of labor costs show relative increases adverse to the four public-sector corporations. Expenditures on labor have not grown more rapidly in the Postal Service than in private mail-type services, but they have been considerably greater as a percent of sales throughout the 1980s (see Table 2.12).[27] Conrail's efforts to cut costs, once it became clear that the company was due for privatization, caused some reductions in its labor costs per unit of sales against the rail industry average.[28] Amtrak's labor costs per

---

[26] Nevertheless, Conrail's success in dealing with its excess labor force is readily apparent in Tables 2.10 and 2.14. The average rate of growth in assets for Conrail is 5.7 percent compared to 13.5 percent for the industry. The average rate of growth in sales per employee for Conrail is 13.2 percent compared to 8.99 percent for the industry. Conrail's favorable performance occurred when railroads in the eastern region of the United States were showing a decline of 13 percent in revenue ton-miles during the period 1976-1985.

[27] Although prior to 1981 TVA's sales-per-employee growth far surpassed that of the electric utility industry. TVA's dominance in this category should be noted with caution, however, due to the presence of substantial economies of scale in the retail development of electricity.

[28] The Northeast Rail Services Act of 1981, which mandated Conrail's return to the private sector, resulted in the transfer of all commuter operations to other agencies, and facilitated the reduction of freight employment. Consequently, the railroad was able to cut the number of employees down from over 70,000 in 1980 to 40,000 in 1984 (Conrail Annual Reports for 1980-1984).

In the Senate confirmation hearings on his re-nomination to the board of Amtrak, labor representative Charles Luna, president of United Transportation Union from 1969-1972, was asked what he thought of management's proposal to eliminate traditional work rules which permitted employees to receive a day's pay for every 100 miles traveled. The question was: "As a member of the Board, would you support management's efforts to reduce labor costs through such means as adoption of an hourly rate of pay?" The nominee responded: "I support reducing

Table 2.11: Return on Assets

(Annual Percent)

| Year | Electric Utilities | | Railroads | | Mail Services | | Passenger Services | |
|---|---|---|---|---|---|---|---|---|
| | Industry | TVA | Industry | Conrail | Industry | USPS | Industry | Amtrak |
| 1975 | 6.56% | 3.16% | 4.63% | n/a | 17.19% | -13.71% | 5.37% | -58.38% |
| 1976 | 7.55 | 3.69 | 6.47 | -4.31 | 19.61 | -10.10 | 7.80 | -46.96 |
| 1977 | 7.39 | 3.52 | 6.38 | -8.19 | 30.61 | -4.88 | 7.94 | -46.20 |
| 1978 | 6.64 | 4.10 | 6.14 | -8.00 | 29.21 | -2.73 | 8.39 | -39.77 |
| 1979 | 6.14 | 4.99 | 8.76 | -3.28 | 24.96 | 1.81 | 10.05 | -33.89 |
| 1980 | 5.92 | 6.47 | 9.10 | -3.32 | 20.90 | -2.28 | 8.45 | -33.12 |
| 1981 | 7.09 | 6.41 | 9.97 | 1.16 | 11.04 | -2.42 | 8.76 | -29.18 |
| 1982 | 7.32 | 6.98 | 5.57 | 0.89 | 11.52 | 2.43 | 4.20 | -21.14 |
| 1983 | 7.93 | 7.40 | 6.70 | 5.05 | 13.66 | 1.38 | 3.50 | -20.29 |
| 1984 | 8.62 | 6.76 | 9.52 | 7.47 | 12.34 | -0.76 | 8.90 | -20.05 |
| 1985 | 8.80 | 6.32 | 8.43 | 6.04 | 7.86 | -1.85 | 7.80 | -19.44 |

SOURCES: COMPUSTAT Annual Industrial and OTC file, Quarterly Utilities file and annual Research file for Industrial data. Various "Annual Reports" for individual company reports.

NOTE: Return on Assets (ROA) is operating income divided by the total assets (both current plus long term assets). The industry ROA is calculated by adding operating income for each firm in the industry and dividing it by the total assets for all the firms in the respective industry.

Table 2.12: Labor Cost as a Percent of Sales

(Annual Percent)

| Year | Electric Utilities | | Railroads | | Mail Services | | Passenger Services | |
|---|---|---|---|---|---|---|---|---|
| | Industry | TVA | Industry | Conrail | Industry | USPS | Industry | Amtrak |
| 1975 | 18.32% | 17.36% | 39.82% | n/a | n/a | 93.53% | 13.70% | n/a |
| 1976 | 16.45 | 16.41 | 42.17 | 80.22 | n/a | 93.32 | 14.96 | n/a |
| 1977 | 16.45 | 16.85 | 40.23 | 61.89 | n/a | 89.22 | 16.00 | n/a |
| 1978 | 15.70 | 15.13 | 39.02 | 60.26 | 37.04 | 88.50 | 16.14 | n/a |
| 1979 | 15.81 | 15.46 | 37.38 | 56.80 | 38.90 | 85.06 | 17.35 | 86.61 |
| 1980 | 16.14 | 17.10 | 38.17 | 55.45 | 41.01 | 86.78 | 16.21 | 108.10 |
| 1981 | 15.78 | 17.35 | 36.72 | 51.25 | 41.09 | 85.65 | 17.02 | 93.62 |
| 1982 | 16.34 | 17.41 | 39.80 | 49.93 | 39.85 | 81.93 | 21.23 | 72.17 |
| 1983 | 16.75 | 17.11 | 37.62 | 44.08 | 41.63 | 82.36 | 29.39 | 78.78 |
| 1984 | 16.81 | 17.49 | 32.29 | 43.71 | 43.35 | 84.59 | 28.07 | 74.23 |
| 1985 | 16.77 | 18.13 | 32.54 | n/a | 44.67 | 84.28 | 27.85 | 68.97 |

SOURCES: COMPUSTAT Annual Industrial and OTC file, Quarterly Utilities file and annual Research file for Industrial data. Various "Annual Reports" for individual company reports.

unit of sales have been more than twice those of the airlines and bus companies offering comparable service; and on a passenger-mile basis, they are more than twice as much as the airlines and more than triple those of the bus companies (Table 2.12). These differences are not because of excessive wages and salaries. Rather, they are the result of substantially higher levels of employment.[29] The Postal Service continued to realize increases in unit labor costs (see Table 2.13).[30] And most directly to the point, unit labor costs for all of these firms have been rising from levels that were higher than those of private-sector service and manufacturing corporations.[31]

The public companies' relative ability has declined in the production of more output from more capital and labor. Total factor productivity in the 1980s has declined for TVA and Amtrak, while their counterpart private-sector companies have been constant (electric power) or increasing at seven percent per annum (passenger services) (see Table 2.15). Only Conrail has done better than its comparable private-sector railroads, but only after 1981 when the privatization transition process had begun.

Although costs for the public and private companies show considerable variation, cost disadvantages seem to prevail for the public companies. Thus both capital usage rates and labor costs have risen, causing

---

costs wherever possible; however, I think it is important that before agreeing to certain reductions or changes, that I fully understand what are the cost savings involved." This was the response from a director who had been on the board for over ten years (U.S. Senate 1982).

[29] The 1980 average annual outlays per worker are as follows: Amtrak - $27,000; bus - $24,000; air - $33,000. The labor costs per passenger-mile are as follows: Amtrak - $0.14; bus - $0.04; air - $0.05 (U.S. Congressional Budget Office 1982a).

[30] The Postal Service also increased its sales per employee, but there is no indication that this was sufficient to compensate for excessive employment since the 1960's (see Table 2.14). With the exception of the mid-1970s, postal labor costs have averaged 85 percent of revenues since the 1971 reorganization. During the mid-1970s, due to labor contracts with generous cost-of-living allowances coupled with high inflation, this percentage increased to over 90 percent, and helped necessitate a $1 billion emergency appropriation from Congress in the 1976 amendment to the Postal Reorganization Act.

[31] With the exception of Postal Service, which had lower unit labor costs given its much higher volume throughput than the specialty express or one-day service corporations.

Table 2.13: Labor Cost per Unit of Production

($ per unit of output)

| Year | Electric Utilities | | Railroads | | Mail Services | | Passenger Services | |
|---|---|---|---|---|---|---|---|---|
| | Industry | TVA | Industry | Conrail | Industry | USPS | Industry | Amtrak |
| 1976 | 0.0411 | 0.0252 | 0.0081 | 0.0203 | n/a | 0.1335 | 0.0277 | n/a |
| 1977 | 0.0455 | 0.0266 | 0.0089 | 0.0220 | n/a | 0.1423 | 0.0299 | n/a |
| 1978 | 0.0515 | 0.0297 | 0.0104 | 0.0227 | 6.9400 | 0.1448 | 0.0303 | n/a |
| 1979 | 0.0579 | 0.0363 | 0.0168 | 0.0241 | 0.0000 | 0.1519 | 0.0322 | 0.0671 |
| 1980 | 0.0652 | 0.0426 | 0.0230 | 0.0265 | 0.0000 | 0.1531 | 0.0332 | 0.1007 |
| 1981 | 0.0796 | 0.0504 | 0.0261 | 0.0273 | 9.8506 | 0.1587 | 0.0396 | 0.0968 |
| 1982 | 0.0940 | 0.0596 | 0.0306 | 0.0266 | 11.5041 | 0.1674 | 0.0488 | 0.1084 |
| 1983 | 0.0992 | 0.0644 | 0.0374 | 0.0193 | 12.5338 | 0.1681 | 0.0506 | 0.1246 |
| 1984 | 0.1089 | 0.0679 | 0.0362 | 0.0192 | 12.0526 | 0.1684 | 0.0527 | 0.1224 |
| 1985 | 0.1060 | 0.0729 | 0.0371 | 0.0193 | 10.5480 | 0.1738 | 0.0520 | 0.1186 |

SOURCES: COMPUSTAT Annual Industrial and OTC file, Quarterly Utilities file and annual Research file for Industrial data. Various "Annual Reports" for individual company reports.

Table 2.14: Sales per Employee

(Thousand dollars per annum)

| | Electric Utilities | | Railroads | | Mail Services | | Passenger Services | |
|---|---|---|---|---|---|---|---|---|
| Year | Industry | TVA | Industry | Conrail | Industry | USPS | Industry | Amtrak |
| 1976 | 111.50 | 63.42 | 49.01 | 24.48 | 54.52 | 18.92 | 59.22 | 15.22 |
| 1977 | 126.62 | 95.30 | 55.98 | 34.75 | 72.14 | 22.45 | 63.65 | 16.60 |
| 1978 | 130.24 | 120.91 | 61.62 | 38.23 | 78.27 | 24.19 | 68.22 | 15.71 |
| 1979 | 132.25 | 136.88 | 74.15 | 44.98 | 93.94 | 26.88 | 75.49 | 18.99 |
| 1980 | 148.34 | 172.54 | 88.80 | 50.03 | 93.20 | 28.12 | 87.00 | 20.91 |
| 1981 | 169.42 | 201.92 | 111.01 | 59.79 | 97.25 | 30.45 | 95.58 | 23.20 |
| 1982 | 175.43 | 228.70 | 95.16 | 62.67 | 95.52 | 34.52 | 100.04 | 33.37 |
| 1983 | 181.47 | 291.31 | 111.92 | 75.00 | 98.61 | 35.90 | 93.76 | 35.91 |
| 1984 | 195.59 | 229.33 | 112.78 | 83.57 | 93.78 | 36.05 | 102.24 | 38.91 |
| 1985 | 204.62 | 228.92 | 115.96 | 85.07 | 94.61 | 37.26 | 102.77 | 39.32 |

SOURCES: COMPUSTAT Annual Industrial and OTC file, Quarterly Utilities file and annual Research file for Industrial data. Various Annual Reports are used for individual company reports; Edison Electric Institute Statistical Yearbook (1981-1985) and Association of American Railroads "Railroad Facts" (1986).

Table 2.15: **Total Factor Productivity**

**(Product per constant dollar of factor costs)**

| Year | Electric Utilities (units KwH) | | Railroads (ton miles) | | Mail Services (pieces) | | Passenger Services (passenger miles) | |
|---|---|---|---|---|---|---|---|---|
| | Industry | TVA | Industry | Conrail | Industry | USPS | Industry | Amtrak |
| 1976 | 29.81 | 52.29 | 28.14 | 19.92 | n/a | 4.07 | 3.32 | 5.67 |
| 1977 | 27.46 | 54.61 | 27.38 | 14.63 | n/a | 4.07 | 3.60 | 5.66 |
| 1978 | 27.86 | 48.30 | 25.51 | 14.95 | 0.01 | 4.34 | 3.89 | 5.57 |
| 1979 | 28.03 | 43.32 | 28.95 | 16.05 | 0.01 | 4.51 | 4.52 | 6.35 |
| 1980 | 26.12 | 40.82 | 18.42 | 16.49 | 0.02 | 4.77 | 4.68 | 6.19 |
| 1981 | 25.24 | 51.03 | 18.51 | 17.85 | 0.02 | 4.94 | 4.75 | 6.16 |
| 1982 | 24.09 | 39.78 | 15.71 | 19.06 | 0.02 | 4.99 | 4.96 | 5.81 |
| 1983 | 24.38 | 39.24 | 15.17 | 26.30 | 0.02 | 5.02 | 7.17 | 5.70 |
| 1984 | 23.68 | 39.71 | 14.16 | 28.48 | 0.03 | 5.24 | 7.38 | 6.06 |
| 1985 | 25.22 | 38.39 | 13.89 | 28.73 | 0.04 | 5.36 | 6.72 | 6.04 |

SOURCES: Annual Reports and COMPUSTAT for the industry and individual firms; "National Income and Product Accounts", Bureau of Economic Analysis, Department of Commerce, for the input price deflator.

NOTE: Total factor productivity is level of production in units divided by constant dollar cost of inputs. The total cost of inputs of total factor cost is direct labor cost, direct material cost, direct overheads and net interest. This total factor cost is divided by specific industry input price deflators to determine constant dollar total factor cost. The input price deflator for railroads and passenger services, from Railroad Facts, is used to deflate total factor cost for Conrail, Amtrak and the corresponding private sector indices. The implicit national income price deflator from the Bureau of Economic Analysis, Department of Commerce is used to deflate total factor costs for the electric utilities and the mail services industry.

prices of these four public-sector corporations to increase beyond those of their counterpart private-sector corporations.[32]

## MANAGEMENT PRACTICE IN THE FOUR PUBLIC-SECTOR CORPORATIONS

Given that public enterprises had higher rates of price appreciation and lower profitability in the 1980s than comparable private-sector organizations, then the question is: What are the structural factors in these corporations that lead to such results? The comparative price increases and profitability levels were traceable to cost increases in excess of those found in the private corporations used as the basis for comparison. But this is only a partial response, suggesting that public-sector enterprises do not perform as well in seeking ways to control cost escalation, while passing through in price increases the cost increases that occur.[33] Efforts to improve the productivity of public enterprises are for some reason not as effective as efforts to improve productivity in the private sector.

One explanation is that there are pre-ordained conditions in public companies which reduce the motivation of managers to pursue cost control and productivity growth. Lacking such mechanisms as the threat of bankruptcy or takeover, the ability to share in growth of equity, and managerial compensation tied to profits, management does not respond to reduced or stagnant productivity and rising wages in collective bargaining.[34] Rather, cost

---

[32] In order to approximate how TVA would price if they were subjected to the constraints faced by private utilities, a least-squares regression model was constructed. The results of this regression showed that if TVA had the same cost of debt and was obligated to pay taxes at the same rate as private utilities, its rates would not have differed significantly from those charged by private utilities. For details of this regression, see Appendix One.

[33] In its 1977 study on the improvement of federal government productivity, including public corporations, McKinsey & Co. identified a number of factors that acted as barriers to increased productivity. Among these are: Productivity improvement is not regarded as having a major payoff; a continuous "higher level" interest in productivity is thought to be lacking; motivation suffers from a lack of incentives; personnel management constraints limit managerial initiative, and productivity suffers from appointees' lack of experience (McKinsey & Company Inc. 1977).

[34] Another structural mechanism that is not available to public enterprises is the transfer of ownership via shares of stock. Individual taxpayers can "sell their shares" in a public enterprise only by moving outside the political jurisdiction of the owning government. Furthermore, individual taxpayer's interests are so diffuse that the incentive to monitor management's performance is reduced (Zeckhauser and Horn, this volume, page 11).

increases are passed through to the consumer or users of services in the form of price increases.

The most significant of these structural and process conditions appear to have such an effect. They include:

1) the responsibilities and priorities of the governing boards;
2) the nature of the contracted responsibility and accountability of the chief executive officer for achieving productivity performance;
3) the responsibility of subordinate managers to exercise productivity discipline;
4) given (1) to (3), the effectiveness of processes for ensuring gains in labor productivity so as to reduce costs; and,
5) the effectiveness of processes for reaching decisions on the execution of capital expenditures and the achievement of productivity improvement.

In the following sections of the paper, we discuss our views with regard to each of the above points.

## Governing Boards

At the highest level in management, the supervisory boards of public corporations have not exercised discipline in the strategic emphasis on productivity improvements comparable to that of the boards elected by beneficial owners.[35] [36] The boards of Amtrak, Conrail, TVA, and the Postal

---

[35] Consider the following testimony of Rep. William D. Ford, Chairman of the House Committee on Postal Service and Civil Service: "The Board of Governors, which Congress created in the Postal Reorganization Act of 1970, was supposed to be akin to a corporate board of directors in the private sector. Our idea worked for a while, but during the last few years we have seen our creation turn into something which isn't remotely similar to a corporate board. Individual governors have interfered unduly with collective bargaining, with financial planning, with service modernization, with procurement, and with direct intervention in personnel matters. During the last 18 months, we have had three Postmasters General -- and it will be four with the imminent departure of Albert Casey. All have found it impossible to do the job because [of the board's meddlings]. We are here today in response to a series of incidents which have caused the members of this committee to question the ability of top management of the U.S. Postal Service to govern effectively. The nation's Postal Service is facing the gravest crisis since the 1970 reorganization, and this crisis emanates from the quality of leadership of its governing board.

"The Board of Governors was set up under the Postal Reorganization Act of 1970 as a general policy making body. They were to function as overseers of the Postal Service. What we have seen in the past few years, however, is an increasing tendency toward micromanagement.

Service have been appointed for diverse purposes. Members have represented the interests of important constituencies such as the employees, the business community of that region, or specific directly-related consumer groups.[37] They have represented the interests of railroad passenger associations, postal and railroad unions, large postal service users, industrial customers of electric

---

"This committee has been concerned for several years now with the governing style of the Board. Certain members seem to be pursuing their own agenda. The recent scandal, where an individual Board member was engaged in various schemes for his own enrichment, highlights this type of thinking" (U.S. House of Representatives 1986a, pp. 2-3).

[36] With respect to TVA, much the same has been stated. This is the opening statement by Senator Gordon J. Humphrey, Chairman of the Subcommittee on Water Resources, at a TVA oversight hearing:

"Today's hearing, again, focuses on the matter of accountability of TVA, and I would observe, having now been immersed in this matter for some weeks, that as far as I can see, at least, TVA is not accountable to its customers in any meaningful way. It is not accountable to the Governors of the TVA states. I would observe that it is not accountable in any meaningful way to the public utilities commissions, to the state legislatures, nor is it accountable to the marketplace, in as much as it can borrow from the Federal Government pretty much when it wants, for whatever purpose it wants, providing it does not exceed its cap line of credit. Nor is it accountable to Congress in a practical sense, because we in Congress are charged to oversee the entire Federal Government, a task which is, frankly, impossible. So as a practical matter, TVA gets superficial scrutiny once in a while, every several years, and as a practical matter, therefore, in my opinion, TVA is not even accountable to Congress" (U.S. Senate 1985a, p. 611).

[37] Similar statements have been made with respect to Conrail: "There were two Boards that oversaw the operation of Conrail: The Board of Directors of the United States Railway Association and the Board of Conrail. The Board of Directors of the USRA was to have three government officials: the Secretaries of Transportation and the Treasury, and the Chairman of the ICC. The remainder consisted of representatives of various interest groups: the National League of Cities and the U.S. Conference of Mayors, the AFL-CIO, the Association of American Railroads, the financial community, the National Governors Conference, large shippers and small shippers. There was also a Finance Committee, which consisted of the Chairman of the USRA and the Secretaries of Transportation and the Treasury" (U.S. Railway Association 1986).

The Rail Passenger Service Act, as amended, states that the Amtrak board shall consist of nine members, all U.S. citizens and selected as follows:

- President of Amtrak, ex officio, Chairman
- Secretary of Transportation, ex officio
- Three members appointed by the President of the United States, by and with the advice and consent of the Senate; one of the three to be selected from a list recommended by the Railway Labor Executives Association; one to be selected from among the governors of states with an interest in rail transportation; and one to be selected as a representative of business with an interest in rail transportation.

power and the construction industry.[38] Still other members have been elected to represent the body politic -- the "public interest" -- having been chosen to reward party service at levels not requiring major ambassadorships or sub-cabinet appointments.

In each of the forms of board supervision used by these four public corporations, responsibility for productivity improvement has been muted by other concerns.[39] [40] It has become more important to ensure sustained levels of employment, and to maintain service for certain constituencies,[41] for example, than to ensure productivity improvement and consequent cost containment. But finding these combinations of conflicting policies has been difficult and prolonged.[42] Since the interests being served are not particularly

---

[38] Zeckhauser and Horn maintain that special groups are rewarded when there is an "available pot". An "available pot" is the surplus that could be generated from resources given to the SOE (State-Owned Enterprise) if it were run as a private, for-profit firm (Zeckhauser and Horn, this volume, p. 14). The larger the surplus, the more benefits will be redistributed to "powerful consumers and employees" (Ibid., this volume, p. 42).

[39] Zeckhauser and Horn point to a number of studies which provide empirical evidence to support that publicly owned utilities charge lower prices and favor large users. They contend that the evidence shows that "publicly-owned utilities are used to favoring consumers over tax-payers, and large industrial users over residential groups whose interests are more diffuse" (Zeckhauser and Horn, this volume, p. 47).

[40] "Amtrak has the authority to add or discontinue routes using Congressionally approved procedures that consider economic, social, and environmental factors; however, it has not used these procedures effectively to discontinue its most unprofitable routes...Under this fragmented route decision process, Amtrak increased its route system from about 23,000 route-miles and 69,000 daily train-miles in 1971 to 27,000 route-miles and 87,000 daily train-miles in 1977. As the system expanded, Amtrak's losses increased,however, so that DOT and the Congress agreed that Amtrak needed more management flexibility to handle its route system and improve its economic performance. Accordingly, a key provision of the Amtrak Improvement Act of 1975 gave Amtrak's Board of Directors responsibility for changing Amtrak's routes and services. The act also specified, however, that the Board must publicly describe the procedures it would use in making its route decisions" (U.S. General Accounting Office 1978a).

[41] The General Accounting Office reported in 1982 that the Postal Service could save over $125 million annually by 1990 if it replaced about 7,000 limited service post offices with rural route extensions or private contractor-operated facilities. These measures would have little or no effect on the quality of mail service, but are not taken because of the requirements of existing law, Postal Rate Commission review procedures, and restrictive postal practices (U.S. General Accounting Office 1982).

[42] Mr. William Chandler of the World Watch Institute:

"... TVA is owned by the Federal Government, and in 1959 the TVA Act was amended to require the users of TVA electricity to bear all the costs of investment. TVA consumers are thus required by law to pay their own way. This is an extraordinary deal for the Federal Government,

clear-cut, much board activity has been directed at reaching compromises among the competing interests of these constituencies.[43] The governing board has operated as a political body structuring compromises to balance constituents with regard to major program issues.[44] Given such an agenda, the boards have subordinated the requirement to perform under policies to keep costs in line with those of private companies operating in the same or similar markets.[45] [46]

---

because it owns and controls the largest utility in the country, but by law, accepts no financial risks for it. Conversely, it is a bad deal for the valley residents to bear all of the risks but none of the decision-making authority. All decisions with respect to power plant construction and rates are determined by the Federal Government's TVA Board" (U.S. Senate 1985a, p. 630).

[43] Mr. Stanley Crane, Conrail CEO, at an oversight hearing:

"At the time that Conrail was formed under the terms of the 3R Act, employment protection was written into that Act which had the effect of guaranteeing everybody who had seniority on Conrail their jobs until age 65. As the reduction in traffic and revenues available to the company occurred from 1976 through 1980 and 1981, there was simply not enough revenue coming in to support that type of payroll. But the management was unable to make the reductions because we were directed by the Congress to keep the people on the payroll" (U.S. Senate 1985b).

[44] John M. Sullivan (Administrator, Federal Railroad Administration) at an oversight hearing for Conrail funding:

"I am happy to sit here and support Conrail's management in the judgement that they are making because we can see they do have the ability to target these moneys, and at a time like this we are happy they are not coming to you for more dollars."

Representative Edward Madigan (Illinois):

"Of course that could just indicate a sensitivity on our part about the burden for us in trying to get the dollars. Instead of making a good management decision they might be making a political judgement and then making a management decision taking into account what the politics are up here" (U.S. House of Representatives 1980a).

[45] In 1985, in the midst of a procurement-contracts kickback scandal which resulted in the jailing of one postal governor, the postal board violated its own resolution regarding the scope of activities by its own committees. The resolution, dated 2/5/85, authorized the committees to gather information on behalf of the Board but not to take action on its behalf. On March 5, 1985, 2 of the 3 members of the board's Technology Committee, with the consent of the chairman of the board, directed postal management to "freeze" a certain procurement action which would not have favored the firm providing kickbacks to the governor later jailed (U.S. House of Representatives 1987, pp. 50-1).

[46] Compared with other common-carrier modes, Amtrak is extremely labor intensive. Amtrak's output (whether measured in seat-miles or in passenger-miles) per labor year compares poorly with that of the airline and bus industries. "The bus and air industries' outputs per labor year (measured in passenger and seat miles) are about triple Amtrak's" (U.S. Congressional Budget Office 1982b).

## The Chief Executive and Productivity Improvement

Without a board directed to the creation of economically beneficial services disciplined by the production of net cash flow, the chief executive of the public enterprise has had relatively greater freedom to set the agenda. Since there has been no commitment in the governing body as to precisely where, in the spectrum of potential objectives, efficiency should be placed,[47] the chief executive has evidently chosen in a number of cases among the objectives of the various constituencies that combination which has best sustained his administration.[48] At the least, given that he was appointed with regard to his skill at reaching compromises, the stage was set for maintaining the support of the various constituencies represented either on the board or in the oversight process. At the most there has been a lack of accountability for market performance,[49] relative to providing service at lower prices, and in

---

[47] Enabling legislation specifies efficiency is to be met by each organization:

i. Conrail: The Regional Rail Reorganization Act of 1973 (45 U.S.C. 771) laid out four broad purposes: "to identify a rail system for the Northeast and Midwest that could meet the needs of the region and of national transportation policy; to reorganize the region's railroads into just such a viable <u>and efficient</u> system; to provide assistance to State and regional and local transportation authorities so that they could continue rail services that were in danger of being halted; and to see that the federal financial assistance required for all this was provided at the lowest possible cost to the taxpayer".

ii. Postal Service: The statute empowers the Postal Rate Commission to enable the Postal Service to break even "under honest, efficient, and economical management" (39 U.S.C., sec. 3521).

iii. The Rail Passenger Service Act of 1970 (P.L. 91-518): Title III, Section 301 required that Amtrak be a "for-profit corporation and not an agency or establishment of the U.S. government"... Section 305 authorized the corporation to "own, manage and operate ... intercity trains ... providing modern, <u>efficient</u> intercity transportation of passengers".

[48] "Conrail's first CEO, Mr. Edward Jordan, was convinced his mandate was to rebuild the railroad to serve as many customers as possible, and to that extent he pushed through an expanded investment program, despite declining economic conditions. The result was an overbuilt or 'gold-plated' railroad" (National Academy of Public Administration 1981).

[49] David M. Boodman, vice president at Arthur D. Little, testifying to Congress in 1982 as a consultant to the USPS: "One must recognize the differences in the avenues to efficiency available to the Postal Service as compared with a private corporation. Few private investors would consider placing funds in an enterprise required to provide so uniform a service at so uniform a price when the costs of serving different segments of the market vary so widely, and when the degree of variation inevitably will increase as the costs of transportation and labor increase" (U.S. Congress. Joint Economic Committee 1982, pp. 313-14).

greater volume, than would be found in markets in the private sector of the economy. These management structures have permitted a forging of narrow interests at the cost of inefficient and high-priced operations.

Even if the boards of the four organizations had made productivity improvement and cost control their objective, they lacked the process for appointment and termination of the chief executive, and the other operating executives of these enterprises, that would have enforced achievement of that objective. In some instances that power has been subsumed by the White House staff appointments process. The electoral victor in the Presidential race has designated particular individuals to the executive position in the TVA and the Postal Service.[50] In a number of instances in the 1980s, that individual had limited qualifications to manage a complex and large-scale organization so as to secure improved productivity, but rather brought to the position an impressive record in national politics.[51] In other instances, particularly influential legislators exercised appointment rights. Only in the extreme case (e.g. the appointment of Albert Casey as Postmaster General)[52] has the price and cost performance of the public company deteriorated to a point where someone of widely recognized managerial force and skill had to

---

[50] Of the two CEOs in Conrail's history, one was chosen by the USRA, and the other (the current one) by the board. There were some difficulties in attracting qualified candidates for the job as the first chief. This was because there was no guarantee that the consolidation would be successful, and tenure in the position might therefore be limited. When the first CEO left in 1980, the board chose a veteran railroad operating man with long experience in dealing with government. The lack of politicization of the selection process may be linked to the company's relatively strong performance compared to other public-sector enterprises (National Academy of Public Administration 1981).

[51] Conversely, the boards of directors for private enterprises are theoretically chosen for their reputation and ability to direct and manage a company profitably for the shareholders. Since there is income to be gained by being a board director, there is an incentive for board members of private enterprises to execute their duties appropriately or else be removed by management or in an unfriendly tender offer (Fama 1980, p. 288-307; Jensen and Ruback 1983, pp. 5-50; Hermalin and Weisbach 1987).

[52] Another example where industry experience improved results is the appointment of W. Graham Claytor, Jr., a former Secretary of the Navy and a former president of Southern Railway, who became Amtrak's president in 1982. Within his first year, he met the Reagan Administration's mandate of covering one half of all operating costs from revenue (Itzkoff 1985), and he managed an important labor agreement covering most of Amtrak's 18,000 workers. Six of fifteen unions agreed to loosen many archaic work rules. He effected a 25-percent reduction in headquarter staff ("Amtrak Gets on Right Track", *Business Week*, June 21, 1982, p. 99).

be brought in to clean up the "mess". But Casey left after nine months,[53] a departure which reflected the continued problem in public enterprise of a lack of continuity of management.

### Subordinate Management Attention to Productivity Gain

The politicization of top levels of management, while having a purpose in solving problems among constituencies often in conflict, does not generate the incentives necessary to achieve operating performance compared to that of private companies.[54] Contracts with subordinate managers regarding priorities in their performance are ambivalent.[55] And contracts that

---

[53] Terms of recent Postmasters General:

| | |
|---|---|
| William F. Bolger | 1978 to 12/84 (retired) |
| Paul N. Carlin | 1/85 to 1/86 (ousted by board) |
| Albert V. Casey | 1/86 to 8/86 (temporary appointment) |
| Preston R. Tisch | 8/86 to 1/88 (resigned) |
| Anthony Frank | 1/88 - |

[54] The Hon. B.F. Sisk, a Congressman from California testifying in 1976 on proposed criteria for discontinuing Amtrak routes:

"I think that all of us can agree that there is a need for the criteria. Amtrak cannot be expected to operate indefinitely under political pressures generated by local interests. At some point there must be a bottom line. But how are we to make those decisions? Are we only to look at the dollars and cents, as the Administration would probably prefer? Or are we to take into consideration other factors, many of which are subjective? I think it is clear that the criteria cannot reasonably be based simply upon economics. If we are to choose that as the sole or primary basis for making route decisions, we would end up with no passenger train service because Amtrak reports that all of its 35 revenue routes have deficits" (U.S. House of Representatives 1976, p. 111).

Rep. James Florio (New Jersey):

"Admittedly, Conrail is a bit different than the rest of the railroad system and network across the country. But we are all hoping that the difference can be removed over whatever period of time. So there is an apparent difference in the thrust of the government's approach to railroads in general and the thrust of its approach to Conrail. Those differences can be reconciled, I suspect. But the immediate fact that sort of leaps out is that we are treating different segments of the railroad industry in a different way with regard to the degree of government involvement -- in a sense going in opposite directions vis-a-vis Conrail versus the rest of the industry" (U.S. House of Representatives 1980b).

[55] From a statement by Hon. Alfonse M. D'Amato, U.S. Senator from New York, at an Amtrak oversight hearing (U.S. Senate 1984):

have given priority to control of cost growth and the productivity improvements have not been put into effect with high expectations for achievement in these areas, nor with the priority that accompanies bonus programs found in the private sector.[56] There have been too many other projects and administrative requirements for cost growth containment to be over-riding, particularly where containment conflicts with the constituency interests of board members and senior management.[57] [58]

---

"This is basically a story of a constituent who first called my Albany office to inform us of something that they had observed ... He related the story that he often rides Amtrak trains from Albany to New York City. He said that he often sees employees, to quote him, ~blitzed on alcohol' ... Of course, we are talking about Amtrak contract workers, but to the public [there is] no distinction about whether these are Conrail employees or Amtrak employees."

Also at the hearing, John H. Riley, the Administrator of the Federal Railroad Administration, spoke further of the lack of supervision:

"Is it not true that today in many cases the conductor, the main man in charge or the woman in charge of that particular train, never sees the engineer or the fireman or the brakeman, neither before they go out of that station, nor on the entire run, because they essentially sue radio communication? And if that is true, might it not be a good idea for management of the railroads and the railroad unions to get together to begin to affix responsibility by having someone who is in charge take a look at these people who are taking these trains out of the stations?"

[56] In 1986, Postmaster General Albert Casey instituted a comprehensive reorganization of Postal Service management, which consolidated operations and decentralized substantial amounts of decision-making authority to the field division levels. In a March 1986 oversight hearing, Casey testified that their intent was to eliminate administrative layers. He said:

"Quite naturally, we are doing everything we reasonably can to complete these changes in a fair and equitable manner. Our intention is to rely on attrition and not disruptive separations or terminations. Of course, sensible relocation provisions will be provided, and we are exploring early retirement benefits for employees who do not wish to be relocated."

In response to an inquiry later in the hearing, Casey stated: "We are not eliminating any jobs. Nobody is going to be summarily dropped from the payroll" (U.S. House of Representatives 1986b).

[57] By shaping Amtrak's route structure to fit Congressional as opposed to public demands for service, the legislative branch damaged operating efficiency. In 1971, when Amtrak proposed its routes, three trains were to stop in Indianapolis, but none in Cleveland. Indiana's Congressional delegation projected a strong interest in national transportation policy. Ohio's did not. Only after the Ohio Congressmen protested was Cleveland restored to the intercity system. The "Harley Staggers Special", nicknamed for the Congressional leader, ran through the state of West Virginia at 22 percent of capacity in 1975. Discontinuance of the route was not considered. In 1977, "Senator Mansfield's Train", which ran across southern Montana, suffered a deficit of almost $25 million. That train, too, continued operation. In a typical Amtrak budget dispute, Secretary of Transportation Brock Adams called for route cuts in 1979, but Congress fought off the proposal by citing among other things a need for "regional balance". Such interference exemplified the difficulty of trying to please legislators in control of federal purse strings (Itzkoff 1985, p. 126).

There is another structural problem in rewarding cost control at the lower levels of the organization. The payment mechanisms for rewarding achievement in reaching stated organizational objectives do not exist to the same degree as in private-sector organizations.[59] And, even where such mechanisms are in existence, the performance standards, particularly in areas of cost control and productivity improvement, are not set as high as in comparable private-sector enterprises.[60]

An important obstructive factor has been the direct relationship of second- and third-level executives to constituent groups. These levels have been filled by managers that are administratively independent in order to have them respond directly to specific constituencies.[61] Separate, informal (but implicitly contractual) relationships have existed between these officials and important customers. As just one example, the rate-setting mechanisms in

---

[58] Although not directly related to the four subject public enterprises, an example of this phenomenon at work occurred when the Western Area Power Administration was formed in 1978 as part of the structure of the Department of Energy. Congressional pressures from both sides of the aisle were brought to bear to add about 200 employees or (10 percent of the work force to the staffing tables of that organization. These additional positions were sought by a coalition of the new Power Administration's managers and various public constituencies. The resistance of the Assistant Secretary of Energy, who exercised responsibility for these activities, and the Office of Management and Budget, was eroded through several Congressional hearings wherein that particular Assistant Secretary was reminded over and over again that other important items on his and the Administration's agenda would be compromised if his resistance continued. The positions, about half of which were not needed, according to that Assistant Secretary, were added (U.S. Senate 1978a).

[59] Performance rewards (through merit-based salary increases, bonuses and promotions) are limited due to the statutory cap on top postal executive pay, an administratively set pool of funds available for management pay increases, and salary compression within and among pay grades (U.S. Postal Service 1986, p. 12).

[60] Certain features of railroad labor agreements contribute to Amtrak's labor intensiveness and, hence, to costs. A railroad engine crew typically receives a full day's pay for a 100-mile trip. So, at an average speed of 40 miles per hour, a two-man crew costs two days' pay for a two-and-a-half-hour run. Similar agreements increase the cost of train crews. For example, a 1978 study by the General Accounting Office examined the costs of Amtrak train No. 355 from Detroit to Chicago (U.S. General Accounting Office 1978b, p. 20). For a five-hour and 40 minute trip, the two two-man engine crews altogether received 5.6 days' pay (an average of 1.4 days' pay per crew member), and the two-man crew each received just under two days' pay. The on-board service crew of three employees was paid on an hourly basis with a guaranteed 180 hours of pay per month. All in all, a trip that required less than 40 labor-hours cost Amtrak more than 66 labor-hours in pay. Not all Amtrak employees work under such costly contract provisions, of course, since labor contracts vary among the operating railroads and the crafts. But such arrangements do pervade the system, and they are very costly to Amtrak (U.S. Congressional Budget Office 1982b).

[61] See footnote 57.

the Postal Service arguably favor second- and third-class mail users. Given the depth of knowledge and political influence of these classes of mail users, they are advantageously positioned to influence the cost allocations which result in rate determinations. The countervailing forces which exist for first-class mail users have been rendered partially impotent largely because second- and third-level executives are realistically responsive to one-sided pressures.[62] Moreover, third-class mailers have alternatives (newspaper delivery, for example) to reach homes, while first-class mailers are bound to the postal services. Thus the motivation of subordinate managers, driven by compensation systems scaled to volume and employment measures, is to sustain utilization of the postal system -- however inefficient it may be with regard to realistically assigned costs.

Therefore, the responsiveness of the public enterprise organization to direction has been limited when it came to the issues of cost allocation and cost growth related to employment levels and organization expansion.[63]

---

[62] The Postal Service Board of Governors proposes new postal rates based on information supplied by postal management. To do so, management must first determine the cost of each class of mail. Each mail class must bear all of its directly attributable costs, as well as a portion of institutional postal costs (those not attributable to specific mail classes). The nine rate-making criteria in the Postal Reorganization Act are sufficiently diverse to allow postal management considerable latitude as to their methodology of allocating these institutional costs (which usually range between 40 and 50 percent of total postal costs). Postal management has taken the position that assignment of these costs should reflect the estimated demand elasticity of each class of mail.

As one example, the Postal Service's billion-dollar National Bulk Mail System, built between 1971 and 1976, handles bulk third- and fourth-class mail, and some second class mail. Because of their costing methodology, the Postal Service was able to charge 58 percent of the bulk mail system's costs to first-class mail (Tierney 1981, p. 125).

[63] From a statement submitted by John S. McQueen, General Manager, Chattanooga Power Board:

"The number of TVA employees continues to rise at a rapid rate. The salaries paid to lower-level TVA employees have continued to outpace the level of salaries available in the private market, while the salaries of top TVA officials are much lower than comparable salaries in private utilities. All too often, the TVA Board does not take full advantage of the skills and expertise available among its staff, instead implementing abrupt changes in policies and often ignoring staff recommendations. TVA's overall personnel policies are a source of great concern, both to consumers of TVA power and to TVA employees. Our consumers do not understand why TVA cannot tighten its belt as we all are required to do in times of economic hardship. The TVA Office of Power added approximately 2,300 additional employees during the eighteen-month period ending 12/31/80, with about 1,600 of these being added during the calendar year 1980. The consumer cannot understand why the number of TVA employees and their salaries continue to escalate at a rapid pace. TVA employees, most of whom are very dedicated to the goals of the Authority, are also bewildered at the rapid shifts in TVA policy and the management style used by the Board. As a result, employee morale cannot help but impact upon

Dysfunction has been a central problem. And the public enterprise corporations seem to have shielded such organizations from retribution or accountability through political processes.[64] No one gets ousted from office because of escalation in first-class postage rates.[65]

But at a basic level, the incentive systems have been lacking to in the achievement of efficiency objectives. Discretion has not been exercised by upper level managers in setting rewards for lower level managers for

---

employee performance" (U.S. Senate 1981).

A 1983 General Accounting Office report was critical of postal management for ineffective control of employee overtime usage (which then cost the Postal Service $1 billion per year). It reported that facility managers budgeted expected overtime based on historical usage, rather than determinations of expected need. As long as the facility's overtime goals were met, no attention was paid to excessive overtime usage by specific employees or work areas. When overtime goals were exceeded, managers took action (such as hiring additional letter carriers) without exploring the underlying causes. In addition, there was insufficient monitoring of employees' arrival and departure times, and as much as 25 percent of overtime was approved retroactively, contrary to postal procedures (U.S. General Accounting Office 1983).

In Congressional testimony during October 1985, GAO Director William J. Anderson reported that between FY81 and FY84, postal overtime use had grown more than twice as fast as mail volume. He noted that overtime started to decline near the end of FY85 due to additional hiring (U.S. House of Representatives 1985, p. 212).

[64] Mr. William Chandler of the World Watch Institute testified:

"... When a company like Coca-Cola makes a mistake, it has to face the market, and a correction is forced. When politicians make mistakes, they have to face that day of reckoning when they stand up before the electorate and explain why they voted as they did. But TVA is not accountable to the marketplace, because it is a monopoly. It is not accountable to the electorate, because its directors do not owe their jobs to the people that they serve. Neither do the politicians who appoint the directors. The directors are appointed for 9-year terms by a President who may or may not understand the problems of the Valley, and their appointments are reviewed by a Senate committee, which at present doesn't even include a representative of the Valley" (U.S. Senate 1985a p. 633).

[65] Rep. Don H. Clausen, at a hearing concerning the effects of TVA electric rate increases:

"What seems to be underlying the bulk of testimony at this hearing is that there is a lack of adequate policy direction that reflects the interests and attitudes of the people who are served, and finally that there seems to be a rate structure that is designed to accommodate some social engineering scheme with a public-be-damned attitude" (U.S. House of Representatives 1982, p. 227).

performance in accordance with the objectives of the enterprise.[66] Most pay scales have replicated civil-service standards,[67] based on experience, job scope (including "sizing" factors) and promotion, which work well only when the organization expands.[68] [69] Systems which have measured performance and

---

[66] From a statement submitted by Congressman John J. Duncan:

"TVA's salary structure needs an overhaul. Top-level executives who manage $5 billion in assets with another $12 billion in construction need to be compensated accordingly. Nor can TVA pay the chief engineer and chief construction manager at a nuclear contruction site only $40,000 when such individuals would receive at least $80,000 elsewhere. TVA's salaries are generally too low at the top, about right in the middle range, and too high at the entry level for non-engineering skills. This highly skewed pay scale is extremely dangerous, considering TVA's high degree of employment in the middle and lower levels" (U.S. Senate 1981, p. 366).

From a report on TVA performance by Robert N. Clement, Director of TVA:

"TVA has entirely too many assistants, assistants-to and staff positions...Most of TVA's rate-payers believe TVA is overstaffed. Based on my observations and discussions with TVA employees, I too believe that TVA could do its work with less people. In my opinion, the overall productivity level could even increase with fewer employees. This phenomenon could happen because the remaining TVA employees would be more motivated and fulfilled because each would have more work to do" (Ibid, pp. 195-6).

[67] Postal wages are determined by pay grade and are uniform throughout the country, regardless of regional variations in cost-of-living and comparable wage rates. Pay-grade segments are relative to job scope and responsibility. Volume and employment levels are used to differentiate grades among comparable responsibility levels.

[68] The Postal Reorganization Act of 1970 limited the compensation of any postal employee to that of Executive Level I in the federal service. As a result, the USPS has experienced salary compression within the Postal Career Executive System (PCES) I schedule salary. Increases were limited to executives in the lower levels to reduce overlap between their salaries and those of mid-level managers in the Executive and Administrative Schedule (EAS). However, this further compressed the PCES I schedule, and significant overlap still remains between the PCES and EAS schedules (U.S. Postal Service 1986, p. 12).

[69] As a result of Conrail's continued inability to meet the objectives set out in its system plan, and due to an increasing level of government investment, the Staggers Rail Act of 1980 directed USRA to make a new examination of the causes of Conrail's problems and the possible solutions. The findings were as follows:

"Besides the indigenous problems that are at the heart of the region's railroad crisis, Conrail also has been plagued internally by insufficient control and poor supervision, problems that the company's new management is now attacking with considerable determination and refreshing vigor. Lower-level supervisors have often been insufficiently trained or motivated. Budget discipline is often lacking at the levels in the organization where costs are authorized or incurred. The work force, although significantly reduced since Conrail's inception, remains abnormally large, so much so that by almost any productivity measure Conrail compares poorly with the industry average. Nor is the problem confined to the unionized work force. Nonagreement (management) employment is also excessive and has grown over the past five years. In all, Conrail has at least 10,000 more employees on the payroll than its tonnage can justify and its

related results to executive responsibility have in general been less effective than in private-sector enterprises.[70]

## Labor Productivity Improvement Efforts

The economic effectiveness of public enterprise management in the past decade has required the realization that unit cost reductions would be forthcoming not by production expansion but from employment reduction in existing systems. And this employment reduction can be only partially accomplished through displacement from new capital investments and partially from meeting higher standards of productivity in managing employment costs. The types of management decisions in private companies which have resulted in substantial productivity improvement have, in fact, involved the displacement of workers, reductions in management, and shifts of capacity to lower-cost locations. Reactions to these attempts to achieve productivity improvement even in the private-sector have been traumatic, not only for those displaced but for the executive structure enforcing such discipline as well. The same types of management decisions in public enterprise for attaining comparable efficiency are much more complicated, given managerial control and incentives practices there.[71] Public enterprise officials have not had the

---

revenues can support" (U.S. Railway Association 1981).

A 1982 report by the National Academy of Public Administration suggested that Postal Service managers who evaluate the junior managers in the Postal Career Executive System (PCES) had too broad a set of criteria to assure accurate ratings (especially for those junior managers in field offices). As a result, the ratings were likely to depend on the execution of one or two aspects of the candidates' tasks (toward which the candidates would be inclined to devote their energies) (National Academy of Public Administration 1982, p. 51).

[70] The McKinsey study found that there is a dearth of useful management information -- including information to measure results of activities carried out, and reports that would help Federal managers initiate and oversee productivity improvement efforts. One interviewee pointed out that "if we can get smart about designing a limited array of productivity-related information needs, we will find that 80 percent of it is already in existence" (McKinsey & Co. Inc. 1977).

[71] "Work rules would not seem to explain Conrail's productivity problems. Despite some cumbersome provisions, the rules governing Conrail employees do not differ markedly from those on other carriers. Neither would wage rates seem to be a significant cause since they are also fairly uniform. The multiplicity of agreements on Conrail has undoubtedly caused problems, but this is difficult to quantify.

"Conrail's productivity problems have stemmed in part from the nature of its traffic, which requires a relatively high number of terminals, and its heavy passenger orientation, along with

means and the motivation to undertake "downsizing" under conditions of stagnant or declining demand.[72] The stomach for trauma of this type without

---

operating constraints caused by out-of-date yards and poor track and equipment. Further, productivity improvements in the face of static or declining traffic volumes are difficult to attain. However, some of Conrail's differences from other carriers are so pronounced that the question of adequate supervision arises. Also, because the extensive rehabilitation effort has had little effect to date, Conrail's choice of capital improvement projects perhaps is also suspect."

1977 Productivity ratios:

| | Conrail | Class I RRs |
|---|---|---|
| Yard Wage Expense per Carload: | $45.58 | $24.99 |
| Road Wage Expense per Carload: | 5.43 | 3.87 |
| Total Freight Wage Expense as a percent of Freight Revenue: | 19.4% | 14.2% |

(Source: U.S. Railway Association 1978)

From a GAO report released in 1981: "Amtrak's productivity has improved since 1977, but it is still not as high as the other railroads'. During 1979, the following results were recorded, and while they are not precisely comparable, they do show that Amtrak's productivity is not as high:

| | Amtrak | Commuter | Four Private Railroads | Conrail |
|---|---|---|---|---|
| Wood ties per hour | 0.50 | 1.11 | 2.20 | 2.75 |
| Track Feet Per hour | 1.13 | 2.08 | 5.25 | 4.14 |
| Surfacing Track ft/hr. | 21.17 | n/a | 55.20 | 32.08 |

(Source: U.S. General Accounting Office 1981a)

[72] The U.S. Railway Association indicated that there were two major opportunities to significantly cut Conrail employee costs: (1) Eliminate overhead employees in excess of those required, and (2) eliminate excessive requests for data that creates nonproductive work and distracts line managers from their responsibilities. The following strong recommendations were also made:

"Further to the extent that Conrail's viability depends on cuts in the labor work force or wage concessions, Conrail's management must be prepared to cut its own ranks and costs accordingly so as to share in the sacrifices. The size of Conrail's management has held steady or increased at the same time that Conrail's agreement employee ranks have declined substantially. Not only has the size of Conrail's management failed to shrink at the same rate as the work force that it manages, but it has become less productive. The same number of nonagreement employees now

any reward other than trouble with immediate constituencies does not exist.[73] The Conrail "challenge" was not to the contrary, since the incentive system there was inherent in attaining privatization.[74] In the other three public-sector corporations, senior officers have been sensitive to the potential for labor and other constituencies to seek redress in ways which can threaten continuity of their organizations.[75] Labor constituencies have been represented directly on

---

manages a smaller business. Such comparisons place a heavy burden upon Conrail's management to justify its current size. While USRA's research has been limited, preliminary findings indicate that the railroad's management work force is swollen well beyond necessity. Conrail should match any productivity improvements that it seeks from organized labor with reductions in the sixe of its own management force" (U.S. Railway Association 1981).

[73] In its 1977 survey of ways to improve federal government groductivity, McKinsey & Company found that productivity improvement in federal enterprises is of such a low priority that "you break your back in improving productivity and it won't even qualify as a footnote in the history book" (McKinsey & Co. Inc. 1977).

[74] "Conrail, because of its able management and cooperative labor groups, has achieved a financial turnaround unparalleled in railroad history. Even though tonnage declined 28 percent from 1977 to 1984, and despite the prolonged 1980-82 recession, Conrail recorded a financial turnaround of over $900 million, from a 1977 net loss of a $412 million to 1984 profit of $500 million. In a 1984 survey of shippers conducted by *Distribution Magazine*, Conrail was voted the best railroad in the country in service, pricing, and communication. Conrail is the low-cost producer of merchandise freight service in the northeast and midwest, largely because of its strong market position, lower train operating costs, modern plant and equipment, labor support and management. A viable Conrail that has returned to the private sector as an independent entity will use its considerable marketing and financial resources to: 1) continue to provide a high level of innovative service; 2) maintain a competitive rail environment in the northeast; 3) generate attractive financial returns to shareholders while continuing to support capital spending and productivity enhancements; and 4) improve employment conditions for the long term (U.S. Senate 1985c).

"By early spring 1981, Crane was instrumental in persuading leaders of Conrail's powerful labor brotherhood that the Reagan Administration was serious about dismantling Conrail and selling the pieces, and Congress might well go along if labor costs were not cut sharply. As a result, employees eventually agreed to wage cuts that would save Conrail $260 million over three years and result in the workers making 12 percent a year less than their counterparts in the rest of the rail industry for several years" (Belden 1987).

[75] The March 1970 postal strike affected 23 percent of all organized postal workers, and required the activation of federal troops to move the mail in New York City. The occurrence of strikes, legal or not, has had a significant impact on postal management's negotiating position in collective bargaining.

In addition to large wage and benefit increases, as well as cost-of-living allowances during the 1970s, postal management was unable to reverse previous agreements of a "no layoff" policy and on limitations to the employment of temporary workers.

Furthermore, unlike steel or auto workers, the postal unions have little incentive to help management streamline labor costs to remain competitive. Throughout the 1970s, the postal unions'

the boards of Conrail and Amtrak. Reductions in manpower have had to be accompanied by cutbacks in management, and both have been limited by blocking actions from mid-level management not subject to senior authority.[76] The management systemitself has diminished the capability of the executive to deal with productivity problems.[77]

As one result, service in these "public" as opposed to "private" companies have typically been subjected to a higher degree of oversight and inspection. Knowing the nature of the structure and control problems which existed in the "public" form of organization, federally owned enterprises have been required to report publicly on almost every activity undertaken, in ways that can be audited and compared.[78] But paperwork has been no substitute

---

labor agreements included general wage increases well in excess of those granted to the federal work force, uncapped cost-of-living adjustments, and substantially increased employer contributions to health insurance, life insurance and pensions. One 1984 study estimated that postal employees are paid a premium of 20 percent over their private-sector counterparts (Perloff and Wachter 1984, pp. 26-35).

76 "The diverging trend between the number of management and nonmanagement employees was corroborated by a review of an internal Conrail manpower planning document. That document showed that while employee ranks have declined every year from an average 1976 figure of 90,612 to an estimated 72,596 employees in 1980, average nonagreement employment increased from 6,997 to 7,505 in 1979. According to the document, there were some cuts in management employment in 1980, but the total number of management employees is still higher than in 1977. One notable example of management's declining productivity is that Conrail moved 141,000 tons of freight in 1976 for each executive or official on its payroll. This ratio was better than that of the Norfolk and Western, and close to the ratio of the Chessie and Southern. But by 1979 Conrail's ratio had deteriorated to one for every 117,000 tons. Meanwhile, the other three roads' ratios had improved or held steady" (U.S. Railway Association 1981).

77 Again, Conrail became the exception as it approached privatization:

"Within weeks of his taking over as Chairman on January 1, 1981, Stanley Crane was gaining ground on Conrail's problems. Formerly head of the Southern Railway, which had its headquarters in Washington, Crane had a keen appreciation of politics. 'With his words and with his actions, Crane was a one-man credibility fix,' said a Conrail VP. With [DOT Secretary] Drew Lewis and others in the administration calling for a quick end to federal involvement in Conrail, what really surprised some people was hearing Crane sound some of the same themes. He shocked even his own executives by using his first news conference to say that as a freight railroad, Conrail should not be in the commuter train business. Conrail had always avoided that position as too politically volatile, because commuter service was considered its duty as a government-funded company. What really happened was that Crane brought a 'for-profit mentality' said a senior Conrail executive" (Belden 1987).

78 Conrail management was required to submit to USRA the following reports:

- Monthly, quarterly, and annual financial statements
- A five-year business plan
- Interim projections tracking the business plan

for economic discipline. The point is that it has not been practical to record and examine the detailed transactions influencing the productivity of the public-service enterprises, assemble the information in numerous different ways and engage quantities of analysts to compare and review performance as an ongoing process. Indeed, the various impositions of these types of control structures themselves have added to the inability of such organizations to perform effectively in an economic sense.

## Capital Productivity

Labor productivity is not the only issue. Similar conditions apply in allocating and ensuring optimal utilization of capital. The recent history of the Postal Service, for example, is fraught with decisions on major capital invest-

---

- Quarterly and monthly maintenance reports
- Variance analysis explaining differences between actual results and the business plan
- Reports to the Securities and Exchange Commission, security exchanges, lenders, ICC and shareholders
- Daily cash receipts and disbursements, and 2-week forecasts of future receipts and disbursements

In addition to the Office of Financial Analysis, the USRA also maintained an Office of Operations, which had the responsibility of identifying the differences between the system plan and actual Conrail performance, together with analyzing the reasons for those differences. The operational staff monitored four functional areas of Conrail's activities: 1) local rail service and manpower; 2) operations and cost analysis; 3) marketing and sales; and 4) facilities and equipment. Within each of these areas, USRA operational staff analyzed and evaluated performance, costs, strategies, and production data and presented their findings to the USRA Board of Directors (U.S. Railway Association 1986).

Regarding public monitoring of Amtrak:

1) The President appoints a majority of the Board of Directors; in the absence of common stockholder representatives, the importance of this appointed majority is substantially magnified.

2) Amtrak is required to submit reports to both the executive and legislative branches.

3) The Federal government retains the right to investigate the financial affairs of the Corporation to ascertain whether or not the public's monies are being prudently managed.

4) The General Accounting Office conducts periodic audits of the Corporation.

5) The DOT annually reviews Amtrak's activities and submits recommendations to the Congress.

6) The ICC mediates disputes between Amtrak and the cooperating railroads and must approve any discontinuance of passenger trains (National Transportation Policy Study Commission 1978).

ments that have had questionable payoff.[79] In some instances these decisions have been directly influenced by political favoritism on the part of board appointees. At TVA a controversy has erupted over the appropriation, timing and pace of investment in new generating capacity -- particularly nuclear power capacity.[80] Certainly, the recent TVA nuclear power development

---

[79] In efforts to win support for large-scale postal projects, postal management has consistently overestimated the volume of new or increased service due to new projects. Their volume projections often fail to take into account the "debugging" problems associated with new technology, the attractiveness of the new service, or the actual costs to mailers. For example:

a) A 1976 study by the General Accounting Office examined the (then) recently completed, one billion dollar National Bulk Mail System. The report documented several major problems of the system, and concluded that the system might not generate savings high enough to justify the investment if the problems went uncorrected. Among the problems were: overestimation of capacity; significant underestimation of the volume of mail that could not be processed by machine; high rates of misdirected mail; high incidence of parcel damage (due primarily to faulty system design); inability to meet delivery standards; and higher rates of accidents and injuries than in the Postal Service as a whole. Estimates of annual costs savings from the system by the Postal Service and its consultants were based largely on significant increases in parcel post volume. The estimates on eventual annual savings ranged from $500 million in 1972 to $138 million in 1975, on expected parcel volume of 400 million pieces (U.S. General Accounting Office 1976). By 1981, the Postal Service had a parcel volume of 200 million, versus United Parcel Service volume of 1 billion parcels (U.S. House of Representatives 1981, p. 214).

b) The Postal Service's 1982 venture into computerized electronic mail service (E-Com) ended in 1984 after losing millions of dollars. In 1983, about 15 million letters were handled, compared with the 50 million first projected by the Postal Service. The service was criticized for being too slow and lacking "the pizazz" to attract business mailers. In addition, the U.S. Justice Department and Federal Trade Commission had charged that the Postal Service improperly subsidized E-Com with monopoly revenue from first-class mail, and the Postal Rate Commission had recommended that E-Com's rates be more than doubled (*Washington Post*, February 25, 1984, p. 12).

c) The Postal Service's projections of nine-digit zip code (Zip+4) adoption by business mailers, which was necessary to support its automated letter-sorting program, have been far overestimated. The USPS had predicted 1985 Zip+4 volume at 21 billion pieces, but the GAO estimated (in 10/85) the actual volume to be 6.5 billion (U.S. House of Representatives 1985, p. 194). Critics charged that the volume was so low because the Postal Service neglected to consider the costs to mailers of converting address directories, despite the Service's promotion of the system with tens of millions of dollars of advertisements and discounts. Charges were also made to the effect that the overestimation of Zip+4 usage coincided with inflated return on investment projections in order to justify the program ("Return Zip Code + 4 to the Sender," *Wall Street Journal*, December 10, 1985).

[80] Dialogue between Ms. Katherine Eickhoff, Associate Director of the Office of Management and Budget, and Senator Gordon Humphrey at a TVA oversight hearing (U.S. Senate 1985a, pp. 614-27):

Senator Humphrey: "...you say that there has been insufficient oversight of the TVA power program. Insufficient oversight by whom, in the eyes of OMB?"

program would have been questionable from a capacity utilization standpoint if the government had continued with the commercialization of the gas centrifuge uranium enrichment program.

Behind the apparent comparative gap in capital productivity performance is the shortfall in use of analytical and performance control mechanisms common in the private-sector.[81] Federally incorporated and governed enterprise is simply not as purposeful and consistent in such use.[82]

---

Ms. Eickhoff: "Almost by anyone. The mechanism really doesn't seem to quite exist. There is an internal audit function, but that doesn't quite have the same sort of outside look at the agency that you would really think of as oversight. FFB asks no questions whatsoever. If you got the authority to borrow, they write the checks."

From further dialogue between Ms. Eickhoff and Senator Humphrey:

Senator Humphrey: "...the concern here with respect to TVA is that they can come and borrow money when they want it in whatever amount they want up to the cap, and they are far from bumping into that constraint. There is a huge line of credit. They can borrow whatever they want whenever they want in whatever amount they want for whatever [purpose] they want, and nobody examines the proposal. That gives the management of TVA enormous flexibility [and] enormous power for which they are accountable to no one, really, in any practical sense."

From an OMB report at the same hearing (Ibid., pp. 677-8):

The reasons behind TVA's performance are no doubt due to a number of factors. However, it appears the lack of oversight has contributed to this situation. For example, more vigorous oversight might have prompted TVA to respond more quickly to changes in the marketplace.

Miscalculations of electricity demand growth have resulted in the cancellation of eight of the seventeen nuclear generating units originally planned by TVA. While this general problem occurred in a number of utilities, some critics have argued that TVA did not move fast enough or as far as it should have to rein in its nuclear construction program. Stronger oversight might have helped TVA to respond faster.

TVA's nuclear fuel inventory is larger than necessary for prudent operations -- five years' supply (down from a ten-year supply) vs. an industry target of one year's supply. Easy access fo FFB money by the Secen States Energy Corporation may have contributed to this problem.

[81] Mr. Ed Jordan (Conrail CEO): "The only place we can improve, and should improve, is what we call "additions and improvements", in the language of the ICC, but for you and me, those are big capital projects. We have been somewhat slow in getting up on those. This is partly a management problem; we simply can't manage enough of them fast enough. However, since some of these projects run as much as $40 million, we have felt that we ought to be very careful in understanding each expenditure" (U.S. Senate 1978b).

[82] "The effect of new equipment purchases on operating costs is not clearly explained in the plan. One of Amtrak's justifications in early five-year plans for new equipment was reduced maintenance costs. Rather than decreasing as more and more new equipment is delivered, the maintenance costs for equipment are increasing. Amtrak's current plan shows a $1.3 million decrease in equipment maintenance costs -- in 1980 only. In the other four years, the maintenance cost will increase by a total of $14.6 million over the 1977 level. Reasons for the

Given the structure and incentive problems discussed above, it is difficult for public-sector managers to measure and adhere strictly to a decision-making discipline assessing returns on investment.[83] Perhaps even more significant, once a capital investment decision is made, project management systems are not as rigorous or disciplined.[84] Control mechanisms used to ensure achievement of on-stream performance goals by certain dates of operation, do not

---

increases are not given in the plan" (U.S. General Accounting Office 1977).

83 "Specifically, Conrail has fallen short of some critical operational objectives. Improved service must be the focal point of Conrail's rehabilitation program. To date, the impact of the $858 million spent on track rehabilitation has not been quantifiable. USRA notes that, as of the end of 1978, there were 876 slow orders remaining on approximately 2400 miles of track where rehabilitation work had been implemented. Many of these slow orders were due to Conrail's failure to complete various aspects of the projects. These failures have resulted in the retention of slow orders, which have a negative impact on train operations and service. This is disturbing because rehabilitation projects are justified, at least in part, by returns on investments directly related to the removal of slow orders. On many projects, budgeted costs have been equaled or exceeded while only a portion of the work has been completed. USRA estimates that the 1978 program, though ostensibly within its budget, incurred a labor cost overrun of about 30 percent for material installed.

"USRA stated in its 1977 Performance Report that 'Conrail cannot afford to continue to permit delays in planning, approval, and construction of capital projects that are critical in order to improve operations and realize planned efficiency savings.' This statement can be applied equally to Conrail's 1978 performance. Conrail's cumbersome decision-making process continued to inhibit the implementation of additions and improvements in 1978. A number of projects were approved later in the year. Very little work was completed, leaving approximately $115 million worth of approved projects for implementation in 1979 out of a planned program of $145 million projected in the company's March 15, 1979, Business Plan" (U.S. Railway Association 1978).

To follow up its earlier study on the Postal Service's National Bulk Mail System, the GAO in 1978 reported that the system was still unable to achieve its objectives. "The Postal Service's parcel post volume and its share of the parcel market continue to decline. Rates generally have been noncompetitive, and deliveries too often are untimely and inconsistent...Recently, the Service estimated annual savings to be $40 million, a return of less than 4 percent annually on the $1 billion invested in the system. If parcel volume further declines as projected, the system may prove to be more costly to operate than alternative means to move bulk mail." In response to the decline in parcel volume, the Postal Service began in 1977 to process some oversize second- and third- class mail through the bulk mail system, which had the advantage of spreading the system's operating costs over a larger mail volume" (U.S. General Accounting Office 1978c).

84 According to Mr. Edmund Jordan, Conrail CEO:

"... It is our view that the discipline required of the management to utilize a [new car utilization] system of this sort is essential. Data processing systems are only as good as the people who make use of them. They do not do the job for you. Our management discipline was inadequate to make better use of a more sophisticated system" (U.S. Senate 1978b).

function to the same degree.[85] The result is that capital productivity, despite the ability of the government enterprise to raise money at advantageous interest rates, is not as high as in the private-sector.

## CONCLUDING REMARKS

Our conclusions can be summarized in the form of Table 2.16. Based on the reports of management and of program analysts in Congress and the Executive Office, the judgement overall has to be that the four public corporations operate at a lower degree of effectiveness in containing costs and increasing productivity than private-sector enterprises. All four are "lower" on the five categories of structure and process. The Postal Service was relatively the worst, and Conrail was relatively best (but not until after passage of the Act to privatize). This ranking is in agreement with a listing from worst to best in price performance -- Postal Service and Amtrak with the largest price and cost hikes, and Conrail with the smallest such increases. Thus poor management practice results in the failure to achieve the mandate for more and better service from the public enterprises.

There are fundamental reasons why these public-sector organizations have had more management problems than have comparable private-sector organizations. Public-sector organizations have not been driven by concern for efficiency of internal operations, but rather by serving the "public interest". But the "public interest" has been difficult to define, except in terms of specific constituencies. Between elections, the public company board members, members of Congressional oversight committees, and the managers of the public enterprises have engaged in seeking that definition as it pertains to their own interests. This process has worked out to protect groups of employees, specific classes of customers, suppliers of capital goods, or influential political spokesmen. As a consequence, the managers have operated with only limited concern for the efficiency interests of the nominal shareholder -- the public at

---

[85] A 1981 GAO report recommended that Amtrak should try to continue to improve its passenger service contracts (U.S. General Accounting Office 1981b). A similar GAO report in 1977 had described how the incentive contracts with other railroads were affecting productivity and efficiency and costing a tremendous amount of money (U.S. General Accounting Office 1977). Still, in 1982 $305 million was spent for these services, which was equal to 25 percent of Amtrak's total operating expenses, and absorbed 70 percent of its operating income. At the time of this report, Amtrak had made amendment agreements with fourteen railroads but continued to operate under the original agreements with five (Conrail; ICG Railroad; Atchison, Topeka & Santa Fe; Baltimore & Ohio; and Chesapeake & Ohio).

Table 2.16: The Degree to Which Cost Control and Concern for Productivity Varies from Private Norms

| | USPS | Amtrak | TVA | Conrail * |
|---|---|---|---|---|
| Board Attention | lower | same | lower | lower/similar |
| Chief Executive Attention | lower | same | same | lower/similar |
| Subordinate Management Emphasis | lower | lower | lower | lower/similar |
| Employed Cost Control Process Effectiveness | much lower | lower | lower | lower/lower |
| Capital Cost Control Process Effectiveness | much lower | lower | lower | lower/similar |

SOURCE: See the Text

* Split before and after <u>The Northeast Rail Services Act of 1981</u>.

large -- that would have kept prices down and sales growing at faster rates than in the private companies.

These results have followed because management has had greater discretion to serve particular purposes and respond to influence group "problems" at the expense of the more broadly conceived market for final goods and services. But discretion when applied has led to forms of behavior which have been detrimental to the basic "public" purposes of the organization. Strategic decisions on service offerings, on the level of investment, and on the matching of labor supply to service demand have all proceeded without an adequate economic discipline. The mechanisms used to substitute for such market-based discipline -- oversight and inspection -- do not work to a satisfactory degree as a substitute. Nor are they likely to, as the record of repetitive "fixes" over the years has shown. Only in the example of Conrail has the pattern of performance relative to the private-sector been corrected.

It is not surprising, then, that the results of the government-sponsored corporation in the last decade have not been adequate. On a very tolerant standard, prices in the public enterprises have been high. Excessive costs have justified high prices, as compared to the averages of private corporations serving similar markets. Our quarrel is not with the freight service in the Northeast, the de facto subsidization of third-class mail or TVA programs for augmenting government-owned hydroelectric generating facilities with nuclear power plants. Nor is it with the original purposes which the Congress pursued in establishing these structured forms. The issue before us is whether these organizations should be continued in a structural mode which has proven to be not as productive as the private structural form. Here it has been argued that the particular and specific workings of the managerial structures of public enterprises have caused both labor and capital costs to expand when both should have contracted. The impetus for excessive resource use is inherent in the structure of these public-sector organizations. With the fault in the public corporate structure so fundamental, then divestiture of the enterprises from government appears to be the only possible means for correction in the long run.

## APPENDIX ONE

### TVA's Relative Price Performance

There are four main factors contributing to TVA's ability to price their electricity lower than their private-sector counterparts:

1) Lower cost of debt
2) Lack of taxation
3) Ease of debt fund procurement
4) Lower cost of fuel

The first three advantages are a direct by-product of government ownership. (Lower fuel costs are due to ownership and proximity to large coal deposits and not directly derived from government ownership)

One question that has arisen frequently in discussions of privatization is: How would government-owned enterprises perform if subjected to the same constraints as private-sector enterprises in the same industry? In order to answer this question, an electricity price predictor was formed using a least squares regression with price (using average revenue per KwH as a proxy) as the dependent variable. Since prices for electric utilities can be loosely defined as Costs + Allowed Return on Investment, the independent variables for this regression are six cost variables -- Depreciation Expense, Total Tax Expense, Maintenance Expense, Operation Expense, Interest Expense and Fuel Cost -- and one return-on-investment variable -- net income.

It is difficult to quantify the advantage TVA derives from its favorable financing relationship with the Federal Financing Bank, and that advantage is therefore ignored in this analysis. The two remaining advantages will be eliminated by raising TVA's cost of debt and taxation to approximate those levels incurred by private utilities.

The data used for this regression were taken from six electric utilities, all of comparable size to TVA. They are Detroit Edison, Ohio Edison, Georgia Power and Light, Carolina Power and Light, Commonwealth Edison and Pennsylvania Power and Light. Eleven years of data (1975-1985) were compiled for each utility. These numbers were run with generalized differences to correct for autocorrelation.

The coefficients for the independent variables were (standard errors in parentheses):

| | | | |
|---|---|---|---|
| Intercept | 0.000261<br>(0.477) | Fuel Expense | 0.747282<br>(4.225)* |
| Depreciation | 1.427826<br>(2.384)* | Maintenance Expense | 1.364244<br>(2.844)* |
| Total Tax Expense | 1.475807<br>(5.271)* | Net Income | -0.023345<br>(-0.061) |
| Operation Expense | 0.544990<br>(2.726)* | Interest Expense | -0.023345<br>(2.725)* |

| | |
|---|---|
| R-square | 0.963 |
| F-Statistic | 256.186 |
| Durbin-Watson | 1.606 |

* Significant at the 95 percent confidence level

After finding the price predictor function, TVA's numbers for each of the variables for each of the eleven years were put into the equation. In order to put TVA and private utilities on an even keel, two changes were made. First, TVA was subjected to the same cost-of-debt constraint faced by private utilities. This was done by adding 77.21 basis points to the cost of debt for TVA in each of the eleven years.[86] Another area where a constraint was added for TVA was taxation. To represent the amount of total taxes that TVA would be obligated to pay, an amount equal to 18.32 percent of TVA's average revenue per KwH was put into the tax coefficient.[87]

86 In prior research it was found that after TVA began receiving its debt funds exclusively from the Federal Financing Bank in 1975, it avoided paying an average market premium of 77.21 basis points on publicly issued debt. This was added to its average cost of debt to compensate for that. It could be argued that this number should be higher because the implicit (albeit erroneous) assumption that TVA debt is guaranteed by the U.S. government seems to keep this market premium even lower.

87 During the years 1975-1985, the average total taxes paid by the utilities in the sample amounted to 18.32 percent of average revenue per KwH.

The following table shows the actual rates charged by TVA and utilities incorporated in this sample, compared to predicted values of TVA rates when subjected to the above constraints:

Results of Least Squares Regression
(cents per kilowatt hour)

| Year | TVA (Actual) | TVA (Predicted) | Private Utilities |
|---|---|---|---|
| 1975 | 1.09 | 1.34 | 2.24 |
| 1976 | 1.54 | 1.85 | 2.79 |
| 1977 | 1.58 | 1.96 | 2.92 |
| 1978 | 1.96 | 2.44 | 3.19 |
| 1979 | 2.38 | 2.79 | 3.51 |
| 1980 | 2.69 | 3.23 | 3.77 |
| 1981 | 3.27 | 4.52 | 4.36 |
| 1982 | 3.81 | 4.91 | 4.97 |
| 1983 | 3.99 | 5.24 | 5.02 |
| 1984 | 4.18 | 5.56 | 5.45 |
| 1985 | 4.34 | 6.09 | 6.08 |

From the above table one can see that in recent years, lack of taxation and lower cost of debt can account for all of the discrepancy in electricity rates between TVA and private utilities. However, the argument does not end here. There are other factors not included in this analysis which might afford TVA rate advantages over private utilities. Because of its ability to acquire capital funds without being subjected to the scrutiny of the capital markets, TVA is able to expand capacity at a rate unparalleled by private utilities. This allows it to capture levels of average cost-reducing economies of scale unavailable to investor-owned utilities constrained by capital market accountability mechanisms. Although TVA's advantage in fuel cost is not directly related to government ownership, could TVA afford (or even justify to its shakeholders) the purchase and operation of such large coal mining operations if it did not have such large amounts of investment capital readily available? If these factors could be directly quantified and included in this analysis, the predicted rates for TVA would be significantly higher.

Given the above analysis, we maintain that the lower rates charged by TVA are due entirely to advantages derived from government ownership and not superior management or production efficiencies. If TVA were subjected to the same constraints faced by investor-owned utilities, it would be forced to price electricity higher than its private-sector counterparts.

Appendix Two Table 2.17: Wages and Salaries per Full-Time Employee

(1982 = 100)

| Year | Government Enterprises | Finance and Insurance | Transportation | Communication | Electric and Gas Utilities |
|---|---|---|---|---|---|
| 1975 | 57.60 | 55.94 | 56.72 | 52.25 | 54.35 |
| 1976 | 62.90 | 60.03 | 63.49 | 58.75 | 59.78 |
| 1977 | 66.84 | 64.24 | 68.62 | 64.19 | 64.60 |
| 1978 | 71.50 | 69.64 | 74.32 | 70.44 | 69.80 |
| 1979 | 76.35 | 75.54 | 80.81 | 76.43 | 75.22 |
| 1980 | 85.30 | 83.68 | 88.59 | 83.07 | 82.88 |
| 1981 | 96.30 | 91.44 | 95.63 | 91.99 | 91.50 |
| 1982 | 100.00 | 100.00 | 100.00 | 100.00 | 100.00 |
| 1983 | 105.96 | 109.44 | 103.58 | 107.78 | 107.08 |
| 1984 | 112.71 | 115.88 | 105.38 | 110.53 | 113.93 |
| 1985 | 118.19 | 123.22 | 106.86 | 117.78 | 120.29 |

SOURCE: Bureau of Economic Analysis: Department of Commerce.

NOTE: The Federally owned government enterprises that are included in the "Government Enterprise" section are listed in an accompanying footnote.

# The Performance and Management of United States Federal Government Corporations: Comment

William Niskanen*

Paul MacAvoy and George McIsaac have provided a valuable summary of the performance of Federal corporations and of some of the institutional reasons why this performance has been unsatisfactory. My brief comments on the paper are restricted to the following issues:

The authors attribute the unsatisfactory performance of Government corporations primarily to agency problems; by that they mean the differences between the incentives of the boards and managers of the corporations from those of the owners -- in this case the voters and taxpayers, presumably. After substantial experience in both a major private corporation and in several government agencies, I'm convinced that the agency problem is substantial in the private sector and severe in the public sector.

There is an alternative explanation, however, for the performance of federal government corporations that the authors do not address -- namely, that the performance of these corporations may be very close to the preferences of the Administration and Congress. In other words, the primary agency problems may be in our political system and not in the government corporations. My own experience suggests that Congressional subcommittees maintain excruciatingly fine monitoring of government corporations when their particular interests are at stake. In September 1982, for example, I was asked to chair an interagency group to evaluate the pricing policies of the power-marketing administrations. We had one meeting and prepared one set of

* Cato Institute

papers that was limited specifically to describing current policies. We had no time even to discuss alternative policies, and we did not have a second meeting. Someone in the group informed Alex Raddin, chief lobbyist for the American Public Power Association, about our gathering. He, in turn, informed a half-dozen key members of Congress. Soon thereafter I got a call from Al Gore, then a member of the House. He said, "Dr. Niskanen, we understand that you have a study of power-marketing administrations underway. I'd like you to come up to my office on the Hill and talk with me and a few of my colleagues about what you expect to do in that study." And because I'm a cooperative type, I said, "Fine -- I'll bring my material." On the morning of the day that the meeting was to be held, I got a call from Gore's secretary. The location of the meeting had been changed, she said. I arrived at the Rayburn Building at the appointed time -- and quickly discovered that the meeting was going to take place in the hearing room of the Military Affairs Committee. There were about twenty Representatives up on a high dais. I went up without an assistant, and there were I think eight television cameras from local stations in the Tennessee Valley and the Pacific Northwest. I was Gored! It was basically a re-election campaign "show trial" that was staged for the voters back in their home districts. And the general spirit of their remarks was that people who consume public power have a property right in low power rates. In one particular case, it was suggested that I was taking bread from the tables of widows.

After twenty years of trying to sort out how much of the agency problem exists at the level of the bureau or the government corporations relative to Congress, and after having written a book about it, I'm still not very clear on that subject. But what is clear is that a substantial part of the problems that we attribute to these Government corporations is a consequence of the rather fine-grain preferences of their immediate monitoring agencies, preferences which may very well differ from the interests of the general population. And I think it is not sufficient to conclude that the problems of organizing the government corporations themselves are the primary source of the agency problem.

The case for privatizing these corporations is not dependent on whether the primary agency problem is at the corporation or the political level. The primary opportunities for privatization, however, may be limited to those government corporations which have a specific agency problem -- that is, where the problem is in the structure of the corporation rather than in the particular preferences of Congress. But this paper does not provide the information that bears upon whether privatization would serve the interests of Congress, and thus whether such measures are likely to be approved.

# The Performance and Management of United States Federal Government Corporations: Comment

Louis De Alessi*

Professors MacAvoy and McIsaac provide an excellent study of the arguments used to justify the establishment of Federal Government corporations and of the actual economic performance of these enterprises over the period 1975-1985.

The first half of the paper contrasts the behavior of the prices, outputs, and costs of federal corporations with those of private firms. For an overall view, various performance indices based on the income statements of eighteen federal corporations are compared with the corresponding indices for their, or similar, U.S. industries (the indices used were computed by the Department of Commerce). The federal corporations in general had prices that increased faster, wages and salaries per unit of output that were higher and increased faster, and both outputs and productivity that increased more slowly.

A more detailed comparison of four individual federal corporations (Tennessee Valley Authority, Postal Service, Conrail, and Amtrak) with the averages for their or similar industries reveals an analogous pattern. Indeed, these four firms apparently were less profitable than their private counterparts -- even though they were subject to weaker government regulation (i.e. the

* University of Miami

TVA is exempt from regulation by state public utility commissions, and Amtrak is exempt from ICC jurisdiction over routes and fares and from state regulation of passenger services), did not have to pay state and local taxes, and enjoyed lower costs of financing. The assets and labor costs of these four firms increased faster than industry averages, escalating production costs and squeezing profits.

Although the rough evidence is clear, the nature of the tables and the procedures used to compute the indices are not always clear. Also troublesome is the use of aggregate rather than individual firms' data. Aggregation masks some information and makes it difficult to control for variables that might bias the results.

Nevertheless, the various independent findings all point in the same direction and are consistent with a great deal of evidence at the state and local levels in the U.S. and elsewhere.[1] Thus, cross-section studies of electric power, water, urban transit, airline, health, fire protection, refuse collection, and other industries indicate that, relative to private firms, municipal firms are less likely to tailor their prices to the demand and supply conditions that they face and to minimize the cost of producing the level of output chosen. For example, municipal firms are more likely to have higher operating costs, give across-the-board rather than selective wage increases, be slower at adopting cost-reducing innovations, and earn rates of return that are lower and have greater variance.

The evidence offered by MacAvoy and McIsaac supports the broad conclusion that, judged by market standards, federal corporations do not perform as well as their private counterparts. The actual performance of federal corporations, however, presumably is worse than the data suggest. First, in some cases the federal corporations were compared to government-regulated private firms. The latter are subject to a profit constraint, and both theory and evidence indicate that the managers of regulated firms have a reduced incentive to choose the wealth-maximizing/price-quantity combination, to minimize the cost of producing the level of output chosen, and to take full advantage of profitable opportunities for enhancing productivity. Relative to wealth-maximizing private enterprises, therefore, the performance of the federal corporations would be even worse. Second, the federal corporations apparently were included in the industry averages to which they were compared. Although the effect presumably is slight, it would reduce apparent differences in performance.

---

[1] For example, see De Alessi (1974) and (1980).

The second half of the paper seeks to explain the poor performance of federal corporations by focusing on their organization.

The structure and decision-making processes of the four federal firms noted earlier are described in some detail. Among other things, members of the governing boards typically are appointed to represent special interests and lack control over the employment of the chief executive officer and other operating executives; these executives do not have clear directions and standards of performance; and Congressmen protect the interests of their friends and constituents who work for, or have dealings with, these firms.

This evidence suggests that federal corporations are highly politicized, which gives their managers a discretionary authority greater than that enjoyed by their counterparts in the private sector, and results in decisions detrimental to the profitability of the enterprises. MacAvoy and McIsaac conclude that, at least in the case of the firms examined, privatization may be the best solution.

The analysis presented reflects a sound understanding of the underlying economic principles. These principles, however, could be made more explicit.

At times there are hints that if incentives were restructured appropriately, federal corporations could be made to work more effectively. If the boards were appointed with clearer profit-making goals, given more authority over the hiring and promotion of the CEO and other operating executives, subject to less interference from politicians, and so on, then these firms could be expected to perform as well as their private-sector counterparts.

Poor performance by market standards, however, is inherent to the nature of political or government-owned enterprises. Individuals, whether consumers or decision-makers within private or political organizations, have the incentive to respond to the opportunities for gain available to them. Political firms, unlike their private-sector counterparts, do not provide anyone with the opportunity to fully capture the wealth gained from improved management. Because property rights in political firms effectively are not transferable, individuals cannot specialize in their ownership and cannot capitalize and capture the future gains from improved performance. Accordingly, the monitoring of managers is less exacting and limited to those characteristics that are more easily observed and of greater personal interest to the monitors.

This analysis implies that managers of political firms have greater opportunity for discretionary behavior, as judged by market standards, than managers of comparable privately owned firms. Not surprisingly, they will take advantage of the opportunity to further their own interests.

MacAvoy and McIsaac have done an excellent job of documenting the political nature of decision-making within federal corporations and the resulting detrimental consequences on economic performance. Moreover, their analysis has highlighted the importance of using market processes to provide a flexible means for coping with change in a world of dispersed and continually changing knowledge.

# CHAPTER THREE

# Privatization at the State and Local Level

Kenneth W. Clarkson*

## INTRODUCTION

Increasingly, state and local officials are seeking ways to cut costs without reducing the level of government-provided services. As a result, many jurisdictions have increased their use of cost-saving privatization techniques, and countless more are investigating the potential outcomes from greater use of the private sector. This paper examines privatization, defined as the methods and strategies designed to transfer the production or provision of public services from government to the private sector, at the state and local level.

This review of privatization options first examines the various forms of privatization utilized in providing public services at the state and local level. The paper then turns to recent experience and trends in privatization, with the results of a comprehensive survey that was focusing on a single state. Next, various elements impacting the feasibility of and potential savings from privatization are discussed. Legal barriers to privatization attempts are then examined. The paper concludes with a review of the more commonly cited objections to privatization.[1]

---

* Law & Economics Center, University of Miami

[1] The Law and Economics Center (L&EC) at the University of Miami and the Local Government Center (LGC) of the Reason Foundation, Santa Monica, CA, have recently completed a research study that examines the extent of privatization in the delivery of Florida's

## SERVICE DELIVERY PRIVATIZATION ALTERNATIVES

Unlike privatization activities conducted by the federal government, privatization at the state and local level encompasses a broader class of activities than the sale of assets or operations, which is commonly referred to as service-shedding or divestiture. The major techniques for privatizing public services are:

**Contracting-out** - Government contracts with a private firm (profit or nonprofit) to produce and/or deliver a service or part of a service.
**Franchise Agreements** - Government grants a private organization either an exclusive or nonexclusive right to provide a particular service within a specific geographical area.
**Grants/Subsidies** - Government makes a financial or in-kind contribution to a private organization or individual to facilitate the private provision of a service at a reduced cost to consumers.
**Vouchers** - Government issues redeemable certificates to eligible citizens, who exchange them for services from approved private providers. The service-providers then return the vouchers to the issuing government for reimbursement.
**Volunteers** - Individuals work without pay to provide all or part of a service usually provided by government.
**Self-help** - Individuals, neighborhood groups, or community organizations supplement or take over a service. Those providing the service are also the ones who benefit from it.
**Incentives** - Local government uses its regulatory and taxing powers to encourage private firms to provide public services

---

public services and identifies service areas that could benefit from further privatization, along with nonprivatized service areas that are prime candidates for privatization. The research project, funded by the Florida Chamber of Commerce Foundation and the Council of 100, is designed to assist Florida's state and local officials in undertaking privatization programs appropriate to their own communities. To fulfill this task, the L&EC and the LGC have produced a manual that helps public officials identify privatization options, quantify the potential gains and losses from implementing those options, and develop general guidelines for selecting a successful privatization program. This article is drawn from that research and is published in Clarkson and Fixler (1987).

or to encourage individuals to reduce their demand for such services.

**User Fees** - Consumers are charged either a flat or a quantity-related fee for the use of a particular service.

**Service-shedding** - Government discontinues or gives up responsibility for a service, which may then be taken over by private service-providers, or which may no longer be provided in the community.

A review of these alternatives points to the conclusion that most of the privatization that occurs at the state and local level is focused on the question of management operation and, in some cases, on the prices paid by consumers (i.e. the mix of taxes, user charges, etc.).

## Contracting-Out

The most common method of privatization is contracting out. Under this approach, state or local governments make a written, legal agreement with a private or other organization for the delivery of a service. The governing body retains a significant degree of control and continues to finance the provision of the service through taxes, user charges, or other means.

Several options are available to governments in contracting-out. First, "producer options" allow the government to determine the number and type of service providers selected. Officials may decide to contract with a single firm or, in order to induce more competition, with several organizations. Government may contract with nonprofit, voluntary, or neighborhood organizations for some types of services. It may also permit in-house departments to bid against private firms.

An examination of the existing form of organization chosen to produce the public service reveals a definite pattern across major service categories.[2] In the environment and public-works areas, for instance, the predominant form is to contract with for-profit firms. Appendix One and Table 3.6 provide information obtained by the International City Management Association (ICMA) in 1982 on alternative methods of utilizing the private sector to deliver public services.

---

[2] For a more extensive discussion of different applications of contracting-out, see Valente and Manchester (1984, Chap. 1 and pp. 161-215).

**Franchise Agreements**

Franchising is a privatization method whereby government grants a private entity (or entities) authority to provide a particular service within a specific geographical area. Users receive and pay for the service directly, but the government may monitor performance with respect to the franchise: price, amount or level of service, and quality. The extent of government involvement ranges from nominal, where private service-providers are licensed without controls on price or quality, to a very extensive role, where conditions of the franchise may include health, safety, price, quality and service-level requirements.[3]

Franchising has great potential for achieving cost savings when applicable and properly implemented. The reason for this is that franchising allows government to remove itself from the actual provision and delivery of a service. Although the savings from relinquishing service-delivery are partly reduced by oversight and monitoring costs, these functions also occur when the service is provided by the government itself. Some governments charge private providers a franchise fee to cover oversight and monitoring costs.

**Subsidy Arrangements**

The use of grants and subsidies is another method for fostering the privatization of public services. Under this approach, government provides financial or in-kind contributions to private organizations or individuals to encourage them to provide a service. In this way, government may avoid producing a particular service and lower the cost of providing it through a private organization. In comparison with other privatization methods, subsidizing the provision of private services is often used when it is difficult to define or measure a service, anticipate demand, or assess service quality. Accordingly, subsidies are often used for governmental activities such as

---

[3] The use of franchises varies widely among public services. The most well known are public utilities. Franchising also occurs frequently in public works and transportation services. There are few franchises in health and human services, and even fewer in parks and recreation services, apparently because it is politically difficult to charge low-income users. In the case of support services, of course, it is not possible to use franchising because the user is the government itself. Appendix One and Table 3.6 provide information on the use of franchising by the cities and counties surveyed to deliver public services.

public safety, health and human services, and recreation/cultural arts. For example, in the health and human services category, 15 percent of the responding cities and counties provided subsidies to day-care facilities, and 13 percent subsidized programs for the elderly. In parks and recreation services, cultural/arts programs received subsidies from 18 percent of the cities and counties surveyed, and 17 percent subsidized the operation of museums. Table 3.6 (see Appendix One) shows the frequency of government subsidization of public service programs.

There are five basic types of subsidies that local governments may provide: unrestricted monetary allocations; restricted or earmarked allocations; matching funds; use of materials, equipment, and personnel; and use of land and capital facilities.[4]

## Vouchers

Under this arrangement, government provides redeemable certificates to eligible citizens requiring a particular service. The users are then free to exchange the certificates or vouchers for services from qualified private organizations that return the vouchers to local governments for reimbursement. State and local governments use vouchers to increase the likelihood that eligible individuals will be able to acquire a given service or product and to permit recipients to select when, where, and from whom to purchase the service, as well as how much of the service to purchase.

The voucher alternative allows the user to choose among services and providers and generally means better monitoring and quality control of services.[5] Monitoring by users and by actual or potential competition among providers helps to control prices and quality. Vouchers have not been widely used.

---

[4] For additional information on various types of subsidy arrangements, see Valente and Manchester (1984, p. 33).

[5] Vouchers may be full or partial. A full voucher refers to a government authorization that is intended to cover the full cost of the designated service to a recipient. Monitoring is enhanced through competition by alternative providers. Recipients of partial vouchers must spend some of their own money, and thus have greater incentive to monitor price and quality of the service.

## Volunteer Personnel

As a privatization strategy, the use of volunteers generally refers to the recruitment of individuals to work for government without remuneration, thereby reducing the degree of tax-supported involvement by government in the provision of public services.

This privatization option has not been utilized extensively in the provision of public works and transportation services. The major exception is the operation and maintenance of paratransit systems (8 percent of the cities and counties surveyed), which typically are directed at the elderly and handicapped and are more citizen-contact oriented than public works and other transportation services.

Volunteers have been used extensively in the provision of various public-safety services, such as fire prevention and suppression (18 percent of the responding cities and counties), emergency medical services (16 percent), ambulance service (15 percent), and crime prevention and patrol (10 percent). There is potential for increased use of volunteers in the provision of other public-safety services, particularly police and fire communication, crime prevention and patrol, and traffic control, especially if such volunteers are given more rigorous training. Some local governments, after careful consideration, have given legal sanction to volunteer crime patrols.

Volunteers are a major resource in the provision of recreational, parks, and cultural arts programs. These activities include the operation of museums, recreational facilities, convention centers and auditoriums, and the provision of park landscaping and maintenance. The cities and counties surveyed showed a range from 2 percent (operation of convention centers and auditoriums) to 32 percent (operation of cultural/arts programs) in the use of volunteers to deliver this category of public services.

## Self-help

Self-help is the most underutilized privatization alternative. Under this approach, the government encourages individuals or groups to provide their own services; that is, the individuals involved become their own clients. Self-help techniques are designed to encourage individuals to find solutions to their own problems, to become more self-reliant, and to provide a service more tailored to local circumstances. There are four basic types of self-help organizations: nonprofit corporation, cooperative, association, and land and building trusts.[6]

## Regulatory, Deregulatory and Tax Incentives

Various regulatory, deregulatory and tax incentives are used to encourage the private sector to provide public services or to reduce public demand for services provided by government.

In some instances increased regulation leads to increased private provision of a public service. For example, property owners could be required to ensure that trees in front of their property are trimmed and dead trees removed. Deregulation, however, is the predominant form of regulatory incentive. For the most part, deregulation is intended to increase the number of providers competing to supply a given service. Examples of local deregulation include abolition of taxi license requirements (beyond minimal health and safety restrictions); termination of cable television regulations limiting competition in franchise areas; and the decontrol of emergency medical services (again, except for minimal health and safety requirements).

Regulatory and tax incentives have not been employed as much as other privatization methods. The most frequent use of incentives occurs in the division of health and human services concerned with the operation of day-care facilities (2 percent of the cities and counties surveyed) and the operation and management of hospitals (1 percent).

## User Fees

In contrast to regulatory and tax approaches, which seek to increase the private supply of public services, user fees are designed to foster financing of public services by the direct beneficiaries. An important distinction between user fees and other charges is that user fees typically are related to the amount of service consumed, making them more like market prices.

Public officials have several options regarding the implementation of user fees and charges. For example, when capacity is limited, time of use may be regulated by charging a higher price during peak demand periods. User fees may also be varied by location and user eligibility. For example, some

---

[6] Additional information on forms of self-help may be found in Valente and Manchester (1984, pp. 73-4).

jurisdictions charge only nonresidents for use of recreational facilities. Moreover, user charges may be set to provide partial or full cost recovery, and may be implemented on a sliding scale (e.g. distinguishing between children and adults, or between high- and low-income individuals). User fees, although widely employed, are still far from being used to their full potential.

User fees traditionally have been applied to a variety of public-works and transportation services. Examples include solid waste collection and disposal, parking lot and garage operation, inspection and code enforcement, and transportation. Public officials might also consider user fees for several public-safety services, including vehicle towing, bus storage, special-events security, alarm response, and emergency medical services.

### Service-shedding or Divestiture

Service-shedding, or divestiture, is the purest form of privatization and has the greatest potential for cost savings. Service-shedding occurs when government shifts the provision of a service entirely to the private sector.

Many of the cities and counties responding to ICMA's 1982 nationwide survey have shed one or more services (Fixler 1986, pp. 18-23). Excluding the service category covering meter maintenance and installation, over two-thirds of the remaining services were shed directly to for-profit and nonprofit agencies rather than discontinued altogether.

Service-shedding may take three forms: shedding to for-profit firms, shedding to nonprofit organizations, and straight discontinuance. Public administrators must determine the most appropriate approach in each case. Service-shedding to for-profit firms occurs most frequently in public works and transportation (except for meter maintenance and installation), public utilities, public-safety, health and human services, and support services. Parks and recreation services are most frequently shed to nonprofit organizations or discontinued altogether. Many health and human services are also discontinued entirely.

## PRIVATIZATION OF PUBLIC SERVICES: EXPERIENCE AND TRENDS

For a variety of reasons, different methods of privatization are associated with alternative types of public services. Nevertheless, there are several broad categories of public services for which the key issues and processes of privatization are very much the same. These categories are the following:

> **Public Works and Physical Environment** - Utilities, waste collection and disposal, street repair, tree trimming, etc.
> **Transportation Services** - Street operation and maintenance, airport management, bus system operation and management, etc.
> **Public-safety Services** - Crime prevention, fire prevention, ambulance service, etc.
> **Health and Human Services** - Animal control, day-care facilities, programs for the elderly, etc.
> **Parks and Recreation/Cultural Arts** - Recreation services, park landscaping and maintenance, library operations, etc.
> **General Government and Support Services** - Legal services, cafeteria management, secretarial services, etc.

The most extensive examination of privatization in the various states was the survey undertaken by ICMA in its 1982 alternative service survey of cities and counties. Responses were obtained from 1,779 local governments in the United States. Since 1982 the LGC has updated this survey through research and review of numerous publications. Results from this effort indicate that several public-service categories have experienced significant increases in the use of the private sector. For further discussion of this survey update, see Appendix Two.

## DETERMINING THE FEASIBILITY OF PRIVATIZATION

Several factors are crucial in determining the feasibility of utilizing various privatization methods. These factors include (a) the "private good" characteristic of the service; (b) level of government expenditures for the service; (c) availability of private suppliers; (d) ability to specify outputs and monitor performance; (e) degree of dissatisfaction with the public service; (f) degree of employee acceptance; (g) extent of political support; and (h) legal authority. Each public service may be ranked as high, medium, or low according to each of these factors, which facilitates the task of identifying those services that are the most likely candidates for privatization.[7]

### Private/Public Good Characteristics

The ability of private firms to provide a good or service depends directly on the degree of "publicness" of the good or service. A pure public good has two important characteristics, both independent of the type of organization providing it: **nonrival** (or **joint**) **consumption** and **nonexclusion.**[8] The second important characteristic of a public good is that, once produced, it may be prohibitively expensive to exclude nonpayers. Nonexclusion may, but need not, occur simultaneously with nonrivalry. Goods or services that have a high degree of **both** public-good characteristics are more likely to be provided by government.

Many services, such as the broadcasting of a major sports event, have a high level of nonrivalry. But exclusion, through scrambling or other technologies, is feasible. Accordingly, they are well-suited to provision by the private sector. Exclusion allows the possibility of financing the provision of the service or good by those who use it. For services where both rivalry and exclusion are high, provision by the private sector is feasible, and the private-good ranking should be high.

---

[7] Clarkson and Fixler (1987) provide various decision tools and IBM-compatible computer programs that enable local government officials to examine the feasibility of the three major privatization options (contracting- out, franchising, and divestiture) not only on purely financial grounds, but also on the basis of more subjective criteria such as availability of suppliers, ease of monitoring the performance of private providers, political interest, public-service programs, legal authority, and acceptance by the public employees. The results give a sense of the services that have the greatest potential for privatization, including total divestiture.

[8] A good or service is characterized as nonrival when its consumption by one person does not diminish the quantity available to anyone else. Thus, a number of individuals may simultaneously consume the same service or good. The nonrival characteristic is also referred to as "jointness of consumption" or "indivisibility of benefits". A classic example is a television signal. Once the program is on the air, tuning in by one more viewer does not detract from any other viewer's ability to watch the program. Mosquito abatement, pollution reduction, and other public health measures that reduce the spread of disease are also examples of services with a high degree of nonrivalry, or jointness of consumption. By contrast, most goods and services in our society are rival in consumption. Thus, consumption of such goods as food, clothes, autos, homes, and jewelry by one individual reduces the amount available to others. Goods sharing this characteristic are frequently described as "private goods."

In considering the feasibility of alternative privatization methods, particularly service-shedding or divestiture, the publicness of the service (i.e., its nonrival and nonexclusionary characteristics) may be decisive.

### Level of Government Expenditures

The level of government expenditures also affects the desirability of privatizing alternative services. If governments are to achieve significant cost savings, public officials must give weight to privatizing those services that comprise a significant part of their budgets. For example, privatization of solid waste collection, which normally comprises anywhere from 5 percent to 20 percent of a local government's budget, should be given higher priority -- other things being the same -- than the privatization of a cultural arts program, which usually accounts for only a small part of a government's budget.

### Supplier/Provider Availability

The availability of actual or potential suppliers is critical. The presence of only one or two suppliers of a particular service, however, should not be taken to imply lack of competition, particularly if potential entrants exist.

### Output Specification and Performance Monitoring

The feasibility of contracting-out, franchising, or utilizing other privatization methods is affected by the ability of local or state governments to specify the desired outputs, prepare and execute agreements, and monitor results.

### Public Service Problems

User satisfaction with the current quality of the service may be critical to a privatization decision. For example, if the government is having difficulty producing adequate garbage collection, then alternative service options would be assigned a high ranking.

**Public Employee Acceptance**

The attitudes of the public employees currently providing the service is extremely important. Strong opposition can block a privatization program or hamper its implementation. As discussed later, however, several approaches are available to mitigate such opposition and even provide incentives for employees to favor privatization.

**Legal Authority**

A jurisdiction may not have the legal authority to contract-out, franchise, or form some other agreement for privatizing a particular service. Sometimes these issues are ambiguous. For example, a city attorney may advise that although state law does not explicitly prohibit contracting-out the service in question, the issue is unclear. In such cases, there is always the possibility of obtaining authority through a legislative act.

An initial review of the evidence on privatization provides some indication of the importance of these variables. First, data from the ICMA survey show considerable variation in the frequency of privatization throughout the United States. Table 3.1 shows the percentage of privatization of several public services for large jurisdictions (250,000 or more residents) in four major regions of the U.S. An examination of the frequency reveals that there is no hierarchy of privatization candidates among regions, and rankings vary among closely related services (e.g. emergency medical service versus ambulance service). Second, a review of Tables 3.2 and 3.7 reveals that governments tend to privatize, though not consistently, those services with a lower degree of publicness (e.g. waste collection and disposal services as opposed to law enforcement). Third, an examination of the survey data from Florida shows that higher levels of government expenditure (adjusted for population) increase the likelihood of privatization, while higher average public employee compensation levels reduce it.[9] Finally, the extent of privatization is partly determined by the institutions governing state and local officials. Some of these factors are discussed in other papers in this conference, and some are discussed in the next section.

---

[9] See Appendix Three for a regression model that tests these relations.

Table 3.1: Regional Variation in Privatization Forms

| Service | No. | Contracting Out Prof | Nghr | Nonpf | Franchise |
|---|---|---|---|---|---|
| | (250,000+ Residents) | | | | |
| Resid Solid Wst Col | | | | | |
| Northeast | 3 | 0% | 0% | 0% | 0% |
| North Central | 11 | 45 | | | |
| South | 31 | 39 | | | 19 |
| West | 12 | 17 | | | 17 |
| Commer Solid Wst Col | | | | | |
| Northeast | 3 | 67 | | | |
| North Central | 5 | 80 | | | |
| South | 22 | 59 | | | 23 |
| West | 9 | 22 | | | 33 |
| Emergency Med Serv | | | | | |
| Northeast | 5 | 23 | | 20 | |
| North Central | 18 | 20 | | 11 | 6 |
| South | 33 | 6 | | 6 | 9 |
| West | 17 | 18 | | 12 | 6 |
| Ambulance Service | | | | | |
| Northeast | 1 | | | | |
| North Central | 12 | 33 | | 17 | 8 |
| South | 30 | 30 | | 10 | 3 |
| West | 14 | 57 | | 7 | 7 |
| Recreation Services | | | | | |
| Northeast | 9 | | | 11 | 11 |
| North Central | 14 | 7 | | | 7 |
| South | 28 | 14 | 7 | 14 | 4 |
| West | 19 | 16 | 16 | 21 | 5 |
| Oper/Main Rec Facil | | | | | |
| Northeast | 12 | 8 | | | 33 |
| North Central | 20 | 20 | | | 25 |
| South | 28 | 14 | | 7 | 14 |
| West | 20 | 55 | 5 | 15 | 40 |
| Oper Cult/Art Prog | | | | | |
| Northeast | 8 | | 13 | 38 | 13 |
| North Central | 13 | 15 | 8 | 46 | 8 |
| South | 25 | 4 | 12 | 52 | 4 |
| West | 15 | 20 | 13 | 40 | 20 |
| Oper Conven C./Audit | | | | | |
| Northeast | 3 | | | | 33 |
| North Central | 9 | 22 | | | 33 |
| South | 19 | | | 11 | |
| West | 14 | 36 | | 7 | 21 |

SOURCE: Valente and Manchester, 1984

Table 3.2: Estimated Annual Savings from Privatization of Government Activities

| Governmental Activity | Budget Level | Estimated Savings Lower | Estimated Savings Upper |
|---|---|---|---|
| General Government Services | ($) | ($) | ($) |
| Legislative | 59,263,695 | 5,670,548 | 4,741,096 |
| Executive | 82,791,845 | 3,351,674 | 6,703,348 |
| Financial & Administration | 524,618,947 | 41,969,516 | 78,692,842 |
| Legal | 45,515,643 | 759,201 | 1,518,402 |
| Comprehensive Planning | 70,614,931 | 2,824,597 | 5,649,194 |
| Judicial | 227,341,317 | 9,093,653 | 18,187,305 |
| Other Govt Services | 640,549,681 | 25,621,987 | 51,243,974 |
| Public Safety | | | |
| Law Enforcement | 1,177,032,012 | 80,320,664 | 150,601,246 |
| Fire Control | 506,843,350 | 67,638,245 | 159,148,812 |
| Detention and/or Correction | 239,895,423 | 29,845,390 | 68,873,976 |
| Protective Inspections | 88,538,239 | 8,526,232 | 21,315,581 |
| Ambulance & Rescue | 82,580,482 | 14,705,932 | 40,441,314 |
| Other Public Safety | 78,565,756 | 6,678,089 | 16,695,223 |
| Physical Environment | | | |
| Electric | 201,236 | 9,257 | 23,142 |
| Gas | 38,077 | 2,033 | 5,083 |
| Water | 5,992,882 | 489,019 | 1,222,548 |
| Garbage/Solid Waste | 134,234,156 | 3,490,088 | 13,087,830 |
| Sewer | 12,736,410 | 743,806 | 2,789,274 |
| Water/Sewer Combination | 10,891,095 | 748,436 | 2,806,635 |
| Flood Control | 94,127,236 | 6,837,402 | 25,640,259 |
| Other Physical Environment | 174,642,282 | 10,478,537 | 39,294,513 |
| Transportation | | | |
| Road & Street Facilities | 749,393,916 | 105,814,421 | 211,628,842 |
| Airports | 6,781,708 | 923,669 | 2,463,116 |
| Water Transportation | 11,997,297 | 1,700,617 | 4,534,978 |
| Transit Systems | 34,942,666 | 4,853,536 | 12,942,763 |
| Parking & Other Transport | 21,713,706 | 2,996,491 | 6,991,813 |
| Economic Environment | | | |
| Employment Opportunity/Dev | 20,037,377 | 1,299,117 | 2,598,233 |
| Downtown/Indust Dev/Improv | 40,879,761 | 1,768,050 | 3,536,099 |
| Housing/Urban Development | 135,968,696 | 5,880,646 | 11,761,292 |
| Other Economic Environment | 98,085,647 | 4,242,204 | 8,484,408 |
| Human Services | | | |
| Hospitals | 32,093,156 | 2,914,059 | 10,199,205 |
| Health | 28,400,865 | 2,578,799 | 9,025,795 |
| Mental Health | 174,973,445 | 14,277,833 | 49,972,416 |
| Welfare | 99,984,303 | 9,138,565 | 31,984,979 |
| Other Human Services | 66,529,141 | 5,654,977 | 19,792,419 |
| Culture & Recreation | | | |
| Libraries | 121,479,435 | 11,030,333 | 33,090,998 |
| Parks & Recreation | 346,579,281 | 24,468,497 | 73,405,492 |
| Other Recreation | 76,262,535 | 6,482,315 | 19,446,946 |
| TOTALS: | 6,334,117,630 | 522,528,436 | 1,220,541,394 |

SOURCE: Clarkson and Fixler 1987, p. 180

A recent survey conducted by Touche Ross & Co. and International City Management Association (Touche Ross & Co. 1987) provides additional evidence regarding the reasons for privatization. The most commonly cited reason for contracting-out (74 percent) or choosing some other form of privatization (47 percent), including divestiture (46 percent), was the level of cost savings. Other reasons for choosing some form of privatization are provided in Table 3.3.

## POTENTIAL GAINS AND LOSSES FROM PRIVATIZATION

The privatization of individual public services frequently results in significantly lower costs or improved output. These gains are the result of differences in the regulations and incentives that distinguish governmental and private organizations. Each kind of organization is best suited to a particular set of activities and straying beyond them yields inefficiencies.

### Potential Savings by Service Function

Estimates of the potential annual savings from privatization are based on the numerous studies and publications identified in Clarkson and Fixler (1987), as well as on the extensive literature addressing the relative efficiency of alternative delivery systems. These sources include case studies of privatization activities implemented by various governmental units and comparisons of coexisting public and private service-providers.[10] In other cases, the estimated annual savings are based on a comparison and interpolation of savings from similar services.[11] Thus, the annual savings from the

---

[10] For a review of some case studies involving one operation, see Teal et al. (1986).

[11] Each range of potential savings was determined by the following methodology: First, when detailed empirical studies were available, they were used in estimating the range of savings. Second, if empirical studies were not available, but an individual case study of an actual privatization activity was reported, that information was utilized. Third, information from studies of governmental operations, such as the 1972 Commission on Government Procurement and the 1983 President's Private Sector Survey on Cost Control, was utilized along with results from studies of specific governmental activities. Fourth, the LGC's Privatization Database, which includes estimated cost savings from private contractors, was also utilized to determine the range of potential savings. It is important to recognize that the actual level of savings that are realized is highly dependent on the degree to which the public sector effectively implements a particular privatization option.

Table 3.3: Why Governments Privatize Services

| Government Reason | Contracting Out | Other Forms of Privatization | Divestiture |
|---|---|---|---|
| | (Percentage Responding) | | |
| Cost Savings | 74% | 47% | 46% |
| Solves Labor Problems | 50 | 19 | 16 |
| Higher Quality of Service | 33 | 15 | 11 |
| Higher Levels of Service | 32 | 28 | 17 |
| Reduced Implementation Time | 30 | 33 | 14 |
| Share Risk | 34 | 39 | 27 |
| Local Political Problems Solved | 21 | 21 | 16 |

SOURCE: Touche Ross & Co., 1987

privatization of residential solid waste collection have been taken to be similar to those obtained from the privatization of commercial solid waste collection. Some of the studies are quite rigorous; they involve various governmental units and corrections for such variables in output characteristics. For example, one study of potential residential solid waste collection involved 145 sites.

The actual annual savings realized from implementing a specific privatization option are determined as much by the public sector as by the private sector. For example, the public sector generally determines the characteristics of the output to be provided. If these characteristics are not properly specified, overall costs can easily be higher than anticipated. Similarly, inappropriate procurement provisions, such as a requirement to accept the "lowest cost bidder" independent of any quality or performance considerations, also may reduce expected annual savings. The structure and provisions of the contractual agreement, as well as the amount and quality of monitoring conducted by the public sector, also affect quality, performance, and annual cost savings. For these reasons, it becomes more appropriate to estimate a potential range of annual savings for each public services as opposed to a single number. Table 3.4 shows the estimated range of annual cost savings for several representative public service categories.

**Estimated Savings from Privatization of Florida's Public Services**

Estimating the potential annual savings from widespread privatization in the delivery of city and county services is, at best, difficult. First, as noted earlier, actual savings are highly dependent on the motives and interests of public officials. It is easy to write a contract that seems well designed to deliver services at low cost; however, the contract may be so deficient that any potential cost savings are offset by lower quality or higher costs of monitoring performance. For this and other reasons, estimates have been calculated as a range of possible savings rather than as a single value.

Second, actual savings depend on the current level of utilization of private organizations and on the nature of the incentives facing public decision-makers. The L&EC/LGC 1986 survey has been used to determine future savings from privatization; savings from activities that are currently fully or partially privatized have been excluded. Thus, potential savings from privatization are underestimated to the degree that further privatization may be possible.

Table 3.4: Estimated Range of Privatization Cost Savings

| Public Service Category | Expected Savings Range Lower | Upper |
|---|---|---|
| | (%) | (%) |
| Public Works & Physical Environment | | |
| Solid Waste Collection: Residential | 22 | 30 |
| Parking Lot/Garage Operation | 14 | 31 |
| Wastewater Treatment | 8 | 30 |
| Transportation | | |
| Road/Street Operation/Maintenance/Repair | 25 | 50 |
| Bus Transit Operations/Maintenance | 20 | 60 |
| Fleet Management/Maintenance | 20 | 40 |
| Public Safety | | |
| Fire Prevention | 17 | 40 |
| Emergency Medical Services | 28 | 77 |
| Correction Facilities Management | 13 | 40 |
| Health & Human Services | | |
| Elderly Program Management | 10 | 40 |
| Operation/Management of Hospitals | 20 | 55 |
| Operation/.Management of Mental Health Facilities | 10 | 40 |
| Parks & Recreation/Cultural Arts | | |
| Recreation Facilities Operation/Management | 19 | 52 |
| Park Landscaping and Maintenance | 10 | 28 |
| Convention Center/Auditorium Operations | 13 | 35 |
| General Government & Support Services | | |
| Building/Grounds Maintenance | 30 | 42 |
| Building Security | 34 | 59 |
| Data Processing | 23 | 40 |

SOURCE: Clarkson and Fixler 1987, Ch. IV and VII

Third, it is difficult to apply a specific range of potential annual savings to several of the aggregated service functions reported by the State of Florida. Accordingly, the expected annual savings for some of the categories have been scaled down. Finally, services that are largely financed through user charges related to the level of service--usually administered as enterprise funds--are subject to more cost-reducing incentives than activities financed from the general fund. In the case of enterprise funds, therefore, the estimates of potential annual savings have been cut in half.

Taking all of these factors into consideration, privatization of public services still yields substantial annual savings. Based on expenditures for the 1985-86 fiscal year, the estimated annual savings from privatizing various governmental activities in Florida range from about $500 million to $1.2 billion for general operating budgets (Table 3.2). For those activities operating with enterprise funds, the expected range of annual savings is lower: ranging from approximately $215 million to $673 million. Florida's potential for achieving additional cost savings through greater privatization remains high.

## LEGAL ASPECTS OF PRIVATIZATION

Before actually implementing a privatization program, the legal aspects involved must be scrutinized. This section explores various constitutional, statutory, regulatory, and other laws pertaining to privatization, and examines them in detail for a single state -- Florida.

### Extent of Laws

An analysis of the legal aspects of privatization begins with a determination of current provisions regarding such matters as authority, implementation, funding, maintenance, and liability. Because privatization typically involves a hierarchy of laws and policy decisions at various levels of government, it is important to understand the interrelation among different government entities. Three types of law must be considered: constitutional law, statutory law, and common law (i.e. court decisions). Each type of law may exist at several levels of government: federal, state, and local such as county, municipality, and special district. It is therefore necessary to analyze each type of law that may influence the process at each level of government. Furthermore, the rights and responsibilities of the government <u>and</u> the private entities involved must be considered, because the position of each side is crucial in determining the feasibility of the relationship.

## Government Units That Affect Privatization

Operating in a federal system, the states have retained power to deal with certain governmental matters not expressly delegated to the federal government. In conjunction with their subdivisions, the states maintain substantial authority over matters of health, safety, morals, and welfare through their "police powers". Because the federal government, the states, and their subdivisions have complementary and sometimes overlapping powers, the lines of government control may be quite complex. It is important to keep each level of government in mind when structuring a privatization project.

**Federal Government.** The Constitution of the United States is the supreme law for determining private rights and administering public authority. The Fourteenth Amendment protects citizens from deprivation of life, liberty, or property without due process of law. It also protects individuals from the power of the states and extends to the latter many of the constitutional limitations on federal government. Such constitutional rights cannot be abolished by a state, its political subdivisions, or its officers or employees. Therefore, any privatization legislation, agreement, or other action must meet the requirements of the United States Constitution.

Federal legislation also affects privatization. Acts such as the Urban Mass Transit Act, the Fair Labor Standards Act (FLSA), the Economic Recovery Act of 1981, the Tax Equity and Fiscal Responsibility Act of 1982, the Deficit Reduction Act of 1984, and the 1985 Omnibus Growth Management Act define or limit what a state can do in carrying out its functions.

For example, some features of the Urban Mass Transit Act[12] may limit local privatization choices. In order to shed its services, a local transit agency may find it necessary or helpful to sell vehicles and other assets to private service companies. Most of the vehicles owned by these public systems, however, were purchased with funds provided by the Urban Mass Transit Administration (UMTA). These funds may have to be returned to

---

[12] Urban Mass Transit Act, ch. 21, sec. 13, 78 Stat. 307 (1964) (current version at 49 U.S.C. sec. 1609(c) (1966)).

UMTA upon dissolution of the local authority. Moreover, the Urban Mass Transit Act protects the interests of employees affected by such assistance. These protective arrangements, which may reduce the local government's ability to privatize mass transit, include:

(1) the preservation of rights, privileges, and benefits (including continuation of pension rights and benefits) under existing collective bargaining agreements or otherwise;
(2) the continuation of collective bargaining rights;
(3) the protection of individual employees against a worsening of their positions with respect to their employment;
(4) assurances of employment to employees of acquired mass-transportation systems and priority of reemployment of employees terminated or laid off; and
(5) paid training or retraining programs.

Federal tax codes may further affect privatization. A private firm is able to realize tax benefits that are not available to a public entity. These benefits include the accelerated cost recovery system (ACRS) and the ability to deduct interest payments on the debt used to finance the project. For example, depreciation deductions allow a private business to reduce the amount of income subject to tax. If a private firm undertakes an activity previously handled by government, its investment in property that is integrally related to the privatization project can be depreciated, using ACRS schedules, at a faster rate than is normally available. The "depreciable life" for tax purposes usually does not reflect the actual life of the items.

Recent tax reform legislation alters the benefits that currently apply to a privatization alternative and thus bears on the advantages or disadvantages of any given privatization program. The Tax Reform Act of 1986, among other things, eliminated the Investment Tax Credit (ITC), lengthened the period of depreciation, retained the volume cap for tax-exempt bonds (including industrial development bonds), and placed new limitations on such bonds.[13]

Congress, through the Tax Reform Act of 1986, has modified the ACRS for most properties placed in service after December 31, 1986. The new depreciation system divides depreciable property into eight classes, with

---

[13] Tax Reform Act of 1986 secs. 211, 201, 1301 amending I.R.C. secs. 49, 168, 103 (1976), respectively.

depreciation periods ranging from 3 to 31.5 years. The new volume caps and limitations on the kinds of projects that may be financed via industrial development bonds (IDBs) will decrease the availability and attractiveness of such funding. Moreover, Congress has repealed the ITC for property placed in service after December 31, 1985. These changes will reduce the incentive for private investment. Certain projects, however, such as solid waste disposal facilities, have been granted transitional relief under this act. Additionally, the act will lower corporate tax rates, making a broader range of investments profitable and at least partially offsetting the reduction in some tax benefits.[14]

The decisions of the Supreme Court and other federal courts may greatly affect the privatization efforts of local government. For instance, in *Garcia v. San Antonio Metropolitan Transit Authority* (1985),[15] state and local employees were brought under the federal minimum wage and overtime regulations of the Fair Labor Standards Act. Accordingly, local governments must now meet the same federal standards that private firms have had to meet for some time. This increased cost to local governments may serve as an impetus to privatize a service.

Another important Supreme Court decision was handed down in *Fibreboard Corp. v. NLRB* (1964).[16] In that case the Court ruled that contracting-out work normally performed by a bargaining unit, resulting in the termination of employment, comes within the meaning of "terms and conditions of employment". Therefore, the employer must bargain with the employees before subcontracting such a service. Following this decision, some states enacted legislation requiring a public employer to bargain with the union to cushion the impact of contracting-out. In many states, a locality may avoid this bargaining requirement only if the union specifically waives its right to negotiate. Florida courts have found that certain express language in a collective bargaining agreement may constitute a waiver of a union's right to bargain over the issue of contracting-out.[17]

Still another potential issue involves the conflict between federal antitrust policy and the authority of a state to regulate certain activities. Over

---

[14] Tax Reform Act of 1986 sec. 601, I.R.C. sec. 11(b) (1976).

[15] 469 U.S. 528 (1985).

[16] 37 U.S. 203 (1964).

[17] *City of Dunedin*, 8 Fla. Pub. Employee Rep. 13102 (Pub. Employee Relations Comm'n 1982).

the years, Congress has passed several antitrust laws based on the Sherman Act of 1890. These laws prohibit price-fixing, market divisions, tying and resale price maintenance agreements, and other contractual arrangements considered to be anticompetitive.

The inherent conflict between federal antitrust policy and state police powers over particular activities gave rise to the state action exemption, also known as the Parker Doctrine. This doctrine, stated by the United States Supreme Court in *Parker v. Brown* (1943),[18] held that state governments are exempt from prosecution under the Sherman Antitrust Act.

Until 1978, local officials generally believed that *Parker* also exempted local governments. In *City of Lafayette v. Louisiana Power and Light Co.* (1978),[19] however, the Supreme Court ruled that *Parker* applies only to a sovereign state. Accordingly, to be exempt a municipality must provide evidence of state authorization or direction.

In *Community Communications Co. v. City of Boulder* (1982),[20] the Court held that a municipality constitutionally vested with "home rule" powers does not meet federal antitrust exemption requirements on that basis alone. As a result of that decision, local government officials lobbied for legislation that would reduce their exposure to antitrust liability. These lobbying efforts and the decision in *Unity Ventures v. Village of Grayslake* (1984),[21] which for the first time awarded treble damages against a local government, resulted in the passage of the Local Government Antitrust Act of 1984.[22] The act bars recovery of damages from local governments for antitrust violations by local government employees acting in their official capacities. Florida local governments may minimize potential antitrust liability by procuring express state authorization for activities that may otherwise be in violation of antitrust laws. Florida localities, however, may be hesitant to follow this course, having so recently acquired some autonomy from the state.[23]

---

[18] 317 U.S. 389 (1943).

[19] 435 U.S. 389 (1978).

[20] 455 U.S. 40 (1982).

[21] 46 Antitrust & Trade Reg. Rep. (BNA) No.1157, at 595 (1984).

[22] Pub. L. 98-544, 98 Stat. 2750.

[23] 56 Fla. B. J. 895 (1982).

**State Government.** In most states, governmental powers are divided among the legislative, executive, and judicial branches with the customary system of checks and balances.

Legislative acts generally fall into one of three categories: general laws, special laws, and general laws of local application. General laws usually are intended to have statewide application. Many laws, however, are considered general laws even though they do not have statewide application. For example, laws relating to the location of the state capital, universities, prisons, or hospitals are regarded as general laws because they directly or indirectly affect all citizens of the state.

Special laws relate to particular persons or apply to a specific area of the state. Special laws differ from general laws in that (1) they need not apply uniformly throughout the state, and (2) they must be enacted in accordance with special procedures or conditions.[24]

A number of general and special laws have been passed in numerous states. These range from overall authorization to establish privatization programs to specific authorization to privatize water services or correctional facilities as shown in Table 3.3.

General laws of local application relate to subdivisions of the state or to subjects, persons, or things as a class, based upon distinctions and differences peculiar to that subdivision or class. The most common basis of classification for such acts is population (e.g. counties of a certain size).

Some states, such as Florida, place a restriction on how the state or its subdivisions can use their funds and resources. Florida Constitution Article VII, sec. 10, provides that "[n]either the state nor any county, school district, municipality, special district, or agency of any of them, shall become a joint owner with, or stockholder of, or give, lend or use its taking power or credit to aid any corporation, association, partnership or person. . ." Although this provision contains certain exemptions,[25] its overall purpose is to protect public funds and resources from being used to assist or promote private

---

[24] For example, in Florida the procedures include publication or referendum under Fla. Const. art. III, 10.

[25] See Par. (a) through (c); par. (d) allows municipalities, counties, special districts, or agencies of any of these to become a joint owner, among other things, for the joint ownership, construction, and operation of electrical energy generating or transmitting facilities with any corporation, partnership, etc.

ventures.[26] The 1968 Florida constitutional revision provides exceptions to the general prohibition against lending public funds to private interests.[27] The revised constitution allows industrial development bond financing for public projects. Recent cases have extended the public purpose doctrine to a broad range of private, for-profit projects.[28]

A regulatory agency is a governmental body charged with monitoring and regulating a particular industry or service. The agency's actions may have an impact on privatization decisions for certain government services. For example, there is some question regarding the authority, if any, of the Florida Public Service Commission over the private provision of certain railroad and other regulated services. Because a privatization decision rests to a great degree on the ability of the parties to negotiate a mutually satisfactory arrangement, third-party control of rates, standards, and other key elements would undoubtedly inhibit the process. In the absence of a clarification of the commission's role, many private entities would be unable or unwilling to evaluate or come to terms with government regarding the privatization of certain activities.

**County and Municipal Governments.** In Florida, counties derive their existence from Fla. Const. art. VIII, sec. 1, which states, in part, that "counties may be created, abolished or changed by law. . ." Traditionally, they have been the administrative subdivisions of the state, created to perform essentially state-related functions on a decentralized basis (Hart 1974). With the advent of home rule, counties have assumed more local service functions.

Municipalities are created to provide a variety of local services desired by the citizens. They include all cities, towns and villages duly incorporated under the laws of Florida. Municipalities derive their authority from Fla. Const. art. VIII, sec. 2(a), which provides in part that "[m]unicipalities may be established or abolished and their charters amended pursuant to general or special law." Section 2(b) further provides that "[m]unicipalities

---

[26] See *Bannon v. Port of Palm Beach District*, 246 So.2d 737, 741 (Fla.1971).

[27] See Fla. Const. art. VII, sec. 10(c).

[28] See J.C. Regan, *Industrial Development Bonds: The Demise of the Public Purpose Doctrine*, 35 U. Fla. L. R. 541, 545 (1983): *State v. Volusia County Industrial Development Authority*, 400 So. 2d 1222 (Fla. 1981) (bond financing of for-profit nursing home serves paramount public purpose and provides only incidental benefits to a private corporation); *State v. Leon County*, 400 So. 2d 949, 951 (Fla. 1981) (legislative declaration that for-profit health facilities serve public purpose is sufficient to satisfy paramount public purpose test).

shall have governmental, corporate and proprietary powers to enable them to conduct municipal government, perform municipal functions and render municipal services, and may exercise any power for municipal purposes except as otherwise provided by law."[29]

**Special Districts.** Special districts usually are formed to provide a single function whose cost is paid by those residing within the district's geographical area. As the authority of the counties has increased, the usefulness of special districts has been somewhat reduced, although the number of districts continues to increase. Undoubtedly, there would be far more special districts had counties not assumed greater responsibility for local services. Special districts are the most widely used form of local government. In Florida, special districts have been created for hospitals, port facilities, water management, fire control, drainage, beach erosion control, and many other functions.

The general rule of law applicable to all special districts is that, as statutory entities, they possess only such powers and authority as have been expressly granted by law or necessarily implied therefrom in order to carry out an expressly granted power.[30] Therefore, special districts have no inherent powers; every action must be specifically authorized by the enabling legislation. Furthermore, the courts have determined that if there is a question regarding the existence of a special district's particular authority or power, the question should be resolved against the existence of such an authority or power.[31]

---

[29] Fla. Stat. sec. 166.021(2) defines "municipal purpose" to mean "any activity or power which may be exercised by the state or its political subdivisions". Fla. Stat. sec. 166.021(4) further provides that the provisions of Fla. Stat. sec. 166.021 shall be construed so as to secure for municipalities the broad exercise of home rule powers granted by the constitution; extend to municipalities the exercise of powers not expressly prohibited by the constitution, general or special law, or county charter; and remove any limitations, judicially imposed or otherwise, on the exercise of home rule powers other than those so expressly prohibited.

[30] See *Forbes Pioneer Boat Line v. Board of Commissioners of Everglades Drainage District*, 82 So. 346 (Fla. 1919); *State v. Smith*, 35 So.2d 650 (Fla. 1948); *Edgerton v. International Co.*, 89 So.2d 488 (Fla. 1956); 55 Fla. Att'y Gen. Ann. Rep. 138 (1980); 200 Fla. Att'y Gen. Ann. Rep. 384 (1976); 169 Fla. Att'y Gen. Ann. Rep. 267 (1974); and 374 Fla. Att'y Gen. Ann. Rep. 629 (1973).

[31] See *White v. Crandon*, 156 So. 303 (Fla. 1934); *State ex rel. Greenberg v. Florida State Board of Dentistry*, 297 So.2d 628 (Fla. 1974); 18 Fla. Att'y Gen. Ann. Rep. 42 (1980).

## Privatization Alternatives

This section reviews the legal aspects of the major approaches to privatization, focusing on laws relating to the permissibility, prohibition, or limitation of particular methods of privatization. There are many administrative, regulatory, and other laws applicable to the provision of public services -- whether provided by the local government or by a private firm.

The rights and obligations of local governmental units vary depending upon the method of privatization and the level of government involved. What is permitted or prohibited in a county may or may not be permitted or prohibited in a municipality or a special district.

**Service Contracting.** Contracting-out is by far the best known and most widely used form of privatization. Its popularity stems in part from the existence of legislative guidelines for the procurement of goods and the management of contracts, and from the great degree of control that a governing body may retain over a service. In contracting-out, the local government arranges with a private organization, either for-profit or nonprofit, to provide a service or part of a service. The major purpose of contracting with the private sector is to reduce costs.

Federal law does not prohibit contracting public services to private entities. If federal aid is used, however, the state or local government may be obligated to meet certain requirements in order to retain or continue to receive such funds. Although state law may permit, or at least not prohibit, contracting-out, specific procedures or guidelines may have to be followed.

The State of Florida has enacted several statutes dealing with the procurement of commodities, including services with the stated purpose of promoting efficiency and economy.[32] To curb any improprieties that would undermine the public trust, these statutes also establish monitoring mechanisms and uniform procedures to be used by the state and its agencies.

To control purchasing, for example, the State of Florida created the Division of Purchasing within the Department of General Services. The division is authorized to delegate or contract for the purchase, lease, or acquisition of all commodities and to establish standards and specifications for the use of volume purchasing. The division issues state contracts and

---

[32] Fla. Stat. sec. 287.01 (1985), sec. 287.05(3) (1985), and sec. 287.0582 (1985).

promulgates purchasing rules that apply to the state agencies of Florida. Most state agencies are allowed to do their own contracting within these general guidelines.

It is a common rule of law that a government entity may not sign contracts extending beyond the term for which its present governing body is elected, unless the nature of the contract is business or proprietary rather than legislative or governmental. With the advent of home rule, however, a municipality may contract for periods longer than the term of office of its present members.[33]

**Franchise Agreements.** A franchise is created when government grants a private organization(s) authority to provide a public service within a specific geographic area. The government's role then becomes primarily regulatory with respect to the quantity, quality, price, and other characteristics of the service.

Franchises emanate from the sovereign power of the state and owe their existence to a grant,[34] which is an act of the state.[35] Formerly, a county or municipality could grant a franchise only if authorized by the legislature, either expressly or by necessary implication.[36] Now, however, counties and municipalities have broad home rule powers granted under Fla. Const. art. VIII and the implementing legislation,[37] including the right to award franchises. Moreover, the legislature has statutory authority to delegate to various state agencies the power to grant franchises in their respective fields.[38]

---

[33] Fla. Stat. Ann. secs. 166.021, 166.021(4); Fla. Const. art. VIII, sec. 2(b).

[34] See *State ex rel. Watkins v. Fernandez* 106 Fla. 779, 143 So. 638, (1932).

[35] See *Cable-Vision, Inc. v. Freeman*, 324 So.2d 149 (Fla. 3d DCA 1975) (power to regulate occupations and businesses by licensed franchises is a peculiar attribute of state sovereignty that requires state legislation).

[36] See *Colen v. Sunhaven Homes, Inc.*, 98 So.2d 501 (Fla. 1957) (counties occupy position analogous to that of municipalities, being limited to, and dependent upon, legislative enactment as basis of their authority to grant franchises).

[37] Fla. Stat. Counties sec. 125 and Municipalities sec. 166 (1985).

[38] See, for example, Fla. Stat. secs. 338.12(2), 347.21 (1985).

**Subsidy Arrangements.** Through grants and subsidies, local government may make financial or in-kind contributions to private organizations or individuals to facilitate the private provision of public services at reduced costs to users. Control over the amount and use of grants and subsidies may be provided in part by restrictions on the types and number of organizations eligible to apply for or receive such funding. Limited control also may be obtained through contractual stipulations regarding how funds may be used, and accounting or other reporting requirements. Such protection may be secured through the selection, drafting, and implementation process in much the same way that it is secured in contracting-out or franchising. However, uncertainty is greater and default measures are not as stringent.

**Vouchers.** The local government provides vouchers to eligible individuals who use them to purchase eligible services from eligible sellers. The sellers then remit the vouchers to the government for payment. Because government entities have made limited use of this alternative, there is little legislation or case law on the subject.

**Volunteer Personnel.** Volunteers are individuals who work without pay to supplement or replace government provision of a public service. Volunteers who work for local governments are exempt from Fair Labor Standards Act requirements and are allowed nominal reimbursement for out-of-pocket expenses. Under the act, local governments may reimburse volunteers for tuition costs of classes germane to their work. Volunteers may receive workers' compensation, retirement benefits, or group health and life insurance, and may also be furnished uniforms or replacement costs for damaged clothes or equipment.

A major issue is the extent of local government liability for the acts of volunteers. The fact that a volunteer serves without pay does not render that person immune from liability for gross, willful, or wanton misconduct. A volunteer is expected to act in the manner that a prudent person would.

At least to the limits provided in Fla. Stat. sec. 768.28(5) ($50,000 per claim, $100,000 per incident), it appears that the provisions of Fla. Stat. sec. 768.28(9) protect volunteers, acting as agents of the State of Florida, from claims by injured parties.

**Self-help.** Individuals, neighborhood groups, and community organizations have used self-help to supplement or take over activities that the government had previously provided for their benefit. Unlike volunteers, those providing the service are also the beneficiaries.

The most important barriers to self-help occur in the implementation stage. Local government may ease these barriers by providing staff assistance and start-up subsidies. Tax credits or rebates can be used to compensate citizens who provide some of their own services.

The legal issues pertaining to self-help are very similar to those pertaining to volunteers. Self-help groups, however, are more autonomous than volunteers and typically do not enjoy the liability protection that local government provides to volunteers on its staff.

**Regulatory, Deregulatory, User Fee and Tax Incentives.** Local governments, through enabling legislation by the state, have regulatory and taxing authority that may be used to encourage the private sector to increase or reduce either the supply of, or the demand for, a particular public service. Changes in legislation may alter costs or revenues, thereby affecting the decisions of private organizations to enter the market or continue to provide a service. Incentives generally rely on the power of local governments to govern rather than on their power to spend. Incentives vary in duration and participation requirements. They may be one-time only, such as tax abatements, or periodic, such as tax exemptions. Local governments may also limit services to certain groups or areas, thus reducing the budgetary burden. Local governments may have limited authority, however, because most regulations originate at the federal or state levels.

By general law, the legislature has authorized certain municipal taxes, fees, and charges,[39] including ad valorem taxes and public service taxes.[40] Fla. Stat. sec. 166.201 authorizes fees or charges for the use of city facilities by taxpayers or members of the public, but does not authorize charges or fees for performance of a governmental duty owed to the public at large.[41] The courts, however, have recognized the authority of a local government to impose "impact fees"; these require new housing developments to pay their

---

[39] See, generally, Fla. Stat. ch. 166, Part III (1985).

[40] See Fla. Stat. secs. 166.211 and 166.231, respectively, (1985).

[41] See 101 Fla. Att'y Gen. Ann. Rep. 278 (1985); and 55 Fla. Att'y Gen. Ann. Rep. 92 (1974).

"fair share" of the anticipated costs of expanding city facilities or constructing capital improvements to serve their inhabitants.[42]

**Service-shedding.** A major problem encountered when shedding a service is the rights of displaced employees. The relationship between a government entity and its employees is often contractual. Once an agreement is made, it may not be altered without the consent of both parties and upon sufficient consideration. The fact that the terms of an agreement might be embodied in an act of the legislature (e.g. civil service provisions) does not change its essential character as a contract. Therefore, although the legislature can alter, change, amend, or render void the laws, it has no power to make any changes that will affect existing contractual rights. Such action would be in violation of both federal and Florida constitutional provisions prohibiting enactment of any law impairing the obligations of contracts.[43] Accordingly, prior to implementation of any privatization alternative, the employment contracts of those workers who may be affected must be inspected to ensure that actions taken will not breach the contractual terms.

## Findings and Recommendations

Privatization is a viable alternative to the provision of public services by local government. Certain legal issues, however, must be resolved if privatization initiatives are to be successful. At present there are no explicit constitutional or statutory privatization provisions in Florida. Moreover, many relevant provisions are ambiguous, posing potential obstacles to privatization. This problem is partially a result of the relative lack of knowledge or awareness of privatization alternatives, coupled with the "newness" of the concept.

A privatization effort, including extensive media involvement, must be conducted in order to enhance understanding and use of available alternative service-delivery options. Although it is the responsibility of legislative and

---

[42] See *Home Builders and Contractors Association v. Board of County Commissioners*, 446 So.2d 140 (Fla. 4th DCA 1983), reh'g denied, 451 So.2d 848 (Fla. 1984), appeal dismissed, 469 U.S. 976, 105 S.Ct. 376, 83 L.Ed.2d 311 (1984); *Hollywood, Inc. v. Broward County*, 431 So.2d 606 (Fla. 4th DCA 1983), reh'g denied, 440 So.2d 352 (Fla. 1983).

[43] U.S. Const. art I, § 10; Fla. Const. art I, § 10.

judicial officials to draw and interpret rules and procedures affecting privatization decisions, this initiative should extend not only to public officials and administrators, but to the concerned public as well.

A government entity must conform its actions to the limitations expressed in the U.S. Constitution. In addition, specific federal legislation may limit local privatization choices. For example, the Urban Mass Transit Act requires that UMTA subsidies to the local transit agency be paid back before the system can be privatized. UMTA also requires that the local government seek an accommodation with potentially displaced employees. These considerations may reduce the local government's ability to privatize mass transit.

Recent tax reform legislation eliminating investment tax credits, changing the accelerated cost recovery system, and restructuring and limiting the use of tax-exempt bonds will have an impact on privatization. These changes will reduce many of the tax opportunities that have facilitated privatization. The decrease in the corporate tax rate will offset some of the detrimental effects of these tax changes, however. Congress must make certain technical revisions and clarifications, which may ameliorate the adverse effects. Additionally, the transitional relief granted to certain programs may cause a shift in interest to those areas.

Federal antitrust legislation may render a local government liable for anticompetitive action if it should decide to restrict the number of private service-providers. In *Community Communications Co. v. City of Boulder* (1982),[44] the Court held that a municipality constitutionally vested with "home rule" powers does not meet federal antitrust exemption requirements on that basis alone. Therefore, especially when franchising, a government agency may be held liable for alleged anticompetitive actions.

A possible source of difficulty in Florida is Fla. Const. art. VII, sec. 10, which prohibits a government agency from participating in a joint venture with a private party and from giving, lending, or using its powers or credit to aid a private party. However, assistance to a private party incidental to furthering a clear public purpose is acceptable. The taking of property through eminent domain must also be for a public purpose, and will be carefully scrutinized if it involves participation by a private party.

There is some question regarding the involvement, if any, of the Florida Public Service Commission with attempts by government entities to privatize particular aspects of public utility services. If the state legislature

---

[44] 455 U.S. 40 (1982).

were to expressly exclude privatization efforts from such regulatory oversight, this potential barrier would be eliminated. On the other hand, if the legislature were to mandate that the commission exercise full control over privately provided utility services, the burdens and uncertainties encountered would pose large financial and operational barriers to the privatization of these services.

Potential legal barriers to privatization also exist at the local level. The authority of municipalities to grant certain franchises is limited to a period not to exceed 30 years. If the service requires large capital investments for facilities expected to last beyond the statutory period, this limitation may inhibit local governments from obtaining the full benefits of privatization. In these cases the statutory barrier should be repealed. Other legislation prohibits a municipality from pledging its ad valorem taxes for longer than 12 months without the approval of the municipal electorate. Moreover, a local government may not delegate or contract away its governmental powers, its police powers, or its power to enforce state and local laws and regulations. The privatization of some of these services is thus inhibited.

Special districts possess only such powers and authority as have been expressly granted by law or may be necessarily implied in order to carry out an expressly granted power. Thus, their opportunities for privatization are inherently limited.

Turning to volunteers, government agencies acquire certain responsibilities once they decide to employ them. Because citizens have a right to expect a certain level of performance in the provision of public services, volunteers must be properly recruited, trained, and supervised. Moreover, a local government may be liable for the acts of volunteers it employs. The fact that a volunteer serves without pay does not make that person immune from liability for gross, willful, or wanton misconduct.

A tightly drawn contract setting out the terms and conditions for the private provision of a public service is the most important document of the privatization transaction. Although each contract is project-specific, there are certain general provisions that should always be included. Thus, the contract should clearly specify the rights and obligations of the parties with respect to such matters as price structure, quantity and quality of service, length of the contract, and liability coverage. Possible issues and ambiguities should be resolved prior to implementing and structuring privatization transactions in Florida.

Local governments have the responsibility to provide adequate public services to their citizens, and to contribute to their health and welfare and to the continued expansion of the state's economy. To these ends, it is desirable that more efficient and innovative techniques be made available to communities. Thus, privatization-enabling legislation should be developed. The intent of such legislation should be not to compel government agencies to privatize their services, but rather to give them a viable alternative for dealing with the problems involved in supplying public services.

It is in the public interest to pass legislation that would remove many of the barriers and uncertainties present in the current statutes. This legislation would allow each local government to decide for itself whether or not to privatize a specific service. For example, there are currently no explicit statutory provisions permitting counties or municipalities to fund privatization efforts. It would be desirable to have enabling legislation to make such power explicit. Moreover, any enabling legislation must define clearly the terms used, in order to facilitate understanding and interpretation. Terms such as "private service-provider" and "privatization" must be defined within the context of the legislation.

One of the major benefits of implementing a privatization alternative is a reduction in the cost of the service. If the local government is being subsidized by the state, privatization may permit the state to reduce the amount of the subsidy. The enabling legislation should allow a portion of the resulting savings to stay within the local government and be applied to other services, so that both the state and the local governments share the benefits of the reduced costs.

Enabling legislation should be given liberal construction to effect the purposes of privatization. None of the powers granted should be construed as precluding any power conferred upon a government entity or private-service provider by other laws. Moreover, the provisions of the enabling legislation should be cumulative and should not be deemed to repeal existing laws, except to the extent that such laws are clearly inconsistent with the model legislation.

## Opposition to Privatization

As in any new approach to improving the delivery of public services, individual reactions to privatization methods and techniques will vary from approval or skepticism to outright opposition. Some skepticism and opposition are inevitable. In general, the mechanics and rationale of privatization are not well understood, and risk-averse individuals resist change and the resulting uncertainty. A recent survey, for example, revealed that a considerable number of individuals in both the public and private sectors are not informed about privatization (Touche Ross & Co. 1987, pp. 6-7). Table 3.5 provides a summary of the major impediments to contracting-out, divestiture, and other forms of privatization. Some criticisms also reflect the proposition that if privatization were an effective method of delivering some public services, it would have been adopted long ago. In these situations, the solution is to educate individuals about the consequences of the growth of government over time and the advantages and disadvantages of privatization, with emphasis on actual examples of contracting-out, divestiture, and other privatization techniques.

Strong opposition to privatization frequently arises from individuals' self-interest as public employees whose jobs appear to be at risk. Union/employee resistance was cited by nearly half of the cities and counties that responded to the Touche Ross-ICMA (Touche Ross & Co. 1987) survey. For this reason, successful privatization programs typically safeguard the incomes of potentially displaced employees by reassigning them to other government departments or by offering them the option to work for the private firm.

Public employees who oppose any form of privatization, even if unsuccessful in preventing it, can raise some serious problems unless appropriate measures are taken early in the privatization process. For example, such employees should not be assigned to regulate, supervise, or generally monitor the performance of the private firm.

**Failure to Comply.** A reason often cited for limiting the involvement of private firms in the provision of public services is that they may fail to comply with the terms of the agreement. This failure may be due to a variety of factors, from a firm's inexperience, poor management, and bad luck (e.g. natural disasters) to the substitution of lower-quality resources and deliberate malfeasance. Numerous studies of these problems reveal a common element: failure of the governmental organization to plan and implement a suitable privatization program, including rigorous monitoring of performance. For example, financial difficulties and even bankruptcy of the private firm usually arise from the failure of the governmental unit to review the previous performance or financial stability of the private provider, to require sufficient bonding or penalties for nonperformance, to specify service standards more carefully, and to take other steps to ensure performance.

Under a well-specified contract concerning a franchise, a subsidy, or some other agreement, private providers will not have the incentive or the opportunity to utilize inexperienced or transient personnel or other inferior inputs. Properly specified agreements also take away a contractor's tempta-

Table 3.5: Major Obstacles to Privatization

| Government Concern | Contracting Out | Other Forms of Privatization | Divestiture |
|---|---|---|---|
| | (Percentage Responding) | | |
| | (%) | (%) | (%) |
| Loss of Control | 51 | 37 | 38 |
| Union/Employee Resistance | 47 | 15 | 16 |
| Lack of Belief in Benefits | 38 | 36 | 34 |
| Political Interest | 42 | 38 | 39 |
| Public Opinion | 24 | 27 | 28 |
| Bureaucratic Inertia | 26 | 21 | 19 |
| Lack of Awareness | 24 | 38 | 28 |
| Lack of Confidence in Private Sector | 13 | 12 | 10 |
| Legal Authority | 8 | 12 | 12 |

SOURCE: Touche Ross & Co., 1987

tion to make artificially low bids with the intention of raising prices or lowering quality afterwards.

**Milking the Public?** Another criticism of the private provision of public services is that private providers seek to extract excess profits. "Lowballing" on the initial bid price with the express intention of increasing prices later on, explicit acts of bribery, and kickbacks or collusive bidding are all actions that every responsible government organization seeks to avoid. Experience has shown that these undesirable outcomes can be eliminated with proper control of acceptable providers, adequate specification of the contract or other formal agreement, specific penalties for nonperformance, and special incentives for superior outputs.

**Higher Costs?** Another common criticism of the private delivery of public services concerns the continued and sometimes hidden public costs associated with monitoring delivery of the service and inducing providers to respond to changes in market conditions. Such costs, however, are also incurred with respect to government providers; they may be controlled by specifying the nature and scope of the performance desired, including explicit definition of the outputs and procedures for modifying them. All costs for both public and private alternatives should be considered. Thus, the administrative costs of monitoring and enforcing performance should be included for <u>both</u> private- and public-sector operations. The identification and inclusion of such costs will also assist in structuring the appropriate agreement, if the decision is to seek a private or other outside supplier, or in establishing the best way of monitoring public-sector activity, if the decision is to retain the provision of the service within government.

**Displaced Public Employees.** A possible problem with any shift to private providers is the displacement of the public employees who currently provide the service. By its very nature, this problem is significantly reduced in governments that are expanding and can easily find new positions for potentially displaced public employees.

Governmental units have developed a variety of options to reduce the impact of potential job displacement, and in some cases they have been so successful that they have resulted in strong employee support of privatization. A number of government entities have either asked or required private providers to offer positions to interested public employees. Arrangements have varied from offering public employees the right of first refusal to requiring that a specific percentage (e.g. 95 percent) of public employees be hired. This requirement is easily met, as some employees usually relocate to positions in government or retire. In fact, government frequently can offer additional benefits for early retirement and still save through privatization. In other situations, public employees themselves have become the owners and operators of the private supplier. Indeed, public pension funds could be used for this purpose, just like public pension funds were used by New York City to help its employees keep their jobs.

## CONCLUSIONS

A vital part of any privatization effort is to fully understand the concept. In order to enhance the effectiveness of privatization for communities and their citizens, it is important that public officials, the news media, business, unions, government employees, special interest groups, and the general public understand the nature and consequences of privatization. Indeed, those initiating such proposals should have thorough knowledge of the general subject of privatization and the particular needs and resources of the specific locality.

## APPENDIX ONE

Table 3.6 lists the service categories surveyed and the incidence of contracting-out to for-profit, neighborhood, and nonprofit firms. Results show that 35 percent of the cities and counties surveyed contracted out for their residential solid waste collection services, and 44 percent employed this method of privatization for their commercial solid waste collection services. The same is generally true for transportation services; one exception is paratransit for the elderly and handicapped, which is often purchased from a nonprofit agency already serving this clientele. Contracting-out to for-profit firms is also prevalent in the provision of public utility services, including utility support services and infrastructure (e.g. wastewater treatment and resource recovery). Similarly, contracting-out to for-profit firms is the predominant form for general government support services. As indicated in Table 3.6, 49 percent of the cities and counties surveyed contracted out to for-profit firms for legal services, 23 percent for data processing and labor relations services, and 20 percent for building and grounds maintenance.

In the case of health and human services, as well as parks and recreation, the predominant form is contracting-out to nonprofit or neighborhood organizations (Valente and Manchester 1984, p. 123). For example, 41 percent of the responding cities and counties contracted-out to nonprofit organizations for their drug and alcohol treatment programs, and 39 percent used nonprofit firms to operate their cultural and arts programs. This approach is used partly because these organizations already provide many parallel or complementary services. Recently, however, there have been indications that for-profit organizations may be more effective in supplying some of these services. For example, a nonprofit organization providing homemaker/chore services to the elderly found that creating a for-profit subsidiary allowed it to raise the capital necessary to dramatically expand its services while retaining discount or free service to those who could not afford it (Cossette 1986, pp. 63-8).

Table 3.6: Alternative Forms of Privatization of Public Services

| Service | Contracting Out Prof | Nghr | Nonpf | 1 | 2 | 3 | 4 | 5 | 6 | Total |
|---|---|---|---|---|---|---|---|---|---|---|
| | (Percentage of Jurisdiction) | | | | | | | | | |
| **Physical Environment & Public Works** | | | | | | | | | | |
| Utility Meter Reading | 10% | 0% | 1% | 10% | 0% | 0% | 0% | 0% | 0% | 21% |
| Meter Maint./Collection | 7 | 0 | 0 | 0 | 0 | 0 | 0 | 0 | 0 | 7 |
| Utility Billing | 13 | 0 | 1 | 9 | 0 | 0 | 0 | 0 | 0 | 23 |
| Residential Solid Waste Collect. | 35 | 0 | 0 | 15 | 1 | 0 | 0 | 1 | 1 | 53 |
| Commercial Solid Waste Collect. | 44 | 0 | 0 | 19 | 1 | 0 | 0 | 1 | 0 | 65 |
| Solid Waste Disposal | 28 | 0 | 2 | 5 | 0 | 0 | 0 | 0 | 0 | 35 |
| Tree Trimming/Planting | 31 | 1 | 1 | 1 | 0 | 0 | 3 | 3 | 0 | 40 |
| Cemetery Administration/Maint. | 11 | 1 | 8 | 1 | 1 | 0 | 3 | 1 | 0 | 26 |
| Inspect/Code Enforcement | 7 | 0 | 1 | 0 | 0 | 0 | 0 | 0 | 0 | 8 |
| Category Average: | 22 | 0 | 1 | 7 | 0 | 0 | 1 | 1 | 0 | 32 |
| **Transportation Services** | | | | | | | | | | |
| Street Repair | 27 | 0 | 1 | 0 | 0 | 0 | 0 | 0 | 0 | 28 |
| Street/Parking Lot Cleaning | 9 | 0 | 0 | 0 | 0 | 0 | 0 | 1 | 0 | 10 |
| Snow Plowing/Sanding | 14 | 0 | 0 | 0 | 0 | 0 | 0 | 0 | 0 | 14 |
| Parking Lot/Garage Operation | 12 | 0 | 2 | 2 | 1 | 0 | 0 | 0 | 0 | 17 |
| Streetlight Operation | 39 | 0 | 2 | 14 | 0 | 0 | 0 | 0 | 0 | 55 |
| Airport Operation | 24 | 0 | 4 | 9 | 2 | 0 | 1 | 0 | 0 | 40 |
| Bus System Operation/Maint. | 24 | 1 | 9 | 5 | 9 | 0 | 1 | 0 | 1 | 50 |
| Paratransit Syst. Operat./Maint. | 23 | 2 | 21 | 4 | 14 | 3 | 8 | 4 | 0 | 79 |
| Traffic Signal Instal./Maint. | 26 | 0 | 2 | 1 | 0 | 0 | 0 | 0 | 0 | 29 |
| Flt Maint. Heavy Equipment | 32 | 0 | 0 | 0 | 0 | 0 | 0 | 0 | 0 | 32 |
| Flt Maint. Emergency Vehicles | 31 | 0 | 0 | 0 | 0 | 0 | 0 | 0 | 0 | 31 |
| Flt Maint. All Other Vehicles | 29 | 0 | 0 | 0 | 0 | 0 | 0 | 0 | 0 | 29 |
| Category Average: | 25 | 0 | 2 | 2 | 1 | 0 | 0 | 0 | 0 | 31 |
| **Public Safety Services** | | | | | | | | | | |
| Police/Fire Communication | 1 | 0 | 3 | 0 | 0 | 0 | 3 | 0 | 0 | 7 |
| Fire Prevention/Suppression | 1 | 1 | 3 | 0 | 1 | 1 | 18 | 1 | 0 | 26 |
| Crime Prevention/Patrol | 3 | 5 | 2 | 0 | 0 | 0 | 10 | 5 | 0 | 25 |
| Emergency Medical Services | 14 | 1 | 10 | 3 | 5 | 0 | 16 | 0 | 0 | 49 |
| Ambulance Service | 25 | 1 | 10 | 4 | 8 | 0 | 15 | 0 | 1 | 64 |
| Traffic Control/Parking Enforce. | 1 | 0 | 1 | 0 | 0 | 0 | 1 | 0 | 0 | 3 |
| Vehicle Towing & Storage | 80 | 0 | 0 | 7 | 0 | 0 | 0 | 0 | 0 | 87 |
| Category Average: | 16 | 1 | 4 | 2 | 2 | 0 | 9 | 1 | 0 | 35 |
| **Health & Human Services** | | | | | | | | | | |
| Operation/Maint. Hospitals | 30 | 1 | 27 | 1 | 4 | 1 | 2 | 0 | 1 | 67 |
| Operat. Mental Health/R.P. Facil. | 7 | 3 | 40 | 1 | 15 | 1 | 5 | 1 | 1 | 74 |
| Day-Care Facility Operations | 35 | 6 | 37 | 2 | 15 | 2 | 4 | 3 | 2 | 106 |
| Public Health Programs | 8 | 2 | 27 | 1 | 9 | 2 | 8 | 2 | 0 | 59 |
| Operation/Maint. Public Housing | 13 | 1 | 18 | 0 | 5 | 0 | 1 | 0 | 2 | 40 |
| Child Welfare Programs | 5 | 2 | 24 | 1 | 8 | 1 | 6 | 2 | 0 | 49 |
| Drug/Alcohol Treatment Programs | 6 | 4 | 41 | 1 | 13 | 1 | 6 | 2 | 1 | 75 |
| Programs for Elderly | 4 | 4 | 29 | 1 | 13 | 3 | 18 | 7 | 1 | 80 |
| Sanitary Inspection | 1 | 0 | 6 | 0 | 1 | 0 | 0 | 0 | 0 | 8 |
| Insect Rodent Control | 14 | 0 | 5 | 0 | 1 | 0 | 0 | 1 | 1 | 22 |
| Animal Control | 6 | 0 | 9 | 1 | 1 | 0 | 0 | 0 | 0 | 17 |
| Animal Shelter Operation | 13 | 1 | 18 | 1 | 3 | 0 | 2 | 0 | 0 | 38 |
| Category Average: | 10 | 2 | 20 | 1 | 6 | 1 | 4 | 2 | 1 | 46 |

Table 3.6: Alternative Forms of Privatization of Public Services (continued)

| Service | Contracting Out Prof | Nghr | Nonpf | 1 | 2 | 3 | 4 | 5 | 6 | Total |
|---|---|---|---|---|---|---|---|---|---|---|
| | (Percentage of Jurisdiction) | | | | | | | | | |
| Parks & Recreation Services | | | | | | | | | | |
| Recreation Services | 4 | 5 | 13 | 2 | 4 | 1 | 20 | 5 | 0 | 54 |
| Operation/Maint. Recreat. Facil. | 8 | 3 | 9 | 9 | 2 | 0 | 10 | 2 | 0 | 43 |
| Parks Landscape/Maintenance | 9 | 1 | 2 | 1 | 1 | 0 | 4 | 1 | 0 | 19 |
| Operation Cultural/Art Programs | 7 | 8 | 39 | 2 | 18 | 2 | 32 | 6 | 0 | 114 |
| Operat. Convention Ctr/Auditorium | 5 | 1 | 6 | 3 | 2 | 0 | 2 | 1 | 1 | 21 |
| Operation of Libraries | 1 | 1 | 10 | 0 | 6 | 0 | 12 | 1 | 0 | 31 |
| Operation of Museums | 4 | 3 | 32 | 1 | 17 | 0 | 21 | 2 | 0 | 80 |
| Category Average: | 6 | 3 | 13 | 3 | 5 | 0 | 13 | 3 | 0 | 46 |
| General Government and Support Services | | | | | | | | | | |
| Building/Grounds Maintenance | 20 | 0 | 1 | 0 | 0 | 0 | 1 | 0 | 0 | 22 |
| Building Security | 8 | 0 | 1 | 0 | 0 | 0 | 0 | 0 | 0 | 9 |
| Payroll | 10 | 0 | 1 | 0 | 0 | 0 | 0 | 0 | 0 | 11 |
| Tax Bill Processing | 11 | 0 | 6 | 0 | 0 | 0 | 0 | 0 | 0 | 17 |
| Tax Assessing | 7 | 0 | 4 | 0 | 0 | 0 | 0 | 0 | 0 | 11 |
| Data Processing | 23 | 0 | 2 | 0 | 0 | 0 | 0 | 0 | 0 | 25 |
| Delinquent Tax Collection | 10 | 0 | 3 | 0 | 0 | 0 | 0 | 0 | 0 | 13 |
| Legal Services | 49 | 0 | 2 | 0 | 0 | 0 | 0 | 0 | 0 | 51 |
| Secretarial Services | 4 | 0 | 0 | 0 | 0 | 0 | 0 | 0 | 0 | 4 |
| Personnel Services | 5 | 0 | 1 | 0 | 0 | 0 | 0 | 0 | 0 | 6 |
| Labor Relations | 23 | 0 | 1 | 0 | 0 | 0 | 0 | 0 | 0 | 24 |
| Public Relations/Information | 7 | 0 | 2 | 0 | 0 | 0 | 1 | 0 | 0 | 10 |
| Category Average: | 15 | 0 | 2 | 0 | 0 | 0 | 0 | 0 | 0 | 17 |

SOURCE: Valente and Manchester, 1984

LEGEND: (1) Franchise
(2) Subsidy
(3) Voucher
(4) Volunteer
(5) Self-Help
(6) Regulation and User Fees

## APPENDIX TWO

Because there is no complete recent survey for the entire United States, this section will concentrate on information for a single state: Florida. Florida represents a good case study for several reasons; included among them are numerous constraints on the ability of its state and local governments to easily raise revenues to finance public services,[45] and a significant increase in the overall demand for public services.[46]

In 1986 a supplementary survey was conducted jointly by the Law and Economics Center (L&EC) at the University of Miami and the Local Government Center. Responses were obtained from 169 of the 380 cities and counties in Florida with a recorded population of 700 or more.[47] Approximately 43 percent of those surveyed, representing about 68 percent of the total population, provided usable information in the 1986 survey.[48] Because the cities and counties responding in 1986 may not be the same cities and counties that had responded in 1982, caution should be used in comparing the results of the two surveys.

The 1986 survey reveals that most of Florida's cities and counties have had some experience with privatization. There were more than 1,200 examples of contracting-out the provision of public services to private firms, 500 cases of private-sector franchising, and 250 examples of other forms of privatization, including the use of volunteers, self-help, regulatory incentives, and subsidies. In addition, more than 300 services were shed to private firms and nonprofit organizations.

Overall, Florida's cities and counties used some form of privatization in approximately 20 percent (an average of 15.4 per jurisdiction) of the 77 service categories covered by the 1986 survey; this represented an increase of

---

[45] Florida's constitution prohibits a tax on income, and despite broad home-rule powers local governments remain highly dependent upon the state, especially for solutions to financial problems. In Florida, all forms of revenue are preempted or regulated by the state government. There is no fiscal home-rule for local government. Even property taxes, a domain of local governments, are limited by state millage caps and heavily regulated by state appraisal rules. Locally perceived needs for additional revenues or modified tax structures, therefore, cannot always be resolved locally.

[46] Florida's population will expect to grow from about 8.6 million residents in 1975 to a projected 12.2 million by the end of 1987.

[47] The ICMA 1982 survey included 88 Florida cities and counties.

[48] Of the 169 cities and counties that responded to the survey, 163 provided usable answers.

1.1 percentage points above the level reported by the 1982 ICMA survey. The latter found that the average number of public services provided through the private sector was smaller for Florida than for the other 49 states in 1982.

## Physical Environment and Public Works

The services in this category include primary public activities such as solid waste collection and disposal, street maintenance, and utility services. These services usually constitute a significant portion of local governments' budgets.

In the case of public works/transportation services (Valente and Manchester 1984, p. 95), which is the ICMA classification most comparable to the physical environment and public works function in Florida's system of accounts, the 1982 survey indicated that contracting-out to for-profit firms was the most extensively used privatization technique.[49] As shown in Table 3.7 at the end of this appendix, Florida's local governments lagged slightly behind their counterparts in the rest of the nation in the extent to which these services were privatized. Thus, cities and counties in Florida provided (in part or in whole) an average of 1.6 activities (out of 9 reported activities in 1982) of their public works/transportation services through private means, compared to an average of 2.0 activities per jurisdiction for the rest of the nation.

With regard to certain public utility services (which are included within Florida's Physical Environment and Public Works category but were treated as a separate Public Utility category in the ICMA survey), Florida's local governments displayed a mixed pattern of privatization relative to the other 49 states. For example, as shown in Table 3.7, Florida's local governments led the way in using private methods to provide utility meter reading, but lagged behind in the privatization of utility billing services.

Turning to public-works services, Table 3.7 shows that Florida's cities and counties have relied more heavily than the rest of the nation on the private sector for residential and commercial solid waste collection, yet lagged behind in the private provision of solid waste disposal.

Florida's local governments lagged behind those in other states in privatizing tree-trimming and planting, administration and maintenance of public cemeteries, and inspection/code enforcement (only one Florida local

---

49 Throughout this chapter the term privatization includes both full privatization (e.g. service-shedding) and partial privatization (e.g. contracting out).

government used some sort of private means of providing this service compared to over 135 cities and counties in the other 49 states).

The 1986 L&EC/LGC privatization survey reveals that, since the 1982 ICMA survey, Florida's cities and counties have increased their use of private means to provide physical environment and public-works services (Table 3.7). The use of private organizations has grown from an average of 1.6 privatized services to an average of 3.0 (figure not shown in Table 3.2) for those physical environment and public works categories surveyed both in 1982 and 1986, and to an average of 4.8 for all service categories surveyed in 1986.[50] Unfortunately, 1986 data are not available for the other 49 states. Table 3.7 also provides a breakdown of the 1986 survey between service-shedding and other forms of privatization, such as contracting-out, franchising, self-help, user fees, and incentives. According to the 1986 survey, Florida's cities and counties have shed more services in the physical environment/public works category than in any other form of public service.

### Transportation Services

In 1982, local governments' provision of transportation services through private firms (Table 3.7) was roughly the same in Florida (an average of 2.1 out of a total of 10 reported transportation activities) and the rest of the U.S. (an average of 2.2 transportation activities). Florida jurisdictions had a distinct lead in privatizing streetlight operation (48 percent versus 38 percent), fleet management and vehicle maintenance activities (32-34 percent versus 27-30 percent), and airport control tower operation/maintenance (13 percent versus 11 percent), but lagged slightly (using contracting-out) in privatizing street repair, maintenance, and cleaning. Florida was also significantly behind the other 49 states (5 percent versus 14 percent) in using the private sector for bus transit.

The 1986 L&EC/LGC survey data indicate that, since 1982, Florida's cities and counties have increasingly privatized a broad range of transportation services. The average use of the private sector rose from 2.1 to 2.7 privatized transportation services for the same activities examined in both periods, and to 2.8 if the additional services covered in the 1986 survey are included. Thus, privatization of road and street maintenance increased by 50 percent (from 19

[50] Additional services surveyed in 1986 include electric, gas, and water utilities, solid waste recycling, wastewater treatment, flood control, and resource management.

percent to 33 percent), traffic signal installation and maintenance more than doubled (from 13 percent to 27 percent), and various other services, including vehicle management/ maintenance, street cleaning, parking lot/garage operation, and bus transit operations/maintenance, also increased. The frequency of privatization in Florida, however, has fallen in the case of airport management and control tower maintenance.

## Public Safety Services

The 1982 ICMA survey data (Table 3.7) suggest that Florida's cities and counties were slightly behind those in the other 49 states in privatizing public safety activities. The number of privately provided public safety services per jurisdiction averages 1.7 (out of a total of 7 surveyed government activities) in Florida versus 1.8 in the other 49 states.

Two of the seven public safety services covered in the 1982 ICMA survey were comparatively less vital than the others. Florida's local governments lagged behind their counterparts elsewhere regarding the private provision of both scheduled ambulance service (34 percent versus 39 percent) and traffic control and parking enforcement (1 percent versus 3 percent). On the other hand, Florida's cities and counties led the rest of the U.S. in privatizing vehicle towing and storage facilities (70 percent versus 65 percent), crime prevention/patrol (22 percent versus 17 percent), and police/fire communication (8 percent versus 7 percent). Florida's cities and counties, however, lagged in the provision of fire prevention/suppression (15 percent versus 20 percent) and emergency medical services (18 percent versus 33 percent).

The 1986 L&EC/LGC survey indicates that Florida's cities and counties have not made progress in privatizing certain public safety services (Table 3.7). The average number of services privatized appears to have risen from 1.7 to 2.0 if the additional services surveyed are included, but remains unchanged at 1.7 if only the services examined in both 1982 and 1986 are considered. The largest decline occurred in the provision of vehicle towing and storage services, followed by crime prevention or patrols. Between 1982 and 1986, however, private-sector involvement increased with respect to police/fire communication, fire prevention/suppression, and emergency medical services.

In some respects, Florida is clearly ahead of the nation in its willingness to experiment with private-sector supply of some public safety services. For example, Florida's Salvation Army Act of 1976 made it one of the first states to permit the private sector to provide some types of probation-counseling services to misdemeanants. Florida was also one of the first states to permit a private, nonprofit organization to manage a juvenile rehabilitation program. Moreover, Florida's Bay County even turned over its jail to a private, for-profit prison management company.

### Health and Human Services

The most common privatization method for health and human services is contracting out, especially to nonprofit organizations. The next most common methods are subsidization of private providers and the use of volunteers (Valente and Manchester 1984, p. 123).

The 1982 ICMA survey data (Table 3.7) indicate that Florida's local governments led those in other states in using private firms to provide health and human services (the average number of services with private-sector involvement was 2.1 in Florida versus 1.9 in the other 49 states). A review of the individual categories indicates that Florida's cities and counties lagged in the private provision of sanitary inspections, insect/rodent control, animal control, and animal shelter operations, but led in the private provision of day-care facilities, programs for the elderly, child welfare services, and drug/alcohol treatment programs.

Moreover, Florida's cities and counties led in the use of private means to provide the management and operation of hospitals and public health programs. At the same time, however, they lagged in privatizing the operation of mental health/retardation programs or facilities. This finding is particularly ironic because Florida is one of the few states that has employed a private organization to manage and operate a state-owned psychiatric hospital (the South Florida Psychiatric Hospital).

The L&EC/LGC 1986 survey suggests that Florida's local governments have reduced their use of private organizations to provide certain health and human services. The average number of privatized services in Florida fell from 2.1 activities per jurisdiction in 1982 to 1.8 activities in 1986, using the ICMA service categories, but remained about the same using the expanded set of services surveyed by L&EC/LGC. The decline affected all services except sanitary inspections, animal control, and the operation and management of hospitals and mental health facilities.

## Parks and Recreation Services

The 1982 ICMA survey data indicate that Florida's local governments were ahead of their counterparts in the other 49 states (1.6 versus 1.4 activities per jurisdiction out of a total of 7 activities) in the private provision of parks and recreation services.

Florida's cities and counties were moderately ahead in using private methods to provide recreation services and in the operation of cultural arts activities, auditoriums, libraries, and museums (Table 3.7). However, they were moderately behind in the private operation/maintenance of recreation facilities and park landscaping/maintenance services. Because these services are comparatively more expensive to provide than other parks and recreation services, significant savings should be attainable through their increased privatization.

The 1982 survey data indicate that Florida's cities and counties were clearly ahead in harnessing the private sector to help provide cultural arts programs, libraries, and museums.

The L&EC/LGC 1986 survey, however, suggests that Florida's cities and counties may have fallen behind in the private provision of certain parks and recreation services. The average number of services that utilize the private sector has fallen from 1.6 to 1.2 services per jurisdiction (the 1982 and 1986 surveys covered the same activities for parks and recreation services).

## General Government and Support Services

The 1982 ICMA survey data indicate that contracting-out with for-profit firms and the use of volunteers were also the most common privatization methods used for Support Services (Table 3.7) (Valente and Manchester 1984, p. 149). This result is not surprising because government itself is the customer, thus ruling out most other privatization methods including franchise/concession, user fees, and vouchers.

The ICMA data indicate that Florida's cities and counties lagged in the private provision of most support services, including records-management services such as payroll, tax bill processing, tax assessing, delinquent tax collection, and data processing. Data processing is particularly important because it can be a significant part of a local government's budget. On the other hand, Florida's cities and counties were slightly ahead in privatizing building/grounds maintenance and building security, two of the most expensive support services.

With regard to the remaining support services, Florida's privatization status is mixed. For example, Florida's local governments (Table 3.7) are more likely than their counterparts elsewhere to use the private sector to supply legal and labor relations services, secretarial services and public relations/information services, whereas they lag in the provision of personnel services.

The 1986 L&EC/LGC survey data indicate that Florida's average use of the private sector in delivering governmental services rose from 1.5 to 2.2 activities out of a total of 12 services surveyed (using the same categories in 1982 and 1986) and to 2.6 when all service functions in the 1986 survey are included. The private provision of support services increased for building/grounds maintenance, building security, payroll, tax assessing, and data processing. Use of the private sector also increased for legal and secretarial services, personnel services, and public relations, but fell for labor relations.

Table 3.7: Privatization of Public Services in Florida and Rest of U.S.

Privately Provided Public Services/Total Services per Jurisdiction

| Public Service Category | 1982 Survey Florida | U.S.(49) | 1986 Florida Survey Total | Partial | Shed |
|---|---|---|---|---|---|
| | (Percentage Responding) | | | | |
| | (%) | (%) | (%) | (%) | (%) |
| Physical Environment & Public Works | | | | | |
| Electric Utility | | | 61 | 54 | 7 |
| Gas Utility | | | 53 | 47 | 7 |
| Water Utility | | | 21 | 18 | 2 |
| Utility Meter Reading | 16 | 14 | 17 | 17 | 1 |
| Meter Maint./Installation | 10 | 10 | 19 | 17 | 2 |
| Utility Billing | 3 | 15 | 15 | 14 | 1 |
| Residential Solid Waste Collection | 42 | 37 | 79 | 68 | 11 |
| Commercial Solid Waste Collection | 50 | 39 | 81 | 69 | 12 |
| Solid Waste Disposal | 16 | 33 | 29 | 25 | 4 |
| Recycling: Solid Waste | | | 12 | 9 | 2 |
| Wastewater Treatment | | | 17 | 14 | 3 |
| Flood Control | | | 10 | 9 | 1 |
| Conservation & Resource Management | | | 3 | 3 | 0 |
| Tree Trimming/Planting | 20 | 31 | 31 | 28 | 4 |
| Cemetery Mgt. & Maint. | 3 | 10 | 14 | 12 | 2 |
| Inspection and Code Enforcement | 1 | 8 | 14 | 10 | 4 |
| Average Number of Services: | 1.6 | 2.0 | 4.8 | 4.2 | 0.6 |
| Transportation Services | | | | | |
| Road & Street Maintenance | 19 | 26 | 33 | 29 | 4 |
| Street/Parking Lot Cleaning | 7 | 11 | 9 | 7 | 2 |
| Parking Lot/Garage Operation | 7 | 7 | 9 | 8 | 1 |
| Streetlight Operation | 48 | 38 | 56 | 50 | 6 |
| Airport Mgt./Control Tower Maint. | 13 | 11 | 10 | 9 | 1 |
| Port & Water Operations | | | 7 | 6 | 1 |
| Bus Transit Operations/Maint. | 5 | 14 | 11 | 7 | 4 |
| Rail Transit Systems Oper./Maint. | | | 1 | 0 | 1 |
| Traffic Signal Installation/Maint. | 13 | 27 | 27 | 26 | 1 |
| Fleet Management/Maintenance: | | | | | |
| Heavy Equipment | 32 | 30 | 34 | 30 | 4 |
| Emergency Vehicles | 33 | 28 | 47 | 40 | 7 |
| All Other Vehicles | 34 | 27 | 38 | 33 | 5 |
| Average Number of Services: | 2.1 | 2.2 | 2.8 | 2.4 | 0.4 |

Table 3.7: **Privatization of Public Services in Florida and Rest of U.S. (continued)**

**Privately Provided Public Services/Total Services per Jurisdiction**

| Public Service Category | 1982 Survey Florida | 1982 Survey U.S.(49) | 1986 Florida Survey Total | 1986 Florida Survey Partial | 1986 Florida Survey Shed |
|---|---|---|---|---|---|
| | (Percentage Responding) | | | | |
| Public Safety Services | | | | | |
| Police/Fire Communication | 8 | 7 | 14 | 12 | 2 |
| Fire Prevention/Suppression | 15 | 20 | 25 | 22 | 2 |
| Crime Prevention or Patrols | 22 | 17 | 16 | 15 | 1 |
| Emergency Medical Services | 18 | 33 | 23 | 17 | 6 |
| Ambulance Service and Rescue | 34 | 39 | 34 | 26 | 7 |
| Traffic Control | 1 | 3 | 9 | 7 | 1 |
| Parking Enforcement | | | 5 | 4 | 1 |
| Vehicle Towing and Storage | 70 | 65 | 49 | 42 | 7 |
| Corrections Facilities Management | | | 5 | 4 | 1 |
| Protective Inspections | | | 4 | 4 | 1 |
| Consumer Affairs | | | 1 | 1 | 0 |
| Adjudication | | | 3 | 2 | 1 |
| Medical Exam | | | 12 | 10 | 2 |
| Average Number of Services: | 1.7 | 1.8 | 2.0 | 1.7 | 0.3 |
| Health & Human Services | | | | | |
| Operation/Mgt. of Hospitals | 18 | 13 | 21 | 12 | 9 |
| Oper./Mgt. of Mental Health Facs. | 11 | 17 | 21 | 18 | 3 |
| Operation/Mgt. of Day-Care Facs. | 30 | 19 | 18 | 14 | 4 |
| Public Health Programs | 17 | 14 | 12 | 10 | 2 |
| Nursing Home & Special Services | | | 15 | 9 | 6 |
| Child Welfare Programs | 16 | 11 | 10 | 9 | 1 |
| Drug/Alcohol Treatment Programs | 25 | 21 | 24 | 20 | 4 |
| Programs for the Elderly | 41 | 33 | 35 | 31 | 4 |
| Education Services | | | 4 | 3 | 1 |
| Sanitary Inspections | 2 | 4 | 6 | 6 | 1 |
| Insect/Rodent Control | 11 | 13 | 9 | 7 | 2 |
| Animal Control | 11 | 15 | 13 | 12 | 1 |
| Animal Shelter Operations | 23 | 26 | 21 | 18 | 2 |
| Average Number of Services: | 2.1 | 1.9 | 2.1 | 1.7 | 0.4 |

Table 3.7: Privatization of Public Services in Florida and Rest of U.S. (continued)

Privately Provided Public Services/Total Services per Jurisdiction

| Public Service Category | 1982 Survey Florida | 1982 Survey U.S.(49) | 1986 Florida Survey Total | 1986 Florida Survey Partial | 1986 Florida Survey Shed |
|---|---|---|---|---|---|
| | (Percentage Responding) | | | | |
| **Parks & Recreation Services** | | | | | |
| Recreation Services | 34 | 28 | 31 | 29 | 1 |
| Recreation Facilities Oper./Maint. | 22 | 26 | 21 | 20 | 2 |
| Park Landscaping and Maintenance | 9 | 14 | 15 | 13 | 1 |
| Cultural Arts Operations | 38 | 29 | 17 | 15 | 1 |
| Convention Center/Aud. Operations | 7 | 5 | 10 | 9 | 1 |
| Operation of Libraries | 25 | 17 | 12 | 10 | 2 |
| Operation of Museums | 27 | 18 | 17 | 15 | 2 |
| Average Number of Services: | 1.6 | 1.4 | 1.2 | 1.1 | 0.1 |
| **General Government and Support Services** | | | | | |
| Building/Grounds Maintenance | 24 | 20 | 48 | 40 | 7 |
| Building Security | 11 | 7 | 19 | 16 | 3 |
| Payroll | 2 | 11 | 5 | 4 | 1 |
| Tax Bill Processing | 3 | 13 | 3 | 2 | 1 |
| Tax Assessing | 1 | 8 | 3 | 2 | 1 |
| Data Processing | 6 | 21 | 13 | 12 | 1 |
| Delinquent Tax Collection | 3 | 10 | 6 | 4 | 1 |
| Legal Services | 50 | 46 | 66 | 58 | 7 |
| Law Library | | | 10 | 9 | 1 |
| Secretarial Services | 5 | 4 | 15 | 12 | 3 |
| Personnel Services | 6 | 7 | 7 | 5 | 2 |
| Labor Relations | 27 | 21 | 25 | 24 | 1 |
| Public Relations/Info. Services | 10 | 9 | 12 | 9 | 3 |
| Cafeteria or Food Service Mgt. | | | 11 | 9 | 2 |
| Grant Administration | | | 15 | 13 | 1 |
| Property Control | | | 6 | 4 | 2 |
| Average Number of Services: | 10.6 | 11.1 | 15.5 | 13.2 | 2.2 |

SOURCES: International City Management Association 1982 Survey, and Law and Economics Center, University of Miami/Local Government Center, Reason Foundation 1986 Survey.

NOTE: All figures exclude service arrangements with other governments.

## APPENDIX THREE

A multiple regression was performed on the number of separate public service categories that had some form of privatization in those Florida counties that responded to the 1986 survey. Specifically, the model estimated was:

$$PRIV = 18.68 - .052TAX + .059SPEND + .0005ASSMT - .171GOVT$$
$$\qquad\qquad (-1.31) \qquad (4.86) \qquad (2.82) \qquad (-4.07)$$

where:

PRIV = Number of Privatized Services

TAX = Direct Taxes (per capita)

SPEND = Current Direct Spending (per capita)

ASSMT = Property Assessment (per capita)

GOVT = Government Personal Compensation (per capita)

$R^2$ = .504

DF = 30

# Privatization at the State and Local Level: Comment

Steve H. Hanke*

Professor Clarkson provides a valuable contribution to the privatization literature. His treatment of the legal complexities that accompany state and local privatization is original and noteworthy because the so-called institutional details with which he grapples often pose significant obstacles to privatization. For example, even after the receipt of a political blessing, privatization has been torpedoed because its proponents either overlooked or failed to understand the legal environment.

Since I am in general agreement with Professor Clarkson, I will focus most of my attention on topics that complement those addressed by him.

## ON THE IMPORTANCE OF TAXONOMY

Professor Clarkson discusses nine "privatization forms". (See the first nine items listed in Table 3.8) Four of these forms (grants/subsidies, vouchers, incentives and user fees) are not privatization <u>per se</u> because they do not represent a shift from public to private supply (ownership of the means of production). Rather, these four items represent policies that alter the mix of finance between public and private sources. Even though these forms of finance do not represent privatization <u>per se</u>, they do determine, in part, the

* The Johns Hopkins University

Table 3.8:
"Privatization Forms": Supply vs. Finance

| "Privatization Forms" | Supply | Finance |
|---|---|---|
| Contracting-Out | * | |
| Franchise Arrangements | * | |
| Grants/Subsidies | | * |
| Vouchers | | * |
| Volunteers | * | |
| Self-Help | * | |
| Incentives | | * |
| User Fees | | * |
| Service-shedding | * | |
| Asset Sales | * | |

Note that an "*" in the "supply" column indicates that the so-called "privatization form" is privatization per se because the supply (ownership of the means of production) is switched from the public to the private sector. An "*" in the "finance" column indicates that the form is not privatization per se, but only that it influences the choice between private and public supply.

desirability (from the suppliers' and/or users' points of view) of privatization, and are important features to consider when designing a privatization program.

We must ask whether this taxonomic error is of any practical significance. I believe that it is. Many privatization proposals become hopelessly bogged down because finance issues are mixed with supply issues. For example, it is often argued that privatization is undesirable because the poor cannot afford the prices that private suppliers would have to charge to recover their costs. Whether the poor can or cannot afford privately supplied goods and services should not bear on the privatization decision. The decision about the appropriate means of supply should be based on which supply alternative -- private or public -- can produce a given quantity and quality of goods and services at the lowest cost.

If private enterprise can supply a given quantity and quality of goods and services by utilizing fewer resources than public enterprise, then private enterprise should be employed. If the broad polity deems that private finance

-- which operates through consumer sovereignty and private charity -- does not allow the poor to purchase adequate quantities and qualities of goods and services from a cost-effective private enterprise, then the polity must choose the method and level of public finance to be used to assist the poor. The choice between private and public finance is separable from the choice between private and public supply.

This separability feature allows the decision about privatization to be unencumbered by a host of issues that are associated with decisions about the means of finance. To the extent that separability is practiced, the prospects for privatization will be improved. Hence, the proper application of taxonomy to the field of privatization has important consequences.

## ASSET SALES

The last privatization form in Table 3.8 is asset sales. Even though this represents the most pure form of privatization, it was not discussed by Professor Clarkson. State and local governments own vast quantities of real assets that are potential candidates for privatization. These range from land and buildings to municipal utilities. Although there are a variety of "reasons" invoked for state and local government ownership of real assets, it is worth noting that there are strong bureaucratic incentives that explain why governments obtain and retain real assets. To appreciate this, just consider public budgets. They grow larger as a government's stock of real assets increases, and this budget expansion benefits bureaucrats. If this were not enough, public bureaucracies, in most cases, do not have to account for the capital carrying-costs that accompany the ownership of real assets. These incentives explain why bureaucrats display the behavior of pack rats.

Before closing my comments on asset sales, I will illustrate the waste that accompanies public asset ownership. I am motivated to focus on timberlands, in part, because most people are unaware of the fact that many state governments have considerable timberland holdings.

These lands are usually subject to a timber-harvesting principle (or in some cases a modification thereof) called "nondeclining even-flow". Non-declining even-flow requires annual timber harvests not to fall below an initially established level. With even-flow, the timber-harvest rate is determined by inventory volumes and timber growth rates. Hence, it is a physical, rather than an economic, concept. Economic costs and demands are not part of the determination of harvest rates. Consequently, even-flow results in the noneconomic under-use of timberlands.

Since timber is a capital asset, it should be managed as an investment and capital costs should be properly considered. These costs are not counted when the nondeclining even-flow is employed. In consequence, timber is allowed to become, in an economic sense, "overripe" before it is harvested. Hence, current output is too low and timber inventories are too large. Moreover, "over-mature" forests are subject to many so-called environmental problems. These range from "blow-down" and disease to forest fires and excessive soil erosion.

Privatization would improve the productivity of these lands because timber would be managed as a capital asset. As such, both commercial and environmental outputs would simultaneously increase.

## FEDERAL COST-SHARING

One method of finance that affects many state and local privatization decisions is federal cost-sharing. As was the case with asset sales, cost-sharing represents an important topic that Professor Clarkson has overlooked.

Federal cost-sharing biases supply away from private provision because public projects qualify and private ones do not. In consequence, even if the private provision of the same quantity and quality of service is less costly than public supply, the private alternative might be less attractive from the local users' point of view because federal cost-sharing exceeds the differential between the real private and public costs.

The bias toward public supply and against privatization is perhaps best illustrated by reviewing the U.S. experience with the supply of wastewater treatment. Federal involvement in the wastewater treatment issue dates back to the 1950s. President Eisenhower believed that water pollution control was important and should be financed by those causing the pollution.

Congress, taken with the argument that the federal government should subsidize the construction of wastewater facilities, opposed the President. In 1956 it overrode his veto and passed the Federal Water Pollution Control Act.

The original program was rather modest -- $50 million a year was appropriated for the entire country, and a limit of $250,000 was placed on any single project. But succeeding Congresses raised the ante dramatically, and the program grew out of control. By 1972 Congress had amended the act and increased the annual authorization to $4.5 billion a year, with the federal government picking up 75 percent of the tab for eligible projects. In less than three decades, the so-called "Construction Grants Program" has now ballooned into the nation's largest public-works effort.

While the program might be well intended, it basically has become a giant, wasteful, pork-barrel operation. Independent professionals have criticized it. In fact, the National Commission on Water Quality has recommended its termination, and last year the Water Pollution Control Federation called for its orderly phaseout.

The amendments to the program, enacted in 1982, lowered the total annual authorization to $2.4 billion a year. They also reduced the coverage and the federal cost-share to 55 percent of eligible projects.

Even though the costs of constructing a private wastewater treatment plant are between 20 and 50 percent lower than a public plant, the nation, prior to 1982, had virtually no private plants. With local governments only required to pay 25 cents of each dollar in public-works costs, the private sector simply could not compete. Since 1982, there have been private plants constructed, even though the public plants receive a subsidy of 55 cents on the dollar.

To correct this bias, the federal subsidy for treatment plants should be eliminated -- or it should be offered on the same basis for public and private supply. If cost-sharing was reformed along either of these lines, we could anticipate a dramatic increase in private provision of wastewater services because the real cost advantages associated with private supply would not be masked by federal subsidies.

## THE NATURAL MONOPOLY PROBLEM

Another issue that Professor Clarkson overlooks is the so-called natural monopoly problem. Proponents of state and local privatization often face opposition because it is argued that certain natural monopolies cannot be made efficient by simply shifting ownership from the public to the private sector.

Even when real natural monopolies exist, I believe that franchise bidding, if properly understood and used, holds great promise and can be used to obtain competitive results that are superior to those in the public sector.

The key to the franchise bidding approach to privatization of a natural monopoly is the following: Bidding for the monopoly franchise would not (or, more precisely, should not) be in terms of a sum to be paid for the franchise. Rather, it should be in terms of the prices that the franchisee would charge and the services the franchises would provide the public on award of the right to be the exclusive seller.

If the franchise were merely awarded to the bidder willing to pay the highest price for this exclusive right, competition would drive bids up to an amount equal to the present value of expected future monopoly profits in the market. This would filter these profits through the franchises to whatever authority granted the franchise in the first place, but the net result would still be overpricing of the product. By contrast, an auction could be held in which the franchise is awarded to whichever bidder promises the best combination of price and quality to consumers. Here, competition would drive bid prices down to competitive levels for each possible level of service quality. So long as this bidding process is open and competitive, and so long as inputs to the production process are available in open and competitive markets as well, there would be no need to fear monopolistic results even though a single firm would indeed be granted rights as an exclusive seller.

Theory is not necessarily reality, however, and some scholars have expressed reservations about such franchise bidding. One set of problems relates to the bidding process itself. Selecting a winner (i.e. determining an optimal price structure and mix of products) may be exceedingly complex and may require the kind of expertise in the franchise-granting authority that one normally associates with a regulatory commission. In addition, there is no guarantee that bidding will be truly competitive; in particular, significant numbers of new firms may be reluctant to bid on a franchise that has expired when the previous franchisee is also in the bidding (since the previous supplier is almost certain to be better informed about actual cost and demand conditions than are the rivals).

Another set of problems relates to the likely behavior of the winning bidder during the term of the franchise contract. First, if the contract is for a reasonably long term, there must be some formula to allow for rate changes as costs, demands, and technologies change over time -- or renegotiation must be allowed. If a formula approach is impractical and renegotiation allowed, the need for some sort of agency similar to a regulatory commission becomes apparent. Such an agency will also be needed to police the franchise contract, since the agreement will not be self-enforcing. Another problem is that as the end of the contract approaches, the franchisee may stint on maintenance and underinvest in new assets, hich might leave "the next guy" to cope with any resulting problems.

These are important but not intractable problems. Three aspects (the difficulty of selecting a winning bidder, the difficulty of specifying or renegotiating contracts, and the need to police the contract) require the existence of some sort of "buyers' agency" to represent consumers. Critics of franchise bidding have asserted that such an agency would, after all, be reduced to performing the same tasks that traditional regulatory commissions now perform -- and with the same difficulties and potential for inefficiency or abuse.

This is not necessarily the case, however. The degree of technological complexity and the swiftness of technological change in the relevant industry are crucial variables here. Selecting a winning bidder may be difficult where technology has created a myriad of potential service options. But where it is possible to specify a limited number of service standards -- as for example, with water supply -- awarding the franchise may not be troublesome at all. And where the pace of technological change is not too rapid -- as, again, with water supply -- it may be quite easy to agree on some sort of formula for rate increases, and the possibility of mid-contract renegotiation may never arise.

Enforcing the contract also will be facilitated in industries where the number of specified service standards is relatively limited. Note also that the enforcement role of the buyers' agency is fundamentally different from that of the traditional regulatory commission. The buyers' agency in franchise bidding is merely enforcing a contract; there is no need for this agency to try to authenticate (as public utility commissions must) the franchisee's costs -- a much more complex and difficult task.

The critics' doubts about the competitiveness of the bidding process are based largely on a misperception about existing suppliers' presumed advantageous position vis-a-vis new bidders. It is true that a current franchisee will know more about the market than a prospective franchisee, but this in no way implies that bidding for franchise renewal must be less than fully competitive. Knowledge is an asset like any other; it must be created at a cost. That the current franchisee already has acquired the asset and paid the associated cost is relevant. Bids of current franchisees will incorporate a return to the knowledge asset that has been created, while bids of prospective franchisees will incorporate the capital cost of acquiring the asset. Any bidder (including prospective franchisees) with a comparative advantage in creating this asset cheaply will be well situated to submit a winning bid.

The issue of a franchise holder's incentive to stint on maintenance may also relate to the technological complexity of the industry. If the fixed assets of the operation may feasibly be inspected and evaluated by the authority, then the problem may be addressed by having the franchises post a bond (to be forfeited and used to replenish any assets found deficient) as part of the contract. This would be similar to the process every tenant must follow in renting an apartment: A "security deposit" is posted as part of the lease agreement and forfeited if the apartment is depreciated more than normal. Obviously, the more complex the production process the more difficult such an approach would be to implement in practice.

It appears, however, that the nature of the water supply industry is well suited to the franchise bidding approach. The technology of water supply is well known and relatively static, and specifications about service standards and quality are readily formulated. All the critics' qualms about the practicability of franchise bidding recede in such a context.

And the benefits of such a system would be considerable. Giving the winning bidder a monopoly franchise will ensure that the firm is able to exploit all possible economies of scale in the provision of service; requiring that the bidding be in terms of price and service standards will prevent the firm from using its market power to overcharge consumers; granting the franchise to private owners will harness the incentives of these owners to control costs efficiently in order to maximize profits.

To implement the system, the local government need only create a "buyers' agency" to conduct the action and devise the contracts for the construction, maintenance, or operation of the facilities. Once the franchise is granted, enforcement of the contract can itself be privatized: An accounting firm, for example, could be retained to audit the franchisee and confirm that the terms of the contract have been observed. To assure that the auditor has the appropriate incentive to monitor compliance closely, the contract might include a "bounty" that would be payable to the auditor in the event non-compliance is proved.

Once in place, the franchisee -- unlike private utilities laboring under rate regulation -- will have every incentive to aggressively control costs, adopt new technologies, etc., since every dollar of cost saved is an extra dollar of profit earned. If the firm's managers are not attentive to cost control, the firm's profits will fall, share prices will decline, and the firm will become a ripe target for takeover by owners seeking to reap the gains which would result from turning out (or better motivating) the inefficient management.

The best evidence that competitive franchising of private waterworks is feasible in practice is its obvious success elsewhere, especially in France.

## CORRUPTION

Possibly the most potent factor limiting the spread of privatization at the state and local level is the specter of corruption. Recall that a great deal of the municipalization that has taken place has resulted from the exposure of corruption.

It is important to recognize that bribes do not occur in competitive markets. Corruption requires market imperfections. In short, if bribes are to be paid there must be excess profits from which to pay them.

To reduce the possibility of corruption, proponents of privatization, as well as members of "good government" reform movements, should explore the economics of detection and punishment. On the detection front, private firms could be employed, as noted in my remarks on the monitoring of natural monopolies. These firms could be hired by the government and compensated on a fee-plus-bounty basis. Also, if private firms contracting with the government were required to post a bond or carry "anti-corruption" insurance, the bonding agent or the insurance carrier would police and detect corruption. On the punishment side, if a firm was caught bribing a public official, its insurance rates would increase. This would be a deterrent. As for public employees, they should be given non-vesting pensions. This would make them less likely to take risks that would lead to their dismissal and loss of their pensions.

# Privatization at the State and Local Level: Comment

Fred Thompson*

This essay raises four questions:

1. What is privatization, that is, how do you recognize it when you see it? The answer to this question seems to be that privatization refers to several distinct phenomena: contracting (buying rather than making), load-shedding (disestablishment),[1] facilities divestiture (the sale of assets to the private sector for operation), and liquidation (see Touche Ross 1987).

---

* Willamette University

[1] Hence, an opponent of load-shedding would be an antidisestablishmentarian. I never actually thought I would have an opportunity to use this word. But there it is. Actually the differences between organized (or perhaps it is disorganized) religion in the United States and the established churches elsewhere vividly illustrate many of the concerning arguments pro-and-con concerning privatization. Adam Smith and David Hume were antidisestablishmentarians (Rabkin 1987, p. 128); Smith, because he thought that religion was too important to be treated like a mere private commodity, to be bought or sold according to individual taste. He concluded that it should be placed in the hands of government to keep it out of the hands of the Jim and Tammy Fay Bakkers of this world. Hume was an antidisestablishmentarian because he was skeptical of the value of religion and believed that government monopoly would render its practitioners suitably indolent, and that "the interested diligence of the clergy is what every wise legislator will study to prevent."

Similar claims are made with respect to a variety of services today -- not just to eduction (see, for example, Rose-Ackerman 1983 or Katz 1988). The results of disestablishing religion in the United States tend to confirm both Smith and Humes's worst fears -- and our Founding Fathers' best hopes. Surveys tell us that 86 percent of Americans claim that their religious beliefs are very or fairly important, while in Britain and Sweden (where national churches are established by law) the comparable figures are 49 percent and 35 percent; in the FRG, where the Christian Democratic Party has dominated government for almost forty years, the comparable figure is 47 percent (Rabkin 1987, p. 124).

Professor Clarkson's presentation is primarily directed to the first of these phenomena -- contracting -- which makes sense, given that over 95 percent of all state and local governments engage in contracting -- although they continue to rely on their own resources for the satisfaction of most of their needs. Professor Clarkson also mentions load-shedding, although he does not stress its potential. For example, he overlooks the application of load-shedding to state and local government's largest obligation: education at all levels -- elementary through postgraduate. He also ignores the rapid expansion of the private justice system. Increasing numbers of personal injury cases, medical malpractice claims, divorce proceedings, and contract and employment disputes are now being litigated before "rent-a-judges" and "increasing numbers of lawyers and litigants are discovering that the world of private justice ... is simply a better place to go for a quick, well-reasoned resolution of a dispute" (Thompson 1988b, p. 42). It is possible that the public sector could shed much of its responsibility for providing civil and administrative justice.

Although Professor Clarkson has elsewhere (1980) dealt with the transfer of assets from governmental entities to the private, primarily proprietary, sector, the essay in question omits mention of this issue; my comments will attempt in part to compensate for this omission.

2. When does privatization promote the efficient allocation of resources -- and, why? Contracting frequently increases operating efficiency -- at the state and local levels, the evidence on this point is practically unqualified (see Poole and Fixler 1987; Lave 1985; Bennett and Johnson 1982; and Savas 1982 & 1987). However, there is reason to attribute this outcome to the commitments of contracting -- increased competition, better performance monitoring, and greater decentralization -- rather than, or not merely to, proprietorship (Pack 1987; Thompson and Jones 1986).

With respect to load-shedding, facilities divestiture, and liquidation, evidence that privatization promotes efficiency at the state and local level is inconclusive, in part because these phenomena are rare. According to a recent survey (Touche Ross 1987, p. 21), "the sale of assets to the private sector for operation of liquidation is not a widely used form of privatization." Where sales occur at all, they usually involve the transfer of real property -- and then only when the property is recognized to be obsolete or redundant.

"[R]elatively few governments have sold other assets such as loan portfolios, recreational facilities, utilities, or hospitals or other health care facilities."[2]

Nevertheless, we have ample reasons to believe that governments, in comparison with proprietary entities, do a bad job of managing assets, and that facilities divestiture and liquidation might be appropriate responses to this failure. In the first place, the evidence shows that public enterprises at state and local levels tend to underinvest in functionally specific plant and equipment. This propensity is reflected in low productivity growth, a characteristic of activities carried out by state and local governments, as well as in a tendency to overstaff (see, for example, Crain and Zardkoohi 1978). In turn, their propensity to underinvest in functionally specific plant and equipment likely reflects the liquidity constraints -- often self-imposed -- under which these entities labor. The most common reason given at the local level for divesting facilities has been a desire to circumvent borrowing restrictions (Touche Ross 1987). Note, however, that privatization is not the only way a state and local government can avoid onerous, self-imposed liquidity constraints. A more direct expedient would be to reform the laws constraining public bureaucracies.[3]

The evidence that state and local governments tend to waste nonspecific assets is even more compelling; that is, they consistently fail to allocate these assets to their best and highest uses. As Clarkson observed in another context (1980, p. 15):

> Sometimes the rules imposed by nonproprietary trustees allow managers to ignore the cost of ... holding resources. The opportunity costs of real property in the U.S. government, for example, are not usually included (explicitly or implicitly) in the effective managerial constraints of the

---

[2] Like a few other states and many municipalities, Oregon is a creditor. It has issued home and farm mortgages with a face value of $5.2 billion. That this debt should be securitized and sold off is increasingly recognized. Treasury officials want to use the cash obtained from selling these loans to reduce Oregon's relatively high general obligation debt, thereby improving its financial ratios. More important, management and servicing of these loans would also be turned over to the private sector and should then become more efficient. In addition, securitization and sale of these assets would reveal the size of the hidden subsidy in such lending.

[3] It is possible that these self-imposed constraints efficiently signal fiscal responsibility to insurers, underwriters, and potential lenders who would otherwise undervalue notes backed only by the "full faith and credit" of the debt-issuing entity -- in which case the use of privatization as a means of avoiding self-imposed restrictions that hamper effective program administration may be of considerable analytical interest.

> agency using the land. Consequently, the U.S. government's real property holdings are idle or in lower valued uses more frequently than holdings of profit-seeking institutions.

This argument obviously does not apply only to the federal government or only to real property, although land is probably the nonspecific asset that is wasted most frequently by local and *afortiori* state governments. In Oregon, for example, the state realizes gross revenues of less than $30 million from more than two million acres of timber, grazing, and submerged lands. In private hands, the same lands would likely generate more than $100 million in property/severance taxes alone. Water resources tend also to be wasted by state and local governments (see Anderson 1983). Liquidation of these assets is therefore a singularly appealing prospect. Indeed, given that the appropriate goal of public policy is the productive efficiency of the economy as a whole, the best policy might be the transfer of these assets to anyone who wants them at low or even zero price (Thompson 1988a).

Cash or working capital is the ultimate non-specific asset; it can be converted into any other asset and devoted to any use. At the end of fiscal 1985, state and local governments held 25 percent of their total financial assets, nearly $170 billion, in bank deposits and cash -- an amount equal to 33 percent of their general revenues. Entities hold cash stocks principally to provide storage for cash inflows until future outflows occur. All entities require a financing source to make up the difference between cash inflows and outflows. Where alternative financing sources are unavailable -- where short-term borrowing is illegal or inconvenient -- entities must hold liquid asset balances to compensate for negative net cash flows. Because state and local governments are frequently prohibited from borrowing (except to acquire very long-lived assets such as plant, equipment, or real estate), they maintain liquid asset balances that are much larger on average than those of similarly sized private entities.

Unfortunately, the retention of liquid assets net of external financing results in substantial opportunity costs. This is so even when funds are invested in interest-paying checking accounts (such as money-market accounts), since these funds could be still more profitably invested elsewhere. Most students of public financial management believe that state and local government in the United States hold excess, idle or underproductive liquid asset balances. The interesting questions: How much? At what cost?

One answer is suggested by the performance of Oregon's consolidated cash pool. In 1985, the Oregon consolidated cash pool earned 6.8 percent on its assets, or $122 million, on an average balance of $1.8 billion.

In contrast, the state earned 22 percent on long-term, fixed-income securities and 29.3 percent on its other productive investments. My analysis shows that the Oregon consolidated cash pool needed an average of only $440 million to meet its systematic cash flow requirements, plus liquid asset stocks of no more than $140 million to minimize the probability of running out of cash; this leaves available more than $1 billion not needed to compensate for negative net cash flows which then can be invested long term in a broad portfolio of productive assets. Had the Oregon consolidated cash pool invested these funds in equities and long-term fixed-income securities, it would have earned $478 million, <u>$350 million more than it actually earned</u>.

Had the cash and bank deposits of all state and local governments in the United States been similarly managed, they would have earned an additional $40 billion in 1985. Of course this result is partly due to the spectacular performance of stock and bond markets during the now defunct bull market of the mid-1980s. Nevertheless, it should be stressed that the <u>relative</u> performance of the stock market during 1985 was not unusual. Over the past 50 years, returns on investments in common stocks have averaged 400 percent of the return on treasury bills. Hence, on average and over the long run, state and local governments could quadruple earnings on their cash holdings. Clearly there is a problem here; that privatization is the only solution to this particular problem, or even an appropriate solution, is less clear, however. Nevertheless, this example offers stark evidence of the failure of state and local governments to manage nonspecific assets wisely.

3. If privatization promotes efficiency, why isn't it more widely used?

4. How do we explain the great increase in the rate of privatization over the last decade documented by Professor Clarkson and others? He does not have the answers to these questions, nor do I. While there is an emerging literature on the political economy of privatization, it seems to me that the answers given to what I have called question 3 generally contradict the possible answers to question 4 (see for example, Chamberlin and Jackson 1987; Thompson and Jones 1986).

# CHAPTER FOUR

# Privatization in Britain

John Vickers and George Yarrow*

## INTRODUCTION

The importance that privatization would come to have in the economic policies of the Thatcher government would have been difficult to foresee in 1979. The Conservative election manifesto of that year had relatively little to say about privatization, although the party's desire to "roll back the frontiers of the state" and promote a "property owning democracy" were prominent themes. In the government's first term in office (June 1979 to June 1983), the sale of public-sector housing was the most important policy in this regard. Between 1979 and 1983 nearly 600,000 houses and flats were sold -- mainly at discount prices to their tenants -- which was more than in the entire post-war period up to that time. In 1982, receipts from housing sales approached £2 billion.

In contrast, the sale of public-sector enterprises experienced a relatively slow start. As Table 4.1 shows, net proceeds from enterprise sales were less than £500 million annually before 1983, but since then they have grown dramatically. Annual proceeds are expected to be in the region of £5 billion over the next few years, over ten times the 1979-83 levels.

---

* Nuffield College and Hertford College, Oxford University, respectively.

Table 4.1: Privatization Proceeds

| Financial Year | £ Million |
|---|---|
| 1979/80 | 377 |
| 1980/81 | 405 |
| 1981/82 | 493 |
| 1982/83 | 488 |
| 1983/84 | 1,142 |
| 1984/85 | 2,132 |
| 1985/86 | 2,702 |
| 1986/87 | 4,750* |
| 1987/88 to 1989/90 | 5,000* annually |

SOURCE: U.K. H.M. Treasury (1985, Table 2.14; 1986, Table 2.23; 1987, Table 2.21 and p. 30).

NOTE: Figures shown are net proceeds. Asterisks denote expected receipts.

The expansion in the scale of the privatization program accorded with a fundamental change in its nature (see Table 4.2). Before 1984, the firms that were sold operated in more or less competitive industries. Firms like British Aerospace, Cable and Wireless, Enterprise Oil, and Jaguar are major companies, but they do not enjoy such market power as to pose serious regulatory problems. The privatization of British Telecom (BT) in November 1984 -- the first in a series of sales of utility companies with dominant market positions -- therefore signalled a radical shift in policy. Regulated private monopoly came to be viewed by the government as superior to monopoly in public ownership (see Moore 1985). Thus, British Gas was sold in December 1986, and the British Airports Authority (now called BAA) in July 1987. Other firms with significant market power that were privatized in 1987 included British Airways and subsidiaries of the National Bus Company. Plans to sell British Steel, the publicly-owned parts of the water industry in England

Table 4.2: The U.K. Privatization Program -- Principal Asset Sales, 1979-87.

| Company | Year(s) of Share Issue |
|---|---|
| British Petroleum | 1979, 1981, 1983, 1987 |
| British Aerospace | 1981, 1985 |
| British Sugar Corporation | 1981 |
| Cable and Wireless | 1981, 1983, 1985 |
| Amersham International | 1982 |
| National Freight Corporation | 1982 |
| Britoil | 1982, 1985 |
| Associated British Ports | 1983, 1984 |
| International Aeradio | 1983 |
| British Rail Hotels | 1983 |
| Wytch Farm Oilfield | 1984 |
| Enterprise Oil | 1984 |
| Sealink | 1984 |
| Jaguar | 1984 |
| British Telecom | 1984 |
| Trustee Savings Bank | 1986 |
| British Gas | 1986 |
| British Airways | 1987 |
| Rolls Royce | 1987 |
| British Airports Authority | 1987 |

SOURCE: Vickers and Yarrow (1988)

and Wales, and the electricity supply industry are now being developed, and coal, railways, and the postal service might follow later.

Alongside policies to promote private enterprise and ownership, the government has introduced measures designed to stimulate competition in a number of public-sector (and soon to be private sector) activities. The use of contracting out and competitive tendering by central and local government was extended in areas such as refuse collection and hospital cleaning. The 1981 Telecommunications Act, the 1982 Oil and Gas (Enterprise) Act, and the 1983 Energy Act sought respectively to reduce entry barriers into parts of the telecommunications, gas, and electricity industries, and the Transport Acts of

1980 and 1985 substantially deregulated the markets for coach and bus services. However, as we will explain below, some of these liberalizing measures have had limited practical effect, and policies to encourage private ownership have tended to take precedence over measures to promote effective competition in the frequent cases of tension between the two objectives.

Since 1984, regulation has been the other main element of privatization policy. The "RPI-X" method of price control now applies to much of the business of BT, British Gas, and BAA, and is likely to be used again when the water and electricity industries are privatized. This method of regulation imposes a limit on the regulated firm's average price increases for some initial period, at the end of which a regulatory review occurs. Superficially, it is very different from rate-of-return regulation, but in practice the two systems may turn out to be quite similar (see "The British Regulatory Model" section below). New regulatory bodies have been established, such as Oftel (the Office of Telecommunications) and Ofgas (the Office of Gas Supply), and the regulatory powers and duties of existing bodies (e.g. the Civil Aviation Authority) have been extended. Apart from monitoring prices, an important responsibility of the regulatory authorities is to promote conditions for effective competition in at least some parts of the industries that have been privatized.

The aim of this paper is to offer an economic assessment of British privatization policies to date, and in particular of policies regarding competition and regulation in industries dominated by newly privatized firms. In the next, section we discuss the economic and political objectives behind the privatization program. "The British Regulatory Model" section examines general features of the emerging regulatory policies, with particular emphasis on the effects of RPI-X price regulation on incentives for productive and allocative efficiency. Competition and regulation in the privatized telecommunications industry is the subject of the next section. The "Competition and Regulation in Other Privatizations" section looks at policies in the gas industry and elsewhere. Finally, in "Conclusions" we summarize our conclusions and suggest that privatization in Britain has not so far been as successful in terms of the promotion of economic efficiency than we believe it to have been politically.

## OBJECTIVES OF PRIVATIZATION

The government has never produced a comprehensive statement about the aims of the privatization program ranked by priority or weight.

Indeed, objectives are likely to differ between government ministers and departments and to change over time as opportunities, constraints and perceptions develop. However, the following list summarizes what appear to have been the principal aims:

(i) improving economic efficiency by introducing competition and removing constraints (e.g. in respect of borrowing) on the firms concerned;

(ii) reducing the public-sector borrowing requirement (PSBR);

(iii) reducing government involvement in enterprise decision making;

(iv) easing problems of public sector pay determination;

(v) widening share ownership;

(vi) encouraging employee share ownership; and

(vii) gaining political advantage.

The last of these objectives has only been implicit, but it has shaped a number of key policy decisions.

Given the nature of the political coalition that has been required to push through the privatization program, we would argue that, by examining the historical evolution of the government's policies, it is possible to identify goals that played particularly important roles at the various stages of the process. That is, an examination of actual behavior reveals information about the objectives that were crucial in shaping the scope and direction of the overall program as it developed over time. In particular, with respect to the sale of state-owned enterprises, the momentum of privatization policies appears initially to have been most heavily influenced mainly by dissatisfaction with the performance of publicly-owned industries, later by short-term budgetary considerations, and finally by share ownership and distributional objectives.

## The Performance of Publicly-Owned Industries

The typical state-owned firm in Britain is a public corporation. This is a corporate body, established by statute, with its own legal existence. In theory, it is free to manage its own affairs without detailed control by Parliament, but the relevant minister of the Crown has powers to give directions of a general character as to the exercise and performance of the functions of the corporation, to give directions in certain specified matters of particular importance, and to appoint the board of management. Management is directly responsible to the minister for the conduct of its affairs, although the relationship is intended to be at "arm's length". In turn, the minister is responsible to Parliament and hence, ultimately, to the voting public.

In practice, this complex set of agency relationships has failed to perform satisfactorily, and its weaknesses have been well documented elsewhere (see U.K. National Economic Development Office 1976, for example). The fundamental problem has been the inability to establish incentives for the relevant agents, chiefly managers and ministers, to act in ways that promote public interest objectives (which themselves have always been vaguely defined). The result has been extensive goal displacement at both the managerial and political levels. Ministers, for example, have frequently intervened in the detailed decisions of the corporations so as to secure outcomes favorable to key interest groups, while managers have frequently indulged their own preferences for the quiet life and/or higher output and investment.

The implications of these failings are clearly visible in the performance record. Taken as a group, the public corporations have been highly unprofitable: in 1979, for example, the gross trading surplus before allowing for depreciation was £5.593 billion, representing a rate of return on net capital stock, valued at replacement cost, of 5 percent. However, subsidies in that year amounted to £1.569 billion, and capital consumption is estimated at £4.977 billion. Hence, the rate of return, net of subsidies, and depreciation was -0.86 percent.

The year 1979 was by no means untypical, and poor financial performance cannot be attributed solely to the pursuit of allocative efficiency objectives in circumstances of scale economies and deviations between private and social costs. Both the NEDO Report (1976) and Molyneux and Thompson (1987) document numerous examples of failures to adopt efficiency-enhancing policies: cross-subsidization of activities has been common, and most public corporations simply ignored the injunctions of the 1967 White Paper on Nationalized Industries (U.K. H.M. Treasury 1967) that they should seek to construct tariff structures based on marginal costs and to achieve a rate of return on new investment of 8 percent real (later increased to 10 percent and then, in 1978, reduced to 5 percent).

Dissatisfaction with this performance record, then, provided the initial impetus for the development of privatization policies, the early outlines of which were set out in the late 1970s when the Conservative Party was in opposition. Privatization was intended to remove politicians from the direct monitoring hierarchy and to replace them with private investors. It was believed that this would greatly simplify the relevant agency relationships and that capital markets would have much greater incentives than politicians to pressure managements into improving internal efficiency. In the early phase of the program, the targeted public corporations were in relatively competitive industries, so there was little need for concern that a greater emphasis on profit objectives would lead to the abuse of market power.

Unfortunately, the public corporations that both operated in competitive markets and were either profitable or soon to be profitable -- and were therefore suitable for sale -- tended to be the smaller state-owned enterprises. In 1979, therefore, the Thatcher government was confronted with the problem of how to handle the great majority of the corporations that, at the time, were envisioned to remain in the public sector. The policy response was a more rigorous implementation of the principles that had been established by the preceding Labour government (1974-79) in respect of the control of nationalized industries.

In 1976, in response to a deteriorating fiscal position, the Labour government had imposed cash-limits -- later known as External Financing Limits (EFLs) -- on many public-sector activities. As they applied to the public corporations, the EFLs placed a constraint on the change in the net indebtedness of the enterprises to the central government in any given financial year. Later, in 1978, the government introduced a White Paper on Nationalized Industries (U.K. H.M. Treasury 1978) that accorded pride of place to financial targets for the corporations -- which were generally expressed as a minimum rate of return on assets -- and downplayed the importance of the pricing and investment criteria (based upon marginal-cost principles) that had been established by the earlier, 1967 White Paper.

The Thatcher government made no substantial changes to this framework, but over time gradually tightened the financial constraints imposed on the public corporations and sought to introduce more market-oriented managements. In one or two cases, most notably steel, it also experimented with the introduction of performance-related incentive contracts for top managers. As Table 4.3 illustrates, in a number of industries (e.g. steel, coal, rail, buses, and postal services), the consequence was a significant improvement in productivity performance. Moreover, the effects of the change in priorities (towards greater emphasis on financial performance) are still coming

Table 4.3: Productivity Trends in Major Nationalized Industries

| | Output per Head | | Total Factor Productivity | |
|---|---|---|---|---|
| | 1968-1978 | 1978-1985 | 1968-1978 | 1978-1985 |
| | (Average annual percentage increases ) | | | |
| British Rail | 0.8 | 3.9 | n/a | 2.8 |
| British Steel | -0.2 | 12.6 | -2.5 | 2.9 |
| Post Office | -1.3 | 2.3 | n/a | 1.9 |
| British Telecom | 8.2 | 5.8 | 5.2 | 0.5 |
| British Coal | -0.7 | 4.4 | -4.4 | 0.0 |
| Electricity | 5.3 | 3.9 | 0.7 | 1.4 |
| British Gas | 8.5 | 3.8 | n/a | 1.2 |
| British Bus | -0.5 | 2.1 | -1.4 | 0.1 |
| National Bus | -0.5 | 2.1 | -1.4 | 0.1 |
| British Airways | 6.4 | 6.6 | 5.5 | 4.8 |
| U.K. Manufacturing | 2.7 | 3.0 | 1.7 | n/a |

SOURCE: Molyneux and Thompson, 1987

through. In the year to 1986-87, for example, British Coal's output per man-year increased by 22.6 percent -- largely as a result of closures of high-cost capacity -- and stood at 39 percent above the highest level achieved (in 1982-83) in the period before the year-long coalminers' strike of 1984-85.

However, it is also apparent from Table 4.3 that the productivity performance of the public corporations showed no similar tendency to improve in the cases of the major utilities (electricity, gas, and telecommunications). Because of their market power these enterprises were much more easily able to respond to the stricter financial regime by raising prices to customers. Thus, while privatization may have seemed most appropriate for enterprises operating in competitive product markets, these were precisely the enterprises whose internal efficiency performance was most readily improved by reforms to the public monitoring system. Indeed, if dissatisfaction with the performance of the nationalized industries had been the only operative factor, it would be difficult to explain the importance that was subsequently attached to privatization in British economic policy: the government might simply have proceeded by selling the smaller corporations, tightening financial constraints on the enterprises that remained in the public sector, and introducing greater competition into the utility industries. Since this was the emphasis in the first years of the Thatcher government, what then led to the later, more radical approach?

### Public-Sector Borrowing

The centerpiece of the government's economic policy in the early 1980s was the Medium Term Financial Strategy (MTFS). Among other things, the MTFS called for steady reductions in the rate of growth of the money supply and the public sector borrowing requirement (PSBR). The monetary targets were aimed at reducing the inflation rate, while the fiscal targets were designed partly to attenuate the consequences of tight money for interest rates and partly to help control the level of government expenditure (one of the government's objectives being to reduce this expenditure relative to GDP).

The relevance of this macroeconomic policy stance to our discussion arises from the fact that privatization of a state-owned enterprise has direct and immediate effects on two of the key target variables (the PSBR and the accounting measure of government expenditure). In fact, there are three separate effects:

(i) When a firm is transferred to the private sector its borrowings no longer contribute to the PSBR. Although central government also loses the associated profit flow, in cases where the firm has a large investment program to finance (e.g. Britoil and British Telecom) the net effect of the two changes will often be a short-term reduction in the PSBR.

(ii) Proceeds from asset sales are not classed as borrowings in the national accounts. Hence, sales proceeds of #X billion in a given year will reduced the PSBR by #X billion in that year.

(iii) By a quirk of the national accounting system in Britain, asset disposals are treated as negative government spending. Hence, in the accounts, sales proceeds of #X billion will show up as a reduction of #X billion in central government expenditure.

These three financial and accounting implications help to account for the attractiveness of privatization to a government that had nailed its colors to the mast of reducing the PSBR. Asset disposals enabled the government to meet its self-selected fiscal targets via more modest decreases in expenditure on goods and services and more modest increases in taxation than would otherwise have been called for. That is, a more expansionary fiscal policy could deliberately be implemented without the loss of face that would have been entailed by formal abandonment of nominal fiscal targets that had been set at earlier dates.

The importance of fiscal objectives is clear from the pattern of the early privatizations (1979-83). The largest flotations in this period involved firms in the oil industry (British Petroleum, Britoil, and Enterprise Oil), and the first (BP) represented the sale of a fraction of the government's stake in a firm that was already partially privately owned and that was already operating as a commercial, quoted company. The BP sales, therefore, had negligible effects on the agency relationships between managers and shareholders (including the government). Moreover, in this case the government was doing no more than following the precedent set by the previous Labour government when, in 1977, the latter had disposed of a part of the state's shareholding to raise finance for its expenditure program. Preoccupation with PSBR effects is also apparent from the history of government dealings with Britoil. In 1979-80 and 1980-81 forward sales of the firm's oil (amounting to £660 million and £560 million, respectively) were made to increase short-term government revenues, and the possibility of introducing an oil revenue bond -- whose interest payments would be linked to the firm's performance -- was contemplated as a means of using private capital to finance exploration and development activities (and thereby reducing public borrowing). However, the creation of a revenue bond would have had a smaller impact on the PSBR than full privatization and, unlike the latter policy, would not have reduced the recorded level of government expenditure. Unsurprisingly, therefore, the option was rejected, and the government disposed of slightly more than one half of the company's shares in November 1982 (in a sense, the ultimate forward sale of oil).

Nevertheless, the fact that the bond option was under consideration serves to link the 1979-83 privatizations with the utility sales that were to follow. In the early 1980s, various methods of introducing private finance into the balance sheets of other nationalized industries in general, and of British Telecom in particular, were under active consideration. Like Britoil, British Telecom had embarked upon a substantial investment program, the PSBR consequences of which the government wished to reduce. The policy decision in respect of Britoil, together with growing confidence that the London stock market could absorb large share issues without major mishap -- at the time the Britoil flotation being the largest that had been attempted and raising about £550 million -- offered encouragement to the government to repeat the exercise in the case of BT.

Pursuit of PSBR objectives, therefore appears to have been a key factor in leading the government to turn its attention from the sale of the more marginal state enterprises to the privatizations of the larger public corporations that have characterized the later part of the program. For, with respect to the major utility industries, the available evidence does not suggest that regulated private monopoly (the option selected by the Thatcher government) is decisively more efficient than public monopoly. (We do not consider this evidence here, but recent surveys include Millward (1982), Kay and Thompson (1986), Yarrow (1986), Boardman and Vining (1987), and Vickers and Yarrow (1988).)

Supporting evidence for the view that PSBR objectives played a major role in the development of the privatization program is also contained in the White Paper on *The Future of the Telecommunications Industry in Britain* (U.K. Department of Trade and Industry 1982) which set out the government's plan to privatize BT. This gave particular attention to the motive of allowing BT access to greater finance for investment without simultaneously increasing the PSBR. Finally, it can be noted that the central coordinating role in the development of the privatization program was allocated to the Treasury, which was also the government department responsible for the implementation of fiscal policy. Thus, although other parts of government may, and almost certainly did, have priorities that differed from those of the Treasury, the bureaucratic arrangements were conducive to the partial displacement of microeconomic goals (e.g. promoting competition) by macroeconomic goals (e.g. reducing the PSBR).

It is, therefore, a sobering thought (to a professional economist at least) that the extent, scope, and pace of privatization policies in Britain have probably been more influenced by their convenient macroeconomic implications -- which themselves derive in part from quirks in the national accounting system -- than by our cumulated knowledge about the effects of property rights, competition, and regulation on economic performance.

## Share Ownership and Distributional Effects

Much of the public attention that has been attracted by privatization in Britain has focused upon the mechanics of the share flotations, rather than upon the likely effects of ownership transfer on economic efficiency. Between 1979 and 1983, there was some experimentation with different methods of flotation: for example, Britoil (1982), British Petroleum (1983), Enterprise Oil, and Cable and Wireless (1983) were tender offers; British Aerospace (1981), Amersham (1982), and Associated British Ports (1983) were offers for sale at a fixed striking price; British Sugar was a private placing; and National Freight was an employee buy-out. Later flotations have, however, been dominated by the offer-for-sale method, and examination of this phenomenon reveals another, highly-significant motive for privatization.

The government discovered early on that when a state-owned company was sold, it would be subject to criticism from opposition political parties no matter what happened in the markets. The Britoil tender offer, for example, was 70 percent undersubscribed, largely because of falling oil prices between the date at which the minimum tender price was struck and the flotation date. Underwriters were left with a large slice of the equity and, on the opening day of trading, the price fell to a discount of 9 percent on the minimum tender price. In this case the government was criticized for over-pricing the shares. On the other hand, the Amersham (fixed price) issue was heavily oversubscribed, the first-day premium was 32 percent, and the government was criticized for under-pricing the shares.

There was, however, a fairly obvious asymmetry between these two flotations. The general public did not show much interest in the technical details of the share issues -- the events having no discernible impact on the economic well-being of most voters -- but, in the case of Amersham, the tens of thousands of investors who had successfully acquired shares at the bargain offer price were delighted with the outcome, whereas Britoil investors were far from happy. What the government discovered was that over-pricing is best avoided, but that under-pricing is a politically-attractive way of redistributing wealth. If the Amersham outcome could be repeated on the grand scale, millions of satisfied investors would thank politicians for the chance to participate in such a profitable exercise, while the effects on the losers (taxpayers not subscribing to the issues) would be thinly spread and concealed. Moreover, successful applicants would have a direct financial stake in the continuation of Conservative government: given past history, the Labour Party would find it difficult to avoid commitments to the renationalization of the major utilities, and it would therefore be seen as a threat to the capital gains of the new investors. (Note, however, that this strategy may not <u>necessarily</u> reduce the likelihood of renationalization. Even if a low offer price impairs the electoral prospects of the Labour Party, it also <u>reduces</u> the financial cost of renationalization at acquisition value, thereby tending to increase the probability of a return to public ownership in the event that a Labour government does come to power. Thus, it raises fewer barriers to *ex post* shareholder expropriation via the alternative, less transparent route of regulatory policy. Indeed, the regulatory structures established by the Conservative government for BT, British Gas, and BAA offer a future Labour government ready-made vehicles for the establishment of close public <u>control</u> of these enterprises.)

Of course, for the strategy to succeed, it would be necessary to ensure that a substantial fraction of shares in each company were allocated to small investors (rather than to the large institutions that dominated the capital market) and that the new owners did not immediately sell their shares. However, these conditions could easily be arranged through allotment rules in the event of oversubscription (which could be guaranteed by a suitably low striking price) and through loyalty bonuses for small investors who held their shares for prescribed periods.

This, then, was the strategy adopted by the government in the second phase of the privatization program. The objective of widening individual share ownership was increasingly stressed in public statements, and the policy did indeed have dramatic effects: between the summers of 1979 and 1987 the total number of shareholders in Britain approximately trebled (although most of the new owners had highly-undiversified portfolios consisting of small holdings of one or two privatization stocks, and the percentage of the London equity market accounted for by individual investors has continued to decline). However, in respect of share ownership objectives, the government had at its disposal a variety of alternative, frequently-superior policy instruments. For example, existing policy-created tax biases in favor of saving via institutions or home ownership could have been eliminated. Relative to these other policies, the real attraction of privatization lay in the politically-advantageous wealth redistribution that was possible via the under-pricing of shares. Once again, while the original impetus for the sale of state-owned enterprises may have been philosophically inspired, the detailed implementation of policy became increasing to be influenced by desirable (to an incumbent government) political side effects.

Table 4.4 indicates the extent of underpricing in the six largest full privatizations to date. Strictly speaking, the spread between the opening and offer prices should be corrected for movements in an appropriate market index between the date the offer price was struck and the first day of trading. In each of the cases shown, however, the adjustment would be small and has therefore been ignored. (The only recent case where the effect is material was the partial privatization of BP in October 1987, about which we will say more below.) The figures in the final column add up to more than #3 billion, and taking into account the rather large transaction costs of the flotations (advertising, advisory fees, etc.), the direct financial cost to taxpayers of the six privatizations has been close to £4 billion.

While some degree of underpricing was probably inevitable -- private new issues typically trading at a first-day premium -- its extent in practice was not. The premiums associated with the privatization issues are far greater than the degree of underpricing typical in private issues. Buckland et al. (1981) estimated that in times of rising equity markets, premiums on private issues for sale averaged 12 percent. In a more recent study of new equity issues on the London stock market between 1983 and 1986, Jackson (1986) found that the average degree of underpricing of larger issues was 5.3 percent in offers for sale. In addition, private issues rarely have the additional shareholder benefits of vouchers and bonuses that have been a feature of the major privatizations.

There is, therefore, good reason to believe that the government could have sold shares at higher offer prices. In particular there was no requirement to dispose of such large blocks of equity at once. For example, British Gas could have been sold in several tranches and, even if the first tranche had been seriously underpriced, the market would have provided a good guide to the pricing of later offerings of stock. (The Japanese have followed this approach in the privatization of NTT). However, the fact that the government chose to forego substantial revenues (despite its desire to reduce the PSBR) underlines the political attractiveness of creating windfall profits for

Table 4.4. Underpricing of Shares

| Company | Date[1] | Gross Proceeds(Lm) | Offer Price(p) | First Installment(p) | Opening Price[2](p) | % Gain[3] | Extent of Underpricing(Lm) |
|---|---|---|---|---|---|---|---|
| BT[4] | Dec 84 | 3,900 | 130 | 50 | 93 | 86 | 1,290 |
| TSB[5] | Oct 86 | 1,360 | 100 | 50 | 85 | 70 | 476 |
| British Gas | Dec 86 | 5,600 | 135 | 50 | 62.5 | 25 | 518 |
| British Airways | Feb 87 | 900 | 125 | 65 | 109 | 68 | 317 |
| Rolls Royce | May 87 | 1,360 | 170 | 85 | 147 | 73 | 496 |
| BAA[6] | Jul 87 | 920 | 245 | 100 | 146 | 46 | 172 |

SOURCE:Compiled by author from data in Financial Times of London

NOTES: (1) First day of trading in the shares. The offer for sale is usually made about two weeks previously.

(2) Opening price of the shares in their partly paid form at the close of the first day of trading.

(3) Percentage gain with respect to the partly paid price.

(4) 50% of BT's shares were offered for sale. In all other cases except BAA (see [6]), 100% of the equity was offered in one go.

(5) TSB (Trustee Savings Bank) was not a privatization in the strictest sense: the proceeds from the sale were retained by the TSB.

(6) The figures above relate to the 75% of BAA sold by an offer for sale. The remaining 25% were offered by tender: the average tender price accepted was 290 pence.

successful applicants for shares. Above all, it has been this effect that has made privatization a political winner.

The only recent case where this strategy has come unstuck was the sale of the government's residual 31.5 percent stake in BP in October 1987. Shares were priced at 330*p*, which was about 6 percent less than the then prevailing market price of BP shares. In fact, the real discount on the market price was rather greater, by perhaps another 6 percent, because the new shares were payable in three installments, and account should be taken of the interest yield on the second and third installments. The prospectus for the new BP shares was issued on 15 October, and the closing date for the offer for sale was 28 October. The crash in world equity markets began on 19 October, and by the close of the BP offer, the London market had fallen by 28 percent from its level two weeks previously. Investors generally avoided the issue and the underwriters (who may have hedged against market risk at least in part) were left with the great bulk of the shares. Partly-paid shares opened at 85*p*, representing a 29 percent loss on the first installment of 120*p*. Thus, despite the dramatic events surrounding the sale, even if investors bought the shares (rather than sensibly avoiding them), the BP issue would not affect our conclusion that, relative to the market, purchase of the portfolio of privatization stocks would have been a highly lucrative investment strategy.

## THE BRITISH REGULATORY MODEL

After the intention to privatize British Telecom was announced in July 1982, the government was confronted with the problem of how to deal with the very substantial market power that would be enjoyed by the resulting private company. The broad principles of the solution that emerged were subsequently applied in the British Gas privatization and are likely also to be followed in the planned privatizations of the electricity and water industries. We have provided a fuller account of the new regulatory structures elsewhere (Vickers and Yarrow 1988) and here will point to only a few general characteristics of the "British model".

Broadly speaking, regulatory duties are divided among three parties: the relevant secretary of state (Minister of the Crown), a specialized regulatory body (e.g. the Office of Telecommunications), and the Monopolies and Mergers Commission (MMC). The secretary of state grants a license to operate to the private monopolist which imposes certain duties upon the firm, including an initial pricing constraint, and which typically lasts for a 25-year period. The regulatory body monitors compliance with the license and has a range of duties that is laid down in statute. License conditions can be varied in a number of ways: for example, the director general of the regulatory body can alter conditions if the regulated firm is agreeable, and the secretary of state also has restricted powers in these matters. However, the most important method of varying license conditions is via a reference to the Monopolies and Mergers Commission. If the director general believes, say, that the pricing constraint should be tightened and if, as is likely in such circumstances, the firm disagrees, the issue is referred to the Commission for adjudication. The recommendations of the Commission must then be implemented by the director general.

In respect of license conditions, there has been considerable debate about the most appropriate method of regulating prices. (Complete deregulation was contemplated for telecommunications but rejected because of the perceived weakness of competitive threats to the dominant company.) Options examined included versions of rate-of-return regulation and an output-related profits tax but, in the event, the government adopted what has become known as "RPI-X" regulation. In its basic form, the RPI-X method of price control requires an average of the firm's regulated products and services to fall in real terms by at least X percent annually for so long as the initial formula (set out in the license) continues to hold. That is to say, the maximum permitted annual increase in average price is equal to the rate of inflation of the retail price index (RPI) minus X percent. The number X is chosen in the light of prospects for technological advance and demand growth in the industry.

On the face of it, the RPI-X method of price control seems to have important advantages over methods of rate-of-return regulation familiar in the United States, and these advantages were stressed in early government documents on the issue (Littlechild 1983). For example, it appears to limit the regulatory burden to simply checking that price changes comply with the formula, thereby reducing the danger that a particular interest group will be able to exert undue influence on regulatory decisions. Moreover, incentives for productive efficiency seem good, because the firm reaps the marginal benefit of any innovation and cost reduction that it achieves. Similarly, strategic over-capitalization in the manner of Averch and Johnson (1962) appears to be avoided. (Whatever the current status of the A-J model in the U.S., its implications have had some impact on the development of regulatory policies in Britain.)

Before assessing the merits of RPI-X regulation, it will be useful to set out some of the details of its operation in the three instances so far -- British Telecom (BT), British Gas (BG), and the British Airports Authority (BAA). Table 4.5 shows for each case:

Table 4.5: The Operation of RPI-X Regulation

| | British Telecom | British Gas | British Airports Authority |
|---|---|---|---|
| (1) Regulated | Local and truck calls, line rentals. | Gas supplied to domestic users (more precisely, those using no more than 25% therms per annum. | Airport charges (for departing passengers, aircraft landings, (Heathrow, Gatwick and Stansted). |
| Unregulated | International calls, payphone calls, customer premises equipment, telex, mobile radio, vans, etc. | Gas supplied to industrial and commercial users. Connection charges, appliance sales, etc. | Airport charges at Scottish airports. Commercial activities (e.g., retail). |
| (2) x = ?; base year prices | x = 3; pre-existing price structure | x = 2; pre-existing price structure | x = 1; pre-existing price structure |
| (3) Price index/average | The weights in the price index for year t are proportional to contributions to turnover in the previous year. | Average price per therm | Average revenue per passenger |
| (4) Scope for relative price changes within overall constraint. | BT has undertaken that RPI+2 will apply to domestic rental charges. Oftel has investigated rebalancing between local and truck call charges, and has investigated some other individual prices. | The standing charge (i.e.,the fixed element of the charge to the user) cannot increase by more than RPI in any year. | RPI-1 applies to airport charges at Heathrow and Gatwick individually, as well as the group of airports. |
| (5) Adjustments for exogenous cost changes. | None | Full adjustment is made for changes in the cost of gas supplies to British Gas. | Adjustment is made for 75% of additional costs arising from Government airport security requirements. |
| (6) Timing of regulatory review | After five years (i.e., after 1989) price control will operate by a license modification either agreed with BT, or or imposed on BT after an MMC recommendation on public interest grounds. | Price control will be reviewed after five years (in 1991) following an MMC investigation. | Price control will be reviewed after five years (in 1992) by the Civil Aviation Authority following an MMC investigation. |

(1) which prices are regulated and which are not;

(2) the level of X and the base-year price structure;

(3) how the price index/average is constructed;

(4) the scope for changes in relative prices within the overall constraint;

(5) whether adjustment is made for changes in "exogenous" factors (e.g. major input costs); and

(6) the anticipated timing and method of regulatory review.

Although some of these matters may appear to be of relatively minor importance, they can in fact have significant implications for economic behavior. Consider, for example, the method of constructing the (regulated) price index for British Gas. A relatively straightforward piece of analysis shows that it generates incentives for a profit-maximizing firm to adopt an inefficient price structure (i.e. relative prices deviate from Ramsey prices). The reason for this can easily be seen if the price constraint in a given year is written as

$$\Sigma s_i p_i \leq p^*,$$

where $p^*$ is the maximum allowed value of the index and $s_i$ is the output share of market/service i. By expanding lower-priced outputs, British gas is able to shift the index weights in such a way as to loosen the price constraint. (The weights attached to lower prices are increased and the weights attached to higher prices are decreased, thus lowering the value of the index for any given set of prices.) As a consequence, therefore, the company faces incentives to overprice peak supplies and underprice off-peak supplies.

Only in telecommunications, where there have now been three years of RPI-3 regulation, is there as yet a significant history of pricing decisions. BT has made extensive use of its rights to alter relative prices within the regulated basket: within two years of privatization it increased peak-time local call charges by around 25 percent and reduced peak-time long-distance call charges by about the same percentage (Oftel 1987, Table 4.2). Oftel conducted a detailed enquiry into whether "rebalancing" of tariffs to that extent was justified, concluding that it was, but that further increases in local call charges would probably not be necessary. Oftel has reviewed other individual prices -- some that come under RPI-3 regulation (e.g. rental charges, differentials relating to time of day, and discounts on some long-distance routes) and some that do not (e.g. access lines, private leased lines, and telex services).

Here several points are worth noting. First, Oftel has certainly not confined its activities in price regulation to checking that annual price increases comply with the RPI-3 formula: it has scrutinized individual pricing decisions (including some outside the scope of the RPI-3 formula) in detail. Second, there is nothing in the legislation that required Oftel to be so active in price regulation. Third, Oftel's formal powers to regulate individual prices are limited. The ultimate step would be for Oftel to go to the Monopolies and Mergers Commission to seek a modification of BT's license to bring the prices in question under control. Thus, there exists a kind of bargaining game between BT and Oftel, in which negotiating strengths depend partly upon assessments of what would happen in the event of an MMC reference. Fourth, information conditions are of particular importance, because Oftel's power diminishes rapidly the less it knows. Oftel has therefore been pressing (an often reluctant) BT to provide regular flows of accounting information about all aspects of its business, although Oftel's rights to acquire information are by no means clearly laid out in the original legislation.

As well as investigating particular prices, in view of BT's profitability record -- the 1986-87 rate of return on capital employed was 21.1 percent in historical cost terms, and rising steadily -- Oftel has also looked at the general level of the company's prices. Although the director general of Oftel has so far decided that BT's rate of profit does not call for a modification of the price control formula so soon after privatization, he has made it quite clear that he would seriously consider exercising his powers to seek a modification if he found BT's rate of return on capital to be significantly above the minimum acceptable level in competitive capital markets (Oftel 1986, p. 9). Therefore, as in the cases of BG and BAA, a regulatory price review could occur before the end of the initial five-year period, and there is every indication that BT's rate of return will be the main consideration whenever regulatory review does take place.

It follows that the British RPI-X system is not dissimilar to American rate-of-return regulation, and contrary views simply reflect a misapprehension of what has happened. It is true that indexation facilitates reliance upon longer periods between regulatory reviews, but, while the legislation creates expectations that price controls will not be varied for five years, it does not require that this be the outcome. The regulatory lag is not exogenous, nor will review decisions be unaffected by rates of return.

Thus, RPI-X by itself does not avoid the incentive problems of rate-of-return regulation. These arise essentially because of the monopoly of information of the regulated firm. In principle, permitted price increases should be related to the potential for internal efficiency gains and cost reduction, but if the only indication of that potential is the actual cost level of the firm, there is an awkward trade-off to be faced. Allocative efficiency requires that the firm's prices should move as its costs change, but incentives for internal efficiency depend on the firm retaining benefits from cost reduction. Roughly speaking, the better the information that is available to regulators, the more favorable will be the trade-off. However, British policy has been particularly weak in this crucial area: legislation has granted only limited powers to regulators in respect of the acquisition of relevant information and, as we will argue below, opportunities to increase information flows by encouraging greater competition in the industries concerned have been missed.

In conclusion, the RPI-X method of price control does not in practice have the apparent advantages mentioned at the beginning of this section. First, the regulatory task is not necessarily limited to simply checking that price changes comply with the formula, and if it were to be so restricted, the methods by which average prices are calculated would likely lead to inefficient tariff structures. However, it is not yet clear what powers Oftel and Ofgas will have to implement their regulatory policies -- the legislation has not given them many teeth -- and much will depend upon the attitudes of the MMC and government if and when the director generals seek tighter regulation. Secondly, the effect of RPI-X regulation on incentives for cost efficiency depends very much upon the timing of regulatory reviews and the information that will be available to the regulatory bodies and the MMC. Given the information monopolies of the regulated firms, if it turns out that reviews occur regularly at five-year intervals, the incentives for cost reductions in the latter parts of the intervals will not be particularly good: the firm will have incentives to pad costs in the hope of being able to induce a more favorable pricing constraint for the following five years than would otherwise have been permitted. On the other hand, if reviews are more sporadic and are triggered by rate-of-return movements, the cost-plus aspect of price regulation is even more apparent. Either way, although the dynamic setting may be different, the British model offers no easy escape from the type of problems that are familiar from the regulatory experience in the United States.

## COMPETITION AND REGULATION IN TELECOMMUNICATIONS

The RPI-X method of price control is just one element of the regulatory policies being developed for privatized firms with market power. Again, because it is the only case for which is there is a significant history of post-privatization decisions, in this section we will focus on the regime of competition and regulation that has evolved for British Telecom.

Table 4.6 provides some background for our brief discussion by listing some of the main recent events in the British telecommunications industry. Throughout the period, there has been a tension in policy-making between two, central objectives: the desire to promote the well-being of BT (and also Mercury), and the desire to encourage competition and more effective regulation. For the most part, the first of these objectives has been given the greater emphasis by the government. Liberalization has occurred to a limited extent, but BT was transferred from public to private ownership with its dominant positions intact, and with a relatively light regulatory rein.

First, there was no restructuring of BT to promote competition, as happened to AT&T in the United States: BT's management -- a crucial interest group whose cooperation was important in what was a bold and, at the time, unprecedented exercise -- was opposed to the idea, and the government's desire to privatize profitably and speedily stood in the way. BT was therefore sold as an integrated national unit with dominant positions in network operation (at local, long-distance, and international levels), the provision of telecommunications services of all kinds, and the supply (though until the MITEL acquisition not the manufacture) of customer premises equipment. However, there are several ways in which BT could have been split up in order to promote greater competition and more effective regulation. The operation of long-distance and local networks could have been separated, perhaps with several local or regional network operators, as in the United States. The division responsible for supplying customer premises equipment could have been made into an independent entity, and the same is true of BT's interest in cellular radio and value-added services. The MITEL manufacturing operation could also be under separate ownership, as it would have been if the merger had been blocked.

Apart from facilitating greater competition in long distance operations, restructuring would have had broken BT's information monopoly: capital markets and regulators alike would have been able to compare the performances of local or regional monopolies, opening up prospects of creating stronger incentives for internal efficiency. Thus, for example, the threat of takeover is

Table 4.6: Recent Events in the British Telecommunications Industry

1981 - British Telecommunications Act: separated telecom from the postal service and established BT; introduced some competition (e.g., in apparatus supply and value added services).

- Beesley Report on liberalization of BT's network: recommended unrestricted resale of BT's capacity.

1982 - White Paper announced Government's intention to privatize BT.

1983 - Littlechild Report on profit regulation recommended version of the RPI-X method of price control.

1984 - Telecommunications Act, together with Government licensing policy, established the framework of competition and regulation for the industry:

(i) no restructuring of BT (as was happening to AT&T in the USA)
(ii) duopoly of BT and Mercury (i.e., no further entry) in public networks at least until 1990
(iii) RPI-3 regulation of BT's prices
(iv) no unrestricted resale for the time being; value added services only
(v) cable companies able to offer telephone services but only in conjunction with BT or Mercury
(vi) Oftel as regulatory body.

- Offer for sale at 130 pence per share of 50.2 per cent of BT's equity.

1985 - Cellnet (owned by BT and Securicor) and Racal-Vodaphone launched rival cellular radio services.

- Oftel ruled that there should be full interconnection between BT's and Mercury's networks.

- BT increased rental and local call charges substantially and reduced many trunk call charges.

1986 - BT acquired a majority stake in Mitel, a Canadian manufacturer of PABX equipment.

- Mercury's public telephone service began.

- BT introduced further sharp increases in local call charges and reductions in trunk call charges.

1987 - Twelve week industrial dispute by engineers.

likely to have had a much more powerful influence on the behavior of a local/regional network operator than it has had on BT. Similarly, regulators would have been able partially to link the allowable prices for any one firm to the performance of other, similar firms, thus mitigating the cost-plus problems associated with the regulation of a single firm.

The separation of network and equipment supply would also have diminished the danger of anti-competitive behavior. Much of recent telecommunications policy has been concerned with the possibility that BT will restrict or distort competition in apparatus supply by virtue of its dominant position as a network operator. Separating the two businesses would have eased this problem by reducing <u>incentives</u> for anti-competitive behavior. Instead the task is now to regulate <u>conduct</u> by seeking to prevent cross-subsidization, the passing of information, and so on. In a sense, this involves attempting to simulate separation, but information and enforcement problems inevitably cause difficulties.

Second, although the government should be credited for the introduction of liberalizing measures in areas such as apparatus supply and value added supplies, in a number of respects it has deliberately limited the extent of competition in the telecommunications industry. The two most important limitations of competition are the decisions not to license any public network operators other than BT and Mercury, and not to allow simple resale of capacity, at least until the end of the decade in both cases.

Two justifications have been put forward for the restrictions on entry into the industry. The first is based upon familiar arguments about the desirability of preventing "destructive competition" or the wasteful duplication of facilities in conditions of natural monopoly. The second, and the one upon which the government has largely relied, is a variation of the "infant industry" argument: Mercury should be protected while it establishes a foothold in the marketplace. Both justifications are relatively weak.

The natural monopoly (duopoly) arguments are speculative in that they depend upon propositions -- about <u>both</u> cost conditions and the non-sustainability of reasonably efficient equilibria in the assumed conditions -- that lack strong empirical backing. Given the potentially-beneficial incentive effects of entry threats in markets that have long been protected by statutory entry barriers, rather stronger evidence would be required to justify the conclusion that the industry should be spared normal market disciplines. In respect of the "infant industry" argument, while there is a good case for protecting Mercury from anti-competitive behavior by BT -- and it is unfortunate that resolution of the question of interconnection was held up for as long as it was -- it is not at all clear that Mercury should receive assistance beyond measures to ensure that competition is on fair terms. Given the relative sizes of the two firms, a ban on further entry gives more assistance to BT than to Mercury and, by increasing incentives for implicit collusion and peaceful coexistence, may weaken the degree of competition between them.

Third, the RPI-3 formula was relatively generous to BT, as its subsequent profit performance has shown. BT enjoys, and has used, wide scope to alter relative prices in the basket of regulated services. Rebalancing of tariffs has thus far been justified on cost grounds but, if it were allowed to go on unchecked, it could seriously jeopardize the competitive challenge from Mercury: BT could finance a price-war in long distance services simply by raising local call charges, and could use this threat to induce more accommodating behavior from its rival. In this context, as in many others, Oftel has emerged as a vital supplement to the price control formula, although, as already argued, its powers will depend partly upon the still unknown attitudes of the MMC. (In September 1987, the director general indicated that he would like the Commission to review the price control conditions of the license in 1988 and, among other things, to consider the possibility of linking allowable prices to measures of service quality, about which there has been considerable public criticism in the post-privatization period.)

It is perhaps not altogether surprising that the desire to promote the well-being of BT was emphasized at the expense of more effective competition and regulation. It was favored by those in government who were most concerned with the objectives of reducing the PSBR and widening share ownership, by their merchant bank advisers, and, of course, by the management of BT. Especially in view of the government's desire to privatize BT speedily, good relations with the company's management were of the highest importance, and managers therefore came to have considerable influence. Although their unions fought vigorously against privatization, employees of BT also had a natural interest in having a competitive and regulatory regime that enhanced the company's profits and prospects. In contrast, the interests of consumers and of some potential competitors in the industry -- groups that would have benefitted from more effective competition and regulation -- were given relatively low priorities. For the moment, these groups must rely on Oftel successfully continuing an actively pro-competitive approach within its limited powers. However, consumer complaints about tariff levels and, more vocally, about service standards have now become a politically-sensitive issue, and it is likely that there will be strong pressure for the competitive and regulatory framework to be substantially revised when it comes up for review by the MMC.

## COMPETITION AND REGULATION IN OTHER PRIVATIZATIONS

The previous section was devoted entirely to BT because it is only in the telecommunications industry that the new regulatory system has been in operation for any length of time. Our assessments of policy in other industries -- gas, airports, airways, road transport, and water -- will therefore be briefer and more preliminary in nature.

### British Gas

The regulatory regime for British Gas has many similarities with that for BT. The legal possibility of competition in gas distribution and sales was created before privatization by the 1982 Oil and Gas (Enterprise) Act, which removed the statutory monopsony position of British Gas in respect of purchases of gas supplies. When privatization occurred in 1986, a version of RPI-X regulation was introduced for charges to domestic and small volume commercial and industrial users (collectively known as tariff customers): X was set equal to two, and the formula allowed full adjustment for changes in the cost of gas supplies to British Gas (i.e. it contained an explicit cost-plus component). The Office of Gas Supply (Ofgas) was established as the regulatory authority along similar lines to Oftel. However, to an even greater extent than in telecommunications, British Gas was transferred to the private sector with its monopoly and monopsony powers (and its vertically-integrated structure) more or less fully intact: the philosophy of "regulation with a light hand" was implemented in a rather extreme form.

Policy weaknesses are evident in at least four major areas. First, there was no attempt to restructure the company before privatization. It would, for example, have been perfectly feasible to split British Gas into a number of independent, regional distribution companies and a national transmission company: the publicly-owned industry had been regionally organized in the period before 1972, and British Gas had preserved major aspects of this earlier structure in its organization. Compared with the creation of a private-sector, national monopoly/monopsony, this would have facilitated: greater competition in wholesale markets; the elimination of the geographic cross-subsidization practiced by British Gas; the acquisition of information by regulators; greater capital market pressures for internal efficiency (because of greater information and more credible threats of takeover); and, since the national common carrier would have had fewer incentives than British Gas to deter new entrants, greater potential competition in the gas sales markets from offshore producers.

Second, the pricing formula for tariff customers enshrined the earlier pricing philosophy of British Gas, which was closer to average cost pricing than marginal cost pricing. The privatized company was allowed to inherit the long-term gas supply contracts of its nationalized predecessor, including many that were negotiated in the 1960s when energy prices were much lower in real terms than market prices today. For most of the recent period, therefore, average purchase prices have been well below marginal opportunity costs, and retail prices have been based on the former. By explicitly linking the maximum allowable average price to average purchase prices, the government chose to maintain this distortion (in the gas privatization, short-term consumer interests appear to have been accorded a greater weight than in telecommunications).

Third, little attempt was made to promote effective liberalization of the market by encouraging actual and potential competitors to the dominant supplier. The privatization legislation barred entry into the (regulated) tariff markets, and the only prospects for greater now competition lie in the (unregulated) markets for larger industrial and commercial users. The fact that the 1982 Act removed legal barriers to entry into the latter markets is of only limited practical significance, because formidable obstacles to potential competition have been left in place. These include: the access of British Gas to low-priced supplies under the terms of older purchase contracts; British Gas' unrestrained ability to respond to entry threats by localized price cutting; and the informational, strategic, and tactical advantages that flow from British Gas' ownership and control of <u>all</u> relevant pipelines. In fact, there has been no entry into the market in the period since the 1982 Act, and the prospects for competition continue to be bleak.

Fourth, Ofgas has been granted only very limited regulatory powers, and the longer-term regulatory framework is undefined and uncertain. For example, British Gas must supply accounting information to Ofgas only in relation to its gas supply business <u>as a whole</u>. Separate accounts for different regions, for the regulated and unregulated parts of the business, and for the operation of the national transmission system are <u>not</u> required. The ability of Ofgas to monitor price-cost variations among different outputs and, in the event of disputes, to make determinations as to the appropriate charges for use of the British Gas pipelines by third-party suppliers is therefore considerably impaired. A remarkable illustration of the weakness of the regulatory regime occurred in July 1987 when, after taking legal advice, British Gas attempted to withhold information about its gas purchase contracts that was needed by Ofgas to determine whether or not the price changes that had just been announced did in fact comply with the pricing formula.

**British Airports Authority (now BAA)**

Many of the same criticisms apply to the privatization of BAA. Its seven airports -- Heathrow, Gatwick, and Stansted in the London area, and the four Scottish lowland airports -- were sold as a group, and no attempt was made to foster competition by restructuring. Separating the ownership of Heathrow and Gatwick, for example, would have increased competition for traffic at off-peak times when capacity constraints do not bind and would have tended to reduce some cross-subsidies in the existing structure of airport pricing (see below). Separation would also have sharpened capital market pressures by facilitating performance comparisons and, by the same token, would have enhanced the effectiveness of regulation by the Civil Aviation Authority.

The regime of price control that has been adopted (see Table 4.5) also perpetuates inefficiencies that have long existed in BAA's pricing structure. BAA's income comes from two sources: traffic activities (the landing, take-off, and parking of aircraft, and the handling of passengers) and commercial activities (franchises to retailers, banks, caterers, and rents from hotels, car parks, etc.). Commercial activities are very lucrative: BAA's terminals are prime site shopping areas; there is little competition among retailers; and the revenues are boosted by the large (and arbitrary) tax concessions given to tax-free and duty-free goods. On the other hand, traffic activities are loss-making and are heavily cross-subsidized by the profits from commercial activities and their associated tax concessions. This state of affairs is not entirely the fault of the British government: it is enshrined by the 1983 Memorandum of Understanding between Britain and the United States, which states that the London airports should make no more than a reasonable rate of return on traffic and commercial activities combined. There are, however, also inefficiencies in the <u>structure</u> of BAA's traffic charges. In relation to marginal costs, charges are lower at peak than at off-peak times, and Stansted in particular is heavily cross-subsidized (Starkie and Thompson 1985).

Given the government's rejection of the idea of separating ownership to promote competition and the limited room for maneuvering on pricing policy, it is hard to see how the privatization of BAA can significantly enhance the efficiency of its operations. Quite apart from pricing behavior, BAA's investment plans will continue to be subject to close government involvement:

airport expansion in densely-populated areas necessarily raises significant public interest issues. Indeed, it is interesting to note that a major round of investment decisions for Britain's airports was announced in the 1985 Airports White Paper in the run up to BAA's privatization. If the privatization of BAA had been motivated by a belief in the superiority of market forces and private decision-making in these matters, it would hardly have been appropriate for the government to initiate such an important investment program so soon before the sale.

We conclude that, above all else, the privatization of BAA was simply the transfer to private hands of a monopoly with valuable property assets and tax concessions. Public borrowing, share ownership, and distributional objectives were to the fore, and efficiency effects were very much a secondary consideration. The government will continue to exert a strong influence on major aspects of BAA's behavior, notably investment programs, and allocative inefficiencies in the pricing structure will persist.

**British Airways**

British Airways (BA) was always a prime candidate for privatization, but its transfer to the private sector was delayed until early 1987 by competition law suits and disputes concerning competition on North Atlantic routes. The company was profitable, and a change in its ownership raised far fewer problems for policy regarding competition and regulation than the privatization of utilities such as BT and British Gas. BA had been managed according to broadly-commercial criteria in the public sector, and an elaborate system of domestic and international regulations already existed.

Nevertheless, a number of significant questions concerning competition and regulation did remain to be resolved at the time of privatization. First, there were fears that BA, as the dominant U.K. airline, might exploit its market power more energetically when it became a privately-owned company -- a danger that could have been reduced by the structural remedy of reducing its relative size (e.g. by route transfers) and/or by tougher measures to prevent anti-competitive conduct. Second, once privatization had taken place, it would become more difficult for the government to change its airline policies. Such changes would bring forth the accusation that the government had broken commitments upon which the share prospectus was based, and, to the extent that they had adverse consequences for BA's profits, would offend the (intentionally) large number of shareholders.

In the event, although the U.K. government has been a strong advocate of deregulation and increased competition in the domestic and international airline industries, precedents set earlier in the privatization program were followed, and BA was sold without any accompanying attempts to reduce its market power. The most important policy statement in the pre-privatization period was the 1984 *White Paper on Airline Competition Policy* (U.K. Department of Transport 1984a), which followed a major review of the question by the Civil Aviation Authority. In the White Paper, the government declared that its aims were to promote competition in all markets and to encourage a sound and competitive multi-airline industry in Britain, but it failed to act on some of the most important recommendations of the CAA. In particular, the CAA had proposed a number of route transfers from BA to other airlines, notably British Caledonian (B-Cal), and a corresponding reduction of BA's position at Gatwick and provincial airports. The government rejected the CAA's proposals under strong pressure from BA's chairman, Lord King: BA and B-Cal swapped some routes, but there was no major restructuring to stimulate competition.

The impending privatization of BA can only have strengthened Lord King's bargaining position -- because his cooperation was important for an early and successful flotation -- and the outcome is another example of a case where preoccupation with ownership transfer was inimical to the implementation of pro-competitive policies. In the event, the limited route swaps that did occur failed to save B-Cal from serious financial difficulties in 1986 and 1987. The value of its routes to the Gulf was reduced by the recent oil price collapse, and transatlantic traffic fell as a result of the Chernobyl and Libyan incidents. In July 1987, less than six months after privatization, BA announced an agreed takeover of B-Cal, its main U.K. competitor. The bid was referred to the Monopolies and Mergers Commission, which concluded that the proposed merger would not operate against the public interest provided that a number of stated conditions were satisfied. After a contest with the Scandinavian airline, SAS, BA announced in December 1987 that it had successfully acquired B-Cal. The government's multi-airline policy is, therefore, now in complete disarray.

**National Bus Company**

The most radical of the government's measures to promote increased competition have been in road and bus services where, significantly, the political influence of incumbent managements has been slight. The Transport

Acts of 1980 and 1985 dismantled the regulatory structure that had lasted for 50 years and opened up new possibilities for competition. The 1980 Act deregulated express coach services, and there followed a bout of intense competition between the dominant incumbent firm, National Express (a subsidiary of the publicly-owned National Bus Company (NBC)), and new entrants. However, National Express soon disposed of most of the challengers: as well as pricing very aggressively, National Express enjoyed important non-price advantages by virtue of its established nationwide network, its customer awareness, and its privileged access to major terminals, such as the Victoria Coach Station in London. Nevertheless, although National Express regained its dominant position, the pattern (including frequency) and quality of services do appear to have been changed more durably for the better by competition, and rivalry between coach and rail has been increased.

The 1985 Act extended deregulation to local bus services. In many areas, deregulation has as yet had little effect, and few challenges to incumbent operators have been forthcoming. But in some places, competition has been extremely vigorous. In Oxford, for example, competition has led to a dramatic increase in the number of buses on major routes -- and hence to greater service frequencies -- and reductions in some fares. A cost has been serious traffic congestion in the city center, and there has been a re-emergence of some of the aggressive tactics that were a feature of parts of the industry before regulation in 1930. These allegedly included racing to stops, blocking rivals' vehicles, duplicating their services, painting over rivals' timetable displays, and even intimidating passengers! In short, in the places where actual, as opposed to potential, competition has come about, it has so far been unstable and at times chaotic. Whether or not the industry will move to a pattern of widespread, stable, and effective competition remains to be seen.

The 1985 Act also provided for privatization of bus services. The NBC is carrying out a program for selling its 70 or so subsidiary companies. Many of these are management buy-outs of local bus operations. Local government authorities have also been empowered to transfer their bus undertakings to private hands. It is too soon to judge the effect that privatization will have on competition in the industry, but the aggressive responses (while still in public ownership) of National Express to competition in long-distance coach services and of local bus undertakings faced with competitive threats suggest that behavior depends more on the competitive environment than upon ownership *per se*. Established incumbent firms may soon be able to see off the competition in many areas, especially in view of the features of bus competition referred to above. Although service to the consumer may be improved by the process, there is also a danger that privatization will simply lead to market power being exercised by private rather than public operators. If that happens, the call will no doubt be for some form of re-regulation, and there is a possibility that the wheel will turn full circle.

**The Water Authorities**

Plans to privatize the 10 water authorities in England and Wales are currently being developed. Natural monopoly conditions in the industry imply that the prospects for competition in the product market are virtually nil, and regulatory policy must safeguard the environment as well as containing market power. Under public ownership, the organization of the industry has been based upon the concept of "integrated river basin management", according to which each water authority is responsible for every aspect of the water cycle in its catchment areas, including river management and pollution control, as well as delivering water to customers and disposing of sewage and other effluence. The government's initial plans for privatizing the industry maintained this principle -- the water authorities to be sold in their existing forms -- but these were changed under pressure from a variety of interest groups (most notably the Country Landowners Association, which carries some weight in Conservative circles) that were concerned about the prospect of environmental regulation being placed in the hands of private companies. Instead, it is now proposed that there should be a National Rivers Authority, responsible for environmental regulation functions, in addition to the 10 water authorities.

The privatization of the water industry again illustrates some of the points we have stressed in relation to the earlier cases. The government's first line of approach was to avoid any restructuring of the industry, thus accommodating the interests of incumbent managements and facilitating the process of flotation (companies could be brought quickly to the market with prospecti based upon established track records). Options that would have favored the development of greater competition -- if not for the business of the industry's customers, then at least for rights to provide services via, for example, various types of competitive franchising -- were correspondingly set aside. However, in this case, because of the environmental dimensions of the policies, the proposals ran into opposition from other, well-organised and politically-influential pressure groups and, for once, management and financial interests did not hold sway. The result has been that most of the incumbent managements have now come out firmly against the revised proposals, and the government is facing an increasingly-difficult political situation.

In respect of the more technical aspects of regulatory policy, it is likely to prove extremely difficult to devise a satisfactory incentive structure for the privatized water companies. Quite apart from the environmental issues, the position is complicated by: the existence, in addition to the 10 water authorities, of 28 privately-owned statutory water companies, currently regulated by dividend controls; the widespread involvement in sewerage services of local government authorities on an agency basis; and the current method of charging for domestic services, which is based upon a fixed charge that is related to property rental values estimated for local taxation purpose, and which is therefore unrelated to service usage. The charging system will necessarily have to be changed if existing government proposals to reform local authority finance eventually enter the statute book and, while water metering may turn out to be the longer-term solution, the immediate implications of these reforms are highly uncertain.

Perhaps of most concern is the question of the incentives for improvements in service quality and investment under privatization. Price controls of the RPI-X type give profit-seeking firms incentives to reduce service quality if, by so doing, they can cut costs since, unlike in competitive industries, customers are unable to switch to alternative suppliers (i.e. the revenue consequences of quality reductions are small in magnitude). Water pipelines and sewers have extremely long asset lives, and if private discount rates exceed social discount rates -- as is likely in view of future regulatory uncertainties in Britain -- investment in building and maintaining such assets may turn out to be sub-optimally low. If these difficulties are to be overcome, therefore, regulators will have to be given considerable powers in respect of the control of service standards, and the explicit introduction of some form of cost-based method for adjusting allowable charges seems inevitable.

## The Electricity Supply Industry

The government is also committed to privatizing the electricity supply industry (ESI) during its current term in office. This will easily be the largest privatization of the program: the industry's assets are valued at a replacement cost of approximately £37 billion. The ESI in England and Wales consists of the Central Electricity Generating Board (CEGB), responsible for electricity generation and high-voltage transmission, and twelve Area Boards, which carry out distribution and retailing activities. The general policy of the industry is discussed in the Electricity Council, a consultative body whose members are mainly drawn from the CEGB and the Area Boards. Scotland has its own electricity boards (two in number), which are fully vertically-integrated in respect of generation, transmission, and distribution.

As in the gas industry, competition in electricity supply has been notable for its absence. The 1983 Energy Act removed certain statutory barriers to entry in electricity generation, but left the CEGB with a substantial influence both over the prices that the Area Boards could offer for the supplies of private companies and over the terms upon which transmission facilities would be available to its potential rivals. As a result, no significant entry has taken place since the Act was introduced.

The most pressing question that the government has to tackle in determining its policies for the future of the ESI is whether or not to embark upon a program of significantly increasing competitive pressures in the industry. One possibility is that the CEGB could be split into a number of independent generating companies. The pressures working against reorganization are similar to those discussed in the telecommunications and gas cases: incumbent managements are strongly opposed; the government's financial advisers would prefer flotation of existing organizations with performance records; and privatization, and hence the realization of sales proceeds, would be delayed by restructuring. In this case, there is also the problem that the existence of several generating companies might not lead to effective competition in any case: the technology of the industry places a high premium on coordination among generators in arranging supplies. However, in view of mounting consumer disquiet about the post-privatization performance of BT, back-bench Conservative members of Parliament are rather keener than they were in the past to see the introduction of measures that would increase competition in the market. Even without restructuring, there are likely to be greater political pressures in this direction than there were in the case of gas privatization.

Natural monopoly conditions in electricity distribution imply that increased competition will be hard to achieve in the downstream parts of the industry -- although the regional structure of distribution would permit "yardstick competition" (Shleifer 1985), and companies could compete for supplies in the wholesale market -- but the obstacles are fewer in electricity generation. In particular, even given the existence of a large incumbent generation and transmission company, it would be possible to increase competitive pressures significantly by allowing new entrants to bid for incremental capacity requirements (since much of the industry's existing stock of generating sets is relatively old and a major investment program is in prospect over the next 10 to 15 years). This would, however, require the implementation of strongly pro-competitive regulatory policies to prevent abuse of the CEGB's dominant market position, and privatization of the ESI will therefore be an interesting test of whether, because of shifting interest group strengths, there has been any substantive change in the government's priorities.

## CONCLUSIONS

The British privatization program has been acclaimed in many quarters as an economic and political success of the first order. It has led to a massive expansion in the number of private shareholders, including a large increase in the number of employees holding shares in their own firms, and state-involvement in industrial decision-making has been drastically reduced. Shareholders and managers of privatized firms, City of London financial institutions, and the government have all been pleased with the results, but has the program really been such an outstanding success?

The answer to this question depends upon the relative importance that is attached to the various objectives of privatization. Our own view is that the main criterion should be the impact of the program on the economic efficiency of the industries concerned. Performance in this respect depends upon the incentive structures faced by decision-makers within the industries, which in turn depend upon the conditions of competition and regulation under which they operate, as well as upon structures of ownership.

On this criterion (promoting economic efficiency), the British privatization program leaves much to be desired. Preoccupation with the question of ownership has directed attention away from issues of competition and regulation: in cases where the firms concerned possess substantial market power, procompetitive policy measures have been weak and frequently ineffective, and the initial regulatory frameworks have shown little appreciation of the complexity of the trade-offs that arise when attempting to prevent monopolistic abuses. Over time, there will be opportunities to correct some of these deficiencies -- Oftel already having a good record in this respect -- but, if anything, the initial legislation is likely to impede this process of adaptation. In short, major opportunities to improve industrial performance have been missed.

Greater economic efficiency has not, however, been the only goal of the privatization program, and the Government's ranking of priorities has been different from our own. Other major objectives have included widening share ownership and reducing the public-sector borrowing requirement.

Privatization has had significant positive effects in both respects but, in any overall assessment, account should also be taken of the existence of alternative policy instruments. Although the number of individual share owners in Britain has been approximately trebled, from around three to nine million, most of the new owners have undiversified portfolios which, in very many cases, consist of only one or two stocks. Moreover, other things equal, there is a steady tendency for numbers to fall as loyalty bonuses expire and investors realize their short-term capital gains. Finally, investing via institutions continues to enjoy fiscal privileges, which a government that was determined to widen share ownership would seek to abolish.

In respect of fiscal objectives, it can be asked why, in the first place, the public-sector borrowing requirement was elevated to such a central place in the Medium Term Financial Strategy. For the most part, asset disposals are a means of financing fiscal deficits, not of reducing them, and the latter effect only arises from the accounting conventions used for calculating the PSBR. At this point in the argument it is possible to set forth some rather Machiavellian arguments in favor of privatization. For example, privatization allowed the government to meet its declared fiscal target without reducing government expenditure or increasing taxation by as much as would otherwise have been necessary. Thus, during the second Thatcher administration, it allowed the government to claim that its fiscal policy was less expansionary than was actually the case. To the extent that it is believed that a mildly expansionary fiscal policy was desirable in this period, privatization might be regarded as having made a contribution to better policy-making, but since one of its aims has been to reduce government expenditure in relation to GDP, it is doubtful that the government would want to claim credit on these grounds.

The tensions between the economic efficiency and other objectives of the privatization program were not so apparent during its first phase (roughly 1979 to mid-1984), because companies like Amersham, British Aerospace, British Petroleum, Cable and Wireless, and Enterprise Oil operate in reasonably competitive environments. There was still the question of whether to sell shares relatively cheaply in order to promote wider share ownership or whether to maximize sales proceeds by tight pricing. On the whole, the latter goal prevailed during this period. Although Amersham shares were seriously underpriced, this was probably more of a technical misjudgment than a deliberate policy choice. In cases such as Britoil, Cable and Wireless, and Enterprise Oil, tight pricing was achieved by the use of tender offers.

Conflicts between policy objectives became more acute when attention was turned to major public utilities, such as telecommunications and gas. The option of restructuring those industries by regional and/or vertical separation in order to promote competition and more effective regulation was turned down, and public monopolies were sold off with their market power substantially intact. British Telecom faces more competition than it did before 1981, but liberalization could have gone much further. In the gas and airports industries, virtually nothing was done in the interests of competition. In public utilities, consumers have been given the protection of RPI-X regulation to hold the fort for the time being. Whether or not this form of regulation will promote greater efficiency in pricing, costs, and service standards is far from clear. The early signs are not altogether encouraging, but much will depend upon the attitudes and actions of regulatory bodies -- such as Oftel and Ofgas, the Monopolies and Mergers Commission, and government ministers. To say the least, the outlook is highly uncertain.

However, the major privatizations since 1984 (BT, British Gas, TSB, British Airways, Rolls Royce, and BAA) certainly *have* done a lot to widen share ownership. Low pricing of shares, together with perks for small investors, has offered irresistible monetary incentives to millions of people to subscribe for shares in privatized companies. Billions of pounds have been transferred, in the form of windfall gains, to successful applicants for shares from taxpayers in general. Windfall profits were highly popular with the millions of successful applicants, while the relative losses borne by taxpayers were thinly spread and much less perceptible. Moreover, the strategy for selling state assets has created difficulties for the Labour Party, because the prospect that they might return privatized firms to public ownership (or introduce tougher regulation) affects the value of the shares held by the millions of new shareholders. Therefore, in the second phase of the privatization program, which has emphasized the goal of wider share ownership, short-term political advantage has gone hand-in-hand with any philosophical desires to push back the frontiers of the state.

The razzmatazz associated with stock market fluctuations is the most immediately-visible aspect of privatization, but in the long run, we believe that the British privatization program will be judged in terms of its effect on economic efficiency. By failing to introduce sufficiently-effective frameworks of competition and regulation before privatizing such industries as telecommunications and gas, the government has lost a major opportunity to tackle fundamental problems experienced in the past under public ownership. By pushing the program too far and too fast, the government is undermining the long-run success of privatization in Britain.

# Privatization in Britain: Comment*

Sir Alan Walters**

Although I find myself in agreement with much of this paper, particularly with the strictures against retaining monopolies, I cannot commend it as a well-balanced account and assessment of the problems, promise, and performance of privatization in Britain.

There are significant errors of omission. Perhaps the most serious is the lack of any systematic consideration of the great legal, administrative, and political problems and obstacles to the process. These, in my view, dominate the issue. Second, although there are many references to the relative efficiency of the privatized compared to the public monopoly, there is no consideration of any substantive evidence from comparisons of state-owned and private monopolies, yet there are many opportunities to observe the differential efficiency of ownership, holding other conditions, even the regulatory system, constant. Third, I find that the claims of the authors are not supported by intervening argument and evidence. For example, I can see no warrant for their asserting that the PSBR was the dominant motive for privatization. Fourth, I am surprised to see no mention of the immense

---

* This is a comment which I wrote in response to the version of the Vickers and Yarrow paper which was delivered by Professor Yarrow at the Privatization Conference. George Yarrow (and presumably John Vickers) appear to have accepted some of my criticisms but are silent on others. I have resisted the temptation to revise my comment, and it is here printed as it was originally presented. I believe the points still stand.

** The World Bank and American Enterprise Institute

changes in organization and management that have accompanied privatization. There is a new ethos -- but one would get no inkling of it from this paper.[1]

## OBJECTIVES OF PRIVATIZATION

The authors claim that the motives for privatization changed from first dissatisfaction with "performance", then "short-term budgetary considerations", and finally by "share ownership and distributional objectives". In discussing "performance", the authors cite the experience of imposing financial targets, "External Financial Limits" (or EFLs) and believe that large-scale privatization was unnecessary and the government need only to have tightened financial constraints on the nationalized industries and introduced greater competition into utilities.[2] But this ignores the corrupting process of political influence, as well as the deadly hand of Treasury control. The distortions of all decision-making in all nationalized industries are well documented. The British Steel investment program of the 1970s, Concorde, the atomic energy program, rail investment, as well as the political protection afforded to favored groups of workers, are all well known examples of the corrupting political process on industry.[3] Similarly, the control by the Treasury on investment was hardly the stuff of which enterprising businesses are made.

A lasting solution for the performance shortfall requires more than financial targets set by government: it requires <u>institutional</u> change to insulate business from pervasive political pressures and bureaucratic redtape. It requires new incentive systems and transformed motivations.

---

[1] The authors only discuss the Thatcher privatization. Yet substantial privatization took place in the Churchill government, in particular the privatization of trucking in the act of 1953. We have a long comparative history of relative efficiency under private and public ownership. The rump of British Road Services (the nationalized trucking concern 1947-53) came down the years, still nationalized and loss-making, as the National Freight Corporation. I carried out a detailed two-volume study of comparative efficiency, particularly with respect to pricing policies, of the private and publicly owned trucking industries. Similar privatizations, such as shipbuilding, occurred during the Heath Government of 1970-74. One would have thought this provided valuable evidence.

[2] The authors use the yardstick year 1979 as "by no means untypical". It was however the top of the boom.

[3] See Pryke (1983). He shows that productivity of both labor and capital was significantly below that in private industry and investment often had a negative return and marginal productivity was negative.

Some idea of the effects of public ownership could have been obtained from comparing publicly-owned and privately-owned businesses in the same environment and, to examine the authors' contention, where the nationalized firm was subject to "financial constraints". There are many such studies.[4] The more or less unequivocal result is that nationalization does matter a great deal. I cannot think why the authors do not even mention such studies.[5]

The PSBR motive is alleged to be the "decisive factor" in the decision to privatize the large nationalized concerns. They reflect on the "sobering thought (sic) that privatization was more influenced by an arbitrary accounting convention than by (the) cumulated knowledge (of economists)".[6] This implies that the Thatcher government was stupid enough to be fooled by its own conventions -- or alternatively, that Mrs. Thatcher cared only for (accounting) cosmetics, not economic substance. Not the Mrs. Thatcher I know!

I can find no evidence for the authors' claim; furthermore, it is quite inconsistent with my experience at No. 10 Downing Street during the period 1981-84. (Moreover, if the authors had looked at the *Financial Statement and Budget Report 1987/88* or the *Financial Times* of last Wednesday, November 4, they would have seen the proceeds of privatization separated from public expenditure (Chart 2.5 and Table 2.4, for example) -- and virtually all of the commentary is in terms of expenditure excluding privatization receipts).[7]

The authors' discussion of the malign effects of PSBR conventions concentrates on BP and Britoil. The use of revenue-bonds, with interest payments linked to the firm's performance, to finance exploration, etc., was certainly rejected in favor of sale of shares, but it was not the PSBR effect that settled or even substantially influenced the issue. Revenue bonds was

---

[4] See Pryke (1983). I have also carried out extensive studies in the trucking, bus, and the airport businesses.

[5] Nor do the authors even mention the daunting changes in management and wholesale reorganization that accompanied privatization in Britain.

[6] The authors do not tell us what, in their view, is the appropriate convention. If we exclude privatization receipts, should we not also exclude, on the other side, the massive government investment which puts corporations in shape for privatization? Would not therefore much of it "net out"?

[7] I do concede, however, that for some politicians and civil servants, the incentive to privatize may have come from PSBR targetry. If it overcame the national lethargy of the bureaucratic process, it was no bad thing!

one of the many similar instruments that were suggested in order to avoid equity market congestion. They were rejected because of various legal, administrative, and management problems. Indeed, so far as I know, no other private oil company has issued any such bond, so it does suggest that it is not a suitable, or even feasible, form of finance. (The authors do not mention that the idea was resuscitated and supported by the Labour Party in the 1987 election as a method of renationalizing! It is a typical Socialist ploy to transfer private capital to government's control. Perhaps that adequately conveys the Thatcher government's attitude to such instruments.)

Britain was very long on oil, and diversification to other assets (or reducing the outstanding Treasury bonds) made great sense.[8] In retrospect, it seems almost the work of a genius (such as Sir James Goldsmith) to have sold off much of our oil and BP, Britoil, etc. near the top price (circa $32 a barrel). The pity is that Britain did not sell all her holdings then, in view of the events since 1984 culminating in the crash of last month (October 1987).[9] The future expected receipts from petroleum tax give Britain too long a position still in oil.

The underlying motives for privatization were, first and foremost, the reduction in politicization of the economy and, second, the view that it would increase the net wealth of the country as a whole. These remain.

## SHARE OWNERSHIP, ETC.

Here the authors invoke the argument of the grand giveaway -- the underpricing of shares -- "not exactly bribery", but near enough! This has "made privatization a political winner". The arguments apply only to "later flotations" from BT (Dec. 1984) onwards.[10]

---

[8] On a personal note, it was well known that I was a supporter of selling as much oil as quickly as we could.

[9] For the record, the U.K. has accumulated massive net foreign assets -- approximately $200 billion -- almost all since 1978. Perhaps some $40 billion or so may be accounted "oil wealth".

[10] I do not know of any privatization program that has not been accused of "giving away" the assets. Chile, France, Turkey, etc. all stand indicted.

But to imply that before December 1984, the government was not primarily interested in the spreading of asset ownership -- particularly among the median-income families -- is to ignore the biggest privatization of all -- the disposal of 650,000 public sector houses.[11] By the end of 1984, more than 500,000 had been sold, largely to their sitting tenants at a discount of up to 35 percent on assessments. Not just the redistribution of wealth, but the increase was as enormous as the political popularity. (After being bitterly opposed and promising renationalization, by 1987 the Labour Party switched to become a supporter of housing privatization. "Emulation is the tribute ... which mediocrity pays to genius.") The "performance" or efficiency gains were also very substantial, and we enjoyed a net increase in wealth for virtually all involved, including the governments.

But the authors have blinkered their vision of privatization to the new issues market. Their calculations show that on opening trade the shares traded at a premium (just as, for example, Britoil traded at a discount, but that does not appear in Table 4.4.) The percentage premium is calculated by the authors only on the first installment and not on the contracted price. On the contract price -- the only relevant basis -- the percentages are much smaller, for example, British Gas has a gain of 25 percent on the first installment, but only 9 percent on the contract price. (If there had been an issue with only, say, a one penny first instalment, the authors' interpretation of capital gain would have been obviously absurd.)

Table 4.4, as amended, does not tell us whether the shares were underpriced *per se*. Equity issues by private profit-seeking corporations also exhibit similar behavior patterns. Most new issues sell at a premium when the market opens. The extent of underpricing of privatization issues can be gauged only with reference to the behavior of the private sector. The authors might have examined private issues, such as STC in 1983, to see what the average premium is on such stocks. This, not a zero, is an approximation to the appropriate standard.

The government, as did STC, took the advice of merchant banks on the form and pricing of these new issues. Since many of the stocks were highly unusual (such as Amersham in atomic medicine) and since new issue advice is congenitally conservative, mistakes were undoubtedly made. And lessons were learned. In my view and with the benefit of hindsight, many more issues

---

[11] Annual disposals are scheduled to increase 25 percent more than forecast and will give rise to more than Stg.2 billion a year in the next three years, i.e. about 40 percent of the Stg.5 billion expected from privatization. (See statement by the Secretary of State for the Environment, Nov. 3, 1987.)

should have been made, at least partly, through tender rather than a fixed-price offer. But I am told by people who should know that the small investor is shy of tenders and will not participate. Since the policy of the government was to encourage those who held no shares, including particularly workers, to participate in the ownership of these enterprises, the predominance of fixed-price issues with bonuses for long-term ownership is easily explained.

The learning process finally resulted in the BAA issue where small shareholders got 75 percent of the total issue at a fixed price, and the remainder was sold at tender to the institutions, foreigners, and large investors. The best of both worlds perhaps. (But the new issues procedures do need changing: in particular, fixing the price two weeks before the issue invites trouble, which came in a big way with the BP issue.)

The authors suggest that a gradual sale (a la NTT) would have avoided underpricing. Clearly, they believe that stock markets have irrational expectations! Given the overhang of future expected sales, it is difficult to see how this would give a higher overall value -- and it would delay private ownership and management until 51 percent is in private hands. This would delay the much needed reforms and reduce the value of the stock.

The authors also omit any mention, let alone calculation, of the probability of renationalization either in the form of expropriation or with low compensation. Clearly the probability of a Labour government, as indicated by the polls, etc., had some considerable effect on the value of shares. Indeed, the renationalization threat was one very good reason for the "bribery" to which the authors object, and such "bribery" may be shown to increase the privatization proceeds, even to maximize the value to the taxpayer!

Suppose that the wider the spread of long-term share holdings -- and, above all, the greater the fraction in the hands of the workers -- the lower the probability, conditional upon a Labour government being elected, of expropriation of one degree or another. The lower this probability, the higher the market value of the shares. It is easy to show that, if the spread of long-term share ownership is the only efficient way to reduce the likelihood of expropriation, there may be some level (or levels) of "bribery" (that is, differential between the issue and market price) at which the value of the whole issue is maximized! Even the discount shares to the workers, etc. may be priced higher than if the issue had been in the form of an open tender!

How important is this "poison-pill" effect? I suspect it is quite large. The evidence is that as the Labour Party has observed the popularity of privatization through the "bribery" of tenants, workers, etc., so has it reduced its program of planned expropriation. The poison pill worked and had an effect not merely on the issue price but also, to a lesser extent, on the price of all other endangered species.

I apologize for parading before you these rather obvious points of elementary economics. But I think it is necessary to reflect on the "sobering thought", at least to a non-economist, that these distinguished economists are deluding themselves, and perhaps others, with an arbitrary accounting convention when they calculate the "cost to the taxpayer" of Stg.4 billion. (Note this is not a present value calculation.) The real figure may well be negative!

One surprising omission by the authors is the criticism of the role of the merchant bank advisers. As major banks, they were not disinterested in the price commanded by the stock. It was difficult for the government to get both experienced and independent advice. In my experience, this is a ubiquitous problem (for example, I have heard of it in France, Chile, and many other countries). It is an important question to raise. Moreover, one may question whether the authors or my contributions are entirely disinterested -- they are, after all, employees of a large nationalized industry (higher education), and I am a vassal of an international bureaucracy. Fortunately, our motives are irrelevant in discussing the validity of our arguments. Contractual advice from bankers, however, is another matter. Alas, however, I have no solution to offer to such conflicts of interest.

And so to the crash of October 19, 1987, the BP issue, etc. The authors' redistribution argument now looks rather threadbare. It is obvious what I am inclined to say -- so let's leave it unsaid!

## COMPETITION

It is a relief to be able to agree with the authors on the desirability of privatizing in as competitive a way as possible. The launching of Jaguar, Amersham, Cable and Wireless, National Freight Corporation, National Bus, etc. into a competitive structure was a great success story. And I agree that some more competition was probably feasible in BT. But I do not share the authors' penchant for ignoring administrative, legal, and political obstacles, nor do I attribute "protectionist" motives to the government, which I served, so confidently as do they.

An example may illustrate this. In planning BT privatization, Mrs. Thatcher was very anxious to split BT into regional companies. (We had the example of the privately-owned Humberside System -- alas, not mentioned by our authors -- in mind, for competition and comparability.) After much detailed investigation, however, we were persuaded that it would take a most optimistic minimum of two, and probably three or even four, years to set up the separate administrative systems, ownership authorities, and accounting records legally required for a new issue.[12] Such a delay would have excluded the BT issue from the 1983-87 Parliament and made it hostage to the (then remote) possibility of a Conservative return in 1987. Our authors, of course, would have preferred that, but it is at least a moot point for the country and a certainty for the Conservatives.

Similarly, the authors pose a choice on an academic blackboard and do not face the reality of the choice of government in their discussion of Mercury and the restrictions on competitive entry. The point was that the government was persuaded that Mercury would enter the market and commit the massive investment required only if it were secure against non-BT competition, at least for a number of years. The government may have been fooled, but experience in these United States suggests that it was not.

But I do agree with the authors that much, perhaps too much, was conceded to BT, BG, and BA. Sir George Jefferson and, even more, Sir Dennis Rourke and Sir Norman Payne, used all their power as the chosen leaders to take their concerns into the private fold, to extract concessions from the government. The dilemma is that you need powerful and ruthless men to impose privatization on a recalcitrant bureaucracy, but, as public choice theory tells us, they will extract their rents in various quid-pro-quos. So they did.

A sense of perspective is, however, needed. In BT's case, the competition from Mercury and elsewhere has turned out to be far more vigorous and extensive than anyone imagined in 1983-84. Mercury (now wholly owned by Cable and Wireless) has been a great success, particularly, for example, compared to MCI in the United States. It is not the first time that economists have underestimated the power of competition.

But even in the absence of competition with an unregulated monopoly, privatization will generate incentives for X-efficiency -- a fact which the authors do not seem to recognize. If the profits are appropriated by the shareholders, then the private board will have an incentive to seek minimum cost ways of production.

As distinct from the public monopoly, which will tend to maximize an amorphous mass of "interests" -- bureaucratic, political, and those of various pressure groups, with the private unregulated monopoly there will be

---

[12] The old telephone authority had a primitive cash system of bookkeeping.

incentives to minimize costs. Furthermore, the expected X-efficiency effect will be reflected in the offer or tender price, etc., of the shares, so the expected value of monopoly power will accrue to the taxpayer, not to the owners. The inefficiency of the private monopoly is the restriction of output below the competitive level. This will persist and gives at least a prima facie case for considering regulation and other institutional changes.

## REGULATION

One surprising feature of the authors' discussion of regulation is that they do not compare the new system of regulation with the system before privatization. The standard by which they examine the (CPI-X) system is not the reality of what existed before, nor indeed any specified, administratively-feasible alternative. Their standard is some ideal form of regulation. But in policy, reality does matter.

And it is particularly relevant, for example, in the BT case. Before privatization, regulation was subsumed within the telephone administration. It was not subject to the antitrust laws or to the restrictive practices court or to any open and transparent restraints or requirements. Political pressures, bargains, threats, and retaliation were exercised behind the closed doors of smoke-filled rooms. Now, one main result of privatization was to bring all this out of the telephone authority and into the light of day. The share prospectus, the license requirements, the (CPI-X) rule, the need for full accounts, are explicit and open contractual arrangements.[13] Regulation has emerged from the closet. Surely no bad thing.

The next omission from the authors' account is that they do not specify the quantitative extent of the (CPI-X) rule. Such regulations cover only about half of the value-added of the industries (see Table 4.7). Furthermore, these percentages are confidently expected to decline in the future.

---

[13] I find it therefore rather odd that the authors complain about the limited information available; of course, complaints of such a kind are always made, but there has been a quantum leap compared with the nationalized era.

Table 4.7: Percentages of Gross Output Covered by (RPI-X) Rule (1986)

| | |
|---|---|
| British Airports | 37 |
| British Gas | 64 |
| British Telecom | 55 |

SOURCE: Beesley (1987)

NOTE: Figures are approximate.

These figures are relevant to the contention of the authors that (CPI-X) is "not dissimilar to the American rate-of-return regulation". Since the "rate-of-return" regulation proposed by the Department of Industry applied, like the American, to the whole of the utility, whereas in the BA case, for example, it applies to only 37 percent, I cannot see how, assuming all the conjectures of the authors, they could be -- even at the most elementary arithmetic level -- similar!

Nor could it conceivably be similar unless one were prepared to commit a cardinal economist's sin and pursue arbitrary allocations of joint cost (as the FTC used to do in its calculations for truck and railroad rate regulations). Then the rate-of-return would be applied quite artificially, not to the enterprise as a whole but only to the monopolized products.

If the rate-of-return and (RPI-X) were similar, then it is difficult to understand why the FCC recently suggested that the federal government switch from its rate-of-return regulation to the British (RPI-X) system. After a close study, the FCC clearly thought the (RPI-X) system was superior to the rate-of-return regulation. I can see why.

The authors, however, have quite properly exercised their imagination to read the tea leaves of Oftel's pronouncements and to take the political temperature to conjecture what might happen in the future. True, the bureaucracy might once again take over, and Oftel's powers may be expanded so that there is an annual review of the rate-of-return of the whole enterprise and even of the "separated" monopolized sector and that the X-screw is turned accordingly. If, in the 21st century, an aging Kinnock comes to power, advised by Messrs. Vickers and Yarrow, this may well happen. On the whole, I doubt it, but conjectures of such a sort seem rather idle.

## CONCLUDING COMMENTS

Even though there is much to be said about the remainder of the paper, I must now conclude. I find it is disconcerting to read such an academic economist's critique of a policy in which I was, albeit modestly, involved. It tends to underline my view that economic theory per se has little to contribute to the privatization policy issue. But what concerns me is that the authors have failed to elicit evidence and pursue an analysis --particularly comparative analyses -- which would shed a partial light on these issues. The rush to judgment is rash.

I am sure, however, that the Vickers-Yarrow mordant view is quite representative of the vast majority of academic economists in the United Kingdom. Yet, by any standards, privatization has been a stunning success. From that, you may draw your own conclusions.

# Privatization in Britain: Comment

M. Bruce Johnson*

Professors Vickers and Yarrow's appraisal of Great Britain's recent experience in privatization offers two principal conclusions: first, the sale of government assets has massively expanded the number of private shareholders, including employees holding shares in their own firms, and second, if the promotion of economic efficiency is the main reason for privatization, the British result "leaves much to be desired", because "preoccupation with the question of ownership has directed attention away from issues of competition and regulation". Professors Vickers and Yarrow allege that the Thatcher government systematically under priced the shares distributed to the public, and they conclude that British privatization has failed to restructure some of the denationalized industries along more competitive lines.

Consider first the alleged under pricing of shares. It is difficult to discover *a priori* what the appropriate price should be for such shares. The "fair market value" of a share is the market-determined value of a share of a privately-owned firm, not the appraised value of the share of a government enterprise. Furthermore, appraisal and forecasting of the post-privatization market price of shares cannot be done with precision prior to denationalization.

In practice, new issues of private companies frequently carry "first day" capital gains bonuses for initial stockholders. Offer prices may consistently be below fair market value (defined to be the average *ceteris paribus* market equilibrium price in subsequent weeks) in order to achieve the issuer's

---

* University of California, Santa Barbara

goal of a broader base of shareholders. Broad distribution can be accomplished by combining allocations (rationing of shares) with a lower initial offer price. Finally, the true extent of the "first day capital gains" presented in Table 4.4 would be more meaningful if Professors Vickers and Yarrow had also presented data for comparable private-sector companies on their initial public offerings.

But if the under pricing technique indeed was used by the Thatcher government by design, I note that accomplishment with amusement and satisfaction. The main obstacles to privatization are political, not economic. Thus, the Thatcher policy of under pricing shares not only breaks the traditional political impasse but also turns the tables by using a classic redistribution technique. For years some observers have complained that the most insidious method governments use to redistribute wealth is to take small amounts of wealth from each of a large number of citizens in order to transfer (part of) the booty to small groups with concentrated interests. That explains, at least in part, why government grows. Comes now the Thatcher administration to use the same technique to shrink government. The poetic justice is undeniable.

A case could be made that the newly-created shares can be given away for nothing, if that is the political ransom to be paid for privatization. Once ownership is privatized and diversified, property rights are redefined and incentives are refocused. Clearly, privatizing share ownership through the sale of government assets is more than simply reducing the public-sector borrowing requirement (PSBR), as Professors Vickers and Yarrow claim. There is indeed a one-time financial gain to the government from an asset sale, but the argument that it is only one-time is not correct. If privatization improves economic performance, asset disposal by government permanently increases the net present value of the asset's future income stream. The permanent impact on the PSBR is net positive. In the extreme, privatization may be so efficient as to replace public-sector expenditure sinks with tax sources.

Professors Vickers and Yarrow's complaint that the Thatcher government failed to restructure specific industries as they were privatized (especially British Telecom, Gas, Airport Authorities, and Water Authorities) is a more troublesome challenge. Certainly, the characteristics of the subject industry must influence the chosen privatization strategy. For example, it is relatively easy to privatize a state-owned steel company that inevitably must operate in a competitive international environment. The amount of modernizing, pruning, and restructuring done before privatization is debatable; indeed, an extraordinarily-bold government could, in the extreme, simply launch an unmodified steel enterprise into the private-sector environment to survive or fail. The markets and the competitive pressures already exist; the market processes already produce information; and the property rights and incentives are well-defined. The decision to privatize is a relatively risk-free decision with respect to the ultimate economic outcome in such cases.

Other industries are more challenging. When dealing with industries that are of the natural monopoly variety, industries that have traditional cross-subsidies built in, where customers have no good alternatives, and where the reliability of services is important, the best privatization strategy is not obvious. If the privatizing agent is expected to create simultaneously the property rights, the incentives, and the markets that are necessary for economic efficiency, heroic assumptions are involved. Natural monopoly industries are not necessarily subject to the full range of incentives for efficiency, and they suffer from the absence of markets that produce information. Given the large potential variance of economic consequences, politicians may prefer to privatize by transferring the state enterprise to private owners and to regulate the new entity by creating an Ofgas or Oftel.

Private sector monopolies do have one incentive that government-sector monopolies do not: the incentive to minimize costs. Hence, there is much to be said in favor of privatizing natural monopolies combined with (1) price regulation and (2) policies to encourage free entry. At worst, such a strategy will minimize day-to-day operations by government monopolies; at best, workably-competitive industries will evolve.

It is easier to judge efficiency *ex post* than *ex ante* but is not a trivial exercise in either case. Consider the history of the personal computer industry as an example. If economists had been asked 10 years ago how to structure the emerging personal computer industry so that the property rights, incentives, and markets would promote efficient investment, pricing, distribution, and product development, most would have no clear idea of what specific steps should be taken. I am not calling for an optimal plan, merely one that would have had a reasonable chance of success. Wouldn't the prudent response have been to suggest unregulated free markets with free and open entry, and then to trust the market process?

Even if we judge the personal computer industry by some *ex post* efficiency standard, we cannot avoid noting the landscape is strewn with the wreckage of dozens of computer companies and hundreds of computer magazines. Many companies were launched, but few survived. Millions of operable but obsolete computers rest abandoned on closet shelves. Yet, most would judge the personal computer industry as fantastically successful and efficient. The apparent waste of resources was not waste at all, but simply the cost of discovering which of many configurations of technology, production, and marketing best served consumers' wants.

Markets create valuable information in realtime. Much of the information probably cannot be known in advance, or at least cannot be discovered as cheaply as through the operation of markets. Thus, it is considerably easier to propose to "restructure this industry and make it more efficient" than it is to achieve the result. Given our primitive ability to design, initiate, and stimulate those market forces that will produce efficient economic performance, perhaps we should be a bit more charitable when we second-guess the privatizing agents for their restructuring decisions. In the long run, the Thatcher government's alleged emphasis on broadly dispersing shares to the public may be far more effective in promoting efficiency than would attempts to fine-tune the regulations and structures of newly-denationalized industries.

# The Political Economy of Privatization in Britain: A Narrative

Sir Ian MacGregor*

Against the background of the papers presented in this book, it might be useful to learn of the experiences that I have had in the United Kingdom which have led up to probably the most publicized political efforts at privatization as an organized political philosophy. The United Kingdom has certainly made a major political issue of the concept of transferring assets and facilities from state ownership into the hands of the private sector. This was not an event which happened suddenly. Privatization has recently become quite a dramatic part of the political scene, not only in the industrial Western world but actually throughout the world. That the academic world should start to carefully study all the implications of this growing trend is extremely timely.

A brief review of Europe's situation will illustrate why the privatization issue arose. Since World War II, Europe's political philosophy moved backward and forward with a great deal of uncertainty between collectivism and the alleged American ideal of property and individualism. Up to the '70s, one could easily have said that if the trends in Europe were extrapolated, then surely within the next two or three decades Europe would have gone collectivist and would become an outpost of the collectivism of Eastern Europe.

The principal problem with the collectivist concept was just straight economics. In the United Kingdom in the mid-'70s, the consequence of

* Lazard Brothers & Co.

increasing government intervention and control of the economy became evident. As a result of the booby trap that was prepared by the National Union of Miners, the Heath government collapsed in 1974. The National Union of Miners was enormously powerful politically and exhibited the strength of its authority over the economy. The Heath government's fall reflected the totality of the union movement to recover in the '70s the kind of power that it attempted to achieve as long ago as fifty years, in the mid-20's. The general strikes of 1926 in Britain lead by coal miners were an effort to take control of the country's political machinery. The strikes did not succeed, but they left a residue of socialism and socialistic concepts which has been pervasive in British society through all these years.

During the '70s, the Labor movement won its victory and re-established itself as the preeminent authority in national policies. The movement tried to bring the benefits of this political supremacy to its members. The United Kingdom ran through an extraordinary period of increasing inefficiency and increasing costs. The United Kingdom's economy ran down to the point where Mr. Denis Healey, that converted communist, had to go hat-in-hand to the IMF to ask for money to keep the U.K. economy going. It was around this time that the famous publication, *Britain's Economic Problem: Too Few Producers* (Bacon and Eltis 1976) appeared. Professor Bacon and Eltis proposed that, if the trends of the '70s were extrapolated, then sometime during the present decade, the majority of people in the United Kingdom would be working for the government. That trend toward government intervention in all phases of production had grown so extensively, there was a reaction, and that was the origin of the Thatcher government.

In the early days of the Thatcher administration, the concept of privatization had not yet crystallized into the political philosophy that they wished to promote. The privatization concept manifested itself as simply a desire to reduce the impact of the government upon the total economy. During the succeeding years this idea of the transfer of state-owned enterprises back to the private sector became increasingly clear as a very important political dogma. As Mrs. Thatcher's administration began to gain confidence from its re-election in 1983 and from the fact that there was no real organized opposition, an opportunity was provided to develop that [privatization] dogma into a very valuable political mechanism for changing the nature of Britain's society and in motivating people to become more interested in the productivity of society. In the early stages of development, it was not as clearly apparent as it is today that the privatization idea would have such important political value.

Great Britain went through the '40s, '50s and '60s with full employment, but with extremely low wages by international standards, even by European standards. Great Britain maintained its position as an exporter of manufactured goods because of its low wage structure, even though that was coupled with enormously-low efficiency in management and in productivity. However, that combination was quite successful in a world which was then expanding and in which the demand for goods, particularly capital goods and later consumer goods, far exceeded the ability of the industrial world to supply. There was a shortage of everything even to the beginning of the 1970s. In the 1960s, I went to Australia and tried to buy equipment for a mining venture. The delivery times from the British suppliers were months. For example, a generator set would take 24 months to be delivered. At that time the Germans started to squeeze into the market by offering much better and much more reliable delivery schedules. There is the interesting example at Mount Whaleback in which we needed to replace our first temporary set of diesel generating engines that had been supplied by one of the British companies. I said we ought to just go back and purchase the same British equipment, as it seemed to be pretty good once we had it running. But the local management said, "We are not going to buy British. We're going to buy German. Although the German equipment is more expensive, it will be delivered on time. We have no idea when the British equipment, even though it is less expensive, will get here. It could be two months late, and by then we will have made up for the price difference." The local management had been correct. Thus, the British manufacturing establishment lost business because of its inability to perform -- even though it had lower costs. A period of inflation compounded the problem in the 1970s. British costs escalated dramatically. Britain finished that decade with a very tragic situation in which most of the basic industrial structure in the United Kingdom was no longer sustainable. There was the sudden discovery that the big industries, which had been the great successes in the international market for heavy capital goods, were losing out to foreign companies that could produce the same goods at the same or lower cost and with better performance on delivery. In many cases, the quality of the foreign-made equipment was actually superior. At that point, the British electorate decided that a change was needed, and the administration of Mrs. Margaret Thatcher was elected. One of the planks in Mrs. Thatcher's platform was to advance the return of state industry to the private sector, but it had not been emphasized.

An explanation of recent British history will illustrate reasons why industries went into the state sector. In the 1920s, the electricity industry was moved into the state sector due to the problems of cross-subsidization and of regulation. The easiest way to control those problems was to move the industry into the public sector. Later in the '20s, the rail system in the United Kingdom was crippled by the explosion of the availability of automobiles, buses, and trucks. As a result, the railway system rapidly degenerated and had to be essentially bailed out by going into the state sector. The same thing happened only a few years ago with the motor car industry. While the great, unsatisfied, post-war global demand for cars existed up through the 1960s, everything was fine. But by the 1970s, the demand had been satisfied. The British motor car industry, which largely consisted of numerous small producers, just did not have the resources to meet the competition. The car industry collapsed and fell into the state sector. The same thing happened to the shipbuilding industry. In 1952, Britain supplied over 50 percent of the world's new tonnage built in that year. By 1972, the number had gone down to under 20 percent and, by 1980, the number was 1 percent. That type of restructuring had an enormous impact, but it affected another industry, the steel industry.

In 1980, when I joined the British Steel Corporation, the United Kingdom's steel industry had just been through a three-month strike. The long strike could not have occurred at a worse time, because the British steel users discovered that continental Europe's steel producers had a huge surplus capacity. The British steel industry had not even known that there were steel producers across the Channel. The Germans, the Belgians, the French, and the Italians all poured into England and took over the steel business, so that when I joined the steel company, the industry was fighting for its life. Only a year or two previously, the management of the enterprise had been contemplating increasing capacity from the then 22 million tons of liquid steel per year to something like 40 million tons. All the plans were in place. In fact, the first of the great new integrated steel plants had been started on Teeside. The first blast furnace was built. The plant was to be a replica of the latest Japanese operations, which could produce on one site close to 6 million tons of steel that would then be made into a number of different products, such as sheet, plate sections, and long products. The first phase was completed. The blast furnace, one of the biggest in the world, was capable of producing 10,000 tons of iron each day. With the sudden reversal of demand the plant was never finished. To this day, one blast furnace stands of the two originally planned. There were a number of reasons why the steel industry was facing such a steep decline in its market. First, there was the competition from European manufacturers, who had discovered the potential of the British market. Second, there was the collapse of the shipbuilding industry, one of the huge consumers of flat steel. Third, the motor car industry was in decline.

What was necessary was to cut back production from 22 million tons to 14 million tons of liquid steel and reduce the company's 185,000 employees.

In South Wales, there were two integrated plants, the Llanwern plant and the Port Talbot plant. Each were set up to make approximately $2^1/_2$ million tons of flat sheet steel for the motor car industry. Together, they were capable of producing about 5 million tons. At each unit, between 16,000 and 18,000 people were employed. Within a matter of months, these plants had to be cut down to size. Employment had to be reduced by about 70 percent. As a measure of the productivity problems experienced, in the third quarter of 1980, the South Wales steel sheet plants' productivity was something like sixteen man-hours per ton of steel. In 1983, productivity had improved to four man-hours per ton. By that time, the British steel industry was only starting to catchup with other producers in the world. (Back in 1980, the Japanese had already been producing steel in their flat products plants on a basis of six man-hours per ton.) I can see very clearly from my own experience that even though the steel industry has not yet been privatized, it is on its way. It will be privatized within the next couple of years, on the basis of the fact that it now performs as well as any privately-owned enterprise in any part of the world. The accomplishment in the British steel industry was a great tribute to the flexibility of management.

Consider the point that is raised: the difference between management in state-owned enterprises and in the private sector. The problems regularly faced by the management of a state-owned enterprise are immense. When I took the job at British Steel, I did an analysis of how much management time was spent on labor matters. I found that right down through the third level under each plant manager, a little over 70 percent of their time was spent in discussions concerning labor matters. This, of course, had a very sizeable impact on staffing, because it required an adequate number of people in the top staff echelons. It could not all be delegated. Unions in the United Kingdom felt offended if they were not able to conduct their business with the very top level, and they were encouraged to do so. As a matter of fact, during the Callaghan administration, labor involvement even went further. There was an attempt to initiate proposals whereby union members would become a part of the management structure. I was cynical enough to say that I thought that was merely an attempt to regularize what was then actually happening. During the '70s, which was a period when the Labour Party was in ascendance in the British scene, most of the union people felt that they were the management, especially in the state-owned enterprises. There are some apocryphal stories about groups of people, which included trade union members, going over to Downing Street and sitting down with the Cabinet and having tea and discussing the future of the industry. The only people missing from such gatherings were those who were supposed to be running the industry. Thus, management had a great deal with which to contend.

Another of my priority tasks when I arrived was to try to push the discussions of labor matters out of the building's top floor and put them back into the hands of the first-line supervisors, whose functions had been preempted by the shop stewards. I remember being told by one fellow, a foreman in one of our steel plants, that he felt very lucky because his shop steward was a good friend and would always come around and tell him what had been jointly decided by the stewards committee and the management. That's a wonderful example of what can happen under these circumstances.

Another great problem with state enterprises is that there are a number of people who have their own stakes in what happens. As a consequence management is not allowed to manage. Everyone else is managing. At one time, Tony Benn was the Minister for Industry, and he had a deputy, Lord Bessick. These two people would call the union leaders over to their offices and discuss what was going on at the steel industry. After they had figured it out with the union, they would call over the chairman of the steel company and tell him what they wanted him to do. This was a totally untenable situation for management, but these poor people had to suffer through this. At British Steel, about the only thing that I guaranteed my associates was that I would be their Mr. Lincoln, that I would emancipate them. And I did. Management is now running the business. The net result is that in this current 12-month period, the British Steel Corporation will probably make about $250 million on a production of about 12 million tons of liquid steel. This ranks the company among the top earners in the world today and may be even ahead of the Japanese. It can be done. The changes can be made. The importance of making the change from state enterprise to the private sector cannot be under emphasized. In the British example, there was an extremely large impact on all sorts of people and on the management of the enterprise.

In 1983, I joined the coal industry, and I found much of the same. After the fracas in 1974 in which the Heath government was destroyed by the miners' union, staggering sums of money had been plowed into the industry. The government agreed to spend something like a billion pounds a year on capital investments over a period of time. In exchange, the unions agreed that productivity should be improved at an annual rate of 1 percent. When I arrived there, some 10 years after that famous plan for coal had been put together by Tony Benn, I found that the money had been spent but that productivity had declined during the period. In other words, the investment had been almost totally wasted.

The coal industry represented another aspect of what can happen to state industry. In 1983, the industry was a huge employer; it had a quarter of a million people. Many of the managers had assumed that their role was to run a sort of social security system that would provide people with full employment in their communities and job opportunities for all. The Welsh area was particularly bad in that case. There was a per-annum loss of about a hundred million pounds on a basis of about 14,000 employees producing 10 million tons or so of coal. The productivity was slightly more than one and a bit ton per man-shift. For perspective, in recent years in United States' underground coal mining, a respectable production rate is about 22 tons per man-shift. Of course, the other side of the coin is that people working in underground mines in the United States were drawing down pay of about $40,000 a year and producing coal at $1.00 per million BTUs. In the United Kingdom, people were paid substantially less, in fact only about a quarter of that, and coal was produced at something near $2.50 per million BTUs.

What Britain tried to do was to introduce incentives. (I should mention that such a formula was also applied to the steel industry.) While the unions in the United Kingdom were totally opposed to the idea of incentives, the individual employees were not, a very interesting dichotomy. Adam Smith was right. People really are more concerned about their own personal interests. Breakthroughs occurred when people were encouraged to focus on their own interests. Where the people were shown how to earn more money, there was success in the industry. I rather shocked some of the individual workers, because to sell this idea, I went out to the mines and went down underground and talked to the people. I told them that management was happy to supply them with the equipment they needed. I also told them that I wanted to stop putting equipment into mines that would never produce coal on an economic basis. Citing Mr. Scargill's[1] promises to them of 10 percent pay increases every year as long as he was permitted to dominate the scene, I asked the miners how they would like to go for an immediate 30 percent. The only way to do that was to increase productivity, which meant producing coal with a lot less people. Thanks to a very enlightened Minister of Energy, Mr. Nigel Lawson, management was able to offer to the workforce a transition structure which presented a person who had been in the industry for 30 years

---

[1] Arthur Scargill became the vocal leader of the National Union of Mineworkers during the 1980s and led the 1984-85 national strike.

an opportunity to retire early with £1,000 for every year of service. (Remember that most of the employees had gone to the mines straight out of school.) Social security benefits would continue, and at age 65, the retired worker would begin receiving a pension. This proposal produced, needless to say, a loud scream from the unions. As Mr. Scargill put it, management was encouraging his members to sell jobs that belonged not to the miners but to the union.

It was a very interesting debate. In the long run, the willingness of the individual to make the decision enabled me to reduce in two years the employment in the coal industry by 125,000 people. There was not a soul who left who did not leave on his own volition. Nobody was fired, even though I was castigated in many quarters for having been a butcher. The transition can be made, if there is an enlightened government that looks at the economic interests of all the parties involved and makes the necessary investment as was done in the coal industry. Britain invested in the future. Unfortunately, Mr. Lawson, who subsequently became Chancellor of the Exchequer, stood before the House of Commons and said that the coal strike might have been Britain's best investment. That did not endear him to the opposition, though it was probably true that Britain had crossed a threshold and the coal industry had started down the right track. It will take two or three more years before these inroads become reasonably effective. Britain will need to continue to work out those inefficiencies in the industry that are a legacy from the period when people like Tony Benn considered coal mining to be an essential part of the government's social security system.

Some of the dangers in state ownership have been outlined. All of these dangers stem from the fact that once a property passes into state ownership, it becomes a victim of a large number of different influences. There is the immediate management who would normally try to avoid constant battling, and one can not fault them for this. Most people like to live a reasonably peaceful life. If enough pressure is applied, one will try to compromise. Many of the past relationships in both the steel and the coal industries where compromises were achieved involved two groups putting enormous pressure on each other. This made for dramatic inefficiencies. Fortunately, over the last few years, Britain has started to see improvements. The civil service also creates problems. When private enterprises passed into state ownership, the civil servants became the de facto managers. Many of them were, if you will, frustrated managers. These civil servants had not entered the managerial ranks through the orthodox way of joining a company and working their way up. They were vicarious managers; they loved to practice managing; and they had one great advantage: they could make the decisions about what to do. But somehow or other, when it came to responsibilities, these civil servants were totally anonymous. The person who was responsible could never be identified and, therefore, there was no accountability. A committee decided things, and the committee was a long list of names. Management of state-owned enterprises progressively becomes management by committee. Nobody is held accountable for what happens. Also, the politicians can bring tremendous pressures to bear on managers in order that a particular objective or interest of theirs might be attained. I assure you that this does not promote what I call dispassionate decisionmaking in matters of policy. Then there is the public. A state-owned industry can become a target for all kinds of public pressure groups.

For example, in 1984 British Coal spent £150 million in compensation for subsistence. Extracting coal from underground leaves a gap of five or six feet that ultimately falls in on itself. That collapse goes all the way to the surface. There are large areas of England where buildings on the surface are slowly sinking and how much they sink depends on how much coal has been removed from below. In some buildings, cracks appear in the ceiling. In others, the windows do not move up and down as they once did. Traditionally, the British Coal people compensated the owners of these properties for such damage. Then, there came political lobbyists touting themselves as professionals. These lobbyists, who depicted the coal industry as totally vulnerable, would take claims for compensation and win large settlements. As this large cadre of subsidies adjusters appeared on the scene, costs started to go up year after year. As one man told me, "You know, in the last few years, we've seen more new Rolls Royces bought in our town." This was because these fellows had found a way to embarrass the state-owned enterprise and thereby obtain maximum payments. The managers could only take the way of least resistance; they did not want to get into the line of fire in the subsistence debate. They wanted to do what good mining engineers do: get the coal out. Consequently, the coal industry was prepared to pay. In some cases for every ton of coal extracted, over 10 pounds were paid for fixing living rooms. These are only a few examples of the pressures that can be brought to bear on state industries, which would not normally apply in the commercial world.

The privatization campaign in the United Kingdom was perhaps motivated in the first instance by an ideological objective. Maybe as time went on, it became clear that there were other collateral advantages. The broadening of share ownership in privatization was an important aspect. There was also the fact that the Treasury was progressively relieved of potential costs. The one-time sale of property reduced the public indebtedness, a very important contribution. The recent unhappy experiences in the stock market may slow down the British process, but I do not think it will stop it. Up to now, the broad ownership of securities in these former state-owned enterprises has been an attractive investment. The distribution of the shares, which has been purposely limited to small numbers per person in order to encourage the breadth of ownership, is part of the Prime Minister's belief that a broader participation in industrial ownership would be a sound and attractive basis for the future political stability of the country. Not to be forgotten is the fact that in Europe, where there is a very large amount of money spent on employment costs, what I call "time not worked", that is, pensions, holidays, life insurance, medical care, and other fringes, the direct costs in employment are a lesser percentage than in Britain. Britain has very large indirect costs, including the state insurance plans. All of that is channeled through the institutions. Thus, the Europeans, the British included, have increasingly become the owners of the industry in their countries. The phenomenon has been reflected in stock markets in recent years in that there has been an emergence of new issues in Britain. Companies, such as chains of dry cleaning or photographic stores, have been going to the public market to raise funds. The fact that people have been interested in buying the new equity shows that there has been a shortage of equities. Fortunately, issuing new equity has been a very attractive program for the United Kingdom and an essential ingredient of the privatization program. With the experience of the British Petroleum sale, there will have to be at least a pause to rethink how the stock is distributed. Maybe there will have to be additional bonuses offered, because the government is intent on continuing to have as many as possible of the state-owned enterprises returned to the private sector.

The privatization idea is no longer confined to the United Kingdom. It is fairly general. In a world in which economies are not expanding at any great rate, governments understand the problem that there is a limit to the resources available to them. Governments will increasingly focus on the necessity to optimize the assets they own, and that in itself is a very great incentive to continue the privatization of state-owned enterprises. The privatization trend is not going to be quickly reversed.

# CHAPTER FIVE

## Privatization in Canada: Ideology, Symbolism or Substance?

W.T. Stanbury*

### INTRODUCTION

This study focuses on privatization in Canada conducted by both the federal and provincial governments from 1983 to May 1988. Privatization has largely taken the form of selling federal and provincial Crown corporations to private investors, although, as noted below, the term has been used to describe a variety of other things.

Privatization is of particular significance for Canada because the nation has aptly been described as a "public enterprise country" in contradistinction to the U.S., the quintessential private enterprise country (Hardin 1974). The Economic Council of Canada (1986, p. 1) echoes the widely-held view that "the concept of public enterprise is deeply embedded in the fabric of Canadian society."[1] Indeed, government enterprises predate Confederation by a half-century. The tradition is not only a long one. It is also a deep one. "Today,

---

* Faculty of Commerce and Business Administration, University of British Columbia. I am indebted to Sandy Carter for efficient word processing services under pressure, and to several persons who commented on an earlier version of this paper -- including Rod Dobell, Walter Block, Richard Schultz and the anonymous referees. See also Stanbury (1988).

[1] The Economic Council (1986, p.1) concluded that "by comparison with other mixed industrialized economies, Canada is more representative of the middle ground than the extremes, in terms of its use of public corporations. Public enterprise is more important in Canada than in Switzerland, Australia, Japan and the United States ... On the other hand, government ownership in Canada is very modest by comparison with Austria ... [and] in France, Italy and the United Kingdom, public corporations have also played a more prominent role than in the Canadian economy."

the federal government is the largest single investor in Canadian industry, and all provinces and many municipalities have major commercial holdings" (ECC 1986, p. 1). Measures of the number and size of Crown corporations in Canada are given in Table 5.1.

**Defining Privatization**

The broadest concept of privatization consists of any effort designed to strengthen the role of the market at the expense of the state. This concept, therefore, includes: selling off Crown corporations to private investors; deregulation in total or in part (particularly the removal of direct or economic regulation);[2] and shifting from compulsory taxation to a voluntary, user-pay approach to public services.

The sale of Crown corporations to private investors may be done in several ways: shifting from 100 percent government ownership to 100 percent private ownership, either by sale or by "bricking", i.e. free distribution of shares (see Ohashi 1980, 1982); or shifting from 100 percent government ownership to a mixed enterprise in which the government keeps a minority interest or even retains legal control.

Privatization may also include taking away the present advantages[3] of commercial Crown corporations by: making them subject to the federal Competition Act;[4] requiring them to borrow in the open market ("de-subsidization" of their debt capital); and making them pay income taxes and property taxes like their private-sector counterparts. Contracting-out is another concept of privatization, i.e. the production of goods/services is transferred to privately-owned firms, but they continue to be publicly financed. See, for example, Hurl (1984, 1986), McCready (1986), and McDavid (1985).

---

[2] See Stanbury (1987) for a review of such deregulation in Canada.

[3] This approach, however, ignores the disadvantages under which some Crown corporations operate. These include: the subsidization of (some) customers/provision of uneconomic services; excessive debt loads as determined by their political masters; and the politicization of the management's decision-making process.

[4] Competition Act, R.S., c. C-23 as amended by c.10 (1st Supp.), c. 10 (2nd Supp.) 1974-75-76, c. 76, 1976-77, c. 28, 1985, c. 19, 1986, c. 26. See Stanbury (1986) for a review of the latest amendments.

Table 5.1:

Measures of the
Number, Size, and Scope of Federal and Provincial
Crown Corporations in Canada

1. Number of Crown Corporations

(a) Federal: 366 (Canada, PCO, 1977); 464, including subsidiaries (Comptroller General, 1980); 306, excluding subsidiaries (Comptroller General, 1981)

(b) Provincial: 233 in 1980, excluding subsidiaries (Vining & Botterell, 1983)

2. Government-Owned or Controlled Commercial Enterprises (Dec. 31, 1985)

-- Federal: 56 parent corporations and 81 subsidiaries
-- Provincial: 203 parent corporations and 187 subsidiaries

Source: Economic Council (1986)

3. Number of Mixed Enterprises in 1983

-- Federal 92 first order + 34 second order
-- Provincial 167 first order + 29 second order
-- Legal control: 64 of 322 (34 controlled by the federal government)
-- No. in Top 500 with effective or legal control: 13 by the federal government; 16 by provincial governments.

Source: Elford & Stanbury (1985)

4. Growth of Total Assets of Federal Crown Corporations, excluding the Bank of Canada

| | |
|---|---|
| 1973 | $19.6 billion |
| 1978 | 33.4 billion |
| 1983 | 54.1 billion |
| 1985 | 61.2 billion |
| 1987 | 59.9 billion |

Source: Baumann (1987)

5. Federal employment, March 31, 1982

-- Crown corporations: 263,225 (including Canada Post, 69,457)
-- Departments: 221,000
-- Armed Forces: 83,000
-- RCMP: 18,000

Source: Auditor-General (1982)

Table 5.1 - continued

6. Largest Federal and Provincial Crown Corporations

No. of Crowns in *Financial Post*, 500 Largest Non-financial Enterprises

| | 1985 | 1984 | 1983 |
|---|---|---|---|
| Federal | 18 | 17 | 18 |
| Provincial | 25 | 27 | 25 |

No. of Crowns in *Financial Post*, 100 Largest Financial Enterprises

| | 1985 | 1984 | 1983 |
|---|---|---|---|
| Federal | 6 | 6 | 6 |
| Provincial | 7 | 11 | 11 |

Source: Stanbury (1988)

7. Relative Size of Largest Commercial Crown Corporations, 1983

| Crown Corp. | Assets | Employees |
|---|---|---|
| -- 50 Federal | $47.0 billion | 209,000 |
| -- 18 Provincial | 77.4 | 129,055 |
| | 124.4 | 338,055 |
| Private | | |
| 1 - 25 | $117.4 billion | 773,509 |
| 26 - 50 | 47.9 | 363,343 |
| | 165.3 | 1,136,852 |

Source: Kierans (1984)

8. Largest Federal Crown Corporations by Assets in March 1987

| | |
|---|---|
| -- Can. Mtge & Housing Corp. | $9,588 Million |
| -- Petro-Canada | 8,329 |
| -- CNR | 7,806 |
| -- Export. Dev. Corp. | 7,156 |
| -- Cdn Wheat Board | 4,583 |
| -- Air Canada | 2,923 |
| -- Canada Post Corp. | 2,451 |

Source: Baumann (1987)

9. Largest Federal Crown Corporations by Revenues in 1986

| | $ million | FP 500 |
|---|---|---|
| -- Petro-Canada | $5,263 | # 11 |
| -- CNR | 4,882 | 12 |
| -- Cdn Wheat Board | 3,757 | 22 |
| -- Canada Post | 3,000 est. | 29a |
| -- Air Canada | 2,885 | 32 |
| -- Royal Cdn Mint | 911 | 107 |
| -- Cdn. Comm. Corp. | 763 | 128 |

**Crowns in Context: Government as Leviathan**

Crown corporations were created, expanded and were in some cases privatized in the context of other governing instruments. These instruments have been used to produce what Howard and Stanbury (1984, p. 94) have called a "government-centred society". Consider the following measures of the size and scope of all governments in Canada:

-- The expenditures of all three levels of government combined amount to about 47 percent of Gross National Product. One-half of total expenditures consist of transfer payments which have recently grown much more rapidly than have exhaustive expenditures (both current and capital).

-- "Tax expenditures" at the federal level have been rising more rapidly than direct expenditures over the past decade or so. They now amount to about one half the level of direct or cash expenditures. In other words, if all tax expenditures were counted as subsidies, federal expenditures -- which now amount to about 23 percent of GNP -- would increase by about 50 percent.

-- Khemani (1986, pp. 140-141) estimates that in 1980 "government supervised or regulated" industries accounted for 38 percent of the Gross Domestic Product or 34 percent if the public administration and defence sector is removed. However, in recent years some direct regulation has been liberalized and there has been a limited amount of deregulation in airlines, railroads, trucking, telecommunications and financial services (see Stanbury 1987).

-- In 1983 there were more than 300 mixed enterprises in Canada, i.e. those market-oriented businesses in which the federal or a provincial government had some equity interest but not 100 percent of the voting shares. Of those enterprises wherein a government had legal or effective control, 22 were among the 500 largest non-financial enterprises in the nation in 1983 (Elford & Stanbury 1986).

-- The value of federal and provincial loans and investments and credit insurance provided to the private-sector amounted to 18.5 percent of GNP in 1980. In certain sectors (e.g. agriculture, export financing, housing), government loans/guarantees are of particular significance (Economic Council 1982).

### Structure of the Study

The first section of this study reviews the limited record of privatization in Canada prior to 1983. The second section examines in some detail the 13 privatizations by the federal government and 24 by provincial governments between 1983 and May 1988. Next, possible candidates for privatization in the near future are discussed -- including the proposed sale, in stages, of Air Canada. The following section examines three hypotheses that may explain the extent of privatization over the past five years. Finally, some conclusions are drawn from Canada's privatization record.

## EARLIER PRIVATIZATION EFFORTS IN CANADA

### Privatization Efforts by the Federal Government: W.W. II to 1983

The idea that federal and provincial governments should sell off some of their Crown corporations is not new. While Canadians are frequently said to be pragmatic rather than strongly ideological on the matter of public enterprises and government intervention in general, there have always been a few critics who have advocated privatization of at least some Crown corporations.

**World War II Corporations.** Perhaps the most systematic effort to privatize Crown corporations occurred in the years after World War II. The government created 11 production and 17 administrative Crown corporations. The production enterprises employed 41,200 persons or only 3 percent of the manufacturing labour force (Borins 1982, pp. 383-384). The administrative corporations were used where a high degree of cooperation between government and all of the firms in the industry was required.

Another Crown corporation, War Assets Corporation, was created to sell-off surplus war materials. By January 1947 some $450 million in revenues had been obtained from the sale of federal assets. The following briefly describes what happened to the most important production corporations:

-- Eldorado Mining and Refining was retained; it became Eldorado Nuclear.[5]

-- Wartime Housing Corporation was combined with the National Housing Administration to create Central Mortgage and Housing Corporation in 1946. Consideration was given to privatizing part of its activities in 1979.

-- Park Steamship Co., which operated the world's third-largest merchant fleet, was sold to both foreign and Canadian purchasers.

-- Polymer Corp. was retained by the government; it later became part of the Canada Development Corporation in which the federal government had a large interest. The government sold its shares between 1985 and 1987.

-- Victory Aircraft: Hawker Siddley set up a Canadian subsidiary, A.V. Roe Canada, which leased its Malton plant for 7 years for 50 percent of the gross profits.

-- Aircraft plant operated by Canadian Vickers - incorporated into a new Crown corporation, Canadair Limited, in December 1945. Canadair was purchased by the forerunner of General Dynamics in early 1947.[6]

-- Turbo Research Ltd. - integrated into A.V. Roe Canada.

-- Research Enterprises Ltd. was broken up and sold to the private-sector just after the war.

-- Canadian Arsenals Ltd. - was created in 1946 out of six munitions plants. It was privatized in 1986.

**The Clark Government, 1979/80.** In 1979 the short-lived minority Conservative Government of Joe Clark announced that it would privatize Petro-Canada, which had begun operations at the beginning of 1976. Clark called for its privatization in the election campaign in the spring of 1979. During that campaign Petro-Canada spent some $800 million to acquire the remaining 52 percent of Pacific Petroleum. Some said it was a way of making it difficult for the Tories to privatize the rapidly growing Crown corporation.

Following a task force report, the Prime Minister proposed to give $100 worth of Petro-Canada shares to every Canadian. The scheme would cost $2.5 billion ($1 billion in Petro-Canada assets and $1.5 billion to pay off

---

[5] The government wanted to sell it off in the mid-1950s, but were not able to do so before the Diefenbaker Conservatives were elected in 1957. Eldorado was put on the for-sale list in 1979 and again in 1984. Its merger with the Saskatchewan Mining Development Corporation was announced in early 1988. See "Future Developments" below.

[6] The federal government bought Canadair from General Dynamics in December 1975 for $46 million (Borins & Brown 1986, pp. 17-18). It was sold in 1986 to Bombardier.

the corporation's debt). The idea was to "give Canadians a stake in their own country". His proposal was to prove to be a political albatross in the election campaign early in 1980 (Foster 1982; Simpson 1980).

Early in September 1979, the Clark government announced it had formed a task force to examine the role of Canada Mortgage and Housing Corp. to determine what aspects of its activities could be placed in the hands of private developers.[7] CMHC is a major mortgage insurer[8] and a very large scale guarantor of residential mortgages.

The president of the Treasury Board, Sinclair Stevens, announced on September 13, 1979, that "at least five other Crown corporations" would be sold off.[9] They were Canadair Ltd. (a maker of executive jets and aero engines), de Havilland Aircraft (a manufacturer of smaller aircraft, including the highly regarded Dash 7 turboprop), Eldorado Nuclear Ltd. (a uranium refiner), Canadian Commercial Corporation (a go-between in trade deals between Ottawa and foreign governments), and Defence Construction Ltd. (a builder for the Department of Defence). Both Air Canada and Canadian National Railways were described as candidates for privatization, but the government claimed they were too big to sell off.

The Clark government announced in November 1979 that it proposed to reduce its holding in the Canada Development Corporation (CDC) to less than 50 percent and to encourage the company to take over some of the Crown corporations it had put up for sale.[10] The CDC had been created in 1971, and over the following five years the government had invested $322 million in the firm. Its policy objectives were to "help develop and maintain strong Canadian-controlled and managed corporations in the private-sector ... and ... give Canadians greater opportunities to invest and participate in the economic development of Canada" (Hampson 1976, p. 281). The legislation provided that in time the government's equity interest would be reduced to 10 percent. In November 1979 the federal government owned 66 percent of

---

[7] Jack Willoughby, "Government forms task force to examine what portions of CMHC can go private," *Globe and Mail*, September 7, 1979, p. B5.

[8] It is now the only one after the departure of its sole private-sector competitor from the field.

[9] Roger Croft, "Five more crown companies heading for the auction block," Toronto *Star*, September 14, 1979, p. A4.

[10] Timothy Pritchard, "Ottawa to reduce holding in CDC," *Globe and Mail*, November 20, 1979, p. B1.

CDC, which earned $73.7 million in the first nine months of 1979 on revenues of $1.4 billion.

Before it was able to sell off any Crown corporations, the Clark Government was defeated on a want-of-confidence motion on its budget (presented in December 1979), which proposed substantial increases in energy prices.

**The Liberals Return, 1980.** On April 30, 1980, the new Liberal Government of Pierre Trudeau announced that it was shelving plans to sell off de Havilland, Canadair, Eldorado Nuclear and Northern Transportation.[11] The announcement followed immediately after Donald Johnston, president of the Treasury Board, had been given responsibility for the matter of privatization. In May 1981 the Prime Minister received a letter from Burns Fry Ltd. proposing to assemble a group of investors to acquire the government's 30.7 million shares of CDC.[12] The proposal was prompted by the government's desire to use the CDC as a vehicle to achieve policy objectives which, Burns Fry said, contradicted its earlier promises about the CDC's role.

**A New Crown to Sell Others: The CDIC.** In March 1982 the Liberal Government announced the creation of the Canada Development Investment Corporation (CDIC).[13] It was to help the federal government manage its role as shareholder of a number of industrial corporations, including Eldorado Nuclear, Canadair and de Havilland Aircraft. One of the CDIC's other tasks was to arrange for the sale of the federal government's shares in CDC, which the federal government announced in May 1982.[14] The Liberals still had not

---

[11] "Liberals call off Crown firms' sale," Ottawa *Citizen*, May 1, 1980, p. 40. In September 1981 the government stated that de Havilland and Canadair were still candidates for sale to private interests, but that they were not being put on the block immediately. See Ken Romain, "Canadair, de Havilland still candidates for privatization, but sale not imminent," *Globe and Mail*, September 30, 1981, p. B3.

[12] See Dan Westell, "Ottawa gets offer for CDC shares," *Globe and Mail*, May 16, 1981, p. B1.

[13] See David Stewart-Patterson, "Reorganization makes CDIC giant holding company," *Globe and Mail*, November 25, 1982, p. B1 and Foster (1983a) (1983b).

[14] See "Ottawa plans to sell its 48.5 percent of Canada Development Corp.," Toronto *Star*, May 28, 1982, p. A3; "Sale of CDC shares will hinge on market," *Globe and Mail*, November 26, 1982, p. B4; "Ottawa's sale of CDC: A prelude to Innocan?" *Globe and Mail*, May 29, 1982, p. 2. But also see Jennifer Lewington, "CDIC feels talk of divesting premature," *Globe and Mail*, November 25, 1982, p. B1.

sold the shares more than two years later when a general election was called in June 1984.[15] They were eventually sold by the Mulroney government in three batches between September 1985 and October 1987 (Stanbury 1988, Ch. 6).

In August 1983 a story in the *Financial Times* stated that the first Crown to be returned to the private-sector under the mandate of the CDIC would be Eldorado Nuclear.[16] However, the only sale the Liberals were able to complete before they were defeated by Brian Mulroney and the Conservatives in September 1984 was that of Nordair Inc. In addition the liberals had set in train the privatization of Northern Transportation Ltd., which was sold in July 1985. In May 1984 the Liberals announced the sale of 86 percent of the shares of Nordair, Canada's fourth-largest airline, for $31.8 million (see below).

## Privatization by Provincial Governments

**British Columbia.** The most visible efforts at privatization prior to the activities of the Mulroney government occurred in British Columbia when W.R. (Bill) Bennett was premier and leader of the Social Credit Party. While his father nationalized the largest power utility in the province (B.C. Electric) in 1961 in order to use it as a vehicle for regional economic development, Bill Bennett made an effort to privatize some Crown corporations.

The largest privatization involved a company whose assets included 79 percent of a pulp company (Canadian Cellulose), two sawmills and 10 percent of a gas pipeline, all of which had been acquired by the NDP government in power between 1972 and 1975. These companies were transferred to a new Crown corporation, the British Columbia Resources Investment Corporation, which then had assets valued at $151.5 million.[17] Then in early 1979 the Province of British Columbia privatized BCRIC in a

---

[15] The reason for the delay in selling the CDC shares was largely for commercial reasons, i.e., the price of the shares in the marketplace. The government had made the decision there was no longer any policy reason to maintain its ownership (Ross 1983, p. 110).

[16] Gordon Pope, "Eldorado Nuclear gears up for privatization," *Financial Times*, August 1, 1983, pp. 5-6. See also Tim Padmore, "CDIC looking for quick sale on Eldorado," Vancouver *Sun*, November 19, 1983, p. E11.

[17] BCRIC was created in September 1977. See Ohashi (1980).

remarkable fashion.[18] It gave each resident five shares for free (see Ohashi 1980; 1982). At the same time BCRIC sold additional common shares at $6 each. About 170,000 persons who received the free shares subscribed for additional shares (4,969 bought the maximum of 5,000 shares). The total value of the new issue was $487.5 million. This was the third-largest common share underwriting in North American history. While the privatization and share offering was deemed to be a success at the time, the new privately-owned company did not fare well. It made some poor acquisitions and soon incurred large losses.[19]

**Alberta.** In 1975 the Province of Alberta sold one half the shares in Alberta Energy Corp, which had been created as a Crown corporation in 1973. When AEC was converted into a public company in 1975, only the province was permitted to own more than 1 percent of the shares. In 1984 AEC had revenues of $494 million and net earnings of $72.3 million. Private investors saw the price of their shares rise from $10 in 1975 to $65.25 in September 1984. In 1987 AEC had revenues of $478 million and net earnings of $60.5 million; that year it ranked #9 on the *Financial Times* Oil and Gas 100. In late 1982 the province reduced its stake in AEC to 44 percent. Presently it holds 35.8 percent.[20]

## EXTENT OF PRIVATIZATION IN CANADA, 1983 TO MAY 1988

The purpose of this section is to identify and briefly describe the public enterprises or commercial investments that have been privatized by federal and provincial governments in Canada between 1983 and May 1988. The proposed privatization of Air Canada, announced on April 12, 1988, is discussed in the section entitled "Future Privatizations".

---

[18] The idea may well have come from the leader of the provincial Liberal Party (Ohashi 1982, p. 114).

[19] See John Twigg, "Tough Wondering Howe," *Equity*, July/August 1986, pp. 30-42. In October 1987 BCRIC shares traded for less than $1.

[20] See Barry Nelson, "Alberta Energy floats an $80-million issue," *Financial Times*, April 4, 1988, p. 14.

**Federal Privatizations**

Between 1984 and April 1988 the federal government effected 13 privatizations (see Table 5.2). Nine of these were Crown corporations (nos. 2, 4, 5, 6, 8, 9, 10, 11 and 13); the others consisted of equity interests in mixed enterprises such as Nordair (85 percent), Canada Development Corporation (47 percent), Fisheries Products International(FDI) (62.6 percent) and Nanisivik Mines (18 percent). One of the sales (Northern Canada Power) is not a privatization, as the buyer was another government -- namely the Yukon Territory.

The largest federal privatization -- in terms of its selling price -- was Teleglobe Canada, which has a monopoly on the provision of telecommunications services between Canada and countries outside North America.[21] Teleglobe, reflecting its previous profitability and the fact that it will have a legal monopoly for five years, fetched over $600 million for the federal government. This amount included a special cash dividend of $106 million issued just prior to the closing of the deal. In 1986 Teleglobe had operating revenues of $274 million (i.e. excluding other carriers' shares of gross revenues) and some $502 million in assets. What was an unregulated de facto monopoly owned by the federal government became a legal monopoly (for 5 years) subject to the regulation of the Canadian Radio-Television and Telecommunications Commission. One governing instrument was substituted for another.

The largest enterprise among the federal privatizations is the Canada Development Corporation. It started life as a Crown corporation, but later became a mixed enterprise when the government began selling shares to the public. In three tranches, between 1985 and 1987, the government sold its 47-percent interest for $377 million. The bulk of the shares were sold in a two-stage process in September 1985 and September 1986; buyers paid one half down and the balance a year later.[22] The rest of the government's shares

---

21 The sale was made subject to a variety of conditions: Teleglobe will reduce overseas telephone and telex rates by 13.5 percent and 10 percent, respectively, on January 1, 1988; Teleglobe management will remain in place, no employees will be laid off and existing collective agreements will continue; Teleglobe's head office will remain in Montreal; Within six months Teleglobe employees will be offered an opportunity to acquire 5 percent of its shares at 90 percent of the price paid by Memotec. See *Globe and Mail*, February 12, 1987, pp. A1-A2.

22 Unfortunately, when the second payment was due, the shares were selling in the market for about one half the price set a year earlier. Yet 90 percent of the 23 million shares were taken up in September 1986. See Patricia Lush, "90 percent of CDC shares taken up at $11.50." *Globe and Mail*, September 18, 1986, p. B1.

were sold in 1987. The government made less than $50 million on its investment of $322 million held for a period of over a decade, a poor return.

Several of the sales were initiated under the previous Liberal administration of Pierre Trudeau. One, the sale of the 85-percent interest in Nordair, a regional airline operating in Ontario and Quebec, was effected by the Liberals -- although the deal closed after the Tories came to power. Nordair had been acquired by Air Canada in January 1979.[23]

The implementation of the first sell-off by the Tories, Northern Transportation, was initiated by the Liberals in 1984. The Liberals also said in 1982 that they planned to sell the government's 47 percent interest in CDC.

By far the most controversial federal privatization was the sale of de Havilland to Boeing, which was announced in December 1985 and completed two months later. The sale aroused the ire of nationalists, the two opposition parties and the friends of an activist government industrial policy to create jobs in hi-tech industries.[24] The sale eleven months later of Canadair to Bombardier, a Canadian company based in Quebec, 11 months later caused much less fuss, in part, because the Tories did a better job of explaining and justifying the sale (Stanbury 1988, Ch. 7).

Several other points should be noted about the federal privatizations listed in Table 5.2. First, several of the deals are small -- whether measured by the revenue of the enterprise sold or the selling price. Pecheries Canada, Nanisivik Mines (18 percent interest), Northern Canada Power, and Northern

---

[23] Even before the tender offer closed, the Minister of Transport announced that the shares would be sold back to private-sector interests within a year. However, the politics of selling Nordair were so convoluted that neither the Liberals nor the short-lived Tory government in 1979/80 could divest until May 31, 1984, when Innocan Inc.'s bid was accepted. It should be noted that Air Canada's pension plan then owned a substantial fraction of Innocan.

[24] Bercuson et al. (1986, p. 141) put it this way: "... it appeared to some observers that the Tories had given de Havilland away ... As soon as the announcement was made, former Transport Minister Lloyd Axworthy claimed that although de Havilland was on the verge of profitability, the government was 'giving it away, virtually...the fix [in favour of Boeing] was in from the start.' The NDP announced a motion of nonconfidence in the government because of the agreement and claimed that the sale would mean the loss of Canadian jobs. They predicted that Boeing would transfer the manufacture of the Dash 7 and Dash 8 to the United States and close de Havilland down. This, in fact, made little sense ..."

Opposition Leader John Turner incorrectly claimed that "Canadian expertise in aeronautics, in space, in short-takeoff-and-landing aircraft [would] no longer belong to [Canada]." The deal was closed on January 31, 1986. According to Bercuson et al. (p. 143), information released by the government showed the deal was better than it looked because of the losses avoided: "...de Havilland's projected losses were placed at $83 million for 1985 and $50 million for 1986. (The original estimates given to prospective buyers were $60 million for 1985 and $14 million for 1986, followed by three years of rising profits.)"

Table 5.2
Summary Data on Federal Privatizations Completed Between 1984 and May 1988

| Crown Corp./Asset Sold | Revenues ($000,000) | Year[1] | Assets ($000,000) | Employ-ment | Purchase Pr. ($000,000) |
|---|---|---|---|---|---|
| 1. Nordair Ltd. (85%) (Dec. 1984) | 181 | 1984 | 111 | 1317 | 34+ |
| 2. Northern Transportation (July 15/85) | 41 | 1984 | 75 | 389 | 27 |
| 3. CDC (47%) (Sept. 16/85, Sept.16/86, June 5/87, Oct. 8/87) | 3,257 | 1985 | 7,259 | 17,808 | 377 |
| 4. de Havilland (Jan. 31/86) | 300 | 1985 | 346 | 4,405 | 90 +65 in notes[2] |
| 5. Pecheries Canada (April 18/86) | 16 | 1985 | 16 | 575 | 5 |
| 6. Canadian Arsenals (May 9/86) | 103 | 1985 | 126 | 879 | 92 |
| 7. Nanisivik Mines (18%) (Oct. 28/86) | 26 | 1986 | 65 | 195 | 6 |
| 8. CN Route (Dec. 5/86) | 145 | 1985 | 40 | 2,227 | 29 |
| 9. Canadair (Dec. 23/86) | 451 | 1985 | 478 | 5,431 | 205[4] |
| 10. Northern Canada Power[3] (March 31/87) | 19 | 1986/87 | 146 | 34 | 20 +56 in notes |
| 11. Teleglobe Canada (March 31/87) | 274 | 1986 | 502 | 1,110 | 488 +106 dividend +17 redeem. prefd. |
| 12. Fisheries Products Int'l. (62.6%) (April 15/87) | 387 | 1986 | 224 | 8650 | 104 |
| 13. CN Hotels (Jan. 1988)[5] | 147 | 1986 | 161[6] | 3400 | 265 |

1. Year for the revenue, asset, employment data.
2. The notes are forgiven at the rate of $1 for each $5 of purchases by the buyer for purposes unrelated to their activities at the time of sale.
3. Not a true privatization as the enterprise was sold to another government, the Yukon.
4. Estimate of present value, based on $120 million in cash plus an estimated $173 million in royalties on future sales, plus a $3 million special dividend, plus undisclosed proceeds of a lawsuit, plus 1 percent royalty on CF-18 systems engineering contract.
5. Date of announcement of the sale.
6. Based on value of properties at cost, less depreciation - an underestimate of total assets.
Source: Stanbury (1988)

Transportation had sales of only $16 million, $26 million, $19 million and $41 million, respectively. These are hardly important enterprises in economic terms. Their collective revenues are less than Canada Post's deficit in 1986/87.

Second, even the larger privatizations such as de Havilland, Canadair and Teleglobe are well down the list of the largest federal Crowns. De Havilland ranked #255 on the Financial Post 500 (FP 500) in 1985, while Canadair ranked #189 and Teleglobe would have ranked #280 if it had been included. The CDC is something of an anomaly. While the federal government had 47 percent of the voting shares, it manifestly was not able to exercise control over the firm since 1981.[25] In 1985 the CDC ranked #28 on the FP 500. In 1986 it ranked #34 after some downsizing (see Olive 1985).[26] The sale of the CDC shares amounts to something quite different than selling true Crowns such as Canadair, de Havilland or Teleglobe. In 1986 there were seven federal commercial Crowns on the FP 500 larger than Canadair, the largest federal firm yet privatized (other than the CDC, which was a mixed enterprise).

Third, if we exclude the CDC as a special case, the revenues of the other 12 firms privatized amounted to $2.1 billion. This is much smaller than the revenues of the fifth largest federal Crown, Air Canada, which had revenues of $2.9 billion in 1986. Excluding the CDC, the 12 federal privatizations disposed of $2.3 billion in assets (at book value). Three sales (de Havilland, Canadair and Teleglobe) accounted for 58 percent of all assets sold. The $2.3 billion figure should be contrasted to the assets of the five largest Crowns as of March 1987 listed in Table 5.1. Their assets total $37.5 billion.

This list omits Air Canada (with assets of $3,085 million at the end of 1987) and Canada Post ($2,451 million).[27] In other words, the assets of the five largest federal Crowns are over 16 times the assets privatized to the end of 1987 (excluding the special case of the CDC with assets of $6,324 million in 1986). Put another way, the sale of Air Canada (promised in April 1988) will be economically more important than all 12 federal privatizations between 1984 and early 1988, excluding the sale of shares in CDC.

---

[25] See Foster (1983a) and Anthony Whittingham, "The seedy assault on the CDC," *Maclean's*, June 1, 1981, pp. 46-47.

[26] In December 1987 CDC was renamed Polysar Energy & Chemical Corp.

[27] Data for Canada Post from Doern and Atherton (1987, p. 173) for 1985/86.

Fourth, until it sold Canadair at the end of 1986, the value of assets sold by the federal government was less than the $886 million purchase of Gulf Canada's assets by Petro-Canada in August 1985.[28] Excluding the CDC, the expansion of Crown assets offset 41.6 percent of the value of assets sold to the private-sector.

Fifth, in its privatizations to date the federal government has shown a marked preference for outright sales to a single buyer. Of the 13 deals, only two (CDC and FPI) have involved wide distribution to the public, although the government promises that Air Canada's shares will be widely distributed. The dominance of the single-buyer method may reflect the smaller size of the transactions so far and the particular firms involved. However, one wonders why Teleglobe was not sold as a wide-distribution public offering. Bell Canada Enterprises (#4 on the FP 500 for 1986), which owns Bell Canada, the largest telephone company in Canada, may have been able to get control of Teleglobe indirectly by acquiring what appears to be effective control of the firm (Memotec Data Inc.) that bought Teleglobe.[29] Those who bought FPI stock at the issue price of $12.50 have done well. It began trading at $15 and rose to $21.25 in the summer of 1987. It fell to a low of $12.25 in October after "Black Monday" and then recovered to a high of $17.25 in January 1988. At the end of March it was $15.12.[30]

Sixth, of the 13 federal privatizations six involved firms that were previously privately owned, i.e. Nordair, de Havilland, Pecheries Canada, Canadian Arsenals, Canadair, FPI. With the exception of Canadian Arsenals and Nordair, these firms were created to take over failing private firms (Pecheries Canada, FPI), or to acquire firms from foreign owners anxious to shut down their Canadian operations (Canadair, de Havilland).

Seventh, two of the 13 privatizations have involved pieces of Canadian National Railways. Both CN Route, a trucking company, and CN Hotels had

---

[28] See Christopher Waddell, "Petrocan will be biggest gas retailer after Gulf purchase," *Globe and Mail*, August 13, 1985, pp. 1-2; Christopher Waddell, "Firms, Ottawa to gain from Gulf deal,"*Globe and Mail*, August 14, 1985, p. B1. Petro-Canada acquired 1800 service stations in Ontario and Western Canada and four refineries. The purchase made Petro-Canada the largest gasoline retailer in Canada (see Bott 1987).

[29] See Ken Romain, "BCE set to acquire one-third interest in Memotec Data," *Globe and Mail*, May 8, 1987, p. A3; Lawrence Surtees, "BCE proposal opens door to major Teleglobe stake," *Globe and Mail*, May 9, 1987, p. B8; "A giant charts its future," *Maclean's*, May 25, 1987, pp. 26-27.

[30] John Saunders, "Beginner's luck of FPI owes much to fish prices, dollar rate," *Globe and Mail*, March 28, 1988, p. B10.

been losing money. CN Route lost $31.9 million on revenues of $163.4 million in 1984, and it lost $42.6 million on revenues of $163.4 million in 1985. Canadian National announced in April 1987 that it was putting CN Hotels up for sale seven months before the Minister of Transport announced that all the non-rail assets of CN would be sold. Between 1982 and 1986 the hotels lost from $500,000 to $5.3 million annually.[31] Revenues in 1986 were $147 million, up from $102 million in 1984. At the end of January 1988 CN announced an agreement to sell its hotels to Canadian Pacific Ltd., Canada's largest conglomerate, for $265 million.[32] The deal made CP the largest hotel chain in Canada.[33]

Eighth, Table 5.2 does not include the incremental privatization of part of its activities by Canada Post Corporation which became a Crown corporation in 1981. It is the nation's sixth largest Crown corporation and 29th largest non-financial enterprise.[34] Canada Post proposed to establish 50 retail franchises in major cities in 1987, but only four were opened by September. In addition, over the next decade Canada Post plans to transfer some 3500 rural post offices to franchise operations and to eventually close another 1700.[35]

The Canadian Union of Postal Workers went on strike in October 1987 to protect the "4200 prized day jobs behind the counters of Canada's post offices".[36] According to a CPC official, "franchising is not a terribly radical situation. It's similar to sub-post stations [which operate in convenience

---

[31] CN Annual Report, 1986, p. 20.

[32] Cecil Foster, "CP beats out 40 other bidders, buys CN hotels for $265 million," *Globe and Mail*, January 30, 1988, pp. A1-A2.

[33] CN said CP had agreed to maintain all existing labour contracts and pension benefits and to absorb all employees, about 3400 in total. CP also agreed to continue operating the properties as hotels of similar class and style, to maintain the two hotels in heritage buildings and to complete the renovation of another.

[34] In 1986 Canada Post's revenues were $3 billion, its deficit was $129 million and it employed some 63,500 persons. Generally, see Stewart-Patterson (1987). Baumann (1987) states that in March 1987 Canada Post had 52,760 employees, but this figure excludes part time workers.

[35] See Graham Fraser, "Liberals attack manual setting out strategy for closing post offices," *Globe and Mail*, October 21, 1987, pp. A1-A2. More generally, see Stanbury (1988, Ch. 7).

[36] *Maclean's*, October 12, 1987, p. 11.

stores, drugstores and other small businesses] which we've been offering for decades."[37] While Canada Post offered guaranteed employment with the corporation, albeit with the possibility of having to move to another city, the union has been adamant that these good jobs -- which do not involve shift work and pay an average $13.43 per hour -- must not disappear through franchising. The union stated that it will not fight the creation of franchise locations so long as they are not used to substitute for existing postal stations, and provided that none of their present wicket jobs are eliminated.[38]

It is clear that franchising could have several benefits for Canada Post. First, it could greatly reduce its future capital requirements for more retail outlets. Given the federal government's announced policy of requiring Air Canada and Petro-Canada to be financially self sufficient, this is an important benefit. Second, franchising may reduce CPC's operating costs at the retail distribution level.[39] Third, by offering greater customer convenience and perhaps more cheerful and helpful across-the-counter service, the post office's abysmal image may be improved. Fourth, franchise operations are easy to adopt; they could impose a useful constraint on the power of the union (CUPW), which has been able to get high wages and restrictive working conditions for its members by exploiting the cracks between CPC administrators, other government departments and the cabinet (see Stewart-Patterson 1987).

In an effort to bolster its position, the union commissioned a public opinion poll of 1200 Canadians.[40] Fifty percent were opposed to "privatization", defined as "the transfer of postal services to the private-sector", while 37 percent supported the idea and 13 percent were undecided. In addition, the postal unions and the Canadian Labour Congress ran a campaign to promote a postal policy that emphasizes increased service to the public rather than financial self-sufficiency.[41] For its part, Canada Post launched a $1

---

[37] Vancouver *Sun*, October 3, 1987, p. A8.

[38] Ibid., p. 11.

[39] The expected savings over the next decade were estimated by CPC to be $1.3 billion, mostly in wages. See *Maclean's*, October 12, 1987, p. 14.

[40] David Stewart-Patterson, "Poll shows split on privatization of postal service," *Globe and Mail*, July 21, 1987, p. A4.

[41] See, for example, the advocacy ad in the *Globe and Mail*, October 6, 1987.

million campaign of full-page newspaper ads in about two dozen dailies on September 5, 1987 in support of its "Retail Franchising Program".[42]

Franchising may be limited as a result of a ruling by the Canada Labour Board on September 1, 1987. The Board ordered the first franchisee, Shoppers' Drug Mart, to pay the same wages and benefits to franchise employees as does Canada Post.[43] Franchise employees earn from $4.50 to $8 less per hour than CPC employees. However, the ruling, which is being appealed to the Federal court, may not make franchising unfeasible, as it was based on the union's successor rights. The franchise in question in effect replaced an existing postal station. Where an entirely new outlet is created, the successor-rights provision might not apply.

## Provincial Privatizations

Between 1983 and May 1988 seven of Canada's ten provinces privatized 24 units -- consisting of 11 sales of all (or substantially all) the shares of a Crown corporation, eight sales of part of the assets or equity of a Crown, three sales of shares in a mixed enterprise, and the sale of two units that previously were part of a line department (see Table 5.3). (This list, of course, does not include the contracting-out of services previously performed by government employees.)[44]

Quebec has accounted for eight of the 24 privatizations, and all of them have occurred in 1986 and 1987 following the election of the Liberals under Robert Bourassa on December 2, 1985. Quebec can claim credit for the largest provincial privatization in terms of the selling price: $320 million

---

[42] "Ad campaign touts Canada Post franchises," *Globe and Mail*, September 16, 1987, p. B8.

[43] "Postal franchise ruling makes strike less likely, union says," *Globe and Mail*, September 3, 1987, p. A8.

[44] For example, during this period the B.C. government contracted-out the following: court reporting, part of the janitorial work for government offices, the laundry service for some hospitals, the operation of some recreational facilities, and some services for children and mental patients (see Stanbury 1988). For this and other reasons, authorized full-time positions in B.C. public service fell from 49,000 in 1982/83 to 34,000 in 1987/88. The cost of consultants and contracted work is budgeted to increase by $100 million to $341 million in 1988/89. The government proposes to reduce the number of full-time positions by 3,424 in 1988/89. See "B.C. government to cut 3,400 civil service jobs," *Globe and Mail*, April 4, 1988, p. A4.

for 56 percent of Donohue Inc.[45] It had sales of $475.6 million, assets of $826.6 million, and profits of $24.5 million in 1986. Donohue ranked #180 on the FP 500 in terms of 1986 revenues. Quebec's 6-percent interest in Provigo Inc. (#10 on the FP 500 for 1986), a food distributor, generated $48.3 million.

Quebec has privatized its Crowns in two ways. The sugar refinery ($48.5 million), Quebecair[46] ($5 million) and Soquip Alberta ($195 million),[47] an oil and gas firm, were sold to single buyers after a competitive bidding process. In the case of the bulk of its mining assets held by Soquem, the province, in effect, sold the enterprise through a wide share offering. It generated $100 million in cash and left the povince with 31.8 percent of the new (mixed) enterprise, Cambior Inc.[48] In mid-October 1987 (before the stock market crash), Quebec's seven million shares were worth another $156.6 million! In mid-April 1988 they were worth $107.6 million.

The Quebec government had said earlier that all of the "strategic commercial" Crowns or investments in mixed enterprises would be sold, e.g. the 44-percent interest in Domtar Inc.[49] and Rexfor Inc. (a Crown corporation producing forest products). Quebec has "blown hot and cold" regarding its Domtar shares,[50] and in February 1988 it announced that they had been taken off the market.[51]

---

[45] See *Globe and Mail*, February 23, 1987, p. B4; Vancouver *Sun*, February 10, 1987, p. E6.

[46] See *Financial Post*, August 9, 1986, p. 2; *Globe and Mail*, August 2, 1986, p. A2. Quebec invested almost $100 million in Quebecair between 1981 and 1987. The consolidation of the airline industry is described in Gillen et al. (1988).

[47] See Deidre McMurdy, "Expanded Sceptre seeks bigger deals," *Financial Times*, August 31, 1987, pp. 8, 39; and "Sceptre to pay $195 million for Soquip unit," *Globe and Mail*, October 29, 1987, p. B14.

[48] See *Globe and Mail*, June 10, 1986, p. B1; *Globe and Mail*, February 23, 1987, p. B4; April 30, 1986, p. B6; May 24, 1986, p. B4; May 3, 1986, p. B1; June 10, 1986, p. 11; and July 29, 1986, p. B4. See also Matuszewski (1988).

[49] In 1986 this forest products firm had sales of $2.3 billion, making it #39 on the FP 500.

[50] See *Globe and Mail*, April 11, 1987, p. B5; Matthew Horsman, "Innovation marks province's privatization spree," *Financial Post*, June 22, 1987, p. S4.

[51] Kimberly Noble, "Quebec denial fails to scotch speculation on Domtar sale," *Globe and Mail*, February 22, 1988, p. B3.

In April 1988 Quebec announced the sale of its Seleine salt mine, in which it had invested $125.4 million between 1979 and 1983, for $35 million.[52] The buyer is required to keep the mine operating for 10 years and fulfill other employment guarantees.

Alberta has effected only one privatization, and that was the sale of 85 percent of its shares in Pacific Western Airlines in December 1983. The province sold another 11 percent in August 1984 to bring in a total of $54 million for 96 percent of a firm it had purchased for $36 million in 1974 and made a Crown corporation. PWA ranked #197 on the FP 500 for 1983 when it had revenues of $328 million, assets of $546 million and profits of $10.8 million. It had 3000 employees. In January 1987 PWA acquired Canadian Pacific Air Lines, the nation's second largest airline, for $300 million, partly on the strength of benefits it received from being a Crown corporation (see Gillen et al. 1988).

Although Vining and Botterell (1983) found that Newfoundland had the most Crown corporations of any province excluding subsidiaries (42 in 1980), it has privatized none of them. It sold off, however, its 26.2 percent of FPI when 85 percent of its shares were sold in a wide distribution in April 1987. At that time the federal government sold its 62.6-percent interest in this mixed enterprise created by the two governments in 1984 to "bail out" several fish-processing operations in Newfoundland. The province received $48.7 million for its shares, but this was only 73.6 cents on each dollar it had put into FPI three years earlier. FPI ranked #213 on the FP 500 with sales of $388.7 million in 1986.

In Saskatchewan, the Conservatives led by Grant Devine have effected four privatizations, two of which are tiny: the sale of a plywood plant for $4 million and two operations of SMC for $16 million. In the case of Saskatchewan Oil and Gas Corp., it has moved from a Crown to a mixed enterprise through two public share offerings which have reduced the province's holdings to 46 percent, and netted the government $125 million.[53] Saskoil ranked #376 on the FP 500 in terms of 1985 sales. It has since acquired an Alberta-based oil and gas company to expand its reserves and production.

---

52 "Quebec to sell ailing salt mine for $35 million," *Globe and Mail*, April 4, 1988, p. B3.

53 Nicholas Hunter, "Saskoil privatization may give model for Petro-Canada sale," *Globe and Mail*, January 21, 1986, p. B1; John Twigg, "Saskoil issue to pay off Alberta buy," *Financial Post*, June 15, 1987, p. 3; Jim Lyon, "Saskoil has cash to shop," *Financial Post*, June 28, 1986, p. 23.

The sale of Prince Albert Pulp Co. (Papco) was a highly complex transaction.[54] The announced selling price was $248 million, but there were a few other terms to consider: (i) The buyer paid nothing down and was given 30 years to pay at 8.5-percent interest (but the rate is adjustable by a "prorating factor"); the minimum payment of principal is only $500,000 p.a. The balance (it could be $233 million) may be paid off by the issue of preferred shares which may not pay a dividend. (ii) The buyer agreed to expand the capacity of the pulp mill by about 10 percent and build a new paper mill at a cost of about $250 million. The province will provide loan guarantees for one-third of the $250 million. (iii) The province agreed to build an average of 32 km. of roads and bridges annually for 20 years to provide access to timber for the mills.

So what were the proceeds of the sale? These are not all the terms of the extremely complicated agreement. Can we even determine if the province has decreased or increased its involvement in the forest industry?

At the end of March 1988 the Saskatchewan government announced the sale of the salt mine and peat moss operations of Saskatchewan Minerals Corp. for a total of $16 million.[55] In the same week, however, the government provided a comparable amount of financial assistance to two high-tech firms.[56]

The Province of Ontario has sold two Crowns to private investors. At the end of 1986, it obtained some $4 million (but only $500,000 in cash) for Minaki Lodge upon which it had spent some $50 million since it was taken over in 1974.[57] The net proceeds to the Province will almost certainly be negative because the buyer obtained tax losses that may be used against other income now estimated to reduce federal and provincial tax revenues by $11 million.

---

[54] Kimberly Noble, "Weyerhauser plans major project in Saskatchewan," *Globe and Mail*, March 26, 1986, p. B2; Geoffrey York, "Saskatchewan called loser over Papco sale," *Globe and Mail*, February 11, 1987, p. B7; Robert Gibbens, "Pulp mill expansion ahead of schedule," *Globe and Mail*, April 16, 1987, p. B8.

[55] "Crown corporation sold," *Financial Post*, March 29, 1988, p. 4.

[56] Paul Jackson, "Saskatchewan helps high-tech industries," *Financial Post*, March 29, 1988, p. 26.

[57] "Province poised to auction off Minaki Lodge," Ottawa *Citizen*, July 18, 1986, p. A5; Stanley Oziewicz, "Four Seasons may purchase Minaki Lodge," *Globe and Mail*, October 24, 1986, pp. A1-A2; Ben Fiber, "Taxpayers give Minaki new lease on life," *Globe and Mail*, December 26, 1986, p. B1.

The sale of the Urban Transportation Development Corp. in mid-1986[58] (it would have ranked #287 on the FP 500 based on 1985 revenues) illustrates the sometimes high cost of divesting Crown corporations. Nominally, the Ontario government could claim it obtained $30 million ($10 million in cash and the balance as a 10-year income debenture) for 85 percent of the shares and 25 percent of the pre-tax profits for 10 years. The less visible cost of getting out of UTDC was as follows: (i) Ontario paid the buyer (Lavalin Inc.) a $10-million management fee to handle existing contracts -- which are expected to result in a loss for which Ontario is responsible. (ii) Ontario will pay the buyer $49.6 million for overhead over 18 months in which the existing contracts will be completed. (iii) Ontario will be responsible for paying the costs of warrantees and performance bonds of previous sales (over $500 million). This could end up costing many millions.

It appears that Ontario is paying at least $60 million plus future warranty claims to divest UTDC after investing some $167 million from 1973 to 1985. A public enterprise set up to do R&D ended up guaranteeing 400 <u>manufacturing</u> jobs and 100 research-related jobs for at least four years.

While it was privatizing two Crowns, in 1983 Ontario created a new one, Stadium Corp. of Ontario, to own and operate the $383 million "Sky Dome" in Toronto. When the stadium opens in 1989 the province will have 30 percent of the equity and 51 percent of the votes.[59]

The "social democratic" (NDP) government of Howard Pawley in Manitoba was not an enthusiastic privatizer. It did, however, sell Flyer

---

[58] Robert Sheppard, "Lavalin pays $51 million for UTDC; Ontario to keep 15% of firm," *Globe and Mail*, March 8, 1986, p. B5; See Thomas Claridge, "Detroit's little train that can't," *Globe and Mail*, July 11, 1986, pp. B1-B2; "Advantage in keeping UTDC," *Globe and Mail*, December 12, 1985, p. A7; Robert Sheppard, "2 companies post $1 million bonds in UTDC bidding," *Globe and Mail*, January 17, 1986, pp. A1-A2. For a profile of Lavalin, see Wayne Grigsby, "Master Builder," *Report on Business Magazine*, September 1986, pp. 58-64; Quoted in Andrew Cohen, "Ontario Liberals facing tough odds on transit firm sale," *Financial Post*, January 18, 1986, p. 21. More generally, see Maule (1985); John Partridge, "Bombardier ready to maintain UTDC jobs," *Globe and Mail*, February 4, 1986, p. B3; Duncan McMonagle, "2 Quebec firms in UTDC bidding expected to sweeten latest offers," *Globe and Mail*, February 28, 1986, p. A3; Duncan McMonagle, "Continuing aid urged for UTDC after sale," *Globe and Mail*, March 1, 1986, p. A11; Thomas Claridge, "UTDC's product guarantees may cost Ontario's taxpayers," *Globe and Mail*, March 17, 1986, pp. A1-A2; Robert Sheppard, "Ontario sweetens pot to sell UTDC to Lavalin," *Globe and Mail*, July 15, 1986, p. A4; Orland French, "The deal outdoes Houdini," *Globe and Mail*, July 16, 1986, p. A7.

[59] "Sky Dome: Anatomy of a dream," *Financial Times*, special advertising feature, April 11, 1988, p. A2.

Industries,[60] the fifth-largest manufacturer of transit buses in North America. The "sale" of Flyer also illustrates the high costs of divesting government enterprises. Indeed, it shows that they can be the stickiest type of tar baby. At first glance it seems the Province of Manitoba sold its 97-percent interest in Flyer for $1 million in cash. In fact, the deal was much more complicated. Some of its other terms were as follows: (i) The province will continue to own Flyer's assets, but lease them to the buyer at $300,000 p.a., after spending $4.6 million to renovate the plant. (ii) The province will be responsible for outstanding warranty and performance bonds at an estimated cost of $53 million. (iii) The province gave the buyer a $3-million loan that is forgivable if the buyer maintains 250 jobs in Manitoba. (iv) The province will be responsible for $30.5 million in guarantees for bank loans.

It appears, therefore, that Manitoba will spend about $100 million to get rid of Flyer. However, it should be noted that even if the province had shut down Flyer, it would have had to pay out some $84 million plus severance pay for the 387 employees. More important, the politicians would have had to contend both with the vociferous objections of those thrown out of work, and also the jibes of the more left-wing members of their own party.

Early in 1988 Manitoba announced it was dropping its plans (made known seven months earlier) to acquire Greater Winnipeg Gas Co., the distributor of about 73 percent of the natural gas in Manitoba from Inter-City Gas Corp.[61] The province had been able to negotiate lower gas prices with Alberta suppliers, but continued its appeal of a National Energy Board ruling designed to obtain still lower prices.[62] As of mid-January 1988 the province was assessing bids for Manfor Ltd., the government-owned pulp company. An estimated $250 million in public funds have been invested in the company. In 1987 it earned about $3 million on revenues of about $100 million.[63] In early

---

[60] "Flyer bus firm loses record $12.3 million," Vancouver *Sun*, June 16, 1984, p. B10. For a more detailed description of the company, see Andrew Nikiforuk, "Winging it," *Canadian Business*, November 1984, pp. 85-94; "Manitoba divests Flyer to Dutch firm," *Globe and Mail*, April 23, 1986, p. B8; "Dutch owners now pilot ailing Flyer," Toronto *Star*, July 17, 1986, p. F8; "Cost to fix Flyer problems increases," *Globe and Mail*, May 1987, p. B5.

[61] Geoffrey York, "Manitoba drops plan to buy gas firm," *Globe and Mail*, January 5, 1988, p. A8.

[62] "Manitoba plans to appeal ruling on gas delivery," *Globe and Mail*, January 13, 1988, p. B3.

[63] Ritchie Gage, "Manitoba studies offers for Crown pulp company," *Globe and Mail*, January 14, 1988, p. B11.

March 1988 the Howard Pawley government was defeated on a non-confidence motion. The Conservatives, who have been highly critical of the performance of Manitoba's Crown corporations, formed a minority government after the election on April 26. The Conservatives and the Liberal Party both promised to privatize more Crowns.[64]

As described earlier, the Province of British Columbia created Canadian history in 1979 when it gave away shares in the B.C. Resources Investment Corp. However, B.C.'s privatizations in the period 1983 to May 1988 have been much more modest -- with the exception of the sale of the Expo 86 lands for $145 million (see Table 5.3). While the province received $9 million for the sale of the general insurance business of the Insurance Corporation of B.C., whose principal business is automobile insurance, one report suggests that the province lost $4.6 million on the transaction.[65] However, as I shall later describe, the Vander Zalm government in B.C. has an ambitious privatization program underway.

Despite all the ruffles and flourishes associated with the privatization efforts of the provinces over the past five years, one overwhelming fact is clear. None of the Crowns or interests in mixed enterprises sold to date rank among the largest 15 provincial Crowns (Stanbury 1988, Ch. 9). The largest ones sold off, in whole or in part, were ranked as follows in the FP 500:

| | # | |
|---|---|---|
| -- Sask. Oil & Gas Corp. | 376 | (1985) |
| -- Urban Transp. Devel. Corp. | 287[66] | (1985) |
| -- Prince Albert Pulp Co. | 475est | (1985) |
| -- Donohue Inc. | 180 | (1986) |
| -- Pacific Western Airlines | 197 | (1983) |
| -- Fisheries Prod. Int'l. | 213 | (1986) |

In other words, the largest enterprise sold by any province ranked #180 on the FP 500 -- and it was not a Crown corporation but rather a 56-percent interest in a mixed enterprise (Donohue Inc.). It seems clear that

---

[64] Andrew Allentuck, "Manitoba's lonely Liberal looks forward to the election," *Financial Post*, April 5, 1988, p. 17.

[65] Der Hoi-Yin, "Socreds sold ICBC division at a loss," Vancouver *Sun*, April 3, 1985, p. F1.

[66] UTDC was not on the FP 500, but if it had been included it would have ranked #287.

Table 5.3

Provincial Privatizations in Canada Completed Between 1983 and May 1988

| Date of Transaction | Crown Corp./Asset | Selling Price |
|---|---|---|
| **Quebec** | | |
| 1. March 1986 | Sugar Refinery | $48.5 million |
| 2. July 1986 | 3 small asbestos mines | $5.6 million, $6.4 million, $2.9 million |
| 3. Aug. 1986 | Soquem assets (Cambior Inc.) | $100 million cash[1] plus 31.8% of Cambior ($107.6 million at April 14/88) |
| 4. Sept. 1986 | Quebecair | $5 million (est.) |
| 5. Feb. 1987 | 6% Provigo Inc. | $48.3 million |
| 6. Feb. 1987 | 56% Donohue Inc. | $320 million |
| 7. Oct. 1987 | Soquip Alberta | $195 million (est.)[2] |
| 8. April 1988 | Seleine salt mine | $35 million |
| **Alberta** | | |
| 1. Dec. 1983 & Aug. 1984 | 96% Pacific Western Airlines | $54 million[3] |
| **Newfoundland** | | |
| 1. April 1987 | 26.2% Fisheries Products Int'l. | $48.7 million |
| **Saskatchewan** | | |
| 1. Jan. 1986 & July 1987 | Saskatchewan Oil & Gas | $125 million[4] (for 54%) |
| 2. Sept. 1986 | Prince Albert Pulp Co. | $248 million[5] (all debt over 30 years, min. $500,000 p.a. on principal, at a concessionary interest rate) |
| 3. 1987 | plywood plant | $4 million |
| 4. April 1988 | salt mine & peat moss operations of Sask. Minerals Corp. | $16 million |
| **Ontario** | | |
| 1. Dec. 1986 | Minaki Lodge | $4 million[6] |
| 2. July 1986 | 85% Urban Transport. Devel. Corp. | $10 million cash plus $20 million debenture over 10 years (but the Province will pay $59.6 million to buyer to finish existing contracts, and assume liability for warrantees and performance bonds on $526 million) |

Table 5.3 continued

Provincial Privatizations in Canada Completed Between 1983 and May 1988 (continued)

| Date of Transaction | Crown Corp./Asset | Selling Price |
|---|---|---|
| **Manitoba** | | |
| 1. April 1986 | 98.3% Flyer Industries (buses) | $1 million, but the Province will be liable for previous warranty claims ($53 million), a bank loan ($30.5 million), make a forgivable loan to the buyer for $3 million, pay $4.6 million to renovate Flyer's plant that it is leasing for $300,000 per annum. |
| **British Columbia** | | |
| 1. Sept. 1983 | Beautiful B.C. magazine | $760,000 |
| 2. 1984 | Pacific Coach Lines | not available |
| 3. Feb. 1985 | General insurance business of ICBC | $9 million |
| 4. Jan. 1988 | Laboratory | $140,000 |
| 5. Jan. 1988 | Publications, dist. of Queen's Printer | $352,000 |
| 6. April 1988 | Dept. of Highways sign plant | $859,674 |
| 7. May 1988 | Expo 86 lands | $145 million [7] |

Notes:
1. It appears the Province of Quebec retained responsibility for Soquem's $90 million debt.
2. The buyer, Sceptre Resources, took over $155 million in debt and gave Soquip 8 million of Sceptre's common shares which traded for $3.50 the day after the transaction (Oct. 27/87). On April 18, 1988, the Sceptre shares closed at $4.65.
3. In December 1983 Alberta sold 3.7 million shares for $10.75. In August 1984 Alberta sold another 1.35 million shares for $10.50.
4. In January 1986 Saskoil sold 41.7% to the public; $75 million went to the Province and $35 million was invested in the company's operations. In July 1987 another 12% was sold for $50 million.
5. The buyer agreed to expand the pulp mill and build a new paper mill for about $250 million, one third in loans guaranteed by the Province. The Province is also required to build 32 km in roads each year for 20 years.
6. $1,000,000 in cash (less $500,000 expenses), plus $3 million over seven years. Federal and provincial government will lose up to $11 million in income taxes because of tax losses transferred to the buyer. The Province will have to continue to pay maintenance on the road it built to the Lodge.
7. Provincial government's specified present value; other estimates are closer to $120 million. See Gordon Gibson, Financial Post, May 16, 1988, p. 19.

Source: Stanbury (1988).

none of the largest provincial Crowns, i.e. the electricity and telephone utilities, will be privatized (Stanbury 1988, Ch. 9). In terms of assets, they rank among the largest enterprises on the FP 500. In 1984, for example, 13 of the 100 largest non-financial corporations in Canada ranked by assets were provincial Crowns and six of the next 100 were provincial Crowns (Stanbury 1986, p. 64).

Thirteen of the 24 provincial privatizations between 1983 and May 1988 involved firms or parts of firms that were previously privately owned. Three of these involved mixed enterprises. The economically most important Crowns sold that were previously entirely owned by private owners are the following: Quebecair, Soquip Alberta, Pacific Western Airlines, FPI and Flyer Industries.

## FUTURE PRIVATIZATIONS

### Federal Candidates for Privatization

By mid-1987 the rate of federal privatization announcements slowed markedly. By the end of the year, several events had occurred that suggested that the volume of privatization activity in Canada is likely to be less in the near future than it was in the period 1985-1987. First, there was the stock market crash of October 1987.[67] It will make it harder to sell Crowns at a good price.[68] Second, the crash cost Canadian brokers who had taken up large blocks of the issue of British Petroleum some $120 million.[69] Moreover, on the last batch of CDC shares, brokers contracted to buy 7.5 million shares at $13.75 on October 8 and on October 27, after the crash, when the sale

---

[67] See "Living With the Crash," *Maclean's*, November 2, 1987, pp. 26-40. "After the Meltdown of '87," *Newsweek*, November 2, 1987, pp. 14-53.

[68] See Cecil Foster, "Ottawa misses the market on privatization," *Globe and Mail*, November 2, 1987, pp. B1-B7; Peter Cook, "Mrs. Thatcher sets sail, but McDougall misses the boat," *Globe and Mail*, November 2, 1987, p. B2.

[69] See "Adding to the Wreckage," *Maclean's*, November 9, 1987, p. 45. Wood Gundy is believed to have lost $60 million alone - see Peter Foster, "Scrambling for cover after BP," *Financial Post*, November 9, 1987, p. 16.

closed the shares were trading for $9.62.[70]. Both events may make underwriters chary of handling further privatizations. Third, on its biggest privatization, Teleglobe, the process was somewhat impugned when the Quebec Securities Commission investigation led to charges of insider trading in September 1987.[71] One of the persons charged, a lawyer for Memotec, is a former president of the federal Conservative Party and a former candidate for its leadership. However, he was acquitted in April 1988.

Fourth, it seems clear that in July 1987 the Prime Minister vetoed the sale of Air Canada[72] despite the fact that there was widespread support to sell the airline prior to full deregulation (in southern Canada) coming into effect on January 1, 1988. He did so, apparently, because he believed his credibility would be further eroded (he was then running <u>third</u> in the public opinion polls) in light of his statement in January 1985 that Canada needed a national airline and Air Canada would not be sold (see Stanbury 1988, Ch. 8).[73]

While these factors may inhibit future privatizations, the new free trade agreement between Canada and the U.S. will not do so. The agreement, signed on January 2, 1988, reduces restrictions on foreign investment in both countries. Canada, however, will continue to be able to impose limits on the holdings by foreigners of shares of existing Crown corporations that may be privatized in the future.[74]

As of May 1988 the federal government had several Crown entities under active consideration for privatization in addition to Air Canada. In June 1987 the Minister of State for Privatization announced that a financial advisor was being retained to evaluate the government's 20-percent equity interest in National Sea Products after the private-sector owners indicated they wanted the government to sell its interest. In mid-April 1988 the shares had a market

---

[70] Philip De Mont, "Timing still key on CDC," *Financial Times*, November 2, 1987, p. 12.

[71] Karen Howlett and Robert Gibbens, "Memotec insiders face charges on trading," *Globe and Mail*, September 26, 1987, pp. B1, B13. See also "The Memotec affair," *Maclean's*, October 5, 1987, p. 38.

[72] See Cecil Foster, "Air Canada sale won't fly," *Globe and Mail*, August 22, 1987, pp. B1, B4.

[73] Another interpretation is offered in Deborah McGregor, "Air Canada won't fly - nor will anything else," *Financial Times*, September 7, 1987, pp. 1-2.

[74] See "Ownership of privatized firms may be limited," *Globe and Mail*, December 12, 1987, p. B5.

value of $22.3 million, but no further announcement had been made. Radiochemical Co. is said to be a likely candidate for privatization in 1988. It had revenues of $111 million and profits of about $14 million in 1986/87. Analysts suggested it might fetch $150 million.[75]

In December 1987 the Minister of Transport announced that all of CN's non-rail assets were to be sold[76] with a view to reducing the Crown corporations's $3.2 billion debt. At its peak in 1952 CN had 131,297 employees, but this number had fallen to 41,000 by the end of 1987. In five years the number is expected to fall to 26,000 (Foster 1988, p. 40). In addition to the hotels, the assets for sale include two small telephone companies, the CN Tower, 50 percent interest in CNCP Telecommunications, and CN Exploration, an oil and gas enterprise. Terra Nova Tel, which serves 50,000 subscribers in Newfoundland, earned $4 million in profit on $46 million in revenue in 1987. Northwestel, with 35,000 subscribers in the Yukon, earned $7.6 million on $67 million in revenues in 1987.[77] In 1986, CN Exploration earned profits of $4.5 million versus $30.6 million in 1985 and $15.9 million in 1984. Revenues in 1986 were $33.9 million.[78] CNCP Telecommunications had revenues of $343 million in 1986.[79] It appears that when all of the non-rail assets of CN are sold, it will amount to the second largest privatization in Canada behind Air Canada.

At the end of February 1988 CN announced it was seeking a buyer for its subsidiary Grand Trunk Eastern Line which operates in New England.[80] CN was also moving to restructure or close down its subsidiary Terra Transport, which operates rail, trucking and bus service in Newfoundland at

---

75 David Hatter, "Crown sell-off decisions get harder to make," *Financial Post*, December 28, 1987, p. 6.

76 "CN's non-rail assets for sale, minister says," Vancouver *Sun*, December 2, 1987, p. F5.

77 Nancy Begalki, "Native groups link to pursue Norwestel," *Globe and Mail*, February 1, 1988, p. B8.

78 CN, Annual Report 1986, p. 26.

79 Canadian Pacific Ltd. has the right of first refusal with respect to CN's 50-percent interest in CNCP. See Fred McMahon, "CP sees bright future in bid for CNCP control," *Financial Post*, January 4, 1988, p. 5.

80 Cecil Foster, "CN considers closing Newfoundland unit," *Globe and Mail*, February 25, 1988, pp. B1-B2.

an annual loss of $50 million. It was reported that Ottawa had offered the province $850 million to close down Terra Transport and upgrade the highways on the island.

On February 22, 1988, the federal and Saskatchewan governments announced an agreement to merge Eldorado Nuclear Ltd. with Saskatchewan Mining Development Corp. The Saskatchewan government will own 61.5 percent of the shares of the merged enterprise.[81] The new corporation will have assets of $1.6 billion, 1000 employees, and sales of about $500 million. The two governments are to reduce their shareholdings by 30 percent within two years, by 60 percent within four years, and by 100 percent within seven years. The rate of sale of shares is to be determined by market conditions.[82] Canadian investors will be permitted to hold no more than 25 percent of the voting shares. Foreigners will be limited to 5 percent individually, and collectively they will not be able to vote more than 20 percent of the shares at annual meetings. The new enterprise is expected to issue $600 million to $650 million in new debt to its government shareholders who, in turn, will pay off part of Eldorado's and SMDC's debt that is backed by government guarantees. The federal government will be reimbursed for only $230 million of Eldorado's $570 million debt. The Saskatchewan government, however, will obtain enough out of the debt refinancing to cover SMDC's debt.[83] The new firm will control over one half of Canada's uranium production, which was 32 percent of world output in 1986.

---

[81] Geoffrey York, "Eldorado-SMDC merger 'world-beater'," *Globe and Mail*, February 23, 1988, pp. B1-B6. The synergies expected from the merger include greater ability to market uranium through greater market power, the rationalization of future of uranium mines and an improved balance between mining and refining operations. One financial advisor said that SMDC's low-cost uranium reserves and Eldorado's refineries represent a "world-beating combination".

The merger follows a turn around for Eldorado. It had profits of $12 million in 1987 versus losses of $64 million in 1986 and $57.2 million in 1985. SMDC paid a dividend of $15 million in 1986 and had a profit in 1985. See Jane Becker, "Crown-owned Eldorado Nuclear posed for return to the private sector," *Globe and Mail*, January 28, 1988, p. B13. Eldorado's assets grew from $361 million in 1980 to $916 million in 1987, while long-term debt rose to $561 million. Because the debt was in foreign currencies, Eldorado has had to provide $240 million for potential foreign-exchange losses. In 1987 SMDC had a profit of $60.3 million versus $30.4 million in 1986 (*Globe and Mail*, April 15, 1988, p. B8).

[82] Philip De Mont, "The emerging uranium giant," *Financial Times*, February 29, 1988, p. 13.

[83] David Hatter, "Merger leaves Ottawa with Eldorado's debts," *Financial Post*, February 29, 1988, p. 7.

On March 31 Don Mazankowski replaced Barbara McDougall as the Minister Responsible for Privatization and Regulatory Affairs. The big news came on April 12, 1988, when Mazankowski announced that up to 45 percent of Air Canada would be sold -- with the balance to follow (as market conditions warrant) in a process that may take from five to ten years.[84] With assets of $3.08 billion and revenues of $3.13 billion in 1987, the sale of Air Canada represents by far the most ambitious privatization by the Mulroney government. Mazankowski claimed the announcement was "fully consistent with the Prime Minister's statement to ensure the existence of a national airline. . ." Privatization, he said, was needed to attract new capital to finance the purchase of new aircraft. Opposition Leader John Turner called the move "a clear breach of faith between the Prime Minister and the Canadian people". NDP leader Ed Broadbent described it as "the triumph of Conservative ideology over good, practical, Canadian common sense" and vowed that his party would "do everything we can to stop the Government". Mazankowski argued that "blind devotion to state enterprises would be the only possible reason for not proceeding at this time."[85] The *Globe and Mail* stated that "in denouncing the sale, the New Democrats and the Liberals exhibit a particularly moldy nationalism. Air Canada serves no public policy purpose in our deregulated transportation system," and hence should be privatized.[86]

The president of the airline division of CUPE said privatization will lead to a deterioration in labor relations and a loss of jobs, and will threaten the company's pension plan. He said, "What the Government fails to realize is that the people of Canada already own Air Canada."[87] President Pierre Jeanniot described privatization as the "financial key to Air Canada's future". It will allow the airline "to plan for fleet expansion and renewal as well as pursue new business opportunities". The head of the machinists union, which represents 8500 Air Canada employees, said that "it's not an economic move.

---

84 Christopher Waddell, "Ottawa to begin selling off Air Canada," *Globe and Mail*, April 13, 1988, pp. A1, A9.

85 Ibid., p. A9.

86 "Selling Air Canada" (editorial) *Globe and Mail*, April 13, 1988, p. A6.

87 For a more detailed critique, see Val Udvartely, "Why should public buy shares in something it already owns?" *Globe and Mail*, April 14, 1988, p. A7. This particular assessment contains numerous errors of fact and logic, but it does assemble in one place all of the bad arguments against privatizing Air Canada. For a counter view, see W.T. Stanbury and M.W. Tretheway, "Selling Air Canada: a no-lose solution," *Globe and Mail*, May 16, 1988, p. A7.

It's a blatantly ideological move."[88] An Angus Reid-Southam News poll in March 1988 indicated 53 percent of Canadians think Air Canada should not be sold while 35 percent favor privatization.[89]

Air Canada announced that despite a 19-day strike in December,[90] its 1987 profits were $45.7 million, up $5.3 million over 1986. The strike, cost the airline some $70 million, however. Revenues in 1987 were $3.13 billion versus $2.89 billion in 1986. At the end of 1987 only $130 million of the airline's $2.1 billion debt was guaranteed by the federal government.

The government has imposed several conditions regarding the privatization of Air Canada:

-- The headquarters must remain in Montreal.
-- The airline must keep, for the indefinite future, its operational and overhaul centers in Montreal, Toronto and Winnipeg.[91]
-- No more than 45 percent of the shares will be sold in the initial offering.
-- Employees must be given the first chance to buy shares through a payroll deduction scheme or similar program. (It is not clear whether they will pay a lower price than others.)[92]
-- Small shareholders are to be next on the list of preferred buyers, followed by institutional investors and, finally, by foreigners.
-- After the initial treasury issue of up to 45 percent, the Government's 55-percent stake will be voted in accordance with the majority

---

[88] Waddell, *Globe and Mail*, April 13, 1988, p. A9.

[89] "Critics slam sale of Air Canada," Vancouver *Sun*, April 13, 1988, p. E1. However, the Deputy Prime Minister has cited a poll that indicates 62 percent of Canadians favor the privatization of Air Canada. See *Globe and Mail*, May 20, 1988, p. B1.

[90] The machinists union, which admitted it was fearful of privatization, struck to obtain the principle of indexation of pensions. Although it obtained only partial indexation for retired members, the union succeeded in making the Crown airline less attractive to a private owner and less valuable to the federal government. It should be noted that the union settled with Canadian Airlines International just before the strike started for 4 percent, 4 percent and 5 pcercent over three years without any indexation of pensions. See Robin Schiele, "Sale of Air Canada is eye of dispute," *Financial Post*, December 7, 1987, pp. 1-2.

[91] See Paul Koring, "Ottawa moves to protect Air Canada bases," *Globe and Mail*, May 20, 1988, pp. B1-B2.

[92] Waddell, *Globe and Mail*, April 13, 1988, p. A9.

of the new private-sector shareholders so that there will be "a clear arms-length relationship".[93]

-- No individual shareholder will be allowed to hold more than 10 percent of the shares sold to private investors (hence 4.5 percent of the initial offering).

-- Total foreign ownership will be limited to 25 percent (or 11 percent of the initial offering).

Several questions immediately come to mind. First, the 10-percent limit on individual shareholdings may or may not constitute a serious constraint on the "revenge of the capital market" in the event that management performs poorly. After full privatization, five individuals could combine to get control and appoint new managers. However, the federal legislation may follow the unfortunate Alberta precedent. When PWA was privatized in December 1983, the legislation provided that no individual or group of associated individuals could vote more than 4 percent of the stock.[94] Such a constraint gives management effective control -- even though it owns no shares at all. If the 10-percent rule for Air Canada is similar to PWA's, we could have the spectre of Canada's two largest airlines being privately owned but effectively controlled by management. The 10-percent constraint may be of little consequence if it is possible for private-sector interests to buy all or substantially all of the assets of Air Canada.

Second, Air Canada could end up in the worst of all possible worlds, a mixed enterprise (see Economic Council 1986; Stanbury 1988, Ch. 8). The Tories could sell off 45 percent, but a Liberal or NDP Government could prevent full privatization. This could also occur if the Tories are only a minority government after the next election. A 55:45 mixed enterprise would either involve the exploitation of the private-sector shareholders as the federal government uses its 55 percent to pursue goals inconsistent with profit maximization, or it would result in management exercising effective control where government fails to exercise its rights as a majority owner to remove inefficient management.

Given the possible obstruction by the Liberal-dominated Senate, and the time needed to prepare the issue for market (about four months), it is

---

93 Generally, see Waddell, *Globe and Mail*, April 14, 1988, pp. A1, A10.

94 Note the Alberta legislation still applies to PWA Corp., the holding company of Canadian Airlines International (CAI). The new name was adopted after PWA paid $300 million for CP Air early in 1987 (see Gillen et al. 1988).

doubtful if the first batch of shares (up to 45 percent) will be sold before the autumn of 1988. That may conflict with the timing of the next general election. If the issue (and the election) do not occur until the spring of 1989, the price of the shares may be hurt by the increase in capacity as CAI's and Wardair's new aircraft arrive and/or by the start of a recession. In short, the partial privatization of Air Canada is far from a sure thing, and its full privatization is even more problematic.

## Provincial Plans for Privatization

Based on reports in the media as of May 1988, only two provinces (Saskatchewan and B.C.) had active privatization programs.[95] In October 1987 Saskatchewan's Minister of Consumer and Corporate Affairs confirmed that the province was planning to sell part of Saskatchewan Government Insurance Corp. -- the general and commercial insurance businesses, but not the compulsory automobile insurance business.[96] It is estimated to be worth $100 million. Shares are to be sold to the public. In November, newspaper reports indicated that a major portion of Saskatchewan Computer Utility Corp. ($1.9 million profit on revenue of $26.9 million in 1986) is to be merged with part of Saskatchewan Telecommunications and then sold to the private-sector.[97] Although re-elected in October 1986, the Devine government in Saskatchewan still has to contend with public opinion. A poll of 1,173 Saskatchewan residents in mid-October 1987 found that 55.4 percent disapproved of further privatization while 33 percent were in favor.[98]

---

[95] A recent newspaper report suggests that Premier Getty has promised his supporters that privatization would soon become a major issue. Don Braid, "Alberta too is planning to attack the cost of social programs," Vancouver *Sun*, april 21, 1988, p. B3.

[96] "Saskatchewan to privatize Crown insurance corp.," *Financial Post*, October 19, 1987, p. 8.

[97] "Two Saskatchewan utilities plan to merge, go public," *Globe and Mail*, November 13, 1987, p. B9.

[98] Data cited in Joe Ralko, "Ignore the opposition to selling crown firms expert advises Tories," Toronto *Star*, November 16, 1987, p. D12.

In January 1988 the Premier appointed a Minister of Public Participation responsible for the province's privatization efforts.[99] He soon suggested several methods of reducing the government's role in commercial activities.[100]

Perhaps the most ambitious privatization program was announced in October 1987 by the Premier of British Columbia when he stated that one Crown corporation, part of another, and 11 government operations would be sold or transferred to the private-sector.[101] The total value of the assets and services was estimated to be $3 billion, and the number of employees affected was put at 7,240 (see Twigg 1987).

The two Crowns put on the block in October are the natural gas distribution, rail, and R&D divisions of B.C. Hydro, and B.C. Systems Corp., which provides computer services to the province. The Lower Mainland natural gas division had revenues of $382 million and operating income of $19.6 million in 1986/87 (British Columbia 1988, p. 2). It is being sought by up to a dozen companies. B.C. Systems was put on the block in September 1983, but a buyer could not be found to take over all the assets. BCSC has 433 employees ($42.8 million in revenue in 1986/87), while the gas, rail and R&D divisions of B.C. Hydro employ 1,140.

In the second phase of the province's privatization program, which still requires some additional work, the following activities will be transferred to the private-sector: liquor distribution branch stores (all beer, wine, spirits) with 10 or fewer employees; the government's warehouses, distribution centres and stores operations; the remaining Queen's Printer operations, i.e. typesetting, printing and binding; and the province's second mortgage program.

---

99 "Saskatchewan Cabinet gets 3 new portfolios," *Globe and Mail*, January 16, 1988, p. A16.

100 Paul Jackson, "Saskatchewan plans peaceful, privatization drive," *Financial Post*, February 1, 1988, p. 7.

101 Gary Mason et al. "Socreds aim to privatize 2 firms, 11 operations," Vancouver *Sun*, October 23, 1987, pp. A1-A2; Jennifer Hunter, "B.C. to sell $3 billion in assets, Vander Zalm says," *Globe and Mail*, October 24, 1987, p. A4; and "Vander Zalm's bold plans," *Maclean's*, November 2, 1987, pp. 14-15. The government operations to be privatized are the following: all bridge and road maintenance operations (3800 employees), three laboratories, the van and ambulance modification unit of the health ministry, the sign shop of the transportation and highways ministry, the marketing of government publications, stationery stores and supply centres of the Queen's Printer, a computer software system created by the Purchasing Commission, nine forestry nurseries (400 employees), and transfer of the Riverview mental hospital to a non-profit society funded by government grants (1400 employees).

In addition, over the next five months several other units were added to the list: most of the valuable landholdings of the B.C. Enterprise Corporation, B.C. Steamships (which operates two vessels between Victoria and Seattle), the operation of provincial campgrounds and recreational facilities, automobile safety testing, and (possibly) ambulance services.[102]

The B.C. government favours privatization proposals from employees that emphasize job creation, job protection, and incentives for employee ownership. Employee bids will be accepted even if they are up to 5 percent less than others.

The most interesting element in B.C.'s program is the proposed privatization of highway maintenance and of liquor distribution. The former represents the largest effort at contracting-out, while the privatization of small liquor outlets (previously a government monopoly) flies in the face of the Quebec government's unsuccessful attempt to do much the same thing (see Hafsi and Demers 1986). Indeed, in May 1988 the province backed off on its plan to privatize small liquor stores.[103]

B.C.'s plans for privatization have produced much controversy. The B.C. Government Employees Union "declared war" on privatization, and sponsored a series of advocacy ads in newspapers to solicit public support for its position.[104] The leader of the official opposition and the officials of the BCGEU have stated that privatization of highway maintenance would result in more deaths on the roads.[105] While not necessarily agreeing with this position, the privatization of highway maintenance has been opposed by both

---

[102] Mark Hume, "Ex-insiders caught in Expo land bid fray," April 8, 1988, p. A3; "A mysterious victory," *Maclean's*, April 11, 1988, p. 37; Gary Mason, "BCEC controversy flares," Vancouver *Sun*, April 14, 1988, pp. A1-A2; "B.C. seeks private partners to help run ferries," *Globe and Mail*, February 2, 1988, p. B11; Glenn Bohn, "Privately run camps urged," Vancouver *Sun*, March 23, 1988, pp. A1-A2; Gordon Hamilton, "Whistler up for sale, Blackcomb bidding," Vancouver *Sun*, March 24, 1988, p. E8; Miguel Moya, "Private tests for cars called open to abuse," Vancouver *Sun*, March 17, 1988, p. A12; Keith Baldrey, "Privatization plan for ambulances mulled," Vancouver *Sun*, March 5, 1988, p. A3.

[103] Keith Baldrey, "Liquor store plan shelved, minister says," Vancouver *Sun*, May 4, 1988, p. A9.

[104] "BCGEU declares war on sale plans," Vancouver *Sun*, November 5, 1987, pp. A1-A2.

[105] Vaughn Palmer, "Union's scare campaign simply silly," Vancouver *Sun*, November 27, 1987, p. B6.

a former minister and deputy minister of highways.[106] At the same time, some government employees are proposing to bid for highways maintenance contracts.[107] The Premier caused quite a stir when he sent a letter to some school teachers and principals which said that "others are counting on you to understand the facts of privatization and to know all sides of the issue."[108]

The political furor over B.C.'s privatization plans resulted in the first emergency debate in the Legislature in over a decade and the first ever to be broadcast on radio.[109] A small public opinion poll (n=475) conducted in November 1987 indicated that 49 percent were opposed to privatization while 44 percent favored it. On the most controversial proposal, the privatization of highway maintenance, 61 percent of the respondents were opposed.[110] In general, support for the Social Credit government had fallen to 27 percent, versus 31 percent for the opposition, but one third were undecided.

The first three sales announced in early 1988 were small (see Table 5.3). All were sold to groups of former employees. However, the fourth transaction -- the sale of Expo 86 lands -- netted $145 million, and the sale of B.C. Hydro's natural gas divisions expected in the fall of 1988 will probably generate several times that amount.

In no other province or at the federal level has privatization produced such a heated debate. Only time will tell if the B.C. government is able to fully implement its extensive privatization plans.

---

[106] Keith Baldrey, "Official highway critics' club grows," Vancouver *Sun*, December 8, 1987, p. A11.

[107] Valerie Casselton, "Union brass split on road bid," Vancouver *Sun*, December 3, 1987, p. A3. The Premier announced that the province would be divided into 28 districts for the privatization of highways maintenance. See Gary Mason, "Highway plan assailed," Vancouver *Sun*, January 22, 1988, pp. A1-A2.

[108] Francis Bula, "Premier's privatization letter blasted," Vancouver *Sun*, March 9, 1988, p. A3.

[109] For a summary of the speeches, see "The battle over privatization," Vancouver *Sun*, December 1, 1987, p. A4.

[110] Gary Mason and Keith Baldrey, "Socreds lose favor, poll shows," Vancouver *Sun*, November 28, 1987, pp. A1, A10.

## EXPLAINING PRIVATIZATION IN CANADA

### Three Hypotheses

In this section I shall advance three working hypotheses designed to explain the nature and extent of privatization in Canada over the past five years:

(1) Privatization is the result of other changes in the ideology of the federal and some provincial governments, or it is the result of electoral decisions in which parties or leaders were elected that were committed to "downsizing the state," largely on philosophical grounds.

(2) Privatization is a political (and bureaucratic) response to the recently identified set of problems associated with the large number of Crown corporations, e.g. Crowns that no longer serve a well-defined public-policy purpose; a demonstrated lack of accountability and control; or the Crowns' funding needs outpaces the ability of the treasury to finance them.

(3) Privatization is a case of symbolic politics designed to appease the critics of government while doing little or nothing to divest the largest public enterprises. It is a case of tacking with the political winds, and of being seen to be in tune with leading political policy developments around the world, notably the manifest success of privatization in the U.K. (Yarrow and Vickers 1988). In practice, therefore, privatization consists of selling-off a few minor appendages of government without arousing the organized opposition of interventionist/nationalists, so that after the enthusiasm wanes the largest public enterprises remain as they were. Moreover, even if the size of the public enterprise component of all government activity is reduced somewhat, the total size of government may well be larger through the expansion of other policy instruments such as expenditures, taxes, loans/guarantees, and tax expenditures.

### Privatization as Ideology

The idea that the recent record of privatization in Canada can be explained by ideology must be based on either a change in the ideology of those in the seats of political power, or on the election of leaders and parties whose ideology favours privatization. With respect to the latter, no right-wing party fervently committed to privatization has been elected in Canada. (The

Vander Zalm Government in B.C. is generally described as populist. Privatization was not one of his promises in the campaign prior to the election in October 1986.) So far, the two largest privatization programs have been effected by the Progressive Conservatives in Ottawa (Table 5.2) and the Liberals in Quebec (Table 5.3). The ideological bent of both is to dominate the "mushy middle" so as to attain and maintain power. The ideological variance (in the sense of the traditional right-left spectrum) within each party is as great as it is between rival parties themselves.[111]

However, on the specific dimension of Crown corporations some observers suggest that, at the federal level, the positions of the federal Liberals and Tories can be distinguished on ideological grounds. Columnist Michael Valpy has argued that in 1983 the Tories were developing an ideology in respect of Crown corporations that was quite distinct from the Liberals. It was seen to have two components: "First, a rejection of the general notion that public enterprise should be used to achieve public policy ends. Second, there is a hardening belief that government, in a major way, should divest itself of a state enterprise that no longer demonstrably serves public policy ends."[112] This has been the principal argument for privatization advanced by the Tories (as noted in the concluding section, "Ex Post Facto Rationalization").

Ideology as the main explanation of privatization in Canada is helpful in the case of Alberta selling almost all its holdings in PWA in 1983 and 1984. But it doesn't explain why the Conservatives under Don Getty have not privatized anything. It seems clear that in Saskatchewan that ideology was the motivation behind the Devine government's privatization of Saskoil, Prince Albert Pulp and some other small holdings. The Conservatives' view of Crown corporations was clearly more critical than their NDP predecessors. Devine, however, has stopped short of selling-off or even publicly proposing to sell off two sacred cows: Sask Tel and Sask Power. In B.C., the Vander Zalm Government is strongly committed to limiting the growth of government, and to shifting both some Crowns and the operations of line departments into

---

[111] On the other hand, Michael Prince (1986) argues that the general thrust of the Mulroney government's economic policy has been a notable shift to the right.

[112] Michael Valpy, "A point of ideology," *Globe and Mail*, July 15, 1983, p. 6. Valpy noted that during the campaigns for leadership of the Conservative Party in 1983, "most candidates... - Brian Mulroney, the victor, being a cautious and notable exception - talked much about privatizing public enterprises." However, Mr. Mulroney did make common cause with the others in calling for stronger accountability to, and control by, parliament, and in criticizing the Liberals' new Crown, CDIC, to be used to manage others. More generally, see the discussion in Doern and Atherton (1987).

private hands. It believes fervently in small business and in reducing the power of public-sector unions. Privatization, it believes, can help both causes.

Ideology certainly cannot explain why the NDP government of Howard Pawley divested Flyer Industries, spending about $100 million to do so! Ideology probably explains why Manitoba has privatized nothing else -- considering that the NDP was in power from late 1982 to April 1988. It is not clear that ideology had much to do with the plan (later dropped) to acquire a privately owned natural gas distribution system.[113]

Given the highly interventionist posture of the Liberals in Ontario under David Peterson from mid-1985 to September 1987 (when he began operating a minority government with the help of the NDP), even two privatizations are surprising. However, in opposition the Liberals had been quite critical of the two Crowns that were sold: Minaki Lodge and Urban Transportation Development Corporation.

## Privatization as a Reaction to the Problems with Crowns

This hypothesis to explain the nature and extent of privatization in Canada over the past five years has been well articulated by Gillies (1984, pp. 10-11)[114] when he said that

> "the movement for privatization in Canada at the present time [late 1984] springs primarily from the concern that many Crown corporations have not been well managed, have often exceeded their mandate, and that they do not have a policy function to fulfill that cannot be fulfilled at less cost to the taxpayer, and with more accountability to parliament, by some other policy instrument. Moreover, there is growing belief that the effectiveness of public-sector corporations in dealing with broad, general economic problems of unemployment, inflation and economic growth, at least in Canada, has yet to be demonstrated."

---

113 It appears that a move was made to overcome certain anomalies associated with the deregulation of natural gas prices in October 1985. Finding a way to lower the heating bills of 200,000 households, probably looked like a popular thing to do. Moreover, it is hard to see how other governing instruments could achieve the same objective (see Stanbury 1988, Ch. 7).

114 As a senior policy advisor to the Clark government of 1979/80, Gillies had personal knowledge of the problems.

It is not hard to find analyses and arguments in support of the idea that the accountability and control regimes for Crown corporations were sadly deficient.[115] (It should be emphasized that the political goals are often deemed more important - see Laux & Molot 1987.) There is considerable evidence that the performance of the Crowns has varied, but in many cases it has been poor in economic terms.[116] Moreover, some efforts had been made to make Crowns more accountable, and in the fall of 1984 when the Mulroney government came to power other measures were likely to follow -- including tighter controls over the funds supplied to Crowns (see Doern and Atherton 1987).

The four main issues around which the debate on Crown corporations in the late 1970s and early 1980s revolved were the following: accountability and control, management, financing, and competition.[117] At the heart of the accountability and control issue is the need to devise a system which balances political accountability with the Crowns'legitimate need for operational independence.

The management issue stemmed from the conflict between behaviour associated with being a "market-driven enterprise" (salaries, sales practices, layoffs, strikes, etc.) and also living in a political world (patronage, regional sensitivities, political visibility).

The financing issue arose because of the Crowns' need for funds to finance expansion (e.g. Petro-Canada, Air Canada, CNR), to finance losses (Canada Post, Canadair, de Havilland), or to offer subsidized programs (e.g. CMHC). As the need grew in the early 1980s,[118] it ran smack into the rising federal deficit -- about $30 billion for the past several years.

---

[115] See Auditor-General (1976), (1979), (1982), and (1985); the Royal Commission on Financial Management and Accountability (1979), Beatty (1981), Canada PCO (1977), Gracey (1985).

[116] See a number of the papers in Tupper & Doern (1981), Hirshhorn (1984), and Prichard (1983). See also Pitfield (1984), Sexty (1979), Thomas (1982), Borins & Brown (1986), Bott (1987), Bruce (1985), Economic Council (1986), Ellison (1983), Foster (1981, 1986), Gordon (1981), Halpern et al. (1987), Hirshhorn (1984), Janisch and Schultz (1985), Kierans (1984), Lermer (1984), Maule (1985), McFetridge (1984), Newman (1976), Olewiler (1986), Olive (1982), Perry (1983), Pesando (1984), Ross (1983), Salter (1987), Solomon (1984), Stewart (1987), Stewart-Patterson (1987), Tarasofsky (1984), Tupper (1978), Zuker and Jenkins (1984).

[117] I am indebted to correspondence with Don Gracey for much of what follows.

[118] Cash budgetary payments to federal Crown corporations increased from $3.1 billion in 1980/81 to $6.0 billion in 1983/84 (Baumann 1987).

The competition issue had several facets: the immunity of Crowns from antitrust laws (before June 1986); their access to "cheap money", "inside information", and exemption from income taxes made them "unfair competitors" for private firms; and the ability to gain access to the treasury to finance poor performance, i.e. no bottom-line discipline.

One of the senior officials guiding the federal government's privatization effort describes it as "a pragmatic[119] initiative which fits into Canada's public policy tradition" (Stein 1988, p. 76). He describes privatization as just another bureaucratic fine tuning in "a tradition of balancing private- and public-sector initiative to provide the best possible benefits to the Canadian public". He continues as follows:

> "In the end it is an exercise in management of government: doing the best with the tools available to achieve certain objectives. The environment changes; the objectives change with it; and so do the tools. Pure and Simple. It is not a reversal of history" (Ibid., p. 76).

But does privatization solve all or at least some of the problems with Crowns? Is it the best alternative among the other initiatives that could be taken? It has been argued, with some empirical support, that moving to put commercial Crowns in a competitive market (perhaps by deregulating or making them subject to the antitrust laws) has a more beneficial impact on their economic performance than simply shifting ownership to the private-sector. Others believe very strongly that the agency problem, together with the absence of a market for control of the firm, implies that privatization is the best remedy for the various problems.

At present, it is too early to say whether privatization will solve the widely-perceived problems with Crown corporations. For one thing, the extent of privatization by the federal and provincial governments has been far less than has occurred in Britain, the leader in the field. But one thing is clear: The federal government was quite strongly motivated to privatize de Havilland, Canadair and Air Canada, and to sell off the non-rail assets of CN, in

---

[119] Peter Foster argues cogently that in Canada "pragmatism has been used as a thin disguise for three different but related mindsets: an interventionist ideology that dares not speak its name; sheer, blinding economic ignorance; and naked, unprincipled expediency." In his view, the term "has become one of the great semantic perversions of our age, a piece of trickery that seeks to win political debate by default, or to excuse political cowardice as obeisance to the public will." Peter Foster, "Government redefines myth of Canadian pragmatism," *Financial Post*, August 31, 1987, p. 16.

order to reduce their need for capital in the future. Air Canada represents the strongest case. It needs at least $2 billion within a few years and another $2 billion by 2000 to purchase new aircraft.[120] One analyst suggests that Air Canada needs $1 billion in new equity over the next five years. It requested $300 million in new equity from the federal government in January 1988. The irony is that if a Crown is successful it is highly likely to need more capital to support its growth. If it is a "loser", the government must inject funds to cover its deficits. Privatization, however, shifts both problems to private-sector investors.

## Privatization as Political Symbolism

Not all public policies are designed to produce a substantive result. Some are designed merely to alter the perceptions of voters without making a substantive change. In politics, perception -- notably the perception of marginal voters -- is reality. Could it be that privatization efforts in Canada have been largely an exercise in symbolic politics designed to give the appearance of change while not really making much change at all?

Tom Kierans (1985, p. 5) reminds us that privatization involves symbols on two levels:

> "...the act of privatization is at least as symbolic as it is substantive. As an exercise in symbolism, it signals the government's intention to respond to the challenges of change by strengthening the market at the expense of the state. As such, privatization initiatives "front" for the truly substantive elements of this policy set, liberalization and deregulation which. . . are much more important than ownership. As well, symbolically it evidences [sic] government's willingness to rethink our mixed economy tradition, a signal which clearly could offend the Canadian psyche."

Some Crown corporations such as Air Canada and Petro-Canada are important symbols or political totems for some Canadians (see Thomson

---

[120] See Cecil Foster, "Share issue likely to top airline agenda," *Globe and Mail*, April 18, 1988, pp. B1, B4.

1985; Baldwin 1985). As noted above, both the federal Liberals and the NDP are strongly opposed to the sale of Air Canada.

It is evident that countries from Austria to Zaire are either privatizing public enterprises or seriously debating the merits of doing so. In Canada, with its tradition of interventionism in the name of pragmatism practised by parties of all stripes, privatization could be a symbol of being part of the "new wave". "Everybody's doing it, so why aren't we?" is likely to be a question raised in political and policy circles. The objective is not to privatize per se, but to be seen to be "doing something" about what everyone seems to believe is a problem: Crown corporations.[121]

Prior to the announcement of the plans to sell all of CN's non-rail assets (in December 1987) and to sell Air Canada in stages (April 1988), it would be hard to disagree with the proposition that federal privatization efforts under the Mulroney government were largely symbolic.

The largest enterprise actually sold prior to April 1988, in terms of annual revenues, was Canadair. Its revenues in 1985 were $451 million. (This ignores the CDC which was not a Crown corporation, but for which the government obtained $377 million for its 47-percent interest. CDC had sales of $3,257 million in 1985.) In terms of assets, the largest sale was Teleglobe. Its book-value assets at the end of 1986 totalled $502 million (see Table 5.2). If the CDC is excluded (and it seems reasonable to do so since it became obvious some years ago that the federal government did not control it), the aggregate revenues of the 12 federal Crowns privatized ($2.1 billion) are far less than those of Air Canada and only one seventh of the total revenues of the three largest federal commercial Crowns.[122] In terms of employment, again excluding the CDC, some 28,612 individuals who were once employees of public enterprises now work in the private-sector. Air Canada alone will add 22,000 when it is privatized.

If we look more closely at the 13 federal privatizations between 1985 and 1987 (Table 5.2) we find that one (Northern Canada Power) was not a

---

121 Privatization of a few Crowns, many of which are quite small, is symbolic in another sense. It indicates that good management of the public sector requires the occasional "spring cleaning" and "garage sale". In this way, politicians demonstrate their willingness to eliminate some of the appendages of the Leviathan they have created (in the public interest in order to please voters) to show they run a "tight ship". The official rhetoric in support of privatization stresses that those corporations that no longer have an essential public policy mandate are the ones being sold (see below).

122 Strictly speaking, the Canadian Wheat Board and Canada Post are larger than Air Canada. However, they are remote candidates for privatization, particularly the Wheat Board, which Ottawa does not consider to be a commercial Crown (see Baumann 1987).

privatization at all, but the transfer of ownership to another government. Three involved the sale of equity interests (CDC, Nanisivik Mines, FPI) in enterprises that were not controlled by the government. And two others involved public enterprises with revenues of only $16 million and $41 million, respectively.

That leaves seven Crowns that were sold to private interests and they ranged in size in terms of revenues from $103 million to $451 million. These are hardly major enterprises compared to the entire set of federal Crown corporations briefly described in Table 5.1. Stronger evidence in support of the privatization as a political symbolism hypothesis can be found at the provincial level. Premier Grant Devine in Saskatchewan has sold off more than one half the shares of Saskoil and all of Prince Albert Pulp. However, he has been careful not to raise the axe above the heads of certain sacred cows, namely Sask Tel and Sask Power. Devine did act first to obtain greater political control over Crowns by making them accountable to specific ministers. Later he sought to reduce intervention on a day-to-day basis by appointing businessmen (and Tories) as chairmen of the boards of Crown corporations (see Stanbury 1988).

In Ontario, Liberal Premier David Peterson made no commitment to privatization; he had not campaigned on the issue. And, not surprisingly, it was not part of the accord he made with the NDP that allowed him to gain power and push out the minority Conservative government of Frank Miller in May 1985.

Peterson did take the opportunity to ride the international privatization wave, but only with a surfboard of very modest dimensions. He sold what he in opposition had called the "white elephant of the north", Minaki Lodge, for $4 million at the end of 1986. He also sold the Urban Transportation Development Corp. in March 1986 to Lavalin Inc. Depending upon how one sees the deal, the province obtained $10 million in cash for 85 percent of the shares, plus a $20-million income debenture paying 25 percent of the pre-tax profits over the next 10 years. Others noted that when the fees to be paid to Lavalin to handle existing contracts are taken into account (about $60 million), Ontario taxpayers ended up <u>paying</u> Lavalin to take UTDC off their hands (Stanbury 1988, Ch. 9).

In Manitoba, it might be argued that a single privatization by the NDP government was also a symbolic act. It was designed to show that the generally interventionist left can take tough action to deal with errant public enterprises. However, the biggest public enterprises (the power and telephone utilities and the auto insurance company) are not even candidates for privatization.

In British Columbia, Premier Vander Zalm appears to be acting on his populist instincts. By proposing to contract-out government services such as the maintenance of highways and bridges, he is engaging in more than political symbolism. The extent to which his plans are realized remains to be seen.

It may well be that the limited amount of privatization in Canada is not a cynical form of symbolic politics designed to fool the voters. Rather, it may simply be evidence of confusion among politicians as to what is the best public policy concerning public enterprises. Economic theory concerning agency costs and property rights points toward private ownership of commercial enterprises if efficiency is the most important goal (Economic Council 1986). However, the theory of the choice among governing instruments which deals with a wider range of objectives, notably political ones, is much more equivocal about government ownership of commercial enterprises (Trebilcock et al. 1982). Even if more detailed research indicated that in terms of prices, costs, and productivity government-owned firms performed more poorly than their privately-owned counterparts prior to privatization, this does not mean that politicians decided to sell them off to improve their efficiency. Where privatized firms do perform better in terms of efficiency, that would be evidence in support of the property rights/agency costs hypothesis. It does not, however, tell us why politicians chose to sell off Crown corporations. The politician's objectives centre around obtaining and maintaining political support in a world in which perception is reality. In such a world, the redistribution of income is usually much more important than efficiency, particularly of public enterprises.

In summary, all three hypotheses find some support from a review of the record of privatizations in Canada. Indeed, it would be quite wrong to attribute privatization to a single cause. Governments act from multiple motives, and all have to consider the effects of their moves on political support. It is safe to say that large-scale privatization is not one of the electorate's top ten priorities. Indeed, most of their priorities involve <u>more</u> government intervention -- not less.

## CONCLUSIONS

### History Counts

Major changes in public policy are seldom made quickly in Canada. Even when this appears to be the case, usually one can find the seeds of that change in earlier discussions of policy. At first glance, it appears that the Mulroney government moved quite quickly regarding privatization. When the Tories were elected in September 1984, they announced in October that several Crowns were for sale, and the first deal was completed in July 1985. A closer look at the record reveals a more complicated picture. First, the initial sale was a small one and had been initiated by the Liberals early in 1984. Second, the Tories' prompt announcement that several Crowns were for sale was really a pre-emptive move by the same minister (Sinclair Stevens) who had proposed the sale of several Crowns in 1979 during the short-lived Clark government. Third, when the Liberals established the CDIC in 1982, they indicated that one of its roles was to arrange for the sale of Crowns no longer serving a public-policy purpose. Fourth, the first true Crown of any significance to be sold, de Havilland, was not sold until the Tories had been in office 17 months. Moreover, it had been on Mr. Stevens' list in 1979. While privatization was not a high political priority for the two previous governments, the fact that the issue had been placed on the policy agenda made it much easier to actually implement in 1985.

History counts also in the sense that the commitment of specific individuals to the sale of a particular enterprise can make the difference. The Mulroney government clearly changed its position between July 1987 -- when Mulroney himself blocked the sale of all the shares in Air Canada -- and April 1988. The key was Don Mazankowski. As the first Tory Minister of Transport, he pushed through deregulation of the transport sector. He was also strongly committed to privatizing Air Canada: He began studies on the issue within weeks of the Tories' assumption of office. He even persisted after the Prime Minister said in January 1985 that Air Canada was not for sale (see Stanbury 1988, Ch. 8). It seems reasonable, in light of Air Canada's requests for $300 million in additional equity capital in January 1988, that Mazankowski made the sale of Air Canada a condition of taking over the privatization portfolio on March 31, 1988. Besides, the PM "owed him one". "Maz" has been a vitally important minister in the Tory cabinet on a wide range of issues. Mazankowski moved very quickly on Air Canada when he had the chance, in order to irrevocably commit the government to this politically ambitious move.

## The Importance of Political Commitment

The Bourassa government in Quebec has shown that where privatization is a political priority it can be implemented quite quickly.[123] The new Minister responsible for privatization had a formal mandate 11 days after the December 2, 1985, election. An advisory committee was appointed in January to report within six months.[124] The Minister announced some targets at the same time. A month later, on February 26, 1986, the Minister published a 71-page document that gave his analysis of the problems, a discussion of policy objectives and a set of principles to guide the privatization effort (Quebec, Minister Responsible for Privatization 1986). No comparable document has yet been issued by the federal government.

Quebec's first privatization occurred in March 1986 when the province's second oldest Crown, a sugar refinery, was sold for $48.5 million. In August, much of the assets of the mining corporation (Soguem) were sold, and the province received $100 million and retained 31.8 percent of the shares (worth $111 million at year end).[125] In September, Quebecair left the fold, although the net proceeds turned out to be only $5 million. In February 1987 the biggest sale occurred, the 56-percent interest in Donohue Inc., which fetched $320 million. The next big sale was SOQUIP Alberta, an oil and gas company, for about $195 million in August 1987.

Certainly the new Bourassa government in Quebec moved quickly in its privatization effort. However, it was able to do so for at least three reasons. First, the issue was already being debated in Quebec prior to the election campaign in which the Liberals advocated substantial privatization. Second, privatization was in the air generally in Canada and in many other countries. The record of the Thatcher government was widely discussed in Canada, and the new Tory government in Ottawa had launched its efforts a year earlier. Third, there was a new, more confident entrepreneurial spirit in

---

[123] It should be noted that the Bourassa government did not privatize SAQ, the liquor distribution monopoly, although this had been proposed by the previous Parti-Quebecois government (see Hafsi & Demers 1986).

[124] See its report, Quebec, Committee on the Privatization of Crown Corporations (1986).

[125] Matuszewski (1988) indicates that in October 1985 Soquem received a report from an investment dealer indicating how the province's mining enterprise could be privatized. The decision it wanted was to proceed in December, the month the Bourassa government came to power.

Quebec which was coming to value private initiative and market forces over the extensive intervention of the state.[126] Indeed, one might argue that both the Quebec nationalism of the 1970s and 1980s and the record of extensive government intervention helped to create an indigenous managerial and technical class capable of, and interested, in owning and running market-oriented enterprises.

### Policy "Connectedness" Complicates Divestment

It is often difficult to sell off the larger Crowns -- even when they are judged to no longer have a public-policy mandate -- because of the policy issues raised by the divestiture. Doern and Atherton (1987, pp. 129-30) note that "they are intricately bound up with the delivery of several programs and the efficacy of other instruments." It is quite clear that the sale of Teleglobe Canada (which closed on April 3, 1987) was delayed twice because Ottawa "couldn't get its act together" on important questions of policy that were central to what bidders were prepared to offer (see Dalfen 1987). Some of the more important questions facing the cabinet were the following: Would Teleglobe be regulated after the sale? By whom? In what way? Would it be given a legal monopoly? If so, for how long? Would the privately- and publicly-owned telephone companies, alone or in some combination, be allowed to acquire all or part of Teleglobe? Would foreigners be allowed to bid?

Teleglobe was among the CDIC assets put up for sale in October 1984. Some 17 bids or letters of intent were received. The first formal invitation to submit bids was issued on August 1, 1985. While bidders were provided with a 10-point "Policy Assumptions and Guidelines", it was acknowledged that the Tories invited bids before resolving key policy issues such as regulation and the corporation's role in national defence.

When bidding closed in mid-October, 18 bids had been received. However, another 11 months passed while the cabinet and bureaucracy (the Departments of Regional Industrial Expansion and Communications) were engaged in a fierce battle over federal policy. In mid-September 1986 the federal government asked the bidders to submit fresh proposals.

On November 19 the government announced revised bidding rules and a new deadline for bids -- January 9, 1987. Federal policy was clarified on

---

126 See Fraser (1987) and Quebec, Minister Responsible for Privatization (1986).

the three important issues: ownership, regulation, and the period for which Teleglobe would have a monopoly.[127] On January 30, only six days before the winner was to be announced, the six final bidders were informed that they could amend their offers to reflect the new assurance that the federal government would legislate to restrict bypass via the U.S. On February 11, 1987, Memotec Data Inc. won the prize. A week later, the Minister of State for Privatization changed the rules again. She announced that one or more of the telephone companies could acquire up to 33 percent of Teleglobe from Memotec or acquire one-third of Memotec. Early in May, Bell Canada Enterprises (#4 on the FP 500) acquired a one third interest in Memotec for $196 million.[128]

The convoluted process, largely attributable to the inability of the federal government to make up its mind about important policy issues, resulted in harsh criticism of the handling of this privatization.[129]

## Privatization as a Political Act

The creation of a new Crown corporation is a political act; so, too, is the decision to privatize. It can be fraught with difficulties not part of a private-sector conglomerate's decision to divest one of its many divisions.

Both the process by which Crown corporations are privatized and the price received must be politically defensible. One of the strongest criticisms of privatization in Britain is that not only has Mrs. Thatcher sold the family silver, but she failed to obtain the best price (see Yarrow and Vickers 1988). These criticisms may well have prompted federal politicians to insist that they are in no rush to sell the taxpayers' patrimony. Therefore there will be no "fire sale" prices (see McDougall 1987a, 1987b).

Of the federal privatizations to date only two have involved widespread distribution to the public; the CDC shares (sold in three tranches) and Fisheries Products International. Although Barbara Mcdougall, the federal

---

127 The government also specified that Teleglobe's telephone and telex rates would be reduced by 13.5 percent and 10 percent, respectively, on January 1, 1988.

128 See Ken Romain, "BCE set to acquire one-third interest in Memotec Data," *Globe and Mail*, May 8, 1987, p. A3; and Mathew Horsman, "BCE moved fast to beat Ottawa on Teleglobe," *Financial Post*, May 18, 1987, p. 2.

129 See Dalfen (1987) and Stanbury (1988, Ch. 6).

Minister of State for Privatization between June 1986 and March 31, 1988, expressed a strong preference for selling Crowns by public issue, no true Crown has been divested using that method. As noted previously, Air Canada is to be widely distributed. The CDC and FPI were mixed enterprises in which the federal government had a large block of shares. (Newfoundland also had 26.2 percent of FPI.)

To be seen to be financially prudent in light of the criticism of the sale of de Havilland to Boeing, the federal government hired no less than four financial advisors to help with the sale of Canadair. More important, the government made a point of releasing their reports when the sale was announced to assure the public that the deal was a good one for the government.[130] To allow both for the "upside" potential of the Challenger jet technology and to reduce the upfront cash requirements for the buyer, the government retained ownership of the technology. It may receive as much as $173 million in royalties over 21 years, depending upon the number of aircraft sold. (Note that 38 percent would go to Challenger's U.S. designer.) However, the government may require Bombardier to pay $20 million in cash within two years in lieu of the stream of future royalties.[131]

The political debate over federal privatizations leads one to conclude that the political flak increases geometrically with the gap between the sum total of taxpayers' money previously spent on a public enterprise (or investment) or which is widely reported to have been spent, and the price received for it when it is sold. The most obvious cases that come to mind are Canadair, de Havilland, Flyer Industries, and Minaki Lodge (see Stanbury 1988).

Another proposition based on Canada's experience so far with privatization is as follows: The reported price at which a Crown corporation or other government asset is sold may be (a) either impossible to determine with a tolerable degree of accuracy, and (b) may, in fact, be large and negative when it is reported to be modest and positive. Perhaps the best example of variant (a) is the sale of Prince Albert Pulp Co. (Papco) by the Province of Saskatchewan, as was described in "Provincial Privatizations"

---

[130] See *Globe and Mail*, August 20, 1986, p. B2.

[131] Alan D. Gray, "Bombardier steps into the billion-dollar class," *Financial Times*, August 25, 1986, p. 6. Note that of the estimated $205 million in present value for Canadair, $120 million was paid in cash on closing, $20 million was for future royalties, and $54 million (estimated) was from the proceeds of the lawsuit against Avco Corp., an engine supplier.

above. The sale of Flyer Industries represents an excellent example of variant (b) of my second law of privatization. It appears that Manitoba will spend about $100 million to get rid of Flyer, while it received $1 million for virtually all of the shares. It seems clear that Ontario will be paying Lavalin about $60 million to complete existing contracts made by UTDC, while receiving only some $30 million for 85 percent of the shares of UTDC. (Recall the discussion in "Provincial Privatizations" above.)

When it comes to the sale of Crown corporations, costs that are sunk in economic terms are not sunk in political terms. One of the most widely-voiced popular criticisms of privatization is that it involves selling off at a low price, or even at a loss (i.e. negative price), enterprises in which taxpayers have invested a great deal of money. Moreover, this argument goes, because of pressure from "right wing fanatics", the government is selling at a low price just as the fortunes of the enterprise are turning around. Large profits are just around the corner, it is said. It is implied that they will justify the taxpayers' previous large "investment" if they were just given a little more time. The all-time champs in this department, of course, were Canadair and de Havilland. They absorbed about $2 billion of federal funds and were sold for a total of less than $300 million (estimated present value). Moreover, the government remains responsible for certain contingent liabilities with respect to previous sales. In political terms, there seems to be a need to throw good money after bad in trying to justify the original (economically bad) decision.

## Privatization Requires Trade-offs

Privatization obviously involves some important trade-offs. If a utility is being sold and is required to become regulated, the proceeds of the sale will be less than if regulation is not imposed. However, creating a privately-owned unregulated monopoly, unless the market is contestable, is an affront to competition policy. In the Canadian tradition of "compromise", Teleglobe moved from being an unregulated Crown corporation with a de facto monopoly to a privately owned firm subject to direct regulation. The federal government did not, however, maximize the selling price: it set a limit of 20 percent on foreign ownership; it limited the interest to be acquired by existing telephone companies; it could have opted for a looser form of price regulation such as that imposed on British Telecom; and the government could have legislated Teleglobe's monopoly for more than five years (Dalfen 1987).

In the case of de Havilland, while Boeing clearly had the expertise and financial strength, it is a highly visible U.S.-owned corporation. The economic nationalists were provoked to high dudgeon. There is a trade-off, too, between job guarantees and the selling price of a Crown. In some cases the Crown was unprofitable and/or inefficient precisely because of overmanning, non-competitive wage rates and restrictive working conditions. Job guarantees, not necessarily at the previous level, were part of the privatization agreement in several cases, e.g. UTDC, Flyer, Papco, CN Route (see Stanbury 1988). It is interesting to note that such guarantees were not part of the deal in the case of de Havilland and Canadair. The test in their case will come during the next down-turn in the aircraft manufacturing industry. Will the unions, local communities and opposition politicians (not to mention local MPs of the government party) succeed in pressuring the government to provide some form of assistance to maintain employment? It is important to appreciate that the political calculus may change very little when a Crown is privatized -- if its plant(s) remain in marginal ridings. It may be, however, that by being at arm's length a privatized firm may have less ability to extract political rents than it could when it was a Crown.

**Ex Post Facto Rationalization**

Privatization by the federal government in Canada indicates that the process of privatization can be implemented prior to any significant effort to provide the conceptual basis for the policy. Privatization as an issue was not given any prominence in the 1984 election campaign (Frizzell & Westell 1985; Prince 1986).[132] When Sinclair Stevens announced the sale of various Crown corporations and other equity interests in the CDIC's portfolio in October 1984, he provided virtually no explanation or justification for the move.[133] One of the reasons why the official rationale for privatization was so ill developed at that time may be the fact that when he was President of the Treasury Board in the Clark government of 1979/80, Mr. Stevens proposed that Petro-Canada and five other Crown corporations would be sold. Three on that list (Canadair, de Havilland and Eldorado) were also on the 1984 list.

---

132 Subsequently, the Minister of State for Privatization claimed that "privatization became an integral part of our [the Tories] 1984 election platform" (McDougall 1987b, p. 4). Yet privatization was not mentioned in the material prepared by the Conservative party for its candidates.

133 See Patrick Nagle, "Crown firms for sale as CDIC boss fired," Vancouver *Sun*, October 31, 1984, p. A10.

In November 1984 the Minister of Finance outlined what was to become the principal rationale for privatization, namely that certain Crowns which no longer served any important public-policy purpose should be sold (Wilson 1984).[134] A year later, the government made the following case for privatization:

> "Privatization will reduce the size of government and leave room for more private-sector initiative; it will promote market competition and the more efficient allocation of resources; it will improve company efficiency through market discipline and by reducing political and bureaucratic impediments; and in some cases, privatization may encourage individual Canadians to take part in the ownership of major corporations through equity investments" (Privatization Secretariat 1986).

However, it was not until May 1987 -- after 11 privatizations -- that the Minister of State for Privatization provided a fairly comprehensive set of reasons why the federal government was pursuing its privatization policy:

-- **The Changing Economic Environment.** For many Crown corporations, the original objectives behind their creation are no longer valid.[135] Some Crown corporations were created to meet public-policy goals that are no longer legitimate. In addition, governments have other options than ownership --taxation, spending, regulation -- available to meet public policy needs;

-- **Effectiveness.** There is abundant evidence to suggest that many Crown corporations are not as effective in serving their clients as are those in the private-sector. Privatization, by putting corporations under the test of the market place, can improve efficiency. . .

---

[134] The Minister of Finance set out the government's economic strategy in terms of four main tasks for the new government: reducing the deficit, making government more efficient and less obstructive to the private sector, fostering investment and a positive climate for business growth, and bringing about changes with equity and fairness (see Wilson 1984).

[135] Later the Minister stated that "Our government believes there is one justification for government ownership and only one: and that is where ownership is essential to achieve a viable public policy purpose, the supply of an essential public service that cannot economically be supplied in any other way" (McDougall 1987c, p. 2).

-- **Public Funds.** Public ownership of Crown corporations places enormous demands on government resources to manage and financially support various enterprises ... On a day-to-day basis, accountability is not always as focussed as it should be. In addition, some Crown corporations cannot expect the infusion of federal funds necessary to expand in the global economy;

-- **Management Styles.** The recognition that a Crown corporation is responsible for public funds often leads to slow,deliberate decision-making and occasional aversion to risk-taking on the part of management. In a commercial milieu, adaptability to rapid changes in markets and technologies is essential. Successful business leaders use a more flexible, market-sensitive approach to meeting their corporate objectives;

-- **Fairness and Equity.** Many Crown corporations compete directly with the private-sector. In effect some businesses see their own tax dollars being used to compete against themselves. Such a practice is hardly fair, or conducive, to a free enterprise system (McDougall 1987b).

In the case of Quebec, the Liberals under Robert Bourassa embraced privatization in their election campaign. Within three months of assuming office, the Quebec Minister Responsible for Privatization tabled a substantial document setting out the government's case for privatization. The central guiding principle for privatization was the following: "The commercial production of goods and services in Quebec belongs to the private-sector, except in extraordinary circumstances justified by the public interest." The Minister, Mr. Fortier, stressed that "Quebec is an integral part of the international movement toward economic reorganization, whose goal is greater efficiency through entrepreneurial vitality" (Quebec, Minister Responsible for Privatization 1986, p. 12).

## Last Words

The privatization record of the federal government between 1984 and May 1988, together with its plan to sell all the non-rail assets of the CNR (two units have already been sold), the plan to sell Air Canada (one of the largest <u>commercial</u> Crowns), and the B.C. government's plans for extensive privatization, suggest that privatization in Canada represents more than the

economic efficiency; and, for that matter on freedom and justice. It is a shortcoming of his paper that none of this is vouchsafed to us. Second, there are several errors and misunderstandings which mar this contribution. I consider several objections to his otherwise very sound paper, in the order of their appearance.

1. Let us begin by considering a confusion as to the meaning of the free enterprise system. Professor Stanbury announces that "the broadest concept of privatization consists of any effort designed to strengthen the role of the market at the expense of the state." This is eminently sensible, to be sure. But then he a more narrow instance of privatization: "taking away the present advantages of commercial crown corporations by making them subject to the federal Competition Act", and to tax payments as well (p. 274). There is a difficulty here. One can, if one wishes, define a narrow sense of privatization as placing the Crowns and their private counterparts on a more equal footing. However, having just defined the most basic concept of privatization in terms of governmental non-interference with the market, it is incumbent upon Stanbury to defend the implicit premise that the two different concepts of privatization are at least compatible with one another. This is a daunting -- not to say insurmountable -- task, since it would be hard to mention activities of the state that are less disruptive of markets than taxes and anti-trust policies.[1]

At first blush, however, this claim sounds plausible. After all, what could be more fair than to have private enterprises and Crown Corporations compete against each other on a "level playing field"? But just as a full free market system would not impose "fairness" onto international trade relations (e.g. by neutralizing "dumping" with countervailing duties),[2] so it would not dictate any particular concentration ratio on a given industry. To do so would be to confuse business concentration with competition. The point is, that as long as there are no legal barriers to entry, it is entirely possible for competition to thrive with a small number of competitors, with only two of them, or, in the extreme case, with only one. As long as entry is free, the forces of profit and loss, and the threat of potential competitors, are sufficient

---

[1] On the issue of taxes as an interference with the free market, and on the myth of the neutral tax, see Rothbard (1970, especially Ch. 12, and 1977). For the view that anti-trust policies are disruptive of the free enterprise system, see Rothbard (1970, chapter 10), Armentano (1972, 1986), Armstrong (1982), and Block (1977, 1982, 1986).

[2] See Friedman (1988).

# Privatization in Canada: Ideology, Symbolism or Substance? Comment

Walter Block*

One of the outstanding elements of Professor Stanbury's treatment is its thoroughness. He tells us everything we ever wanted to know about Canadian privatization -- even more.

The paper is encyclopedic, knowledgeable, systematic, complete, voluminous and detailed. This is especially noteworthy since one of the main conclusions he derives, with which I agree, is that there has been very little privatization in Canada. There has been a lot of talk, but very little action. Stanbury documents virtually every case, every conceivable point of view, every interested party and every discussion that ever took place on this topic. Further, this chapter is well written, informative, entertaining, and especially valuable given the fact that the knowledge about Canada on the part of Americans is rather low.

I have several problems, however, with his contribution. First, I find very little critical analysis of the case for or against privatization. Virtually all of the paper is devoted to description. I would have welcomed more of his own analytical input. He never really comes to grips with the issues explicitly. Instead, we are forced to look for his analysis on an implicit basis -- through asides, innuendoes, tone of voice, and throwaway comments oft times obscurely buried in footnotes.

For example, he steers away, as if from the plague itself, from assessing privatization as a public policy. As a discussant, I want to know what, in his view, is the impact of privatization on consumer welfare; on

* The Fraser Institute, Vancouver, B.C.

to maintain rivalry, cost cutting behavior, and other attributes of rivalrous (but of course not "perfect") competition.

2. Yet another problem arises with regard to what might be called Stanbury's sudden bouts of agnosticism, or his excessive intellectual modesty. Consider his statement "At present, it is too early to say whether privatization will solve the widely-perceived problems with Crown corporations. For one thing, the extent of privatization by the federal and provincial governments has been far less than has occurred in Britain, the leader in the field" (p. 315). It is all well and good, and entirely appropriate, to adopt a policy of scholarly detachment and understatement. This is especially true where the economic principles on a particular issue are unclear, and/or when there is a lack of economic evidence. Indeed, this is the earmark of the sober and cautious economist. In this case, however, there appears to be a bias. For one thing, Stanbury himself cites no less than 34 studies on the effects of privatization. For another, he neglects to mention numerous, very important additional scholarly examinations of privatization, many of which are well known in the profession, and virtually all of which supply evidence strongly supporting the view that this process will indeed "solve the widely-perceived problems with Crown Corporations".[3] Thirdly, this academic hyper-timidity is applied only in casting doubt on the case for privatization; I can find no counterpart regarding the case for public-sector status. Fourthly, and perhaps most important, there is the disquieting implication in Stanbury's words that Canada is scientifically unique -- that economic findings in other countries need not, or are unlikely to, apply to this country. But surely economic principles are universal and apply equally to all human beings; surely Canada need not go through the process of privatization itself before it can learn from the examples which have already taken place elsewhere. The very different incentive structures in private and public enterprise that have been studied in other jurisdictions apply to Canada as well as anywhere else on the globe.[4]

---

[3] See Ahlbrandt (1973); Allison (1982); Baim (1985); Bennett and DiLorenzo (1983); Bennett and Johnson (1980, 1981); Blankart (1985); Block (1979); Bolick (1985); Borcherding (1978); Bridge (1977); Butler (1981, 1985); DeHoog (1984); Downs (1967); Drucker (1973); Fisk, et al. (1978); Fitch (1974); Frech (1980); Hanke (1985); James (1984); Kristensen (1983); Logan (1985); Logan and Rausch (1985); McDavid and Butler (1984); Meyer (1982); Mullen (1985); Ohashi and Roth (1980); Pirie (1985); Poole (1980); Rainey (1983); Roth (1966, 1967, 1987a, 1987b); Rothbard (1973); Savas (1977, 1978, 1979a, 1979b, 1987); Savas and Stevens (1977a, 1977b); Schlesinger, et al. (1986); Waters (1968); Wolf (1979); and, Woodson (1982a, 1982b, 1985).

[4] The view that economic laws apply in different ways to different countries, races, sexes social classes, etc., has been called "polylogism" by von Mises (1966).

3. Professor Stanbury comes perilously close to excusing government failure to privatize Teleglobe -- "It is often difficult to sell off the larger Crowns" (p. 322) -- on the grounds that in order to engage in this activity, it would have to answer several important, complicated and complex questions. But these questions are by no means as daunting and difficult as our author implies. Indeed, given the mandate toward free enterprise which underlies the move toward privatization in its broadest definition, the answers are simple and obvious. Here, then, with his questions are the answers which follow from a commitment to the marketplace.

> "Would Teleglobe be regulated after the sale? By whom? In what way?"
> -- "No. By no one, and in no way."
> "Would it be given a legal monopoly? If so, for how long?
> --"When pigs fly; never. A legal monopoly over any commercial venture is at the absolute opposite pole from the free enterprise philosophy, which even Stanbury sees as intrinsic to the concept of privatization."
> "Would the privately- and publicly-owned telephone companies, alone or in some combination, be allowed to acquire all or part of Teleglobe? Would foreigners be allowed to bid?"
> -- "First of all, there should be no 'publicly-owned' telephone companies. The very concept of public ownership is an oxymoron. The people who really own so-called 'public property' are those who exercise control over it: the civil servants, the politicians, the regulators, the managers, the employees; any claim to the effect that 'we all own a crown corporation' is no better than economic sophistry. Secondly, of course all other privately owned telephone companies, and domestic firms and individuals of all sizes and descriptions, would be allowed to make offers to purchase all or part of any company, Teleglobe included. This is part and parcel of the 'bartering and trucking' of which the marketplace consists. And thirdly, of course foreigners should be allowed to bid for domestic corporations. A free market means just that: All are free to engage in commercial transactions between consenting adults, foreigners, as well as citizens.

4. In the opinion of Stanbury, "One of the strongest criticisms of privatization in Britain is that not only has Mrs. Thatcher sold the family silver, but she failed to obtain the best price" (p. 323). This is indeed a strange and faulty argument, for at least in the view of the Thatcher critics who advocate public enterprise, "we all own" the resources in question. If so, there can be no question of selling off the Crowns at <u>any</u> price, let alone the best available price. On the contrary, the logical implication is that these Crown corporations should be <u>given back</u> to us, the citizen-owners. The point is that it is impossible to get rid of "the family silver" in this case, for we would be giving it to ourselves!

States Milton Friedman in this regard: "One suggestion a number of people have made, which I think makes a great deal of sense, would be not to auction it (a British nationalized industry) off, but to give it away by giving every citizen in the country a share in it. After all, the supposed argument is that the people of Great Britain own the steel industry; it is the property of all the citizens. Well, then, why not give each citizen his piece?"[5]

Secondly, given that a sale and not a give-away is to take place, there is a pragmatic reason for "failing to obtain the best price". As Madsen Pirie never tires of telling us, if the privatization movement is to succeed it must be, and must be perceived to be, safe from the spectre of a new socialist government which threatens to renationalize the property (Pirie 1985). But if this is to be accomplished, share ownership must be spread out to include as many people as possible. Only in this way will be it be politically difficult to re-impose Crown corporation status. And what better way is there of assuring widespread ownership than by selling at a lower price -- or, better yet, by giving out the shares to all and sundry?

5. Stanbury describes Crown corporations as "enterprises in which taxpayers have invested a great deal of money" (p. 325). Perhaps it is somewhat harsh to upbraid him for allowing this to pass without criticism; we all tend to speak loosely, upon occasion. But it is important that the exact moral and legal status of the Crowns not be hidden by obfuscatory language.

Taxpayers no more invest in public enterprises than do hold-up victims "invest" in the automobiles and yachts that are later purchased by the gunmen. The point is that the transfer of monies which allows a public enterprise to come into being is not a voluntary one; on the contrary, it is

---

[5] Friedman (1977, p. 55). This "give away" model is roughly the one that was undertaken by the government of British Columbia, when it gave 5 free shares of the British Columbia Resource Investment Corporation to each of its citizens in 1979. See in this regard Ohashi and Roth (1980).

coercive. Now it may be that in some circumstances such forced transfers are justified.[6] But it is needlessly misleading to erase the distinction between the voluntary investment which occurs in the private-sector, and the compulsory payments which give birth to the Crowns by utilizing the word "investment" to apply to the latter case.

---

[6] If so, however, it must be shown.

# Privatization in Canada: Ideology, Symbolism or Substance? Comment

Richard Schultz*

My first comment on this paper is that it is a comprehensive, indeed encyclopaedic, review of privatization developments in Canada. As such the paper constitutes a rich source of information that is useful in addressing the more important issues raised by privatization, such as the aims and alternative processes for privatization and particularly the consequences of privatization for the size and operations of the Canadian state at both the federal and provincial levels. Secondly, as a student of politics, I am delighted that Stanbury in his analysis clearly appreciates the complexities of the political process and in particular the independent leadership role that politicians and state officials can and do exercise. One important conclusion to Stanbury's paper is that political leaders are not simply, or even primarily, "clerk-like aggregators of consumer preferences", to use Steven Rhoads' most felicitous phrase (Rhoads 1985, p. 200).

When we turn to his explanations for Canadian privatizations, it is important to note Stanbury's refusal to succumb to simple-minded, unidimensional causation. He offers what he calls a three-pronged explanation: ideological, functional and symbolic; although he does not say so explicitly, Stanbury is aware of the interrelated nature of these three causal factors and the influence of "circular causation". In terms of his specific discussion of the individual hypotheses to explain the nature and extent of privatization in

* Centre for the Study of Regulated Industries, McGill University

Canada, I think he could have developed further the discussion of the role of ideological forces. While I would not want to claim that all privatizations were ideologically motivated by concerns about the size and role of the state or that any individual privatizations were solely motivated by such concerns, I think there is a danger that the role of ideological predispositions -- and I use this term deliberately -- may be underemphasized especially within the current federal government in Canada. Although this government is not as coherently, consciously or even single-mindedly ideological as the Thatcher government in the United Kingdom, it has nevertheless shown itself to be determined to re-evaluate and recast where necessary the relationship of the Canadian state to the economy. This has been true not only with respect to privatization but in the area of economic regulation as well. More than any Canadian government in the post-War period, this government is predisposed, albeit cautiously and somewhat defensively, to favour market-oriented solutions and to eschew economic intervention.

Having suggested that a greater emphasis should be placed on ideological concerns, let me backtrack somewhat by noting a further causal factor to which Stanbury only alludes in his discussion of the financing issue as part of his functional explanation. That factor is the need to reduce the federal deficit. The issue here is not only reducing the financial demands placed on the treasury by public enterprises, but obtaining, through privatization, funds to apply to the deficit-reduction program. This was clearly a fundamental consideration, for example, in the sale of Teleglobe. For many Ottawa decision-makers, it was the sole concern; indeed the final evaluation of bids was rushed to permit a sale to be concluded just prior to the 1987 federal Budget.[1] The significance of this objective in the privatization process in Canada and elsewhere needs further study.

My major concern with the paper is with the rather limited discussion of privatization as political symbolism. Stanbury asks the question: "Could it be that privatization efforts in Canada have been largely designed to give the appearance of change while not really making much change at all?" In the original version of this paper Stanbury answered this question in the affirmative, while in this version he is somewhat more qualified. The problem I have is not with the conclusion but with the meaning assigned by Stanbury and other commentators to the concept of political symbolism.

---

[1] On the privatization of Teleglobe, in addition to the Dalfen paper cited in Stanbury's text, see also my analysis of the Teleglobe privatization process (Schultz 1988).

It is undoubtedly true that political action *qua* symbol may be mere tokenism or smoke and mirrors, to employ some of the terms used by Stanbury. It is important to note, however, that such action can be much more complex and rich and therefore of greater long-term significance. In the former use of the term, privatization as symbolic political action may be used to preempt or preclude further, more fundamental or profound political change. On the other hand, as a political symbol privatization can be used to challenge existing stereotypes or cultural predispositions in order to create a receptive environment and the necessary preconditioning for a more profound structural and ideological realignment. Clearly Margaret Thatcher's long-term objectives in Great Britain through the use of privatization and other policy instruments are symbolic as well as substantive. Although it is far too early to say in which sense privatization as symbol is being employed in Canada, especially at the federal level, or whether such action will be successful, whatever the purpose I would not rule out, as Stanbury appears to do, the possibility that the reorganizing, rationalizing and rearranging of the Canadian state that has already resulted from privatization may have significant long-term consequences for the role of the Canadian state in the economy.

My final comment on the Stanbury paper, and it is one that I believe to be pertinent in varying degrees to the other papers in this collection, is that insufficient discussion and weight were given to the larger context within which states operate in the analysis of the forces leading to privatization. Economic interdependence and comparative/competitive advantage have become cliches in modern economic and political analysis. And yet I believe insufficient attention has been paid to these concepts as they impact on government instruments, such as public enterprises and regulation, as well as the concomitant need for governments to reassess basic assumptions about the efficacy of such instruments. Traditionally governments have employed such instruments on the assumption that they can control the economic environment within which they operate, and that they can insulate public enterprises and regulatory regimes from external forces. This is clearly no longer the case (if it ever was) and consequently governments have had to reassess the capacity of such instruments. One of the reasons for this has been identified by Molot and Laux in their recent excellent analysis of Canadian public enterprises, namely the "internationalization of production", and I would add consumption in the case of previously closely regulated services such as domestic transportation and telecommunications (Molot and Laux 1987). The complexity of the contemporary environment compels governments to reassess the utility and indeed viability of particular public enterprises.

This reassessment and possible demise is relevant to one of the more simple-minded assumptions about privatization, namely that it entails a "shrinking" of the state. Analysts who make such an assumption as well as advocates of reversing the growth of the state are often perturbed that, contrary to their assumptions and advocacy, privatization may result in the continuance of the status quo, or even growth in state activity. This should not really be all that surprising, however. Economists have long appreciated that economic actors do not necessarily retreat or withdraw because of basic changes in their environment; they adjust, sometimes profoundly, the form and manner in which they structure their operations. I suggest that a similar process may be at work in privatization.

To return to Stanbury's discussion of privatization as political symbol and his concern that the figures suggest that little has really changed in Canada, I would contend that there may be more going on here that immediately meets the eye. Stanbury quite rightly notes that Canada has a "public enterprise" culture. Changing that deep-rooted culture can only take time. As a result of the willingness of some governments -- and the imposition on others -- to accept the need to reassess the utility and capacity of particular public instruments, there is the potential for long-term change to occur, and not only in the methods by which governments operate and intervene in the economy but in public acceptance of and/or pressure for such intervention. When it comes to addressing well-entrenched attitudes and assumptions and the need for change, we would all do well to remember the words of a Southern preacher as recalled by the Rev. Dr. Martin Luther King, Jr.: "We're not where we ought to be, and we're not where we want to be, and we're not where we're going to be. But thank God almighty we're not where we was!"

# REFERENCES


Aharoni, Y. 1986. *The Evolution and Management of State-Owned Enterprises*. Cambridge, MA: Ballinger Publishing Company.

Ahlbrandt, Roger S., Jr. 1973. *Municipal Fire Protection Services: Comparison of Alternative Organizational Forms*. Beverly Hills CA: Sage Publications.

Alchian, A. and H. Demsetz. 1972. Production, Information Costs and Economic Organization. *American Economic Review* 62:777-95.

Allison, Graham T. 1982. Public and Private Management: Are they fundamentally alike in all unimportant respects? *Current Issues in Public Administration*, 2d ed., ed. by Frederick Lane. New York: St. Martin's Press.

Anderson, T.L., ed. 1983. *Water Rights: Scarce Resource Allocation, Bureaucracy, and the Environment*. San Francisco: Pacific Research Institute for Public Policy.

Armentano, Dominick. 1972. *The Myths of Antitrust*. New Rochelle, NY: Arlington House.

Armentano, Dominick. 1986a. *Antitrust and Monopoly: Anatomy of a policy failure*. Washington, D.C.: The Cato Institute.

Armentano, Dominick. 1986b. *Antitrust Policy: The Case for Repeal*. Washington, D.C.: The Cato Institute.

Armstrong, Donald. 1982. *Competition and Monopoly: Combines policy in perspective*. Vancouver: The Fraser Institute.

Arrow, K. and R. Lind. 1970. Uncertainty and the Evaluation of Public Investment Decisions. *American Economic Review* 60:364-78.

Atkinson, S. and R. Halvorsen. 1986. The Relative Efficiency of Public and Private Firms in a Regulated Environment: The case of U.S. electric utilities. *Journal of Public Economics* 29(April): 281-94.

Auditor General of Canada. 1976. *Report to the House of Commons*. Ottawa: Minister of Supply and Services, Ch. 5, and Appendices C and D (re financial control).

Auditor General of Canada. 1979. *Report to the House of Commons*. Ottawa: Minister of Supply and Services, Ch. 8, "Control and Accountability of Crown Corporations".

Auditor General of Canada. 1982. *Report to the House of Commons*. Ottawa: Minister of Supply and Services, Ch. 2, 43-88.

Auditor General of Canada. 1985. *Report to the House of Commons, 1984/85.* Ottawa: Minister of Supply and Services, Ch. 5, "Mixed Joint Enterprises".

Averch, H. and L. Johnson. 1962. Behavior of the Firm under Regulatory Constraint. *American Economic Review* 52:1052-69.

Bacon, Robert and Walter Eltis. 1976. *Britain's Economic Problem: Too Few Producers*. London: MacMillan.

Baim, Dean. 1985. *Comparison of Privately and Publicly Owned Sports Arenas and Stadiums.* Chicago, OH: Heartland Institute.

Baldwin, John R. 1985. The Privatization of Air Canada. In *Papers on Privatization*, ed. by T.E. Kierans and W.T. Stanbury, 144-66. Montreal: The Institute for Research on Public Policy.

Baumann, Harry. 1987. Between Ideology and Ad Hocery: A pragmatic approach to the management of energy Crown corporations. Notes for a seminar presented at the Faculty of Commerce, University of B.C., November 26. Mimeo.

Beatty, G.H. 1981. Bridling the Beasts: How Saskatchewan combines accountability and management freedom in its Crown corporations. *Policy Options* 2(3):35-8.

Becker, G. 1976. Comment. *Journal of Law and Economics* 19:245-48.

Beesley, Michael. 1987. *Privatization: Reflections on the U.K. Experience*, paper delivered at ADEBA Conference, Buenos Aires, August. (Forthcoming)

Belden, T. 1987. The Way to Run a Railroad. *Philadelphia Inquirer Magazine*, June 14.

Bennett, James T. and Manual H. Johnson. 1981. *Better Government at Half the Price: Private production of public services.* Ottawa, IL: Caroline House, 53-54.

Bennett, James T. and Manual H. Johnson. 1980. Tax Reduction without Sacrifice: Private-sector production of public services. *Public Finance Quarterly* 8(4):363-96.

Bennett, James T. and T.J. DiLorenzo. 1983. *Public Employee Unions and the Privatization of "Public Services".* Journal of Labor Research 4(Winter):41-42.

Bercuson, David, J.L. Granatstein and W.R. Young. 1986. *Sacred Trust?* Toronto: Doubleday Canada.

Blankart, Charles. 1985. Market and Non-Market Alternatives in the Supply of Public Goods: General issues. In *Public Expenditures and Government Growth,* ed. by F. Forte and A.T. Peacock. Oxford: Blackwell.

Block, Walter, ed. 1986. *Reaction: The new Combines Investigation Act.* Vancouver: The Fraser Institute.

Block, Walter. 1977. Austrian Monopoly Theory: A critique. *Journal of Libertarian Studies* 1(4):271-79.

Block, Walter. 1979. Free Market Transportation: Denationalizing the roads. *Journal of Libertarian Studies* 3(2).

Block, Walter. 1982. *The Combines Investigation Act.* Vancouver: The Fraser Institute.

Boardman, A.E. and A.R. Vining. 1987. A Comparison of the Performance of Private, Mixed and State Owned Enterprises in Competitive Environments. Working Paper No. 1206, Faculty of Commerce, University of British Columbia.

Bolick, Clint. 1985. Solving the Education Crisis: Market Alternatives and Parental Choice. In *Beyond the Status Quo,* ed. by David Boaz and Edward H. Crane. Washington, D.C.: The Cato Institute, 207-21.

Borcherding, Thomas E. 1978. Competition, Exclusion and the Optimal Supply of Public Goods. *Journal of Law and Economics* 21:III-32.

Borins, Sanford F. and Lee Brown. 1986. *Investments in Failure: Five government corporations that cost the Canadian taxpayer billions.* Toronto: Methuen.

Borins, Sanford F. 1982. World War Two Crown Corporations: Their wartime role and peacetime privatization. *Canadian Public Administration* 25(3):380-404.

Bott, Robert. 1987. Would You Buy a Piece of This Company? [re Petro-Canada]. *Report on Business Magazine*, September, 56-64.

Bridge, Gary. 1977. Citizen Choice in Public Services: Voucher systems. In *Alternatives for Delivery of Public Services: Toward improved performance,* ed. by E.S. Savas. Boulder, CO: Westview, 57-78.

British Columbia. 1988. *Mainland Gas Service of British Columbia Hydro and Power Authority: Information memorandum.* Vancouver: Province of British Columbia.

Brittan, S. 1984. The Politics and Economics of Privatization. *Political Quarterly* 55(April-June):109-28.

Bruce, Alexander. 1985. Where Coal is King [re Cape Breton Development Corp.]. *Report on Business Magazine*, July/August, 66-72.

Buckland, R., P.J. Herbert and K.A. Yeomans. 1981. Price Discounts on New Equity Issues, in the *U.K. Journal of Business, Finance and Accountancy* 8:79-95.

Butler, Stuart M. 1981. *Enterprise Zones: Greenlining the inner cities.* New York: Universe Books, 24-74.

Butler, Stuart M. 1985. *Privatizing Federal Spending: A strategy to reduce the deficit.* New York: Universe Books, 136-48.

Canada. Privy Council Office. 1977. *Crown Corporations: Direction control accountability - Government of Canada's proposals.* Ottawa: Supply and Services Canada.

Caves, D. and L. Christensen. 1980. The Relative Efficiency of Public and Private Firms in a Competitive Environment: The case of Canadian railroads. *Journal of Political Economy* 88:958-76.

Chamberlin, J.R. and J.E. Jackson. (1987). Privatization as Institutional Choice. *Journal of Policy Analysis and Management* 6/4:586.

Cheung, S. 1983. The Contractual Nature of the Firm. *Journal of Law and Economics* 26(April):1-21.

Clark, R.C. 1986. *Corporate Law.* Boston, MA: Little, Brown and Company.

Clarkson, Kenneth C. and Philip E. Fixler, Jr. 1987. *The Role of Privatization in Florida's Growth.* Tallahassee, FL: Chamber of Commerce.

Clarkson, K.W. (1980). Managerial Behavior in Nonproprietary Organizations, *Research in Law and Economics*, ed. by R.O. Zerbe. Greenwich, CT: JAI Press Inc.

Coase, R.H. 1937. The Nature of the Firm. *Economica* 4(Nov.):386-405.

Comptroller General of Canada. 1980. *Government of Canada Corporations in Which the Government Has an Interest.* Ottawa: Minister of Supply and Services.

Comptroller General of Canada. 1981. *Government of Canada Corporations in Which the Government Has an Interest.* Ottawa: Minister of Supply and Services.

Conrail. 1981. *Options for Conrail: Conrail's response to Sec. 703(c) of the Staggers Rail Act of 1980.* Philadelphia.

Cossette, Margaret. 1986. Missouri Home Care: Home health care in a rural area. *Caring* April.

Crain, M.W. and A. Zardkoohi. (1978). A Test of the Property Rights Theory of the Firm: Water Utilities in the United States. *Journal of Law and Economics* 14/2:149.

Dalfen, Charles M. 1987. *Deregulation and Privatization in the Canadian Telecommunications Sector: The case of Teleglobe Canada*. Paper presented to the International Colloquium on Privatization and Deregulation in Canada and the United Kingdom, Gleneagles, Scotland, November 2-4. Mimeo.

Davies, D.G. 1981. Property Rights and Economic Behaviour in Private and Government Enterprises: The case of Australia's banking system. *Research in Law and Economics* 3:111-42.

De Alessi, L. 1974. An Economic Analysis of Government Ownership and Regulation: Theory and the evidence from the electric power industry. *Public Choice* 19:1-42.

De Alessi, L. 1977. Ownership and Peak-Load Pricing in the Electric Power Industry. *Quarterly Review of Economics and Business* 17:7-26.

De Alessi, L. 1980. The Economics of Property Rights: A review of the evidence. *Research in Law and Economics* 2:1-47.

de Cotret, Hon. Robert. 1985. Notes for the Keynote Address to the Financial Post Conference on Crown Corporations and Regulated Industries. Toronto, April 11. Mimeo.

DeHoog, Ruth H. 1984. *Contracting Out for Human Services.* Albany: State University of New York Press.

Demsetz, H. and K. Lehn. The Structure of Corporate Ownership: Causes and consequences. *Journal of Political Economy* 93(6):1155-77.

Demsetz, H. 1983. The Structure of Ownership and the Theory of the Firm. *Journal of Law and Economics* 26(June):375-90.

Demsetz, H. 1986. Corporate Control, Insider Trading, and Rates of Return. *American Economic Review* 76(May):313-16.

Doern, G. Bruce and John Atherton. 1987. The Tories and the Crowns: Restraining and privatizing in a political minefield. In *How Ottawa Spends, 1987-88: Restraining the State*, ed. by M.J. Prince, 129-69. Toronto: Methuen.

Donahue, J. 1987. Private Agents, Public Acts: The architecture of accountability. Unpublished Ph.D. diss., Harvard University.

Downs, Anthony. 1967. *Inside Bureaucracy.* Boston: Little, Brown and Company.

Drucker, Peter F. 1973. Managing the Public Service Institution. *Public Interest* 33(Fall):43-60.

Eccles, R. 1985. Transfer Pricing as a Problem of Agency. In *Principals and Agents: The Structure of Business*, ed. by J. Pratt and R. Zeckhauser. Harvard Business School Press.

Eckel, C. and A. Vining. Toward a Positive Theory of Joint Enterprise. In *Managing Public Enterprises*, ed. by W.T. Stanbury and F. Thompson. New York, NY: Praeger Publishers, 209-22.

Economic Council of Canada. 1982. *Intervention and Efficiency: A study of government credit and credit guarantees to the private sector.* Ottawa: Minister of Supply and Services.

Economic Council of Canada. 1986. *Minding the Public's Business.* Ottawa: Minister of Supply and Services.

Elford, Craig and W.T. Stanbury. 1986. Mixed Enterprises in Canada. In *Economic and Industrial Structure*, ed. by D.G. McFetridge, 261-303. Toronto: University of Toronto Press.

Ellison, A.P. 1983. Air Canada: The cuckoo in Canada's aviation nest. (Treasury Board Canada, Office of Regulatory Reform, June, and McGill University Centre for the Study of Regulated Industries Working Paper No. 1983-32.)

Fama, E.F. 1980. Agency Problems and the Theory of the Firm. *Journal of Political Economy* 89(5):288-307.

Fama, E.F. and M.C. Jensen. 1983. Separation of Ownership and Control. *Journal of Law and Economics* 26(June):301-26.

Fama, E.F. and M.C. Jensen. 1983. Agency Problems and Residual Claims. *Journal of Law and Economics* 26(June):327-50.

Fare, R., S. Grosskopf and J. Logan. 1985. The Relative Performance of Publicly Owned and Privately Owned Electric Utilities. *Journal of Public Economics* 26(Feb.):89-106.

Feigenbaum, S. and J. Teeples. 1983. Public versus Private Water Delivery: A hedonic cost approach. *Review of Economics and Statistics* 65(Nov.):672-78.

Fisk, Donald, Herbert Kiesling and Thomas Muller. 1978. *Private Provision of Public Services: An overview.* Washington, D.C.: The Urban Institute.

Fitch, Lyle C. 1974. Increasing the Role of the Private Sector in Providing Public Services. In *Improving the Quality of Urban Management,* ed. by Willis D. Hawley and David Rogers. Beverly Hills, CA: Sage, 501-59.

Fixler, Philip E., Jr. 1986. Service Shedding -- A New Option for Local Governments. *The Privatization Review* 2(Summer):10-23.

Fixler, Philip E., Jr., ed. 1987. *Annual Report on Privatization of Government Services: Privatization 1986.* Los Angeles, CA: Reason Foundation.

Foster, Cecil. 1988. The Rule of Lawless [re CNR]. *Report on Business Magazine* February:38-44.

Foster, Peter. 1981. The Power of Petro-Can. *Saturday Night*. October:56.

Foster, Peter. 1982. *The Sorcerer's Apprentices: Canada's super-bureaucrats and the energy mess.* Toronto: Collins.

Foster, Peter. 1983a. Battle of the Sectors [re CDC]. *Saturday Night* March:23-32.

Foster, Peter. 1983b. Strong Politics [re Maurice Strong, CDC and CDIC]. *Saturday Night* August:17-23.

Foster, Peter. 1986. The Empire Builder [re Bill Hopper of Petro-Canada]. *Saturday Night* June:17-24.

Fraser, Matthew. 1987. *Quebec Inc.: French Canadian Entrepreneurs and the New Business Elite.* Toronto: Key Porter Books.

Frech, H.E. III. 1980. Health Insurance: Private, mutuals or governments. In *Proceedings of the Seminar on the Economics of Nonproprietary Organizations,* ed. by K.W. Clarkson and D.L. Martin. Greenwich, CT: JAI Press.

Friedman, Milton. 1977. *On Galbraith and on Curing the British Disease.* Vancouver: The Fraser Institute.

Friedman, Milton. 1988. In Defense of Dumping. *Journal of Economic and Monetary Affairs* 2(1):96-100.

Frizzell, Allan and Anthony Westell. 1985. *The Canadian General Election of 1984.* Ottawa: Carleton University Press.

Funkhauser, R.N. and P.W. MacAvoy. 1979. A Sample of Observations on the Comparative Prices in Public and Private Enterprises. *Journal of Public Economics* 11(June).

Gillen, D.W., W.T. Stanbury and M.W. Tretheway. 1988. Duopoly in Canada's Airline Industry: Consequences and policy issues. *Canadian Public Policy* 14(1):15-31.

Gillies, James. 1984. Privatization of Public Enterprise: The case of Canada. Paper presented to the African Association for Public Administration and Management, Blantyre, Malawi, December 3-8. Mimeo.

Gordon, Marsha. 1981. *Government in Business.* Montreal: C.D. Howe Research Institute.

Grace, William D. 1985. The Case for Implementing Privatization. Speech to the Conference, "Implementing Privatization," Ottawa, June 25. Mimeo.

Gracey, Don. 1985. The Real Issues in the Crown Corporation Debate. In *Public Administration in Canada* (5th ed.), ed. by K. Kernaghan, 122-39. Toronto: Methuen.

Hafsi, Tareb and Christiane Demers. 1986. State Divestment in Quebec. Paper presented at the ASAC Conference, Whistler, B.C., June 1-3. Mimeo.

Halpern, P., A. Plourde and L. Waverman. 1987. *Petro-Canada, Its Role, Control and Operations.* Ottawa: Minister of Supply and Services.

Hampson, H.A. 1976. The Canada Development Corporation. In *Business and Government in Canada,* ed. by Rae and McLeod, 280-89. Toronto: Methuen.

Hanke, Steven H. 1985. Privatization: Theory, evidence and implementation. In *Control of Federal Spending,* ed. by C. Lowell Harris. *Proceedings of the Academy of Political Science* 35:10-13.

Hansmann, H.B. 1980. The Role of Nonprofit Enterprise. *Yale Law Review* 89(5):835-901.

Hardin, Herschel. 1974. *A Nation Unaware: The Canadian economic culture.* Vancouver: J.J. Douglas.

Hart, D.S., Jr. 1974. Municipal and County Ordinances: Looming Difficulties Under Florida's New Judicial Article. *University of Florida Law Review* 26:255,258.

Hermalin, B. and M. Weisbach. 1987. Why do Firms Change Their Boards of Directors? Managerial Economics Research Center, No. 87-9. University of Rochester.

Hirschman, A.O. 1970. *Exit, Voice, and Loyalty.* Cambridge: Harvard University Press.

Hirshhorn, Ron, ed. 1984. *Government Enterprise: Roles and rationale.* Ottawa: Economic Council of Canada.

Howard, J.L., and W.T. Stanbury. 1984. Measuring Leviathan: The size, scope and growth of governments in Canada. In *Government and the Market Economy,* ed. by George Lermer, 87-110, 127-223. Vancouver: The Fraser Institute.

Hurl, L.F. 1984. Privatized Social Service Systems: Lessons from Ontario children's services. *Canadian Public Policy* 10(4):395-405.

Hurl, L.F. 1986. Privatization of Social Services: Time to move the debate along. *Canadian Public Policy* 12(3):507-12.

Itzkoff, Donald M. 1985. *Off The Track: The Decline of the Intercity Passenger Train in the U.S.* Greenwood Press.

Jackson, P.D. 1986. New Issue Costs and Methods in the U.K. Equity Market. *Bank of England Quarterly Bulletin* 26:532-542.

James, Estelle. 1984. Benefits and Costs of Privatized Public Services: Lessons from the Dutch Educational System. *Comparative Educational Review* 28(4):605-24.

Janisch, Hudson, and Richard Schultz. 1985. Teleglobe Canada: Cash cow or white elephant? In *Papers on Privatization,* ed. by T.E. Kierans and W.T. Stanbury. Montreal: Institute for Research on Public Policy, Ch. 13.

Jensen, M.C. 1983. Organization Theory and Methodology. *Accounting Review* 8(April):319-39.

Jensen, M.C. and W. Meckling. 1976. Theory of the Firm: Managerial behavior, agency costs and ownership structure. *Journal of Financial Economics* 3(October):305-60.

Jensen, M.C. and Kevin J. Murphy. 1988. Are Executive Compensation Contracts Structured Properly? Harvard Business School and University of Rochester working paper, February.

Jensen, M.C. and R. Ruback. 1983. The Market for Corporate Control: The scientific evidence. *Journal of Financial Economics* 11:5-50.

Karpoff, Jonathan M. and Edward M. Rice. 1987. Organizational Form, Share Transferability, and Firm Performance: Evidence from the ANCSA Corporations. University of Washington working paper, August.

Katz, M.Z.N. 1988. The Judicial Gold Rush: Rent-a-Judge and Arbitration Programs are Harming the Judiciary. *California Lawyer* 8/1:10.

Kay, J.A. and D.J. Thompson. 1986. Privatisation: a Policy in Search of a Rationale. *Economic Journal* 96:18-32.

Khemani, R.S. 1986. The Extent and Evolution of Competition in the Canadian Economy. In *Canadian Industry in Transition,* ed. by D.G. McFetridge, 135-76. Toronto: University of Toronto Press.

Kierans, Thomas E. 1984. Commercial Crowns. *Policy Options/Options politiques* 5(6):23-29.

Kierans, Thomas E. 1985. Privatization: Strengthening the market at the expense of the state. *Choices.* Montreal: The Institute for Research on Public Policy, April.

Kitchen, Harry M. 1986. Local Government Enterprise in Canada. Ottawa: Economic Council of Canada, Discussion Paper No. 300.

Knight, F.H. 1965. *Risk, Uncertainty, and Profit.* Hart, Schaffner and Marx, 1921; republished New York, NY: Harper and Row, 1965.

Kornai, J. 1986. The Hungarian Reform Process: Visions, hopes and reality. *Journal of Economic Literature* 24(Dec.):1687-1737.

Kornai, J. and A. Matits. 1984. Softness of the Budget Constraint - An Analysis Relying on Data of Firms. *Acta Oeconomica* 32(3-4):223-49.

Kristensen, Ole P. 1983. Public versus Private Provision of Governmental Services: The Case of Danish Fire Protection Services. *Urban Studies* 20:1-9.

Kydland, F. and E. Prescott. 1977. Rules Rather Than Discretion: The inconsistency of optimal paths. *Journal of Political Economy* 85:473-87.

Langford, John and Kenneth J. Huffman. 1983. The Uncharted Universe of Federal Public Corporations. Ch. 4 in *Crown Corporations in Canada: The calculus of instrument choice,* ed. by J.R.S. Prichard. Toronto: Butterworth.

Lave, C.E., ed. 1985. *Urban Transit: The Private Challenge to Public Transit*. Cambridge, MA: Ballinger Publishing Company.

Lermer, George. 1984. AECL - An Evaluation of a Crown Corporation as a Strategist in an Entrepreneurial, Global Scale, Industry. Paper presented to the Economic Council of Canada's Conference on Government, Toronto, November.

Lewin, A. 1982. Public Enterprise, Purposes and Performance: A survey of Western European experience. In *Managing Public Enterprises*, ed. by W.T. Stanbury and F. Thompson. New York, NY: Praeger Publishers, 51-78.

Littlechild, S. 1983. *Regulation of British Telecommunications Profitability.* London: HMSO.

Logan, Charles H. 1985. Competition in the Prison Business. *Freeman* (August):469-78.

Logan, Charles H. and Sharla P. Rausch. 1985. Punish and Profit: The Emergence of Private Enterprise Prisons. *Justice Quarterly* 2(3): 303-18.

Mann, P. 1974. User Power and Electricity Rates. *Journal of Law and Economics* 17:433-43.

Mann, P. and J. Mikesell. 1971. Tax Payments and Electric Utility Prices. *Southern Economic Journal* 38:69-78.

Mann, P. and E. Siefried. 1972. Pricing in the Case of Publicly Owned Electric Utilities. *Quarterly Review of Economics and Business* 12:77-89.

Manne, H.G. 1965. Mergers and the Market for Corporate Control. *Journal of Political Economy* 73:110-20.

Matuszewski, Pierre. 1988. Partial Public Privatization in Quebec: Soquem/Cambior. In *Privatization Tactics and Techniques*, ed. by Michael Walker, 185-99. Vancouver: The Fraser Institute.

Maule, Christopher J. 1985. *The Urban Transportation Development Corporation: A case study of government enterprise.* Ottawa: Economic Council of Canada, Discussion Paper No. 281.

McCraw, T. 1984. Business and Government: The origins of the adversary relationship. *California Management Review* 26(Winter):33-52.

McCready, D.J. 1986. Privatized Social Service Systems: Are there any justifications? *Canadian Public Policy* 12(1):253-57.

McDavid, James C. 1985. The Canadian Experience with Privatizing Residential Solid Waste Collection Services. *Public Administration Review* 45(September/October):602-8.

McDavid, James C. and Evelyn Butler. 1984. *Fire Services in Canadian Municipalities.* University of Victoria, School of Public Administration.

McDougall, Hon. Barbara. 1987a. Excerpts from Statements Made by the Honourable Barbara McDougall on the Reasons for Privatization. Ottawa: Ministry of State for Privatization, May 1. Mimeo.

McDougall, Hon. Barbara. 1987b. Luncheon Address to the B.C. Politics and Policy Privatization Conference. Vancouver, May 21. Mimeo.

McDougall, Hon. Barbara. 1987c. Privatization in an Information Age. Speech to The Institute for Political Involvement. Toronto, September 21. Mimeo.

McFetridge, D.G. 1984. The Federal Business Development Bank. Paper presented to the Royal Commission's Symposium on Crown Corporations, Ottawa, June.

McKinsey & Company, Inc. 1977. *Determining a Strategy for Improving Federal Government Productivity*. February.

Meyer, Marshall W. 1982. "Bureaucratic" versus "Profit" Organizations. In *Research in Organizational Behavior*, vol. 4. Greenwich, CT: JAI Press, 89-125.

Millward, R. 1982. The Comparative Performance of Public and Private Ownership. In *The Mixed Economy,* ed. by E. Roll. London: MacMillan.

Molot, Maureen and Jeanne Laux. 1987. *State Capitalism in Canada.* Ithaca, NY: Cornell University Press.

Molyneux, R. and D. Thompson. 1987. Nationalised Industry Performance: Still third rate? *Fiscal Studies* 8(1):48-82.

Moore, J. 1985. The Success of Privatisation. HM Treasury Press Release 107/85.

Moore, T. 1970. The Effectiveness of Regulation of Electric Utility Prices. *Southern Economic Journal* 36:365-75.

Mullen, Joan. 1985. *Corrections and the Private Sector.* Research in brief. Washington, D.C.: National Institue of Justice (March).

Murphy, K.J. 1985. Corporate Performance and Managerial Remuneration: An empirical analysis. *Journal of Accounting and Economics* 7:11-42.

Musolf, L. 1983. *Uncle Sam's Private, Profitseeking Corporations*. Toronto: Lexington Books.

National Academy of Public Administration. 1981. *An Administrative History of the United States Railway Association*. Washington, D.C.

National Academy of Public Administration. 1982. *Evaluation of the United States Postal Service*. Washington, D.C.

National Transportation Policy Study Commission. 1978. *Amtrak: An Experiment in Rail Service*. Special Report No. 2.

Newman, Walter. 1976. *What Happened When Dr. Kasser Came to Northern Manitoba?* Winnipeg: Newman Publishing.

New Zealand Minister of Finance. 1987a. *Budget Speech: Parliamentary Paper B.6*. Wellington, N.Z.: Government Printer.

New Zealand Minister of Finance. 1987b. *Economic Commentary and Budget Tables: Parliamentary Paper B.6A*. Wellington, N.Z.: Government Printer.

Niskanen, W. 1971. *Bureaucracy and Representative Government*. Chicago: Aldine.

Oftel. 1986. *Annual Report*. London: HMSO.

Oftel. 1987. *Annual Report*. London: HMSO.

Ohashi, T.M. 1980. Privatization in Practice: The story of the British Columbia Resources Investment Corporation. In *Privatization: Theory and practice,* ed. by T.M. Ohashi and T.P. Roth. Vancouver: The Fraser Institute.

Ohashi, T.M. 1982. Selling Public Enterprises to the Taxpayers: The case of the British Columbia Resources Investment Corporation. In *Managing Public Enterprises,* ed. by W.T. Stanbury and Fred Thompson, 111-20. New York, NY: Praeger Publishers.

Ohashi, T.M. and T.P. Roth, eds. 1980. *Privatization: T heory and practice.* Vancouver: The Fraser Institute.

Olewiler, Nancy D. 1986. The Potash Corporation of Saskatchewan: An assessment of the creation and performance of a Crown corporation. Ottawa: Economic Council of Canada, Discussion Paper 303, April.

Olive, David. 1982. Caisse Unpopulaire. *Canadian Business* May:94-101.

Olive, David. 1985. Turnaround Travails at the CDC. *Report on Business Magazine* May:28-43.

Olson, M. 1965. *The Logic of Collective Action*. Cambridge MA: Harvard University Press.

Park, J.R. 1987. Privatization of Public Sector Services in Theory and Practice. *Journal of Policy Analysis and Management* 6/4:523.

Pashigian, B. 1976. Consequences and Causes of Public Ownership of Urban Transit Facilities. *Journal of Political Economy* 84:1239-59.

Peltzman, S. 1971. Pricing in Public and Private Enterprises: Electric utilities in the United States. *Journal of Law and Economics* 14:109-47.

Peltzman, S. 1976. Toward a More General Theory of Regulation. *Journal of Law and Economics* 19:211-40.

Perloff, J. and M. Wachter. 1984. Postal Service Wage Comparability. *Industrial and Labor Relations Review* 38(1):26-35.

Perry, Robert L. 1983. The CDIC: Jobs for the boys or jobs for the country? *Financial Post* June:46-56.

Pesando, James E. 1984. An Economic Analysis of Government with Investment Corporations, with Attention to the Caisse de Depot de Placement du Quebec and the Alberta Heritage Fund. Paper presented to the Economic Council of Canada's Conference on Government, Toronto, November.

Pirie, Madsen. 1985. *Dismantling the State.* Dallas, TX: National Center for Policy Analysis.

Pitfield, M. 1984. The Limits of Public Enterprise. Address to the Couchiching Conference, August.

Poole, Robert W., Jr. 1980. *Cutting Back City Hall.* New York, NY: Universe Books, 101-2.

Poole, R.W. and P.E. Fixler. 1987. Privatization of Public Services in Practice: Experience and Potential. *Journal of Policy Analysis and Management* 6/4: 612.

Pratt, J. and R. Zeckhauser. Principals and Agents: An overview. In *Principals and Agents: The structure of Business,* ed. by J. Pratt and R. Zeckhauser. Cambridge, MA: Harvard Business School Press.

Prichard, J.R.S., ed. 1983. *Crown Corporations in Canada: The calculus of instrument choice.* Toronto: Butterworth.

Priest, G. 1975. The History of Postal Monopoly in the United States. *Journal of Law and Economics* 18:33-80.

Primaux, W. 1977. An Assessment of X-efficiency Gained Through Competition. *Review of Economics and Statistics* 59:105-8.

Prince, Michael J. 1986. The Mulroney Agenda: A right turn for Ottawa. In *How Ottawa Spends 1986-87, Tracking the Tories,* ed. by M.J. Prince, 1-60. Toronto: Methuen.

Privatization Secretariat. 1986. The Privatization of Crown Corporations. Ottawa: Privatization Secretariat, Treasury Board, June. Mimeo.

Pryke, Richard. 1983. *The Nationalized Industries.* Oxford: Martin Robertson.

Quebec, Committee on the Privatization of Crown Corporations. 1986. *From the Quiet Revolution. . .to the Twenty-First Century* [submitted to Mr. Pierre Fortier, Minister Responsible for Privatization]. Quebec: Gouvernement du Quebec, June.

Quebec, Minister Responsible for Privatization. 1986. *Privatization of Crown Corporations: Orientation and prospects.* Quebec: Minister of Finance, February.

Rabkin, J. 1987. Disestablished Religion in the United States. *The Public Interest* 86(Winter):124.

Rainey, Hal. 1983. Public Agencies and Private Frims: Incentive structures, goals and individual roles. *Administration and Society* (August): 207-42.

Regan, J.C. 1983. Industrial Development Bonds: The Demise of the Public Purpose Doctrine. *University of Florida Law Review* 35:541, 545.

Rhoads, Steven E. 1985. *The Economist's View of the World.* Cambridge University Press.

Rodrik, D. and R. Zeckhauser. 1987. The Dilemma of Government Responsiveness. Mimeo.

Rose-Ackerman, S. 1983. Social Services and the Market: Paying Customers, Vouchers, and Quality Control. *Columbia Law Review* 83/4:1405.

Ross, Alexander. 1983. Strong Medicine [re CDIC and Maurice Strong]. *Canadian Business* April:38-41, 107-112 .

Roth, Gabriel. 1966. *A Self-Financing Road System.* London: Institute for Economic Affairs.

Roth, Gabriel. 1967. *Paying for Roads.* Middlesex, England: Penguin.

Roth, Gabriel. 1987a. *Private Provision of Public Services in Developing Countries.* New York, NY: Oxford University Press.

Roth, Gabriel. 1987b. Private Ownership of Roads: Problems and opportunities. *Transportation Research Record* (December).

Rothbard, Murray N. 1970. *Man, Economy and State.* Los Angeles: Nash.

Rothbard, Murray N. 1973. *For a New Liberty.* New York, NY: MacMillan.

Rothbard, Murray N. 1977. *Power and Market: Government and the economy.* Kansas City, KS: Sheed, Andrews and McMeel.

Royal Commission on Financial Management and Accountability. 1979. *Report.* Ottawa: Supply and Services Canada.

Salter, Michael. 1987. Bad Idea [re Ontario's Idea corporation]. *Report on Business Magazine* August:45-52.

Savas, E.S. 1978. *On Equity in Providing Public Services.* Management Science 24(8).

Savas, E.S. 1979a. Public vs. Private Refuse Collection: A critical review of the evidence. *Journal of Urban Analysis* 6.

Savas, E.S. 1979b. How Much Do Government Services Really Cost? *Urban Affairs Quarterly* 15.

Savas, E.S. 1982. *Privatizing the Public Sector: How to Shrink Government.* Chatham, NJ: Chatham House Publishers, Inc.

Savas, E.S. 1987. *Privatization: The key to better government.* Chatham, NJ: Chatham House House Publishers, Inc.

Savas, E.S. and Barbara J. Stevens. 1977a. *Evaluating the Organization of Service Delivery: Solid waste collection and disposal.* Columbia University Graduate School of Business.

Savas, E.S. and Barbara J. Stevens. 1977b. *The Organization and Efficiency of Solid Waste Collection.* Lexington, MA: Lexington Books.

Savas, E.S., ed. 1977. *Alternatives for Delivery Public Services: Toward improved performance.* Boulder, CO: Westview.

Schlesinger, Mark, Robert A. Dorwatt, and Richard T. Pulice. 1986. Competitive Bidding and States' Purchases of Services. *Journal of Policy Analysis and Management* 5(2):245-63.

Schultz, Richard. 1988. Teleglobe Canada: The sale of the jewel of the Crowns. In *Privatization, Public Corporations and Public Policy in Canada*, ed. by Allan Tupper and G. Bruce Doern. Montreal: Institute for Research on Public Policy.

Sexty, Robert W. 1979. Direction, Control and Accountability of Crown Corporations: Review and analysis of government proposals. *Osgoode Hall Law Journal* 17(1).

Shleifer, A. 1985. A Theory of Yardstick Competition. *Rand Journal of Economics* 16:319-27.

Short, R. 1984. The Role of Public Enterprises: An international statistical comparison. In *Public Enterprise in Mixed Economies: Some macroeconomic aspects*, by R. Floyd, C. Gray and R. Short, 110-94. Washington, D.C.: International Monetary Fund.

Simpson, Jeffrey. 1980. *Discipline of Power.* Toronto: Personal Library.

Solomon, Lawrence. 1984. *Power at What Cost?* Toronto: Energy Probe Research Foundation.

Spann, R. 1977. Public versus Private Provision of Governmental Services. In *Budgets and Bureaucrats: The Sources of Government Growth*, ed. by T. Borcherding, 71-89. Durham, NC: Duke University Press.

Stanbury, W.T. 1986. The New Competition Act and Competition Tribunal Act: Not with a bang but a whimper. *Canadian Business Law Journal* 12(1):2-42.

Stanbury, W.T. 1987. Reforming Direct Regulation in Canada. In *The Age of Regulatory Reform,* ed. by K.J. Button and D. Swann. Oxford University Press (in press).

Stanbury, W.T. 1988. *Reducing the State: Privatization in Canada* (book manuscript to be published by The Institute for Research on Public Policy, Montreal).

Starkie, D. and D. Thompson. 1985. *Privatising London's Airports.* IFS Report Series 16. London: Institute for Fiscal Studies.

Stein, Kenneth C. 1988. Privatization: A Canadian perspective. In *Privatization Tactics and Techniques,* ed. by Michael Walker, 69-76. Vancouver: The Fraser Institute.

Stevens, B. 1984. Comparing Public- and Private-Sector Productive Efficiency: An analysis of eight activities. *National Productivity Review* 3(4):395-406.

Stewart, Walter. 1987. *Uneasy Lies the Head: The truth about Canada's Crown corporations.* Toronto: McClelland and Stewart.

Stewart-Patterson, David. 1987. *Post Mortem: Why Canada's mail won't move.* Toronto: MacMillan.

Stigler, G. 1971. The Theory of Economic Regulation. *Bell Journal of Economics and Management Science* 2:3-21.

Tarasofsky, Abraham. 1984. The Canada Development Corporations 1973-83. Paper presented to the Economic Council of Canada's Conference on Government, Toronto, November.

Teal, R.F., G. Giuliano and E. Morlok. 1986. *Public Transit Service Contracting.* Report prepared for Urban Mass Transportation Administration, U.S. Department of Transportation, March.

Teeples, J., S. Feigenbaum and D. Glyer. Public versus Private Water Delivery: Cost comparisons. *Public Finance Quarterly* 14(July): 351-66.

Thomas, David. 1982. Tough Enough to Hurt [re CNR]. *Canadian Business* November:28-34.

Thompson, F. and L.R. Jones. 1986. Controllership in the Public Sector: Normative and Positive Aspects of Public Sector Control System Design. *Journal of Policy Analysis and Management* 5/2:514.

__________. 1988a. Why America's Military Base Structure Cannot be Reduced. *Public Administration Review* 48/1:557.

Thompson, M. 1988. Rented Justice. *California Lawyer* 8/2:32.

Thomson, John. 1985. Politics and the Process of Privatization. In *Papers on Privatization,* ed. by T.E. Kierans and W.T. Stanbury. Montreal: Institute for Research on Public Policy, Ch. 5.

Tierney, John T. 1981. *Postal Reorganization: Managing the Public's Business.* Boston, MA: Auburn House.

Tierney, John T. 1984. Government Corporations and Managing the Public's Business. *Political Science Quarterly* 99(1):73-92.

Touche Ross & Co. 1987. *Privatization in America: An Opinion Survey of City and County Governments on Their Use of Privatization and Their Infrastructure Needs.* New York, NY: The Privatization Council.

Trebilcock, M.J. et al. 1982. *The Choice of Governing Instrument.* Ottawa: Minister of Supply and Services.

Tullock, G. 1965. *The Politics of Bureaucracy.* Washington, D.C.: Public Affairs Press.

Tupper, Allan and G. Bruce Doern. 1981. Public Corporations and Public Policy in Canada. In *Public Corporations and Public Policy in Canada,* ed. by Tupper and Doern, 1-50. Montreal: The Institute for Research on Public Policy.

Tupper, Allan. 1978. Public Enterprise as Social Welfare: The case of the Cape Breton Development Corporation. *Canadian Public Policy* 4(4):530-46.

Twigg, John. 1987. Going, Going, Gone [re B.C. Privatization]. *Equity* December:27-31, 40-41.

U.K. Civil Aviation Authority. 1984. *Airline Competition Policy.* Paper 500. London.

U.K. Department of Energy. 1986. *Authorisation Granted by the Secretary of State for Energy to British Gas under Section 7 of the Gas Act 1986.* London: HMSO.

U.K. Department of the Environment. 1986. *Privatisation of the Water Authorities in England and Wales.* Cmnd. 9734. London: HMSO.

U.K. Department of Trade and Industry. 1982. *The Future of Telecommunications in Britain.* Cmnd. 8610. London: HMSO.

U.K. Department of Trade and Industry. 1984. *Licence Granted by the Secretary of State for Trade and Industry to British Telecommunications under Section 7 of the Telecommunications Act 1984.* London: HMSO.

U.K. Department of Transport. 1984a. *Airline Competition Policy.* Cmnd. 9366. London: HMSO.

U.K. Department of Transport. 1984b. *Buses.* Cmnd. 9399. London: HMSO.

U.K. Department of Transport. 1985. *Airports Policy.* Cmnd. 9542. London: HMSO.

U.K. H.M. Treasury. 1967. *Nationalised Industries: A Review of Economic and Financial Objectives.* Cmnd. 3437. London: HMSO.

U.K. H.M. Treasury. 1978. *The Nationalised Industries.* Cmnd. 7131. London: HMSO.

U.K. H.M. Treasury. 1985. *The Government's Expenditure Plans.* Cmnd. 9428-II. London: HMSO.

U.K. H.M. Treasury. 1986. *The Government's Expenditure Plans.* Cmnd. 9702. London: HMSO.

U.K. H.M. Treasury. 1987. *The Government's Expenditure Plans.* Cmnd. 56. London: HMSO.

U.K. National Economic Development Office. 1976. *A Study of U.K. Nationalised Industries.* London: HMSO.

U.S. Congress. Joint Economic Committee. 1982. *The Future of Mail Delivery in the U.S.* 97th Cong., 2d sess., June.

U.S. Congressional Budget Office. 1982a. *Federal Assistance to Rail Passenger Service* . Washington, D.C.: GPO.

U.S. Congressional Budget Office. 1982b. *Federal Subsidies for Rail Passenger Service: An Assessment of Amtrak.* Washington, D.C.: GPO.

U.S. Department of Commerce. 1983. Bureau of Economic Analysis. *The National Income and Product Accounts of the United States, 1929-82; Survey of Current Business.* Washington, D.C.: GPO.

U.S. General Accounting Office. 1976. *Problems of the New National Bulk Mail System*. Report No. GGD-76-100. Washington, D.C.: GPO.

U.S. General Accounting Office. 1977. *Analysis of Amtrak's Five Year Plan.* Washington, D.C.: GPO.

U.S. General Accounting Office. 1978a. *Should Amtrak's Highly Unprofitable Routes Be Discontinued?* Washington, D.C.: GPO.

U.S. General Accounting Office. 1978b. *Should Amtrak Develop High-Speed Corridor Service Outside the Northeast?* Report No. CED-78-67. Washington, D.C.: GPO.

U.S. General Accounting Office. 1978c. *Grim Outlook for the USPS's National Bulk Mail System*. Report GGD-78-59. Washington, D.C.: GPO.

U.S. General Accounting Office. 1981a. *Amtrak's Productivity on Track Rehabilitation is Lower than Other Railroads' - Precise Comparison Not Feasible.* Washington, D.C.: GPO.

U.S. General Accounting Office. 1981b. *Further Improvements are Needed in Amtrak's Passenger Service Contracts, But They Won't Come Easily.* Washington, D.C.: GPO.

U.S. General Accounting Office. 1982. *Replacing Post Offices with Alternative Services*. Report No. GGD-82-89. Washington, D.C.: GPO.

U.S. General Accounting Office. 1983. *Postal Service Needs to Strengthen Controls over Employee Overtime*. Report No. GGD-83-36. Washington, D.C.: GPO.

U.S. House of Representatives. 1976. Subcommittee on Transportation and Commerce,*Amtrak's Criteria and Procedures for Making Route and Service Decisions*. 94th Cong., 2d sess., February 3, 4, and 6.

U.S. House of Representatives. 1980a. Subcommittee on Transportation and Commerce. *Future Funding for Conrail*. 96th Cong., 2d sess., April 15.

U.S. House of Representatives. 1980b. Subcommittee on Transportation and Commerce. *Reauthorization for U.S. Railway Association for FY1981*. 96th Cong., 2d sess., March.

U.S. House of Representatives. 1981. Committee on Post Office and Civil Service. *Effectiveness of Postal Reorganization Act of 1970, Part I.* 97th Cong., 1st sess., December 10.

U.S. House of Representatives. 1982. Committee on Public Works of Transportation. Subcommittee on Water Resources. *The Effect of the TVA Rates on Homeowners, Business and Industrial Activities and the TVA Board Structure and Functions*. 97th Cong., 2d sess., April 30.

U.S. House of Representatives. 1985. Committee on Post Office and Civil Service. *Oversight on Operations of U.S. Postal Service*. 99th Cong., 1st sess. Serial No. 99-34.

U.S. House of Representatives. 1986a. Committee on Post Office and Civil Service. *Oversight Hearing on U.S. Postal Service Board of Governors*. 99th Cong., 2d sess., June 25. Serial No. 99-61.

U.S. House of Representatives. 1986b. Committee on Post Office and Civil Service. *Oversight on Reorganization of Postal Service*. 99th Cong., 2d sess. Serial No. 99-78.

U.S. House of Representatives. 1987. Committee on Post Office and Civil Service. *Oversight on Operations of U.S. Postal Service.* Excerpts from U.S. Attorney's "Conspiracy Investigation". 100th Cong., 1st sess., July.

U.S. Postal Service. 1984. *Competitors and Competition of the U.S. Postal Service.* Washington, D.C.

U.S. Postal Service. 1986. *Comprehensive Statement on Postal Operations.* Washington, D.C.

U.S. Railway Association. 1978. *1978 Report to Congress on Conrail Performance.*

U.S. Railway Association. 1981. *Conrail at the Crossroads: The future of rail service in the northeast.* April.

U.S. Railway Association. 1986. *The Revitalization of Rail Service in the Northeast.*

U.S. Senate. 1978a. Subcommittee on Energy Production and Supply. *Fiscal Year 1979 Authorization Energy Production and Supply.* Department of Energy. 95th Cong., 2d sess., April.

U.S. Senate. 1978b. Subcommittee on Surface Transportation. *Authorization for the United States Railway Association.* 95th Cong., 2d sess. Serial No. 95-83.

U.S. Senate. 1981. Committee on Environment and Public Works. *Tennessee Valley Authority Oversight.* 97th Cong., 1st sess., March 16. Serial No. 97-H9.

U.S. Senate. 1982. Committee on Commerce, Science and Transportation. *Nomination of Charles Luna to the Board of Directors, National Railroad Passenger Corporation.* 97th Cong., 2d sess., April 13.

U.S. Senate. 1984. Subcommittee on Commerce, Science and Transportation. *Amtrak Safety.* 98th Cong., 2d sess., July 26.

U.S. Senate. 1985a. Committee on Environment and Public Works. Subcommittee on Regional and Community Development. *Tennessee Valley Authority Oversight.* 99th Cong., 1st sess., July 16 and 30. S. Hrg. 99-239.

U.S. Senate. 1985b. Committee on Commerce, Science and Transportation. *Sale of Conrail.* 99th Cong., 1st sess., February 28.

U.S. Senate. 1985c. Committee on Commerce, Science, and Transportation. *Morgan Stanley Proposal to Purchase Conrail* . Report No. 99-227. July 12.

Valente, Carl F. and Lydia D. Manchester. 1984. *Rethinking Local Services: Examining Alternative Delivery Approaches.* Management Information Service Special Report No. 12. Washington, D.C.: International City Management Association.

Vernon, R. 1981. Introduction to *State Owned Enterprise in Western Economies*, ed. by R. Vernon and Y. Aharoni. New York: St Martins Press.

Vickers, J.S. and G.K. Yarrow. 1988. *Privatization: An Economic Analysis.* Cambridge, MA: MIT Press.

Vining, Aidan R. 1981. Provincial Hydro Utilities. In *Public Corporations and Public Policy in Canada*, ed. by Allan Tupper and G. Bruce Doern, 149-88. Montreal: The Institute for Research on Public Policy.

Vining, Aidan R. and Robert Botterell. 1983. An Overview of the Origins, Growth, Size and Functions of Provincial Crown Corporations. Ch. 5 in *Crown Corporations in Canada: The calculus of instrument choice,* ed. by J.R.S. Prichard. Toronto: Butterworth.

von Mises, Ludwig. 1966. *Human Action: A treatise on economics.* Chicago: Henry Regnery.

Walker, Michael, ed. 1988. *Privatization: Tactics and techniques.* Vancouver: The Fraser Institute.

Walsh, A.H. 1978. *The Public's Business: The politics and practices of government corporations.* Cambridge, MA: MIT Press.

Waters, A.A. 1968. *The Economics of Road User Charges.* Baltimore, MD: Johns Hopkins Press.

Weisbach, M.S. 1987. Outside Directors and CEO Turnover. University of Rochester, April. Mimeo.

Williamson, O.E. 1975. *Markets and Hierarchies: Analysis and antitrust implications.* New York, NY: Free Press.

Williamson, O.E. 1983. Organization Form, Residual Claimants, and Corporate Control. *Journal of Law and Economics* 26(June):351-66.

Wilson, J.Q. 1980. The Politics of Regulation. In *The Politics of Regulation*, ed. by J.Q. Wilson. New York, NY: Basic Books, 357-94.

Wilson, Hon. Michael. 1984. *A New Direction for Canada: An agenda for economic renewal.* Ottawa: Department of Finance, November 8.

Wolf, Charles, Jr. 1979. A Theory of Non-market Failures. *Public Interest* no.55 (Spring): 114-33.

Woodson, Robert L. 1982a. The Importance of Neighborhood Organizations in Meeting Human Needs. In *Meeting Human Needs: Toward a new public philosophy,* ed. by Jack A. Meyer, 132-52. Washington, D.C.: American Enterprise Institute.

Woodson, Robert L. 1982b. Child Welfare Policy. In *Meeting Human Needs: Toward a new public philosophy,* ed. by Jack A. Meyer, 455-65. Washington, D.C.: American Enterprise Institute.

Woodson, Robert L. 1985. *Tenant Control of Public Housing: An economic opportunity.* Washington, D.C.: National Forum Foundation.

Yarrow, G.K. 1986. Privatization in Theory and Practice. *Economic Policy* 2:324-77.

Yarrow, George and John Vickers. 1988. This volume.

Zeckhauser, R. and M. Horn. 1988. The Control and Performance of State-owned Enterprises. This volume.

Zeckhauser, R. 1981. Using the Wrong Tool: The pursuit of redistributior through regulation. In *Trends and Perspectives*, U.S. Chamber oı Commerce. Washington, D.C.: GPO.

Zeckhauser, R. 1986a. The Muddled Responsibilities of Private and Public America. In *American Society: Public and private responsibilities*, ed. by W. Knowlton and R. Zeckhauser. Cambridge, MA: Ballinger Publishing Company.

Zeckhauser, R. 1986b. Rational versus Behavioral Economics: What you see is what you conquer. *Journal of Business* 59:435-49.

Zuker, Richard C. and Glenn P. Jenkins. 1984. *Blue Gold: Hydro-electric rents in Canada.* Ottawa: Minister of Supply and Services.

# INDEX

Privatization is being embraced by governments of different political orientations with resulting higher productivity, a smaller public sector, and savings for the taxpayers. The Bradley Policy Research Center at the University of Rochester hosted a conference on Privatization in November, 1987 and this volume is developed from the papers presented at the conference and the ensuing discussion.

*Privatization and State-Owned Enterprises* is divided into three major sections. The first presents a theoretical discussion that introduces the topic to the reader. The second section deals with privatization issues from the U.S. perspective. The third describes research addressed to the U.K. and Canada. The papers and comments presented all focus on the efficiency and management of government and private enterprises.

Kluwer Academic Publishers 0-89838-297-1

606019